The Muslim Brotherhood in Jordan

Since its founding in 1945, the Jordanian Muslim Brotherhood has enjoyed decades of almost continuous parliamentary presence and state acceptance in Jordan, participating in elections, organising events and even establishing a hospital. In this detailed account of the Muslim Brotherhood's ideological and behavioural development in Jordan, Joas Wagemakers focusses on the group's long history and complex relationship with the state, its parliament and society. It shows how age-old concepts derived from classical Islam and the writings of global Islamist scholars have been used and reused by modern-day Jordanian Islamists to shape their beliefs in the context of the present-day nation-state. Far from its reputation as a two-faced global conspiracy bent on conquering the West, the Muslim Brotherhood is a deeply divided group that has nevertheless maintained a fascinating internal ideological consistency in its use of similar religious concepts. As such, it is part of, and continues to build on, trends in Muslim thought that go back hundreds of years.

Joas Wagemakers is Associate Professor of Islamic and Arabic Studies at Utrecht University. He has published extensively on Islamist ideology and Islamic movements, including *A Quietist Jihadi: The Ideology of Abu Muhammad al-Maqdisi* (2012) and *Salafism in Jordan: Political Islam in a Quietist Community* (2016), which won the British-Kuwait Friendship Society Book Prize in 2017.

Cambridge Middle East Studies has been established to publish books on the nineteenth- to twenty-first-century Middle East and North Africa. The series offers new and original interpretations of aspects of Middle Eastern societies and their histories. To achieve disciplinary diversity, books are solicited from authors writing in a wide range of fields including history, sociology, anthropology, political science and political economy. The emphasis is on producing books affording an original approach along theoretical and empirical lines. The series is intended for students and academics, but the more accessible and wide-ranging studies will also appeal to the interested general reader.

A list of books in the series can be found after the index.

The Muslim Brotherhood in Jordan

Joas Wagemakers
Utrecht University

CAMBRIDGE
UNIVERSITY PRESS

CAMBRIDGE
UNIVERSITY PRESS

University Printing House, Cambridge CB2 8BS, United Kingdom

One Liberty Plaza, 20th Floor, New York, NY 10006, USA

477 Williamstown Road, Port Melbourne, VIC 3207, Australia

314–321, 3rd Floor, Plot 3, Splendor Forum, Jasola District Centre, New Delhi – 110025, India

79 Anson Road, #06–04/06, Singapore 079906

Cambridge University Press is part of the University of Cambridge.

It furthers the University's mission by disseminating knowledge in the pursuit of education, learning, and research at the highest international levels of excellence.

www.cambridge.org
Information on this title: www.cambridge.org/9781108839655
DOI: 10.1017/9781108884778

First published 2020

A catalogue record for this publication is available from the British Library.

ISBN 978-1-108-83965-5 Hardback
ISBN 978-1-108-81353-2 Paperback

Contents

Preface

It is not very often that, a few weeks before finishing a book, one realises that one has been writing about something that apparently barely even existed, yet this is what happened to me with this study. After having read about, researched and written on the Jordanian Muslim Brotherhood for years – an organisation founded in 1945 and still in existence today – it was reported in June 2019 that a court of cassation in Jordan had ruled that the group was actually dissolved in 1953 for failing to rectify its status. As a result, the Brotherhood has been illegal since that year. This was somewhat surprising, as the Brotherhood has frequently participated in parliamentary elections, organised numerous events and even founded a hospital – among other activities – since 1953, which is surely an extraordinary feat for an organisation that does not actually exist.

If the Jordanian Brotherhood had really only existed for eight years, it might not have merited a book, but the reality is, of course, that the organisation has a long history in the Kingdom of Jordan and that the court ruling mentioned above is merely the latest chapter in a much longer saga of the state's relationship with the organisation. Unlike in some other countries, the Brotherhood in Jordan has never experienced mass military repression, but has always enjoyed a more complex relationship with the Jordanian state, its parliament and its society. This book deals with how the Jordanian Muslim Brotherhood has negotiated its way through this relationship in the Islamic terms that characterise the organisation. As such, it shows that – ideologically speaking – the group relies on a discourse and a tradition that is far broader and deeper than the Brotherhood itself and also much older than the eight years the court gives the organisation credit for.

Acknowledgements

In 2011, when I received a Veni grant from the Netherlands Organisation for Scientific Research (NWO) to start a research project on Islamic activism in Jordan, I had a pretty good idea about what I wanted to do. It became clear to me rather quickly, however, that the subject of Salafism, which was included in my original research proposal, did not really fit in with my specific plans. I therefore decided to write a book on Salafism in Jordan first (published by Cambridge University Press in 2016) and then focus on my original plans with regard to the Muslim Brotherhood. The present publication, which deals with this organisation, is close to my original research plan and, in its set up at least, represents more or less the book that I had initially wanted to write. Although the grant ran from 2012 to 2016, I would still like to thank the NWO for providing me with the funds to make this book possible.

The initial research for the proposal that formed the basis of this book was done at the International Institute of Social History in Amsterdam. I thank the staff there for helping me to get started and for providing me with sources I could not find elsewhere. The research for the book itself was partly done while working at the Department of Religious Studies at Radboud University in Nijmegen and I thank my colleagues there for providing me with a pleasant working environment. Further research was done at the Department of Philosophy and Religious Studies at Utrecht University, where I started working in 2015 and where the book was also written, and at the Department of Near Eastern Studies at Princeton University, where I was a visiting fellow in 2016. I thank my colleagues at Utrecht, particularly Nico Landman, Christian Lange, Kadir Türkmen, Corné Hanssen and Mehdi Sajid, for helping to make our Islamic and Arabic studies section a joy to work at. I also thank the staff at Princeton, particularly Bernard Haykel, for putting up with me for a few wonderful months.

During my fieldwork in Jordan, I stayed at the Institut Francais du Proche Orient (IFPO), the American Center for Oriental

Research (ACOR) and the British Institute in Amman (BIA). I thank the staff at all of these institutes for their hospitality and help. Part of my research involved work at the newspaper archive of the University of Jordan in Amman, where Lama al-ʿUsayli, Faris al-Zaghal and particularly Afnan al-ʿAlawina and ʿAbdallah Damdum helped me sort through literally thousands of copies of *Al-Kifah al-Islami* and especially *Al-Sabil*. Thanks are also due to Hasan Abu Haniyya, Marwan Shahada and Usama Shahada, who were always willing to discuss my findings with me. I am particularly grateful to Usama for providing me with several issues of the Islamist daily *Al-Ribat* from his impressive personal archive. My greatest thanks, however, go out to the many members of the Muslim Brotherhood and experts in Jordan who were willing to talk to me about the organisation and without whom this book would not have seen the light of day.

As was the case with my previous book, this one was also enthusiastically received by Cambridge University Press's African and Middle Eastern Studies editor, Maria Marsh, for which I am truly grateful. While Maria was away on leave, Daniel Brown took the helm and did an excellent job. Also, Lisa Carter, Vigneswaran Viswanathan and Muhammad Ridwaan guided the book through the various stages of the production process, for which I thank them. I would also like to thank the anonymous peer reviewers for reading and commenting on the manuscript. I am particularly grateful to Shadi Hamid, Roel Meijer, Jillian Schwedler and Morten Valbjørn for taking time out of their busy schedules to read large parts of the manuscript or even the entire text and providing me with useful and sometimes quite detailed comments. This book has become better because of them, although all remaining mistakes are, of course, my own.

On a more personal note – and as usual – AccuJazz.com as well as lots of other jazz accompanied me throughout my research. After finishing a chapter, I always rewarded myself by listening to Rachael Price's truly wonderful rendition of Fred Coots and Haven Gillespie's 'You Go to My Head', which – to me at least – is as great as Billie Holiday's version. I can think of no greater compliment for a jazz singer. Unfortunately, finishing this book also more or less coincided with the passing of Harald Motzki, a former professor of mine, the supervisor of my dissertation and a lasting source of influence. Although the subject of the Muslim Brotherhood is far removed from what his research focussed on, I sincerely hope that traces of his impact on my academic work can still be seen in this book. Finally, I would like to thank my wife and children, who not only had to cope without me for several months when I was doing field work in Jordan, but who also had to put up with my being in my study for most of the day for a period of five months or so when I was writing this book. I do not know if they think the end result was worth it, but I hope they will understand that I think it was.

Note on Transliteration

The system of transliteration used in this book generally follows that of the *International Journal of Middle East Studies* (IJMES) though, as a notable exception, the Arabic *alif maqṣūra* is transliterated as '-á' to distinguish it from a *tāʾ marbūṭa* ('-a') and an *alif ṭawīla* ('-ā'). Like IJMES, however, I have fully transliterated common words (e.g. Qurʾan/Qurʾān), names and titles of books in the notes, but not in the text itself. Finally, some words, such as *ḥadīth*, have not been given their accurate Arabic plural forms (*aḥādīth*) but anglicised equivalents instead (*ḥadīth*s).

Introduction

'Is there a problem with your car?' I asked. A member of the Muslim Brotherhood in Amman, whom I had just interviewed, insisted on driving me home, but we were moving so slowly that I could not help but think that his car was not in mint condition anymore. We were certainly not going any faster than 40 kilometres per hour and other cars were passing us left and – this being Amman – right, often loudly sounding their horns. Moreover, the car was producing such an amount of noise that suggested it was being powered by a jet engine, which – given our lack of speed – was clearly not the case. Despite all this, my host answered my question by saying: 'Oh, the car is fine. I am just driving slowly because Islam teaches us not to break the speed limit.'

At first glance, such a response may look odd. My sense was, however, that this was merely the umpteenth example of a member of the Muslim Brotherhood in Jordan trying to reassure this non-Muslim researcher that Islam – despite what I might possibly think – was really a force for good and that the Brotherhood itself was a law-abiding organisation. Although I do not believe that I had given the group's members the impression that I thought anything to the contrary, this reassurance, that the Muslim Brotherhood and Islam in general were not evil, was an almost constant refrain in my meetings with them, which should not come as a surprise. Despite its being repressed in much of the Arab world, the Brotherhood has a reputation of being a powerful and conspiratorial group, working behind the scenes to infiltrate Western governments such as the administration of former American president Barack Obama.[1] As several scholars have pointed out, such a tendency to ascribe secret agendas and hidden conspiracies to the Brotherhood is by no means exceptional.[2] This impression

[1] Examples include 'Muslim Brotherhood Infiltrates Obama Administration', *Investor's Business Daily* (www.investors.com/politics/editorials/radical-islamist-officials-find-home-in-white-house/, accessed 3 September 2018), 5 December 2013; Frank Gaffney, *The Muslim Brotherhood in the Obama Administration* (Sherman Oaks, CA: The David Horowitz Freedom Center, 2012).

[2] Roel Meijer and Edwin Bakker, 'Introduction', in *The Muslim Brotherhood in Europe*, ed. Roel Meijer and Edwin Bakker (London: Hurst & Co., 2012), 4–11; Frank Peter, 'Muslim

has probably only grown since 2012, when the Egyptian branch of the Muslim Brotherhood rose to power through presidential and parliamentary elections, only to be overthrown in a military coup a year later.[3]

Such conspiratorial ideas about the Muslim Brotherhood being a unified international plot striving for world domination are belied by the far more complex reality on the ground, as many studies have shown. This book seeks to contribute to this growing body of analysis on the Muslim Brotherhood by concentrating on one context in which the organisation operates: the Kingdom of Jordan. As I will explain in greater detail later in this introduction, this study focusses on how and why the Jordanian Islamist movement (encompassing the Muslim Brotherhood and its political party, the Islamic Action Front (IAF)) has moderated its views and positions on the topics of the state, political participation and societal rights and freedoms in the period 1946–2016. Before delving into this, however, I will first give an overview of the academic literature on the Muslim Brotherhood and how this book contributes to these publications. I then explain the theoretical framework, methodology and sources used for this study and conclude with an overview of the rest of the book.

The Study of the Muslim Brotherhood

Founded in 1928 by an Egyptian school teacher called Hasan al-Banna (1906–1949), the Muslim Brotherhood (Jamāʿat al-Ikhwān al-Muslimīn) quickly grew into a political force to be reckoned with in the 1930s and 1940s and, from then on, also spread to other countries in the Arab world and even beyond. At a time of colonial occupation and the dictatorial Arab regimes that followed British and French rule in the Middle East, the Brotherhood's simple but activist slogan that 'Islam is the solution (*al-Islām huwa l-ḥall*)' motivated and mobilised many for the cause of Islamisation through missionary work (*daʿwa*), party politics (*ḥizbiyya*) and sometimes even jihad.

The Muslim Brotherhood in Egypt has been dealt with extensively in the literature with regard to the organisation's origins and early development,[4] its conflictual relationship with the military rulers during the reign of Egyptian President Jamal ʿAbd al-Nasir (Nasser;

"Double Talk" and the Ways of the Shariʿa in France', in *The Muslim Brotherhood in Europe*, ed. Roel Meijer and Edwin Bakker (London: Hurst & Co., 2012), 127–48.

[3] Elizabeth Iskander Monier and Annette Ranko, 'The Fall of the Muslim Brotherhood: Implications for Egypt', *Middle East Policy* 20, no. 4 (2013): 117.

[4] Olivier Carré and Michel Seurat, *Les frères musulmans (1928–1982)* (Paris: L'Harmattan, 1983), 11–47; Ishak Musa Husaini, *The Moslem Brethren: The Greatest of Modern Islamic Movements* (Westpoint, CT: Hyperion Press, 1986 [1956]), 1–124; Ella Landau-Tasseron, *Leadership and Allegiance in the Society of the Muslim Brothers* (Washington,

r. 1954–1970)[5] and its internal make-up and workings.[6] The group has garnered further attention for its role in the so-called Arab Spring, the revolts against dictatorial rule in the Arab world starting in 2011, during which it moved to the forefront of the revolution against Egyptian President Husni Mubarak, a position it subsequently lost when a coup overthrew the Brotherhood-led government in 2013.[7]

Egypt is by no means the only country whose branch of the Muslim Brotherhood has received academic attention, however. Other countries' Brotherhoods or Brotherhood-like groups have also been dealt with in the literature, such as those in the Palestinian territories[8]

DC: Center on Islam, Democracy, and the Future of the Muslim World at the Hudson Institute, 2010); Brynjar Lia, 'Autobiography or Fiction? Ḥasan al-Bannā's Memoirs Revisited', *Journal of Arabic and Islamic Studies* 15 (2015): 119–226; Brynjar Lia, *The Society of the Muslim Brothers in Egypt* (Reading, UK: Ithaca Press, 1998); Beverley Milton-Edwards, *The Muslim Brotherhood: The Arab Spring and Its Future Face* (London and New York: Routledge, 2016), 13–27; Richard P. Mitchell, *The Society of the Muslim Brothers* (Oxford: Oxford University Press, 1969), 1–104; Christina Phelps Harris, *Nationalism and Revolution in Egypt: The Role of the Muslim Brotherhood* (Stanford, CA: The Hoover Institution on War, Revolution, and Peace, 1964), 143–94.

5 Carré and Seurat, *Frères*, 49–82; Husaini, *Moslem Brethren*, 125–43; Milton-Edwards, *Muslim Brotherhood*, 27–33; Mitchell, *Society*, 105–62; Phelps Harris, *Nationalism*, 195–225; Barbara H. E. Zollner, *The Muslim Brotherhood: Hasan al-Hudaybi and Ideology* (London and New York: Routledge, 2009), 25–49.

6 Khalil al-Anani, *Inside the Muslim Brotherhood: Religion, Identity, and Politics* (Oxford: Oxford University Press, 2016); Hazem Kandil, *Inside the Brotherhood* (Cambridge: Polity Press, 2015), 5–118; Mitchell, *Society*, 163–84.

7 Khalil al-Anani, 'Upended Path: The Rise and Fall of Egypt's Muslim Brotherhood', *Middle East Journal* 69, no. 4 (2015): 527–43; Shadi Hamid, *Islamic Exceptionalism: How the Struggle over Islam Is Reshaping the World* (New York: St. Martin's Press, 2016); Stig Jarle Hansen, Mohamed Husein Gaas and Ida Bary, eds, *The Muslim Brotherhood Movement in the Arab Winter* (Cambridge, MA: Harvard Kenney School Belfer Center for Science and International Affairs, 2017); Philipp Holtmann, 'After the Fall: The Muslim Brotherhood's Post Coup Strategy', *Perspectives on Terrorism* 7, no. 5 (2013): 198–204; Ibrahim El Houdaiby, *From Prison to Palace: The Muslim Brotherhood's Challenges and Responses in Post-revolution Egypt* (N.p.: Fride/Hivos, 2015), 6–15; Milton-Edwards, *Muslim Brotherhood*, 34–60; Monier and Ranko, 'Fall', 111–23; Samuel Tadros, 'Egypt's Muslim Brotherhood after the Revolution', in *Current Trends in Islamist Ideology, Vol. 12*, ed. Hillel Fradkin, Husain Haqqani, Eric Brown and Hassan Mneimeh (Washington, DC: Hudson Institute, 2011), 5–20; Samuel Tadros, 'Islamist Responses to the "End of Islamism"', in *Current Trends in Islamist Ideology, Vol. 16*, ed. Hillel Fradkin, Husain Haqqani, Eric Brown and Hassan Mneimeh (Washington, DC: Hudson Institute, 2014), 33–64; Eric Trager, 'Egypt's Looming Competitive Theocracy', in *Current Trends in Islamist Ideology, Vol. 14*, ed. Hillel Fradkin, Husain Haqqani, Eric Brown and Hassan Mneimeh (Washington, DC: Hudson Institute, 2014), 27–37.

8 Ziad Abu-Amr, *Islamic Fundamentalism in the West Bank and Gaza: Muslim Brotherhood and Islamic Jihad* (Bloomington and Indianapolis, IN: Indiana University Press, 1994); Abd Al-Fattah Muhammad El-Awaisi, *The Muslim Brothers and the Palestine Question, 1928–1947* (London and New York: I.B. Tauris, 1998), 150–71; Beverley Milton-Edwards, *Islamic Politics in Palestine* (London and New York: I.B. Tauris, 1996); Milton-Edwards, *Muslim Brotherhood*, 61–85; Emile Sahliyeh, 'The West Bank and Gaza Strip', in *The*

(including Hamas),[9] the Gulf,[10] Sudan,[11] Tunisia[12] and especially Syria,[13] as well as the organisation's branches outside the Muslim world, such as in

Politics of Islamic Revivalism: Diversity and Unity, ed. Shireen Hunter (Bloomington and Indianapolis, IN: Indiana University Press, 1988), 88–100; Mohammed K. Shadid, 'The Muslim Brotherhood Movement in the West Bank and Gaza', *Third World Quarterly* 10, no. 2 (1988): 658–82.

9 Paola Caridi, *Hamas: From Resistance to Government*, trans. Andrea Teti (New York: Seven Stories Press, 2012 [2009]); Zaki Chehab, *Inside Hamas: The Untold Story of the Militant Islamic Movement* (New York: Nation Books, 2007); Jeroen Gunning, *Hamas in Politics: Democracy, Religion, Violence* (London: Hurst & Co., 2007); Michael Irving Jensen, *The Political Ideology of Hamas: A Grassroots Perspective*, trans. Sally Laird (London and New York: I.B. Tauris, 2010 [2009]); Khaled Hroub, *Hamas: A Beginner's Guide* (London and Ann Arbor, MI: Pluto Press, 2006); Khaled Hroub, *Hamas: Political Thought and Practice* (Washington, DC: Institute for Palestine Studies, 2000); Matthew Levitt, *Hamas: Politics, Charity, and Terrorism in the Service of Jihad* (New Haven, CT, and London: Yale University Press, 2006); Loren D. Lybarger, *Identity & Religion in Palestine: The Struggle between Islamism & Secularism in the Occupied Territories* (Princeton, NJ, and Oxford: Princeton University Press, 2007); Beverley Milton-Edwards and Stephen Farrell, *Hamas* (Cambridge and Malden, MA: Polity Press, 2010); Shaul Mishal and Avraham Sela, *The Palestinian Hamas: Vision, Violence, and Coexistence* (New York: Columbia University Press, 2000); Andrea Nüsse, *Muslim Palestine: The Ideology of Hamas* (Abingdon, UK: RoutledgeCurzon, 1998); Sara Roy, *Hamas and Civil Society in Gaza: Engaging in the Islamist Social Sector* (Princeton, NJ, and Oxford: Princeton University Press, 2011); Jonathan Schanzer, *Hamas vs. Fatah: The Struggle for Palestine* (New York: Palgrave Macmillan, 2008); Azzam Tamimi, *Hamas: A History from Within* (Northampton, MA: Olive Branch Press, 2007).

10 Courtney Freer, The Changing Islamist Landscape of the Gulf Arab States (Washington, DC: The Arab Gulf States Institute in Washington, 2016); Courtney Freer, Rentier Islamism: The Influence of the Muslim Brotherhood in Gulf Monarchies (Oxford: Oxford University Press, 2018).

11 Mustafa A. Abdelwahid, *The Rise of the Islamic Movement in Sudan (1945–1989)* (New York: Edwin Mellen Press, 2008); Abdelwahab El-Affendi, *Turabi's Revolution: Islam and Power in Sudan* (London: Grey Seal Books, 1991); J. Millard Burr and Robert O. Collins, *Sudan in Turmoil: Hasan al-Turabi and the Islamist State* (Princeton, NJ: Markus Wiener Publishers, 2010).

12 François Burgat and William Dowell, *The Islamic Movement in North Africa* (Austin, TX: University of Texas Press, 1993), 182–246; Susan Waltz, 'Islamist Appeal in Tunisia', *Middle East Journal* 40, no. 4 (1986): 651–70. See also François Burgat, *Face to Face with Political Islam* (London and New York: I.B. Tauris, 2005 [1996]).

13 Elena Arigita and Rafael Ortega, 'From Syria to Spain: The Rise and Decline of the Muslim Brothers', in *The Muslim Brotherhood in Europe*, ed. Roel Meijer and Edwin Bakker (London: Hurst & Co., 2012), 199–202; Hanna Batatu, 'Syria's Muslim Brethren', in *State and Ideology in the Middle East and Pakistan*, ed. Fred Halliday and Hamza Alavi (London: Macmillan, 1988), 112–32; Petra Becker, 'Die syrische Muslimbruderschaft bleibt ein wichtiger Akteur', *SWP-Aktuell* 52 (2013): 1–7; Carré and Seurat, *Frères*, 125–203; Dara Conduit, *The Muslim Brotherhood in Syria* (Cambridge: Cambridge University Press, 2019); Dara Conduit, 'The Syrian Muslim Brotherhood and the Spectacle of Hama', *Middle East Journal* 70, no. 2 (2016): 211–26; Raphaël Lefèvre, *Ashes of Hama: The Muslim Brotherhood in Syria* (Oxford: Oxford University Press, 2013); Raymond A. Hinnebusch, 'Syria', in *The Politics of Islamic Revivalism: Diversity and Unity*, ed. Shireen T. Hunter (Bloomington and Indianapolis, IN: Indiana University Press, 1988), 41–56; Aron Lund, *Struggling to Adapt: The Muslim Brotherhood in a New Syria* (Washington, DC: Carnegie Endowment for International Peace, 2013); Alison Pargeter, *The Muslim Brotherhood: The Burden of Tradition* (London: Saqi Books, 2010), 61–95; Alison Pargeter, *The Muslim Brotherhood: From Opposition to Power*

various European countries[14] (France,[15] Germany,[16] Great Britain,[17] the Netherlands[18] and Spain[19]) and the United States.[20] Some studies portray the Muslim Brotherhood as a fundamentalist movement that takes the Qur᾽an, the Sunna (the Prophet Muhammad's example) and Islamic legal texts as its frame of reference and favours Islamic law (*sharīʿa*) over

(London: Saqi Books, 2010), 65–102; Robert G. Rabil, 'The Syrian Muslim Brotherhood', in *The Muslim Brotherhood: The Organization and Policies of a Global Islamist Movement*, ed. Barry Rubin (New York: Palgrave Macmillan, 2010), 73–88; Johannes Reissner, *Ideologie und Politik der Muslimbrüder Syriens: Von den Wahlen 1947 bis zum Verbot unter Adīb aš-Šīšaklī 1952* (Freiburg: Klaus Schwarz Verlag, 1980); Yvette Talhamy, 'The Syrian Muslim Brothers and the Syrian–Iranian Relationship', *Middle East Journal* 63, no. 4 (2009): 561–80; Joshua Teitelbaum, 'The Muslim Brotherhood and the "Struggle for Syria", 1947–1958: Between Accommodation and Ideology', *Middle Eastern Studies* 40, no. 3 (2004): 134–58; Joshua Teitelbaum, 'The Muslim Brotherhood in Syria, 1945–1958: Founding, Social Origins, Ideology', *Middle East Journal* 65, no. 2 (2011): 213–33.

14 Steven Brooke, 'The Muslim Brotherhood in Europe and the Middle East: The Evolution of a Relationship', in *The Muslim Brotherhood in Europe*, ed. Roel Meijer and Edwin Bakker (London: Hurst & Co. 2012), 27–49; Brigitte Maréchal, 'The European Muslim Brothers' Quest to Become a Social (Cultural) Movement', in *The Muslim Brotherhood in Europe*, ed. Roel Meijer and Edwin Bakker (London: Hurst & Co., 2012), 89–110; Lorenzo Vidino, 'The European Organization of the Muslim Brotherhood: Myth or Reality?', in *The Muslim Brotherhood in Europe*, ed. Roel Meijer and Edwin Bakker (London: Hurst & Co., 2012), 51–69; Lorenzo Vidino, 'The Muslim Brotherhood in Europe', in *The Muslim Brotherhood: The Organization and Policies of a Global Islamist Movement*, ed. Barry Rubin (New York: Palgrave Macmillan, 2010), 105–16.

15 Cédric Baylocq, 'The Autonomisation of the Muslim Brotherhood in Europe: *Daʿwa, Mixité* and Non-Muslims', in *The Muslim Brotherhood in Europe*, ed. Roel Meijer and Edwin Bakker (London: Hurst & Co., 2012), 149–68; Farhad Khosrokhavar, 'The Muslim Brotherhood in France', in *The Muslim Brotherhood: The Organization and Policies of a Global Islamist Movement*, ed. Barry Rubin (New York: Palgrave Macmillan, 2010), 137–47; Pargeter, *The Muslim Brotherhood: The Burden of Tradition*, 136–49; Pargeter, *The Muslim Brotherhood: From Opposition to Power*, 140–52.

16 Stefan Meining, 'The Islamic Community in Germany: An Organisation under Observation', in *The Muslim Brotherhood in Europe*, ed. Roel Meijer and Edwin Bakker (London: Hurst & Co., 2012), 209–33; Pargeter, *The Muslim Brotherhood: The Burden of Tradition*, 160–71; Pargeter, *The Muslim Brotherhood: From Opposition to Power*, 162–74; Guido Steinberg, 'The Muslim Brotherhood in Germany', in *The Muslim Brotherhood: The Organization and Policies of a Global Islamist Movement*, ed. Barry Rubin (New York: Palgrave Macmillan, 2010), 149–60.

17 Innes Bowen, 'The Muslim Brotherhood in Britain', in *The Muslim Brotherhood in Europe*, ed. Roel Meijer and Edwin Bakker (London: Hurst & Co., 2012), 111–26; Pargeter, *The Muslim Brotherhood: The Burden of Tradition*, 150–60; Pargeter, *The Muslim Brotherhood: From Opposition to Power*, 152–62; David Rich, 'The Very Model of a British Muslim Brotherhood', in *The Muslim Brotherhood: The Organization and Policies of a Global Islamist Movement*, ed. Barry Rubin (New York: Palgrave Macmillan, 2010), 117–36.

18 Edwin Bakker, 'The Public Image of the Muslim Brotherhood in the Netherlands', in *The Muslim Brotherhood in Europe*, ed. Roel Meijer and Edwin Bakker (London: Hurst & Co., 2012), 169–88.

19 Arigita and Ortega, 'Syria', 202–5.

20 Alyssa A. Lappen, 'The Muslim Brotherhood in North America', in *The Muslim Brotherhood: The Organization and Policies of a Global Islamist Movement*, ed. Barry Rubin (New York: Palgrave Macmillan, 2010), 161–79.

democracy.[21] Others view the Brotherhood as an organisation that is essentially the same as terrorist groups like al-Qaʿida, or at least bears a strong ideological resemblance to them.[22] Most studies show, however, that the Brotherhood is dynamic, susceptible to societal changes, more democratic and willing to work within the systems of countries such as Egypt,[23]

[21] Uriya Shavit, 'Islamotopia: The Muslim Brotherhood's Idea of Democracy', *Azure*, no. 46 (2011): 35–62; Mariz Tadros, *The Muslim Brotherhood in Contemporary Egypt: Democracy Redefined or Confined?* (London and New York: Routledge, 2012); Tadros, 'Egypt's Muslim Brotherhood', 6, 18; Trager, 'Egypt's Theocracy'.

[22] Amira El-Azhary Sonbol, 'Egypt', in *The Politics of Islamic Revivalism: Diversity and Unity*, ed. Shireen Hunter (Bloomington and Indianapolis, IN: Indiana University Press, 1988), 31; Burr and Collins, *Sudan*; Cynthia Farahat, 'The Muslim Brotherhood, Fountain of Islamist Violence', *Middle East Quarterly* 24, no. 2 (2017); Daniel Pipes, 'Islamism's Unity in Tunisia', www.danielpipes.org/12103/islamism-unity (accessed 6 September 2018), 30 October 2012; Barry Rubin, 'Comparing Three Muslim Brotherhoods', in *The Muslim Brotherhood: The Organization and Policies of a Global Islamist Movement*, ed. Barry Rubin (New York: Palgrave Macmillan, 2010), 7–18; Nachman Tal, *Radical Islam in Egypt and Jordan* (Brighton, UK, and Portland, OR: Sussex Academic Press, 2005).

[23] Sana Abed-Kotob, 'The Accommodationists Speak: Goals and Strategies of the Muslim Brotherhood of Egypt', *International Journal of Middle East Studies* 27, no. 3 (1995): 321–39; Khalil al-Anani, 'Egypt's Muslim Brotherhood: From Opposition to Power and Back Again. A Study in the Dynamics of Their Rise and Fall', in *The Prospects of Political Islam in a Troubled Region: Islamists and Post-Arab Spring Challenges*, ed. Mohammed Abu Rumman (Amman: Friedrich Ebert Stiftung, 2018), 75–87; al-Anani, *Inside the Muslim Brotherhood*; Gehad Auda, 'The "Normalization" of the Islamic Movement in Egypt from the 1970s to the Early 1990s', in *Accounting for Fundamentalisms: The Dynamic Character of Movements*, ed. Martin E. Marty and R. Scott Appleby (Chicago, IL, and London: University of Chicago Press, 1994), 375–7, 379–81, 385–91; Hesham Al-Awadi, *In Pursuit of Legitimacy: The Muslim Brothers and Mubarak, 1982–2000* (London and New York: I.B. Tauris, 2004); Nathan J. Brown, *When Victory Is Not an Option: Islamist Movements in Arab Politics* (Ithaca, NY, and London: Cornell University Press, 2012); Katerina Dalacoura, *Islamist Terrorism and Democracy in the Middle East* (Cambridge: Cambridge University Press, 2011), 130–40; Olaf Farschid, 'Hizbiya: Die Neuorientierung der Muslimbruderschaft Ägyptens in den Jahren 1984 bis 1989', *Orient* 30, no. 1 (1989): 53–74; Martin Forstner, 'Auf dem legalen Weg zur Macht? Zur Politischen Entwicklung der Muslimbruderschaft Ägyptens', *Orient* 29, no. 3 (1988): 386–422; Mona El-Ghobashy, 'The Metamorphosis of the Egyptian Muslim Brothers', *International Journal of Middle East Studies* 37 (2005): 373–95; Shadi Hamid, 'Arab Islamist Parties: Losing on Purpose?', *Journal of Democracy* 22, no. 1 (2011): 68–80; Chris Harnisch and Quinn Mecham, 'Democratic Ideology in Islamist Opposition? The Muslim Brotherhood's "Civil State"', *Middle Eastern Studies* 45, no. 2 (2009): 189–205; Marc Lynch, *The Brotherhood's Dilemma* (Waltham, MA: Crown Center for Middle East Studies at Brandeis University, 2008); Marc Lynch, 'Young Brothers in Cyberspace', *Middle East Report* 245 (2007): 26–33; Roel Meijer, 'The Majority Strategy of the Muslim Brotherhood', *Orient*, no. 1 (2013): 22–30; Roel Meijer, 'Moslim Broederschap maakt zich op voor de democratie van morgen', *ZemZem* 1, no. 2 (2005): 56–8; Pargeter, *The Muslim Brotherhood: The Burden of Tradition*, 15–60; Pargeter, *The Muslim Brotherhood: From Opposition to Power*, 15–64; Carrie Rosefsky Wickham, *Mobilizing Islam: Religion, Activism, and Political Change in Egypt* (New York: Columbia University Press, 2002); Carrie Rosefsky Wickham, *The Muslim Brotherhood: Evolution of an Islamist Movement* (Princeton, NJ, and Oxford: Princeton University Press, 2013); Bruce K. Rutherford, *Egypt after Mubarak: Liberalism, Islam, and Democracy in the Arab World* (Princeton, NJ, and Oxford: Princeton University Press, 2008), 77–99; Samer S. Shehata, 'Political

Morocco,[24] the Palestinian territories,[25] Syria[26] and Tunisia.[27] Some

Da'wa: Understanding the Muslim Brotherhood's Participation in Semi-authoritarian Elections', in *Islamist Politics in the Middle East: Movements and Change*, ed. Samer S. Shehata (London and New York: Routledge, 2012), 120–45; Amr Elshobaki, 'The Muslim Brotherhood – Between Evangelizing and Politics: The Challenges of Incorporating the Brotherhood into the Political Process', in *Islamist Politics in the Middle East: Movements and Change*, ed. Samer S. Shehata (London and New York: Routledge, 2012), 107–19; Ana Belén Soage and Jorge Fuentelsaz Franganillo, 'The Muslim Brothers in Egypt', in *The Muslim Brotherhood: The Organization and Policies of a Global Islamist Movement*, ed. Barry Rubin (New York: Palgrave Macmillan, 2010), 39–56; Denis J. Sullivan and Sana Abed-Kotob, *Islam in Contemporary Egypt: Civil Society vs. the State* (Boulder, CO: Lynne Rienner Publishers, 1999), 41–70; Mohammed Zahid, *The Muslim Brotherhood and Egypt's Succession Crisis: The Politics of Liberalisation and Reform in the Middle East* (London and New York: I.B. Tauris, 2010), 83–103, 109–27.

24 Idriss al-Kanbouri, 'Morocco's Islamists: Action Outside Religion', in *The Prospects of Political Islam in a Troubled Region: Islamists and Post-Arab Spring Challenges*, ed. Mohammed Abu Rumman (Amman: Friedrich Ebert Stiftung, 2018), 67–74; Vish Sakthivel, *Al-Adl wal-Ihsan: Inside Morocco's Islamist Challenge* (Washington, DC: Washington Institute for Near East Policy, 2015); Emad Eldin Shahin, *Political Ascent: Contemporary Islamic Movements in North Africa* (Boulder, CO: Westview Press, 1998), 166–201, especially 172, 178–9; Eva Wegner, *Islamist Opposition in Authoritarian Regimes: The Party of Justice and Development in Morocco* (Syracuse, NY: Syracuse University Press, 2011).

25 Gunning, *Hamas*; Khaled Hroub, 'Die Aktuelle Politik von Hamas: Überleben ohne Strategie', *Inamo* 8, no. 32 (2002): 15–17; Hroub, *Hamas: A Beginner's Guide*; Khaled Hroub, 'A "New Hamas" through Its New Documents', *Journal of Palestine Studies* 35, no. 4 (2006): 6–27; International Crisis Group (ICG), *Dealing with Hamas*, Middle East Report no. 21 (Amman and Brussels: ICG, 2004), 13–19; International Crisis Group (ICG), *Enter Hamas: The Challenge of Political Integration*, Middle East Report no. 49 (Amman and Brussels: ICG, 2006), 19–22; Menachem Klein, 'Hamas in Power', *Middle East Journal* 61, no. 3 (2007): 442–59; Jean-François Legrain, 'Hamas as a Ruling Party', in *Islamist Politics in the Middle East: Movements and Change*, ed. Samer S. Shehata (London and New York: Routledge, 2012), 183–204; Shaul Mishal, 'The Pragmatic Dimension of the Palestinian Hamas: A Network Perspective', *Armed Forces and Society* 29, no. 4 (2003): 569–89; Shaul Mishal and Avraham Sela, *Palestinian Hamas*; Shaul Mishal and Avraham Sela, 'Participation without Presence: Hamas, the Palestinian Authority and the Politics of Negotiated Coexistence', *Middle Eastern Studies* 38, no. 3 (2002): 1–26; Muhammad Muslih, 'Hamas: Strategy and Tactics', in *Ethnic Conflict and International Politics in the Middle East*, ed. Leonard Binder (Gainesville, FL: University of Florida Press, 1999), 311–26; Joas Wagemakers, 'Legitimizing Pragmatism: Hamas' Framing Efforts from Militancy to Moderation and Back?', *Terrorism and Political Violence* 22 (2010): 357–77.

26 Meijer, 'Moslim', 58–61; Itzchak Weismann, 'Democratic Fundamentalism? The Practice and Discourse of the Muslim Brothers Movement in Syria', *The Muslim World* 100 (2010): 1–16.

27 Francesco Cavatorta and Fabio Merone, 'Moderation through Exclusion? The Journey of the Tunisian *Ennahda* from Fundamentalist to Conservative Party', *Democratization* 20, no. 5 (2013): 857–75; Dalacoura, *Islamist Terrorism*, 140–5; Abdul Latif al-Hanashi, 'Tunisia: The Impact of Democratic Transition on the Ennahda Party', in *The Prospects of Political Islam in a Troubled Region: Islamists and Post-Arab Spring Challenges*, ed. Mohammed Abu Rumman (Amman: Friedrich Ebert Stiftung, 2018), 53–65; Milton-Edwards, *Muslim Brotherhood*, 111–36; Monica Marks, 'Tunisia's Islamists and the "Turkish Model"', *Journal of Democracy* 28, no. 1 (2017): 102–15; Rory McCarthy, 'Protecting the Sacred: Tunisia's Islamist Movement Ennahda and the Challenge of Free

studies have even focussed on 'new' or 'post'-Islamist movements, which emphasise flexibility, the compatibility of Islam with democracy and full citizenship for non-Muslims and a general discourse of rights (rather than duties).[28]

The Study of the Muslim Brotherhood's Moderation in Jordan

While the trajectories of the Muslim Brotherhood in these rather diverse countries are all quite different, the situation is different still in Jordan, where the Brotherhood has always enjoyed a legalised and integrated spot in Jordanian politics,[29] unlike in, for example, Egypt and Syria, where the organisation has suffered from military and political repression. With regard to the Jordanian Muslim Brotherhood, too, many studies have shown that it has accepted the monarchy in its country, has shunned the use of violence, does not seek the revolutionary overthrow of governments and is willing to work within the system to achieve its goals.[30]

Speech', *British Journal of Middle Eastern Studies* 42, no. 4 (2015): 447–64; Shahin, *Political Ascent*, 63–111.

28 Raymond William Baker, 'Invidious Comparisons: Realism, Postmodern Globalism and Centrist Islamic Movements in Egypt', in *Political Islam: Revolution, Radicalism or Reform?*, ed. John L. Esposito (Boulder, CO: Lynne Rienner Publishers, 1997), 115–33; Raymond William Baker, *Islam without Fear: Egypt and the New Islamists* (Cambridge, MA, and London: Harvard University Press, 2003); Asef Bayat, *Making Islam Democratic: Social Movements and the Post-Islamist Turn* (Stanford, CA: Stanford University Press, 2007); Asef Bayat, ed., *Post-Islamism: The Changing Faces of Political Islam* (Oxford: Oxford University Press, 2013); Carrie Rosefsky Wickham, 'The Path to Moderation: Strategy and Learning in the Formation of Egypt's *Wasat* Party', *Comparative Politics* 36, no. 2 (2004): 205–28; Joshua Stacher, 'Post-Islamist Rumblings in Egypt: The Emergence of the Wasat Party', *Middle East Journal* 56, no. 3 (2002): 415–32.

29 This partly changed in 2016, as we will see later on.

30 Mohammad Suliman Abu Rumman, *The Muslim Brotherhood in the 2007 Jordanian Parliamentary Elections: A Passing 'Political Setback' or Diminished Popularity?* (Amman: Friedrich Ebert Stiftung, 2007), 44–55; Nathan J. Brown, *Jordan and Its Islamic Movement: The Limits of Inclusion?*, Carnegie Papers no. 74 (Washington, DC: Carnegie Endowment for International Peace, 2006); Juan José Escobar Stemmann, 'The Crossroads of Muslim Brothers in Jordan', in *The Muslim Brotherhood: The Organization and Policies of a Global Islamist Movement*, ed. Barry Rubin (New York: Palgrave Macmillan, 2010), 57–71, especially 64–5; Hamid, 'Arab Parties', 69–71; Shadi Hamid, 'New Democrats? The Political Evolution of Jordan's Islamists' (paper presented at the CSIC Sixth Annual Conference 'Democracy and Development: Challenges for the Islamic World', Washington, DC, United States of America, 22–23 April 2005); Shadi Hamid, *Temptations of Power: Islamists & Illiberal Democracy in a New Middle East* (Oxford: Oxford University Press, 2014); Mansoor Moaddel, *Jordanian Exceptionalism: A Comparative Analysis of State–Religion Relations in Egypt, Iran, Jordan, and Syria* (New York: Palgrave, 2002), 33–6; Glenn E. Robinson, 'Can Islamists be Democrats? The Case of Jordan', *Middle East Journal* 51, no. 3 (1997): 373–87; Rosefsky Wickham, *Muslim Brotherhood*, 204–18; Jillian Schwedler, 'A Paradox of Democracy? Islamist

Several of these studies on the Jordanian Brotherhood concentrate on the organisation's integration in the country's political system and its ideological flexibility or 'moderation'. The latter is a tricky term, however, because it is not always clear what people who moderate their views should be moderating towards: does the term refer to subservience to the powers that be and a general unwillingness to upset the apple cart, thereby playing into the hands of dictatorial rulers who want to preserve the status quo, or does it denote a tendency to strive for liberal and democratic reforms, which may be quite destabilising?[31] Given the fact that this book deals with Jordan, where the Muslim Brotherhood has been allowed to participate in a pluriform yet ultimately weak parliament in the framework of a dictatorial yet comparatively mildly repressive regime, it seems right to combine these different dimensions of 'moderation' for this study since the Brotherhood's trajectory contains elements of both. For the purposes of this study, 'moderation' is split up into three different dimensions that do not necessarily correlate:[32] a tendency towards a peaceful and non-revolutionary attitude to the state; an inclination towards a democratic view of political participation; and a move towards greater freedom on a societal level. This cluster of dimensions – as well as their 'radical' opposites: (support for) violent rebellion, less democracy and less societal freedom – will be fleshed out more specifically in the Jordanian political context later on.[33]

In political science publications, the term 'moderation' is often treated in the context of the so-called inclusion-moderation thesis, which holds that strongly ideologically inspired groups are likely to moderate if they are included in the political process by allowing them to fully and fairly participate in the state's institutions, specifically parliament and government. The cooperation with other political parties, the need to compromise, the desirability of setting realistic and attainable goals and the accountability one has to voters are, this theory holds, consequences of political inclusion and constitute incentives for groups to moderate. This, in turn, allows governments and regimes to provide more space for these

Participation in Elections', *Middle East Report*, no. 209 (1998): 25–9, 41; Quintan Wiktorowicz, 'Islamists, the State and Cooperation in Jordan', *Third World Quarterly* 21, no. 4 (1999): 1–16; Quintan Wiktorowicz, *The Management of Islamic Activism: Salafis, the Muslim Brotherhood, and State Power in Jordan* (New York: State University of New York Press, 2001), 93–110.

31 Hamid, *Temptations*, 46–7; Jillian Schwedler, 'Can Islamists Be Moderates? Rethinking the Inclusion-Moderation Hypothesis', *World Politics* 63, no. 2 (2011): 350–1.

32 Schwedler, 'Can Islamists Be Moderates?', 351.

33 It should be stressed that this definition of moderate with regard to the Muslim Brotherhood in Jordan was inspired by that specific context, not by what I see as desirable or undesirable.

'moderates', which will then increase their number, while simultaneously decreasing the number of 'radicals', according to this theory. Conversely, the opposite – radicalisation – is likely to happen if groups are repressed and excluded through the arrest and/or imprisonment of their members, the closure of their buildings and media, electoral measures taken to reduce their parliamentary presence and bans on their activities.[34]

The inclusion-moderation thesis has been specified throughout the years, however, and scholars differ in their emphasis and approach to it. As Schwedler has pointed out, some political scientists focus on the moderation of groups' behaviour, whereas others concentrate on the moderation of a group's ideology, while still others direct their attention towards the ideological moderation of individual Islamists.[35] Another difference among scholars pertains to the outcome of their research. While some conclude that inclusion can or does lead to moderation (or that repression leads to radicalisation) in certain countries,[36] this same result is doubted in others,[37] while some believe that repression and exclusion, rather than causing radicalisation, may even lead to moderation.[38]

Interestingly, political scientists dealing with the Muslim Brotherhood in Jordan through the prism of the inclusion-moderation thesis do not even agree on whether this theory holds up in this context. Some approach the theory as a whole in a critical way, but do not dismiss its validity altogether.[39] Those who have made an extensive effort to apply the thesis to the Muslim Brotherhood in Jordan sometimes conclude that

[34] An excellent overview of research on the 'inclusion-moderation' thesis across movements and groups can be found in Jillian Schwedler, *Faith in Moderation: Islamist Parties in Jordan and Yemen* (Cambridge: Cambridge University Press, 2006), 1–26.

[35] Schwedler, 'Can Islamists Be Moderates?', 348, 352–64.

[36] Khalil al-Anani, 'Rethinking the Repression-Dissent Nexus: Assessing Egypt's Muslim Brotherhood's Response to Repression since the Coup of 2013', *Democratization* 26, no. 8 (2019): 1329–41; Khalil al-Anani, 'Understanding Repression-Adaptation Nexus in Islamist Movements', in *Adaptation Strategies of Islamist Movements*, POMEPS Studies 26 (Washington, DC: Project on Middle East Political Science (POMEPS), 2017), 4–7; Matt Buehler, 'The Threat to "Un-moderate": Moroccan Islamists and the Arab Spring', *Middle East Law and Governance* 5 (2013): 213–57; Jillian Schwedler, 'Why Exclusion and Repression of Moderate Islamists Will Be Counterproductive', in *Adaptation Strategies of Islamist Movements*, POMEPS Studies 26 (Washington, DC: Project on Middle East Political Science (POMEPS), 2017), 8–11.

[37] Janine A. Clark and Jillian Schwedler, 'Who Opened the Window? Women's Activism in Islamist Parties', *Comparative Politics* 35, no. 3 (2003): 293–5; Dalacoura, *Islamist Terrorism*, 130–47; Schwedler, *Faith*, 194–7.

[38] Cavatorta and Merone, 'Moderation', 857–75; Courtney Freer, 'Exclusion-Moderation in the Gulf Context: Tracing the Development of Pragmatic Islamism in Kuwait', *Middle Eastern Studies* 54, no. 1 (2018): 1–21.

[39] Brown, *Victory*, 3–5; Rosefsky Wickham, *Muslim Brotherhood*, 282–8.

inclusion does, indeed, lead to moderation,[40] although they, too, acknowledge that it does not in other countries.[41] Some have argued that even in Jordan, inclusion of or cooperation with Islamists does not always lead to moderation[42] while others have gone so far as to say that it is actually exclusion and/or repression that has caused the Brotherhood to moderate in Jordan.[43] Still others claim that both inclusion and repression contribute to the Muslim Brotherhood's moderation.[44]

Moderation through Division

This book is not about political science and does not primarily seek to contribute theoretically to the inclusion-moderation thesis, nor does it strive to fundamentally challenge any of the applications of this thesis to the Brotherhood in Jordan. As such, this book does not go into the theoretical intricacies of the theory as it has been developed by political scientists. Yet the inclusion-moderation thesis is clearly relevant with regard to the subject of this book. Moreover, the moderation referred to, as mentioned above, is not just one of political behaviour but also – and perhaps even primarily – one of ideological change. Given the fact that the Muslim Brotherhood is an organisation with a strongly Islam-flavoured ideology that has to justify its actions by means of that ideology, even if it may have non-ideological motives, my academic field (Islamic studies) can also contribute to the debate on whether inclusion leads to moderation. It does so by focussing not only on the behaviour of the organisation, but primarily on the ideological arguments and concepts used by the Brotherhood and its individual members to legitimise its changes.

As of yet, no academic study has fully focussed on how the moderation of the Jordanian Brotherhood has been justified in the Islamic terms used by the organisation itself, despite the fact that this provides fascinating insight into how people who subscribe to a seemingly homogeneous ideology nevertheless reach quite different conclusions. This book seeks

40 Dalacoura, *Islamist Terrorism*, 124–30; Schwedler, *Faith*, 194.
41 Clark and Schwedler, 'Who Opened the Window?', 293–5; Dalacoura, *Islamist Terrorism*, 130–47; Schwedler, *Faith*, 194–7.
42 Janine A. Clark, 'The Conditions of Islamist Moderation: Unpacking Cross-ideological Cooperation in Jordan', *International Journal of Middle East Studies* 38, no. 4 (2006): 539–60.
43 Hamid, *Temptations*, 38–60, especially 48–53.
44 Neven Bondokji, 'The Prospects of Islamic Movements and Parties in Jordan', in *The Prospects of Political Islam in a Troubled Region: Islamists and Post-Arab Spring Challenges*, ed. Mohammed Abu Rumman (Amman: Friedrich Ebert Stiftung, 2018), 164.

to fill this gap and, by doing so, engages particularly with the ideas put forward by Hamid, who points to the Jordanian Brotherhood's ideological moderation despite repression,[45] and Schwedler, who ascribes the group's moderation to political inclusion and internal debates.[46] This book shows how these two diverging results from research on the Brotherhood's moderation can be reconciled.

By using a detailed analysis of the Jordanian Muslim Brotherhood's discourse, this study seeks to show how and why the Brotherhood and its political affiliate, the IAF, have moderated their ideas about the state, political participation and societal rights and freedoms in the seventy-year period of 1946–2016. This time frame was chosen because the Muslim Brotherhood was officially recognised in Jordan in 1946, marking its formal beginning in the country, and was partly declared an illegal organisation in 2016, which was also the year the IAF last participated in parliamentary elections. This study traces the ideological development of the Muslim Brotherhood back to its theoretical Islamic sources of inspiration found in the Qurʾan, the life of the Prophet Muhammad, Islamic law and Muslim reformers as well as the practical Jordanian political context in which it operates. Moreover, it analyses the Muslim Brotherhood's developing ideology by placing it in the broader context of contemporary Islamist debates among scholars (*ʿulamāʾ*) and thinkers (*mufakkirūn*) that have inspired Jordanian Brothers.

Special attention will be given to divisions within the Jordanian Muslim Brotherhood, which are quite important in explaining not only its ideological moderation but also why political scientists can draw such different and even opposing conclusions with regard to the inclusion-moderation thesis in this context. Building on Schwedler, I argue that the space the regime has given the organisation (inclusion) has often led to moderation. This process was aided, however, by – among other things – the divisions within the Brotherhood, which provided it with the ideological flexibility that allowed it to moderate. In line with Hamid, I also argue that the regime, in turn, has used some of these divisions to put pressure on the Brotherhood (repression), also causing it to moderate. This 'moderation through division' dimension adds a crucial layer to our knowledge of the Muslim Brotherhood in Jordan, why it moderated the way it did and, as such, how it fits in the inclusion-moderation thesis.

[45] Hamid, *Temptations*, 107–12, 129–37.
[46] Schwedler, *Faith*, 195–6. A third factor in this process is the lack of a ruling party in Jordan. See ibid., 194.

Theoretical Framework, Methodology, Sources and Overview

The Theoretical Study of Ideology

The study of social movement[47] organisations such as the Muslim Brotherhood has not always paid sufficient attention to ideas or ideology. In the 1950s and 1960s, social movements were often viewed as 'long-lasting panics or crowds' by collective behaviour theorists, only to give way to sociological explanations of the success of such movements like resource mobilisation and political processes in the 1970s and 1980s.[48] Ideology as an explanatory factor for people's behaviour was entirely missing in many analyses of social movements, perhaps – in the case of religious ideology – as a result of a refusal to take religion seriously as an independent variable, a secular bias that ascribes religious positions to material or political motives or deep-rooted pejorative views of ideology, particularly in Marxist discourse.[49] This changed, however, when the concept of 'framing' was introduced in the study of social movements, mostly by Benford and Snow, in the 1980s. Their work tried to bring ideas back in by focussing on the ways movements 'frame' their views to appeal to and mobilise others. These frames, which – following Goffman[50] – they define as '"schemata of interpretation" that enable individuals "to locate, perceive, identify, and label" occurrences

[47] Social movements can be defined as movements that 'are involved in conflictual relations with clearly identified opponents; are linked by dense informal networks; [and] share a distinct collective identity'. See Donatella della Porta and Mario Dani, *Social Movements: An Introduction* (Malden, MA: Blackwell Publishing, 2006 [1999]), 20–2. The quotation can be found on page 20.

[48] Pamela E. Oliver and Hank Johnston, 'What a Good Idea! Ideologies and Frames in Social Movement Research', in *Frames of Protest: Social Movements and the Framing Perspectives*, ed. Hank Johnston and John A. Noakes (Lanham, MD: Rowman & Littlefield Publishers, 2005), 185. Examples of such publications include Adrian F. Aveni, 'Organizational Linkages and Resource Mobilization: The Significance of Linkage Strength and Breadth', *Sociological Quarterly* 19, no. 2 (1978): 185–202; J. Craig Jenkins, 'Resource Mobilization Theory and the Study of Social Movements', *Annual Review of Sociology* 9 (1983): 527–53; Doug McAdam, *Political Process and the Development of Black Insurgency, 1930–1970* (Chicago, IL, and London: University of Chicago Press, 1999 [1982]); John D. McCarthy and Mayer N. Zald, 'Resource Mobilization and Social Movements: A Partial Theory', *American Journal of Sociology* 82, no. 6 (1977): 1212–41.

[49] Michael Freeden, *Ideology: A Very Short Introduction* (Oxford: Oxford University Press, 2003), 1–11; Oliver and Johnston, 'What a Good Idea!', 187, 190.

[50] Erving Goffman, *Frame Analysis: An Essay on the Organization of Experience* (New York: Harper & Row, 1974). The passage cited by Snow et al. can be found on page 21.

within their life space and the world at large',[51] function to diagnose a problem, propose a solution and call people to action.[52]

Although the focus on framing shone a light on the importance of ideas to social movements, and major studies on social movement theory (SMT) from the 1990s and 2000s incorporated this perspective,[53] it has also been criticised. The reasons for this criticism include the belief that frames do not really do justice to the ideational complexity of movements, reduce ideas to mere mobilisation strategies and – most importantly for this study – are equated with or used as substitutes for ideology.[54] While frames appeal to aspects of people's beliefs and emotions ('Change we can believe in', 'Make America Great Again') and may convey important messages, they are relatively simple and shallow or, in the words of one author, 'the bumper-sticker version of how issues get interpreted within a certain ideological context'.[55] Ideology, on the other hand, is usually seen as describing a deeper and broader set of more or less coherent ideas[56] and may be minimally defined as referring to 'a set of idea-elements that are bound together, that belong to one another in a non-random fashion'.[57]

To analyse these 'idea-elements' and how they 'belong to one another' in the case of the Muslim Brotherhood in Jordan, I make use of the work of Freeden, a British political theorist and one of the leading scholars of ideology.[58] His theory of ideology is ideal for the purposes of this book

[51] David A. Snow, E. Burke Rochford, Jr., Steven K. Worden and Robert D. Benford, 'Frame Alignment Processes, Micromobilization, and Movement Participation', *American Sociological Review* 51 (1986): 464.

[52] David A. Snow and Robert D. Benford, 'Ideology, Frame Resonance, and Participant Mobilization', in *International Social Movement Research, Vol. 1 – From Structure to Action: Comparing Social Movement Research across Cultures*, ed. Bert Klandermans, Hanspeter Kriesi and Sidney Tarrow (Greenwich, CT, and London: JAI Press, 1988), 199–204.

[53] See, for example, Bert Klandermans and Suzanne Staggenborg, eds, *Methods of Social Movement Research* (Minneapolis, MN: University of Minnesota Press, 2002); Enrique Laraña, Hank Johnston and Joseph R. Gusfield, eds, *New Social Movements: From Ideology to Identity* (Philadelphia, PA: Temple University Press, 1994); Aldon D. Morris and Carol McClurg Mueller, eds, *Frontiers in Social Movement Theory* (New Haven, CT, and London: Yale University Press, 1992); Sidney Tarrow, *The New Transnational Activism* (Cambridge: Cambridge University Press, 2005).

[54] Oliver and Johnston, 'What a Good Idea!', 185–90, 193–5.

[55] Glenn E. Robinson, 'Hamas as Social Movement', in *Islamic Activism: A Social Movement Theory Approach*, ed. Quintan Wiktorowicz (Bloomington and Indianapolis, IN: Indiana University Press, 2004), 116.

[56] For a long list of diverse definitions of ideology, see John Gerring, 'Ideology: A Definitional Analysis', *Political Research Quarterly* 50, no. 4 (1997): 958–9; see also Teun A. van Dijk, *Ideology: A Multidisciplinary Approach* (London: Sage Publications, 1998).

[57] Gerring, 'Ideology', 980.

[58] His many publications include Freeden, *Ideology*; Michael Freeden, *Liberal Languages: Ideological Imaginations and Twentieth-Century Progressive Thought* (Princeton, NJ, and

since it focusses precisely on the dynamic and changing nature of ideology that is also central to the Jordanian Muslim Brotherhood dealt with in this study, yet it has only rarely been used for the analysis of the Brotherhood.[59] One of Freeden's basic assumptions about ideology – in this instance liberalism, but the same applies to the Brotherhood's ideology – is that it is not static, but

> a plastic, changing thing, shaped and reshaped by the thought-practices of individuals and groups; and though it needs to have a roughly identifiable pattern for us to call it consistently by the same name, 'liberalism,' it also presents myriad variations that reflect positions posed, and positions adopted, by various liberals.[60]

In order to analyse how ideologies are shaped and how their 'myriad variations' relate to its 'roughly identifiable pattern', Freeden focusses on what he labels the morphology of an ideology, which displays core, adjacent and peripheral concepts. The first are central and hugely important to an ideology (such as 'liberty' in liberalism) and are the concepts around which adjacent ones revolve. The latter give meaning and direction to core concepts and are therefore essential to the formation of an ideology as a whole. In liberalism, to use Freeden's example again, 'democracy' might act as adjacent to the core concept of 'liberty', resulting in an ideological preference for self-determination. Peripheral concepts, finally, though not vital in and of themselves, contribute an important flavour to the more important core concepts and can, with time, become more central to the ideology.[61]

Given the fact that 'ideologies constitute semantic fields in that each component interacts with all the others and is changed when any one of the other components alters',[62] it is of great importance to pay attention not only to the morphology of ideologies, but also to the morphology of concepts. Freeden writes that political concepts consist of ineliminable features and quasi-contingent ones. The former derive from the linguistic usage of a concept, meaning that nobody uses the concept without somehow, implicitly or explicitly, referring to this feature, but the concept as a whole cannot be reduced to this ineliminable feature as such. An

Oxford: Princeton University Press, 2005); Michael Freeden, ed., *Reassessing Political Ideologies: The Durability of Dissent* (London and New York: Routledge, 2001).

59 An exception is Roel Meijer, 'The Muslim Brotherhood and the Political: An Exercise in Ambiguity', in *The Muslim Brotherhood in Europe*, ed. Roel Meijer and Edwin Bakker (London: Hurst & Co., 2012), 295–320.

60 Freeden, *Liberal Languages*, 20.

61 Michael Freeden, *Ideologies and Political Theory: A Conceptual Approach* (Oxford: Oxford University Press, 1996), 77–80.

62 Ibid., 67.

example Freeden mentions is 'raised surfaces on which objects can be placed' with regard to the concept of 'table'. While this is certainly an ineliminable element of the latter, it cannot carry the full meaning of 'table' by itself. Quasi-contingent features, by contrast, are not individually essential to concepts, but they occupy categories that are. To use Freeden's example again: a table can have different means to elevate its surface and different colours, meaning that – unlike with regard to the table's ineliminable feature – variation is quite possible, but tables must have *a* means of elevation and *a* colour. As such, quasi-contingent features give meaning and direction to ineliminable features on the level of concepts in ways that adjacent concepts do to core ones on the level of ideologies as a whole.[63]

Freeden's morphologies on both the ideological and the conceptual level will be applied to the Jordanian Muslim Brotherhood in this book. As such, the changes in the Brotherhood's ideology and the divisions within the organisation will be mapped in a comprehensible way, showing how concepts change and change position within the larger ideological framework espoused by the Brotherhood's members. Since all these concepts, as well as their positions within an ideology as a whole, are contested by the different exponents of an ideology, each participant in these ideological contestations tries to make his or her own interpretation of or place ascribed to a concept seem like the right one.[64]

This specific ideological process of redefining and rearranging concepts in an effort to make oneself appear the true exponent of an ideology is referred to as 'decontestation' by Freeden and accounts for how different people come up with different ideological outcomes on the basis of the same concepts.[65] As we will see later on, some Muslim Brothers in Jordan have a strong tendency to focus on the *sharīʿa*, which I label a *sharīʿa*-centred approach, while others concentrate far more on the community (*umma*) of Muslims and/or Jordanians (an *umma*-centred approach), while still others oscillate between these two approaches (a balanced approach), with each group decontesting adjacent and peripheral concepts in different ways. Although this process will be analysed mostly among Jordanian Muslim Brothers, a similar distinction between *sharīʿa*-centred, *umma*-centred and balanced approaches can be discerned among earlier Muslim Brothers outside Jordan and even in classical Sunni Islamic political thought. As such, this book will use the same terminology with regard to these two subjects, both because of structural

[63] Ibid., 61–7. [64] Ibid., 55–60. [65] Ibid., 76.

parallels between them and the Jordanian Brotherhood and in order to facilitate the comparison between all three.[66]

Methodology and Sources

An ideology, as Freeden states:

> cannot be wholly explained as a reflection of cultural, spatial, and temporal occurrences, or as a predictable epistemological response to those occurrences. Nor is it to be explained wholly as an internally sustained grammar or morphology of logical or functional connections, independent of its consumers. It is instead, the quasi-contingent interplay between these variable factors.[67]

In the case of the Muslim Brotherhood in Jordan, this means that both its ideological framework and the sources underpinning it as well as the context in which these are shaped and (de)contested matter. This is precisely why, in seeking to contribute to our understanding of Islamist moderation through the prism of Islamic studies, I have decided to focus on the writings produced by Jordanian Brothers and their various sources of inspiration as well as to concentrate on fieldwork in Jordan itself.

In my research for this book, I tried to discover what writings, scholars and thinkers were influential and important through a combination of historical and empirical methods by building on existing publications on the Muslim Brotherhood in Jordan and doing fieldwork. During the latter, I talked to or interviewed virtually all of the (former) leaders and prominent members of the organisation still alive at the time. Based on their statements as well as my own search, I collected the relevant writings by Jordanian Muslim Brothers, scholars that inspired them and local experts of Jordanian Islamism. Inevitably, after reading and analysing these writings, I ended up with more questions, which I then sought to get answered during subsequent fieldwork. I repeated this process several times until I felt I had a firm grasp of the subject matter.

While this combination of textual analysis and fieldwork provided me with a well-rounded view of the Muslim Brotherhood's ideology, there are at least two relevant topics in which I was somehow constrained in my research that deserve to be mentioned here. The first pertains to local

66 This terminology bears some resemblance to Anjum's 'community-centered vision of the Qur'an' and his 'ruler-centered vision'. His analysis focusses on classical Islamic theology, however, while mine concentrates on modern-day Islamist politics. In any case, Anjum's study did not catch my attention until after I had thought of these terms and, as such, they were conceived entirely independently of Anjum's terminology. See Ovamir Anjum, *Politics, Law, and Community in Islamic Thought: The Taymiyyan Moment* (Cambridge: Cambridge University Press, 2012), 50–92.

67 Freeden, *Ideologies*, 552.

branches of the Muslim Brotherhood. My informants were from different parts of Jordan, but my research – simply because of time constraints – was nevertheless very Amman centred. Given that I wanted to focus on ideological divisions and not so much on local ones, this is not a problem, but local dimensions and differences are nevertheless interesting and deserve the attention of another researcher.

The second constraint concerns women. Although women's rights are certainly dealt with in this book, I had very few encounters with female members of the Brotherhood. This was partly because I am a man and, as such, could not interview the more conservative women in the organisation, but also simply because I did not have many contacts who were female. This means that my discussion of women's rights later on is mostly informed by what men had to say about them. Since the movers and shakers within the Brotherhood are overwhelmingly male, this means I still managed to discern the main positions on women's rights within the organisation, although I realise the lack of female voices remains a drawback. I can only hope that one of the many excellent female researchers of Jordanian Islamism whose work has inspired and helped me so much will be able to fill this gap.

The sources I have used for this project consist not only of secondary literature, but also of Arabic book(let)s written by (members of) the Jordanian Muslim Brotherhood and the IAF that I bought, photocopied or was given in Jordan. Another important source for this book consists of the Jordanian newspapers and news websites I consulted throughout the period during which I did research (2012–2018). I also did research at the newspaper archives of the University of Jordan in Amman, where I collected relevant articles from the Muslim Brotherhood's 1950s weekly newspaper *Al-Kifah al-Islami* and from the Brotherhood's weekly (and later daily) newspaper *Al-Sabil*, which has been published since the 1990s. I was also able to obtain selected issues of *Al-Ribat*, the short-lived Brotherhood weekly newspaper from the early 1990s.

Another important source consists of the many communiqués the organisation has published through its website and which I printed out. Unfortunately, however, this website did not produce searchable URLs and was shut down several years ago, making these communiqués entirely unavailable to the public. I have therefore not used these in the notes of this book. Finally, I have conducted over thirty semi-structured interviews with members of the Muslim Brotherhood and the IAF, as well as with relevant experts in journalism and academia during five months of field work over the period 2012–2014. Most of these interviews were on the record, but a few people requested that their names be withheld, which I have respected, of course.

Overview

The goal of this book is threefold: firstly, through the prism of Freeden's theory of ideology, it intends to show how and why Islamist ideology changes and how Islamists justify such changes. This way, it shows how early Islamic thought continues to be a source of contested and decontested ideological concepts for highly diverse yet ideologically connected contemporary Islamist thinkers and organisations; secondly, within this framework, it seeks to present a detailed study of the Jordanian Muslim Brotherhood and its historical and transnational ideological trajectories; and thirdly, as such, it seeks to contribute to the wider debate on the inclusion-moderation thesis with regard to Islamist movements and organisations.

Through the pursuit of this three-pronged goal, this book – in a wider sense – also deals with the pluriformity of Islam in general. Many people outside academia worry about 'intolerant' texts in the Qur'an or the Sunna and, while they realise that Muslims may be fine people, wonder if the problem of religious intolerance is perhaps inherent to Islam. This suggests that (interpretations of) the sources of Islam are rigid and frozen, which they are not. The Muslim Brotherhood is an ideal case study to show the pluriformity of Islam and the wide differences of interpreting 'difficult' Islamic texts because the organisation is very broad and has members with wide-ranging ideas that build on historical and transnational Islamic and Islamist traditions, as we will see below. It also shows that the idea of the Muslim Brotherhood single-mindedly conspiring to take over power, either in the Muslim world or the West, is – quite frankly – rather ridiculous.

To achieve all this, the book is divided into two parts with three chapters each. Part I deals with the ideological and political context in which the views of the Jordanian Muslim Brotherhood have been shaped. Chapter 1 presents the historical, theoretical context that Jordanian Muslim Brothers themselves have indicated as having shaped their views. It deals with how the subjects of the state, political participation and societal rights and freedoms have been presented in the Islamic tradition from the seventh to twentieth centuries in order to show the pluriform basis on which the Brotherhood's ideology builds. Chapter 2 deals with how the early (and mostly Egyptian) Muslim Brotherhood dealt with the same three issues through the writings of Hasan al-Banna and other early leaders of the organisation. This is analysed because the early Muslim Brotherhood has clearly served as an example to the Jordanian branch of the organisation. Chapter 3 analyses the political and practical context of Jordan and how the Muslim Brotherhood has played a role in its history and has, in turn, been shaped by that country's (political) environment, ending with an overview of how and on what issues the Jordanian Muslim Brotherhood is divided today.

Part II deals with the development of the Jordanian Muslim Brotherhood's ideology itself. As Muhammad Abu Rumman, an expert on Jordanian Islamism, points out, the Muslim Brotherhood in the kingdom does not really have major thinkers of the same level as other branches of the Brotherhood.[68] When expressing their own ideas, its members therefore not only rely heavily on classical Islamic tradition and the early Muslim Brotherhood, but also on contemporary Islamist ideologues such as the Tunisian Rashid al-Ghannushi (b. 1941)[69], the Sudanese Hasan al-Turabi (1932–2016)[70] and especially the Egyptian Yusuf al-Qaradawi

[68] Muḥammad Abū Rummān, cited in Markaz Ḥimāyat wa-Ḥurriyyat al-Ṣaḥafiyyīn, *Qamʿ bi-Quwwat al-Qānūn: Ḥālat al-Ḥurriyyāt al-Iʿlāmiyya fī l-Urdunn 2012* (Amman: Markaz Ḥimāyat wa-Ḥurriyyat al-Ṣaḥafiyyīn, n.d.), 245.

[69] Stig Jarle Hansen and Mohamed Husein Gaas, 'The Ideological Arena of the Wider Muslim Brotherhood', in *The Muslim Brotherhood Movement in the Arab Winter*, ed. Stig Jarle Hansen, Mohamed Husein Gaas and Ida Bary (Cambridge, MA: Harvard Kenney School Belfer Center for Science and International Affairs, 2017), 7. For references to him by Jordanian Islamists and articles by al-Ghannūshī himself in the Jordanian Islamist press, see Ḥāzim ʿAyyād, 'Rāshid al-Ghannūshī wa-l-Istithmār fī l-Dīmuqrāṭiyya', *Al-Sabīl*, 25 March 2014, 12; Bassām al-ʿUmūsh, 'Rāshid al-Ghannūshī wa-Ḥikmat al-Qiyāda', *Al-Dustūr*, 19 January 2014, 14; Yāsir al-Zaʿātira, 'Al-Ghannūshī: Al-Islām Laysa Ḍidd al-Gharb wa-Innamā Ḍidd al-Markaziyya al-Gharbiyya wa-l-ʿUdwān ʿalá Ummatinā', *Al-Sabīl*, 4–10 January 1994, 17; Rāshid al-Ghannūshī, 'Al-Aḥzāb Ghayr al-Islāmiyya fī l-Dawla al-Islāmiyya', *Al-Sabīl*, 1–7 March 1994, 17; Rāshid al-Ghannūshī, 'Mushārakat al-Islāmiyyīn fī Ḥukm Ghayr Islāmī', *Al-Sabīl*, 29 March–4 April 1994, 14; Rāshid al-Ghannūshī, 'Al-Ḥarakāt al-Islāmiyya Ḥarrarat al-Islām min al-Ṭabaqāt al-Ḥākima li-Yuṣbiḥa Mulkan li-l-Shaʿb', *Al-Sabīl*, 19–25 April 1994, 15; Rāshid al-Ghannūshī, 'Yanbaghī an Narfuḍa l-Dīktātūriyya fī Kull Ashkālihā wa-Law Mārasahā Muslim Yaddaʿī annahu Yurīdu an Yaḥmilu al-Nās ʿalá l-Islām', *Al-Sabīl*, 26 April–2 May 1994, 14. For more on al-Ghannūshī and his views, see Burgat, *Face to Face*, 28–37; Nazek Jawad, 'Democracy in Modern Islamic Thought', *British Journal of Middle Eastern Studies* 40, no. 3 (2013): 327–339; Shahin, *Political Ascent*, 203–8, 211–13, 216–17, 218, 220–5; Azzam S. Tamimi, *Rachid Ghannouchi: A Democrat within Islamism* (Oxford: Oxford University Press, 2001).

[70] For references to him by Jordanian Islamists and articles by al-Turābī himself in the Jordanian Islamist press, see the Brotherhood communiqué 'Jamāʿat al-Ikhwān al-Muslimīn fī l-Urdunn Tanʿá al-Shaykh Ḥasan al-Turābī', published on the occasion of his death on the Brotherhood's website www.ikhwan-jor.com/Portals/Content/?info=YVdROU5UZzNNQ1p6YjNWeVkyVT1VMVZDVUVGSFJTWjB1WEJsUFRFbSt1.ikhwan (accessed 8 March 2016; no longer available), 5 March 2016; Ruḥayyil Muḥammad al-Gharāyiba, 'Al-Turābī Najm Sāṭiʿ', *Al-Dustūr*, 8 March 2016, 20; Ḥasan al-Turābī, 'Al-Dawla wa-l-Mujtamaʿ wa-l-Dīmuqrāṭiyya', *Al-Sabīl*, 18–24 January 1994, 15; Ḥasan al-Turābī, 'Al-Dawla wa-l-Mujtamaʿ wa-l-Dīmuqrāṭiyya', *Al-Sabīl*, 19–25 April 1994, 15; Ḥasan al-Turābī, 'Al-Marʾa, al-Qawmiyya, Ḥuqūq al-Insān', *Al-Sabīl*, 31 May–6 June 1994, 16.

(b. 1926).[71] These and other thinkers will therefore be used in Part II to contextualise the Jordanian Brotherhood's own ideas and to help explain why academics reach such different conclusions with regard to the inclusion-moderation thesis when it is applied to this organisation.

In the context of these contemporary Islamist thinkers' ideas, Chapters 4, 5 and 6 deal with the Jordanian Muslim Brotherhood's views on the state, political participation and societal rights and freedoms, respectively. Chapter 4 shows that the Brotherhood's views on the role of the state and its character range from caliphate-inspired beliefs to the idea of a civil state with an Islamic authority. Chapter 5 presents the same divisions with regard to political participation, ranging from the rejection of democracy to its whole-hearted acceptance. Finally, Chapter 6 shows how Jordanian Muslim Brothers are united with regard to three societal issues: religious minority rights, women's rights and civil liberties. In the Conclusion, I summarise my findings on the development of Islamist ideology, show how the divisions within the Jordanian Muslim Brotherhood help explain its moderation as an organisation, how this contributes to our understanding of the inclusion-moderation thesis and what the wider implications of all of this are.

[71] Ana Belén Soage, 'Yusuf al-Qaradawi: The Muslim Brothers' Favorite Ideological Guide', in *The Muslim Brotherhood: The Organization and Policies of a Global Islamist Movement*, ed. Barry Rubin (New York: Palgrave Macmillan, 2010), 19–37; Husam Tammam, 'Yusuf al-Qaradawi and the Muslim Brothers: The Nature of a Special Relationship', in *Global Mufti: The Phenomenon of Yusuf al-Qaradawi*, ed. Bettina Gräf and Jakob Skovgaard-Petersen (New York: Columbia University Press, 2009), 55–83; David H. Warren, 'The ʿUlamāʾ and the Arab Uprisings 2011–12: Considering Yusuf al-Qaradawi, the "Global Mufti", between the Muslim Brotherhood, the Islamic Legal Tradition, and Qatari Foreign Policy', *New Middle Eastern Studies* 4 (2014): 2–32. For references to him by Jordanian Islamists and articles by al-Qaraḍāwī himself in the Jordanian Islamist press, see Yūsuf al-Qaraḍāwī, 'Al-Taʿaddudiyya al-Ḥizbiyya Ḍarūra Islāmiyya', *Al-Sabīl*, 29 March–4 April 1994, 17; 'Al-Qaraḍāwī: Al-Islām al-Ḥaqq Lā Yumkinu Illā an Yakūna Siyāsiyyan', *Al-Sabīl*, 21–27 January 1997, 14; 'Al-Qaraḍāwī: Al-Markaz Yuʿná bi-Tanmiyat al-Fikr al-Wasaṭī al-Muʿabbir ʿan al-Iʿtidāl al-Dīnī li-Muwājahat al-Taṭarruf', *Al-Sabīl*, 9 September 2009, 7; '"Al-ʿAmal al-Islāmī" Yuhanniʾu l-Qaraḍāwī bi-Iʿādat Intikhābihi Raʾīsan li-Ittiḥād ʿUlamāʾ al-Muslimīn', *Al-Sabīl*, 28 August 2014, 6; Sālim al-Falāḥāt, 'Naʿam al-Qaraḍāwī Irhābī!!', *Al-Sabīl*, 22 June 2017, 2. For more on al-Qaraḍāwī and his views, see the contributions to Bettina Gräf and Jakob Skovgaard-Petersen, eds, *Global Mufti: The Phenomenon of Yusuf al-Qaradawi* (New York: Columbia University Press, 2009); Aaron Rock-Singer, 'Scholarly Authority and Lay Mobilization: Yusuf al-Qaradawi's Vision of Daʿwa, 1976–1984', *The Muslim World* 106, no. 3 (2016): 588–604; David H. Warren and Christine Gilmore, 'Rethinking Neo-Salafism through an Emerging Fiqh of Citizenship: The Changing Status of Minorities in the Discourse of Yusuf al-Qaradawi and the "School of the Middle Way"', *New Middle Eastern Studies* 2 (2012): 1–7; David H. Warren and Christine Gilmore, 'One Nation under God? Yusuf al-Qaradawi's Changing Fiqh of Citizenship in the Light of the Islamic Legal Tradition', *Contemporary Islam* 8 (2014): 217–37.

Part I

Context

1 Sunni Islamic Political Thought until the Twentieth Century

In the writings produced by members of the Jordanian Muslim Brotherhood as well as in my interviews with the organisation's leaders, there were frequent references to their sources of inspiration. These included the Qur'an, the Prophet Muhammad, Islamic law and historical reformist Muslim thinkers. These sources form the historical, theoretical context in which the Jordanian Muslim Brotherhood operates: *historical* because it forms a long, time-honoured tradition of which the Brotherhood considers itself part and on which it seeks to build, but also *theoretical* because it provides the organisation with an ideological framework that serves as a point of departure for negotiations with the political, practical context of Jordanian society.

This chapter deals with Sunni Islamic political thought with regard to the state, political participation and societal rights and freedoms (religious minority rights, women's rights and civil liberties) from the time of the Prophet Muhammad to the twentieth century. Suffice it to say, no single chapter in any book can do justice to this huge subject. Moreover, much has already been written on classical Islamic political thought, so there appears to be little need for a chapter on this subject in a book on the Jordanian Muslim Brotherhood. Yet – apart from the fact that this chapter provides a new analysis of classical Islamic political thought – an overview of this subject is nevertheless necessary for three reasons: firstly, classical Islamic political thought forms an important source of the Brotherhood's ideas, as we will see in Chapters 4–6, and therefore requires to be dealt with in some detail; secondly, dealing with the classical tradition also shows the continuity and change of Sunni Islamic political thought from the advent of Islam to modern-day Jordan, which is essential in a work of intellectual history such as this one; and thirdly, this chapter introduces many of the basic concepts that will be dealt with in greater detail later on and therefore also serves as an introduction to the ideological framework analysed in this book.

The goal of this chapter is thus not to give a full overview of Islamic political thought or to discuss a seemingly irrelevant subject, but to provide essential background information on the Brotherhood's ideas and to facilitate the understanding of the organisation's ideological decontestation later on. As such, this chapter concentrates on Islamic political thought until the twentieth century, showing that *sharīʿa*-centred, *umma*-centred and balanced approaches to Islamic political thought could already be discerned in classical times with regard to the three themes mentioned above.[1] These serve as the basis for the analysis of the problems that the modern-day Jordanian Muslim Brotherhood has to deal with. Based mostly on secondary sources, this chapter is divided into three main sections: the first concentrates on the state; the second focusses on political participation; and the third deals with societal rights and freedoms.

The State

The development of Islamic political thought can be said to have started almost from the very beginning of Islam. Islamic tradition has it that the Prophet Muhammad (570–632) and his early followers fled from Mecca to Medina in 622 (the so-called *hijra* (emigration)) to escape persecution by polytheist Meccans. In this new environment, the Prophet – as leader of the community of the believers there – is said to have had to deal with a variety of issues of governance that concern us here, such as how to deal with non-Muslim minorities. The Prophet's example in such matters proved an important source of inspiration for Muslim scholars who wanted to establish rules for what Islamic political thought should look like.[2] After the Prophet's death, some of his most prominent followers succeeded him as leaders of the community (caliphs) in what became known as the caliphate, the name used for the political system applied by the early Muslims and one that lasted for almost 1,300 years, at least theoretically. It is also with the caliphate that we must start our analysis of what Muslim scholars have written about Islamic political thought.

The Caliphate as State

The caliphate is strongly connected with the various Muslim empires that have existed over the centuries. Yet perhaps the main platform of politics

[1] This means that some important topics, such as polygamy, will be consciously left out because they are not a major issue for the Jordanian Muslim Brotherhood today.

[2] The Prophet Muḥammad can therefore be said to have been, in the words of William Montgomery Watt, a 'Prophet and statesman'. See W. Montgomery Watt, *Muhammad: Prophet and Statesman* (Oxford: Oxford University Press, 1961). Even Muslim critics of the caliphate, such as ʿAlī ʿAbd al-Rāziq (see below), did not deny that the Prophet (also) had a political position.

today is not the empire, but the state: 'a political association that establishes sovereign [. . .] jurisdiction within defined territorial borders and exercises authority through a set of permanent institutions.'[3] The Muslim empires were not states in this sense because they had no defined territorial borders, but they did share states' other characteristics as defined above. Moreover, the Arabic term used for 'empire' and 'state' today is the same: *dawla*. Therefore, despite the fact that there is a clear difference between the Muslim caliphates that have existed throughout Islamic history and modern states, it makes sense to discuss the question of the caliphate in the context of Islamic thought on the state.[4]

The word 'caliphate' is derived from the Arabic *khilāfa*, which in turn stems from the verb *khalafa* (to succeed). This makes it tempting to interpret the caliphate simply as the institution of the successors (*khulafāʾ*, sing. *khalīfa*) of the Prophet. While this sounds obvious, there are indications that the meaning of the term caliph is more complicated. The term *khalīfa* occurs twice in the Qurʾan. The first of these occurrences (Q. 2:30) says, in apparent reference to Adam, '[. . .] "I [God] am setting in the earth a viceroy" [. . .]', while the second (Q. 38:26) states: 'David, behold, We have appointed thee a viceroy in the earth [. . .].'[5] The use of the term *khalīfa* in these verses, translated here as 'viceroy', suggests that God himself appointed a person to rule on earth.

Since the term *khalīfat Allāh*, derived from the Qurʾanic verses cited, is unlikely to have meant 'the successor of God', Crone and Hinds claim that these words actually refer to a 'deputy of God'. This implies that the caliph ruled on God's behalf and did not just have political but also religious authority.[6] In fact, they claim that the title *khalīfat Allāh* was used to label caliphs well into the Abbasid Empire (750–1258) and that 'deputy of God' was actually the original meaning of the term.[7] The title *khalīfat rasūl Allāh* (successor of the messenger of God), Crone and Hinds state, was the meaning given to the term 'caliph' by Muslim scholars,

[3] Andrew Heywood, *Politics* (New York: Palgrave, 2002 [1997]), 87.

[4] For more on the discussion of Muslim conceptions of 'state' as an impersonal entity, which – though different from the above – is still relevant, see also Patricia Crone, *God's Rule – Government and Islam: Six Centuries of Medieval Islamic Political Thought* (New York: Columbia University Press, 2004), 3–4. See also Wael B. Hallaq, *The Impossible State: Islam, Politics, and Modernity's Moral Predicament* (New York: Columbia University Press, 2013).

[5] All translations from the Qurʾān have been taken from A. J. Arberry's *The Koran Interpreted* (New York: Touchstone, 1955). The more common verse numbering used by other translations of the Qurʾān has been adopted, however, rather than the one Arberry uses.

[6] Patricia Crone and Martin Hinds, *God's Caliph: Religious Authority in the First Centuries of Islam* (Cambridge: Cambridge University Press, 2003 [1986]), 4–5.

[7] Ibid., 6–19. See also W. Montgomery Watt, *Islamic Political Thought* (Edinburgh: Edinburgh University Press, 2007 [1968]), 33–4.

whose explanation was subsequently adopted by academics as historically accurate.[8] Others, however, have criticised this thesis as containing errors and making use of a selective reading of sources.[9]

'Sharī'a', 'Umma' *and* 'Sulṭa' *as Adjacent to the Core Concept of 'Caliph'*

Whatever the word 'caliph' may have meant in early Islam, Lambton has pointed out that the caliphate ultimately had God as its authority because it was based on the *sharī'a*,[10] but simultaneously had the *umma* as its heart.[11] Although these two issues are not necessarily contradictory in Islamic thought, they do account for the possibility of two very different points of emphasis and, as a result, two very different ideas of what an Islamic state should look like. To use Freeden's terminology, 'caliph', as the ruling authority, functions as the core concept in Islamic political thought. The caliph needs *sulṭa* (power) to be effective, needs adherence to the *sharī'a* to be legitimate and needs to listen to the *umma* to be just. As such, both '*sharī'a*' and '*umma*' (as well as '*sulṭa*') act as adjacent concepts to the core concept of 'caliph', together forming much of what an Islamic state looks like.

Again, '*sharī'a*' and '*umma*' need not be unequal in their distance to 'caliph', but there is at least the theoretical possibility that the scholarly interpretation of the former clashes with the will of the latter. As a result, they can only be equally important to the core concept of 'caliph' if the *sharī'a* is viewed as adaptable to the wishes of the (inevitably changing) *umma*. If, however, the *sharī'a* is viewed as unchanging, it cannot possibly be aligned with the will of the *umma* at all times and must therefore take precedence over the *umma*, pushing the latter to a peripheral position, or the other way round. It is this choice between (a) opting for equality between '*sharī'a*' and '*umma*' vis-à-vis the core concept of 'caliph' (a balanced approach); (b) allowing '*sharī'a*' to take precedence over '*umma*' in this respect (a *sharī'a*-centred approach); or (c) vice versa (an *umma*-centred approach) that is crucial to analysing modern Islamist debates on what an Islamic state should look like.

This tension and the lack of clarity between these three options can also be seen in early ideas on the caliphate. The latter is described in the literature as having its roots in pre-Islamic tribal custom, with the caliph's job somewhat resembling that of a tribe's chief, whose position was not one of absolute power but rather that of a first among equals.[12] The job of

8 Crone and Hinds, *God's Caliph*, 19–23.
9 For an overview of critical views on Crone and Hinds' theory, see Anjum, *Politics*, 42–8.
10 Ann K. S. Lambton, *State and Government in Medieval Islam – An Introduction to the Study of Islamic Political Theory: The Jurists* (New York: Routledge, 1991 [1981]), 1.
11 Ibid., 13. 12 Watt, *Islamic Thought*, 40.

caliph was therefore limited and was directed towards following the Prophet Muhammad in trying to establish justice (*'adl*) for the *umma.*[13] This justice was not rooted in the caliph's own sense of right and wrong, but in the rights and duties that emanated from God himself as known through the *sharī'a.*[14] According to this line of thinking, the caliph should not be seen as an absolute ruler but as subservient to and bound by the *sharī'a.*[15]

Such an arrangement seems geared towards or at least open to the possibility of limiting the power of the ruler by making him subject to God's own rule through the *sharī'a*, thereby providing room for other actors – such as the *umma* – to somehow be involved in this system as well. This impression of the *sharī'a* acting as a divine check on executive power is strengthened further when one sees the criteria various scholars believed a new caliph had to fulfil, which included that the caliph had to be just, scrupulously observant and knowledgeable of Islamic law.[16] If one views the *sharī'a* as fundamentally just and requires caliphs to adhere strictly to its rules and regulations, this scenario seems a recipe for just and pious leadership that would serve the *umma.* In fact, some scholars describe the caliph as an agent (*wakīl*) or a representative (*nā'ib*) acting on behalf of the *umma* in the sense that he is merely the one implementing the *sharī'a* – Muslims' supposedly preferred system of law – for them.[17]

Yet this scenario also assumes that two of the concepts mentioned as adjacent to the core concept of 'caliph' – '*sharī'a*' and '*umma*' – behave in a rather unrealistic way. Firstly, it is assumed that the *sharī'a* is not only adhered to by the caliph but is also enough in and of itself to prevent him from abusing his powers without further institutional checks. The fact that religious scholars believed they should advise the caliph and ought to be consulted by him[18] could cause the caliph to change course, but there was no guarantee that it would; secondly, it is assumed that the *umma* wishes the application of the *sharī'a* and, once this wish is expressed, does not change its mind about this and gives the caliph a mandate to govern for years or even decades. While the power of the *umma* to influence this situation is dealt with in the next section, the application of the *sharī'a* merits more attention here.

[13] Anke Iman Bouzenita, 'Early Contributions to the Theory of Islamic Governance: 'Abd al-Raḥmān al-Awzā'ī', *Journal of Islamic Studies* 23, no. 2 (2012): 159.

[14] Crone, *God's Rule*, 263–6.

[15] Lambton, *State*, 14; E. I. J. Rosenthal, *Political Thought in Medieval Islam: An Introductory Outline* (Cambridge: Cambridge University Press, 2009 [1958]), 23–4.

[16] Crone, *God's Rule*, 224–6; Lambton, *State*, 64, 79–80, 89.

[17] Crone, *God's Rule*, 277; Lambton, *State*, 76, 112–13.

[18] Antony Black, *The History of Islamic Political Thought: From the Prophet to the Present* (New York: Routledge, 2001), 32–3, 104–5, 110–11; Lambton, *State*, 115, 139.

Given the perceived necessity of the caliph's application of the *sharīʿa* to ensure that it is actually lived by, the caliph's position in an Islamic state was of paramount importance.[19] Such a system naturally vested a lot of power in the hands of the caliph, but without 'authoritative devices for signalling breach of the rules, and no official mechanisms for the imposition of sanctions either', which – Crone states – really amounted to 'government by appeal to the ruler's conscience'.[20] This system, in other words, was easily abused by the caliphs who wanted to, with little that could be done about it. It is likely for this reason that Muslim scholars have written on the need to accept the rulers, even if they did not live up to the criteria set for a caliph or did not abide by the *sharīʿa*, simply because they had the power to enforce their will. While '*sulṭa*' had always been an adjacent concept to the core one of 'caliph', it slowly but surely grew into its main adjacent concept, thereby pushing '*sharīʿa*' to the periphery. This meant that it reached the point at which *ʿulamāʾ* became increasingly willing to simply accept whoever was in power.[21] As such, rather than a balanced or *sharīʿa*-centred approach (or an *umma*-centred approach, which is dealt with below), Muslim scholars – out of necessity – opted for a *sulṭa*-centred approach.

Modern Reformist Islamic Thought

The developments described above all took place under the rule of various Muslim empires. Yet with the rise of Western influence in the Muslim world in general and Western colonialism in particular, the Ottoman Empire slowly but surely crumbled, giving way to colonial mandates and, later, independent states. Partly as a result of this, the traditionalist Sunni educational system of studying legal texts and passing on their knowledge to students was increasingly being challenged by more modern forms of education. This led to the rise of a class of intellectuals who had not always enjoyed traditionalist religious training, but who were nevertheless highly educated. Simultaneously, Muslims began challenging the traditionalist legal doctrines of their forbears as outdated, rigid and incompatible with the challenges of modern times. It was in this environment, which gained momentum in the nineteenth century, that several reformist scholars came to the fore, the most famous of whom are Jamal al-Din

[19] Crone, *God's Rule*, 270. [20] Ibid., 284.
[21] Lambton, *State*, 56–7, 114, 138–42, 308–9.

al-Afghani (1838/1839–1897), Muhammad ʿAbduh (1849–1905) and Muhammad Rashid Rida (1865–1935).[22]

Reformist scholars such as those mentioned also wrote about some of the aspects of political thought dealt with in this book, including the caliphate, which was abolished by the new republic of Turkey in 1924.[23] Opinion in the Muslim world was divided on the abolition of the caliphate: various reformers applauded it for nationalist or modernist reasons, while other, more traditionalist Muslim scholars were less enthusiastic but showed a willingness to come to terms with the new situation.[24] One reformer who clearly rejected the caliphate as a religious duty was the Egyptian *sharīʿa* judge ʿAli ʿAbd al-Raziq (1888–1966) in his book *Al-Islam wa-Usul al-Hukm* (Islam and the Principles of Governance).[25] He argued that neither the Qurʾan nor the Sunna mentions the duty to establish a caliphate and that this system was merely the result of historical developments, not a duty incumbent upon modern-day Muslims.[26] These turned out to be highly controversial conclusions, however, and several traditionalist scholars criticised him because of them, while others proved more supportive of his views.[27]

More important for this book are Rida's views on the caliphate, on which he wrote extensively. The reason Rida is so important in this respect is that he was a major source of influence on Hasan al-Banna, the founder of the Muslim Brotherhood, who even became the editor of *Al-Manar*, Rida's famous journal, after the latter had died.[28] Like his Egyptian fellow reformer ʿAbduh (as well as many others), Rida – who was originally from Tripoli in what is now Lebanon – rejected the blind following (*taqlīd*) of the various schools of Islamic law (*madhāhib*, sing.

22 The literature on these reformers is vast. Examples include Albert Hourani, *Arabic Thought in the Liberal Age, 1798–1939* (Cambridge: Cambridge University Press, 1983 [1962]), 103–60, 222–44; Nikki R. Keddie, *Sayyid Jamal Ad-Din 'Al-Afghani': A Political Biography* (Berkeley and Los Angeles, CA, and London: University of California Press, 1972); Elie Kedourie, *Afghani and ʿAbduh: An Essay on Religious Unbelief and Political Activism in Modern Islam* (London: Frank Cass & Co., 1997 [1966]).

23 Hamid Enayat, *Modern Islamic Political Thought* (Austin, TX: University of Texas Press, 1982), 52–6.

24 Ibid., 56–61.

25 ʿAlī ʿAbd al-Rāziq, *Al-Islām wa-Uṣūl al-Ḥukm* (Beirut/Cairo: Dār al-Kitāb al-Lubnānī /Dār al-Kitāb al-Miṣrī, 2012 [1925]).

26 Asma Afsaruddin, 'Loyalty and Obedience to the Ruler: Religious Obligation or a Practical Necessity?', *The Muslim World* 106 (2016): 371–2; Leonard Binder, *Islamic Liberalism: A Critique of Development Ideologies* (Chicago, IL, and London: University of Chicago Press, 1988), 128–43; Black, *History*, 316–19; Enayat, *Modern Thought*, 62–8.

27 Binder, *Islamic Liberalism*, 144–69.

28 Mehdi Sajid, 'A Reappraisal of the Role of Muḥibb al-Dīn al-Khaṭīb and the YMMA in the Rise of the Muslim Brotherhood', *Islam and Christian–Muslim Relations* 29, no. 2 (2018): 193–5. See also Marion Boulby, *The Muslim Brotherhood and the Kings of Jordan, 1945–1993* (Atlanta, GA: Scholars Press, 1999), 126–9.

madhhab) and advocated independent reasoning on the basis of the Qur'an and the Sunna (*ijtihād*). This was an important aspect of reformers' toolkit to renew Islam and Rida also applied this to his views on the caliphate to ensure that – while aware of, influenced by and respectful towards the Islamic legal tradition on this subject – he was not beholden to what others had decided before him in any way.[29]

Rida essentially agrees with the classical Islamic tradition that having a ruler is not just a rational but also an Islamic legal duty incumbent upon all Muslims[30] in order to prevent chaos.[31] Yet Rida also criticises the caliphate as it developed throughout the centuries. He distinguishes between the ideal caliphate of the first four 'rightly guided' caliphs (*al-khulafā' al-rāshidūn*) and the flawed 'imamate' (which he uses interchangeably with 'caliphate') as it developed thereafter.[32] Rida subdivides the latter into the 'necessary imamate' (*al-imāma al-ḍarūriyya*), which – in the absence of the ideal caliphate – was the next best thing available, and 'mastery by force' (*al-taghallub bi-l-quwwa*), which he deems undesirable, but less bad than chaos (*fawḍá*). Both systems are not ideal, but people should strive to make them so. In the meantime, the rulers of such systems should be obeyed.[33]

Rida thus seems to differ little from his scholarly predecessors. Yet he is also confronted with the question of what to do with the caliphate at a time when it was about to be abolished. It is with regard to this question that he shows his reformist credentials and does so in a manner that not only reinterprets Islamic political thought on this point, but also guides the way to what the Muslim Brotherhood would do later. Rida, in fact, envisages the founding of a new caliphate. He surveys the qualities a new caliph should have,[34] assesses several candidates for this position (including the leader of the 1916 Arab Revolt, Sharif Husayn b. 'Ali (c. 1853–1931)) and concludes that they all fall short of the ideal.[35] He does the same with the location of the new caliphate's capital, which he finds would be ideally situated somewhere between the Arabian Peninsula and what would become Turkey, like in the Iraqi city of Mosul.[36]

Rida thus tries to decontest his views of the core concept of 'caliphate', thereby differing quite substantially from his contemporary 'Abd al-

[29] Muḥammad Rashīd Riḍā, *Al-Khilāfa aw al-Imāma al-'Uẓmá* (N.p.: Maṭba'at al-Manār bi-Miṣr, n.d.), 80–7. Several publications indicate that this book was published in 1922–1923, so right before the abolition of the caliphate. See, for instance, Black, *History*, 314; Enayat, *Modern Thought*, 70.
[30] Riḍā, *Al-Khilāfa*, 10. [31] Ibid., 125. [32] Enayat, *Modern Thought*, 71.
[33] Ibid.; Riḍā, *Al-Khilāfa*, 36–8.
[34] Enayat, *Modern Thought*, 76; Riḍā, *Al-Khilāfa*, 18–24.
[35] Enayat, *Modern Thought*, 74; Riḍā, *Al-Khilāfa*, 74–6.
[36] Enayat, *Modern Thought*, 74–5; Riḍā, *Al-Khilāfa*, 69–78.

Raziq, who was far more dismissive. Yet Rida clearly takes the new situation of colonialism and nation-states into account by calling for a caliphate that is different from the previous ones. Rather than desperately trying to resurrect a form of government that was on its way out, Rida describes a caliphate that does not replace existing states, but acts as a confederation, a commonwealth or a spiritual office that serves as a symbolic leadership of all Muslims. In such a situation, the job of caliph would likely be largely ceremonial or at least not explicitly political.[37] Moreover, Rida even seems to shift his discourse from one focussing on the caliphate to one concentrating on an Islamic government.[38] This not only underlines that Rida had come to terms with the new, 'caliphate-less' situation, but also that he was willing to incorporate this into his political thinking. In Freeden's terminology, Rida targeted the core concept of 'caliph' head on and decontested its meaning, partly by reinterpreting it as merely spiritual, but also by implicitly allowing it to recede to the background in favour of a similar but vaguer concept that is more relevant in colonial times: 'ruler'.[39]

Political Participation

As we saw above, adherents to the classical theory of the caliphate assumed that the *sharīʿa* would prevent the ruler from abusing his power, which turned out to be wrong. How about the second assumption mentioned earlier, which relies on the *umma*'s consent to the caliph's rule by the *sharīʿa* without any further influence or participation? Did Muslim scholars assume the *umma* would just accept things as they were or did they leave room for greater political participation by the community of believers? Answers to both questions can, in fact, be found in Islamic tradition, but just as the increasing emphasis on the adjacent concept of '*sulṭa*' pushed '*sharīʿa*' to the periphery, as we saw above, so too can we discern a trend of '*umma*' becoming increasingly peripheral as time went by.

The caliph had several tasks, such as maintaining divine law and order, ensuring the validity of the communal Friday prayers by being present himself or sending a governor to attend them in his stead and waging

[37] Black, *History*, 314–15; Enayat, *Modern Thought*, 75–6.
[38] Enayat, *Modern Thought*, 76–7.
[39] I have consciously used the term 'ruler' without giving the original Arabic term, simply because different terms have been used for ruler, depending on the time and the circumstances, ranging from *ḥākim* (ruler), *sulṭān* (power, ruler) and *walī al-amr* (the person in charge, ruler) to more specific terms like *malik* (king) and *raʾīs* (president).

jihad.[40] The increased emphasis on '*sulṭa*' as an adjacent concept at the expense of '*sharīʿa*' and the less than pious rule that came about as a result caused some Muslims to resent the caliph. Although Islamic history is full of examples of revolts and insurrections as well as the usurpation of power by rival rulers and dynasties, it is not so much the practice but rather the theoretical Islamic political thought that interests us here. Muslim scholars can be said to have distinguished four different links between the adjacent concept of '*umma*' and the core concept of 'caliph', with each one also being strongly connected to the adjacent concept of '*sharīʿa*': commanding right and forbidding wrong (*al-amr bi-l-maʿrūf wa-l-nahy ʿan al-munkar*); consultation (*shūrá*); an oath of fealty (*bayʿa*); and obedience (*ṭāʿa*). Each of these will be analysed on a conceptual level, together showing how '*umma*' – like '*sharīʿa*' – became a peripheral concept vis-à-vis the core concept of 'caliph'.

Commanding Right and Forbidding Wrong

The most obvious thing the *umma* could do against a caliph it did not like was to depose him in some way.[41] Several Muslim scholars have stated that removing a caliph was allowed if he did not fulfil his duties as an Islamic leader or actively ruled against the *sharīʿa*,[42] although they were often careful to add that the solution (deposition) must not be greater than the problem (a bad caliph) and that one must avoid civil strife (*fitna*). Muslim scholars were therefore highly unlikely to call for open rebellion against a caliph.[43] Moreover, they rarely – if ever – stipulated a procedure to actually depose a ruler, which essentially meant that they allowed for the theoretical possibility of removing a caliph, but did not call or provide guidelines for doing so in practice.[44] It is here that commanding right and forbidding wrong provided the *umma* with a *sharīʿa*-based alternative to outright rebellion to check the caliph's power.[45]

The phrase 'commanding right and forbidding wrong' occurs several times in the Qurʾan, such as in Q. 3:104 ('Let there be one nation (*umma*) of you, calling to good, and bidding to honour (*wa-yaʾmurūna bi-l-maʿrūf*), and forbidding dishonour (*wa-yanhawna ʿan al-munkar*); those are the prosperors'). This Qurʾanic verse makes clear that it is the

[40] Crone, *God's Rule*, 286–300.

[41] Perhaps the most comprehensive work on the subject of rebellion against the ruler is Khaled Abou El Fadl, *Rebellion & Violence in Islamic Law* (Cambridge: Cambridge University Press, 2001).

[42] Black, *History*, 29; Lambton, *State*, 77.

[43] Lambton, *State*, 124; Rosenthal, *Political Thought*, 55.

[44] Black, *History*, 85; Crone, *God's Rule*, 231–2; Lambton, *State*, 64, 77, 80.

[45] Lambton, *State*, 313.

umma that should be doing the bidding/commanding and forbidding and that this is something positive ('those are the prosperors'). This is not always obvious in other verses and neither is it clear what one should command or forbid and towards whom. Qurʾanic exegetes seem to have expanded on the textual references to this duty to create a broader practical meaning of the term.[46] Perhaps this has to do with the many *ḥadīth*s (traditions of the Prophet Muhammad) it occurs in and one in particular, in which the Prophet is credited with saying: 'Whoever among you sees a wrong (*munkaran*), let him change it with his hand. If that is not possible, let him change it with his tongue. If that is not possible, [let him change it] with his heart. That is the weakest faith (*aḍʿaf al-īmān*).'[47]

In practice, commanding right and forbidding wrong towards supposedly sinful rulers was often avoided by ordinary Muslims because they believed it was no use or out of fear that they would be punished or even killed by the caliph. As a result, commanding right and forbidding wrong usually seems to have taken the second form mentioned in the *ḥadīth* cited above: private advice or a verbal reprimand, but no physical action.[48] In fact, it was the caliphate itself that seems to have monopolised the use of violence with regard to *al-amr bi-l-maʿrūf wa-l-nahy ʿan al-munkar* in society. The admonition to command right and forbid wrong was sometimes seen as a collective duty (*farḍ ʿalá l-kifāya*), meaning that only a limited number of Muslims needed to act upon it.[49] In practice, this often meant that the rulers appointed a so-called *muḥtasib* (censor), who patrolled the streets ensuring that Muslims adhered to rules of public morality, attended Friday prayers, abided by the rules when trading at markets and abstained from wine, among other things.[50]

All of this means that commanding right and forbidding wrong – though useful as a duty towards other Muslims and perhaps applicable to rulers in verbal form – was not seen as a viable way to depose or even hold to account a caliph deemed sinful or otherwise incompetent. The ineliminable feature of the duty – that right be commanded and wrong forbidden – remained, of course, but the quasi-contingent features (the role of commander/forbidder and that of the person commanded/forbidden) were increasingly applied by rulers themselves in a way that benefitted the caliphate. As such, 'commanding right and forbidding

[46] Michael Cook, *Commanding Right and Forbidding Wrong in Islamic Thought* (Cambridge: Cambridge University Press, 2001), 13–31.

[47] Versions of this *ḥadīth* occur in many collections of *ḥadīth*s. See, for instance, *Ṣaḥīḥ Muslim*, 'Kitāb al-Īmān', *bāb* 'Bayān Kawn al-Nahy ʿan al-Munkar min al-Īmān wa-anna l-Īmān Yazīdu wa-Yanquṣu wa-anna l-Amr bi-l-Maʿrūf wa-l-Nahy ʿan al-Munkar Wājibān'. For more variations and version of this tradition, see Cook, *Commanding Right*, 32–3, notes 2 and 6. For entirely different *ḥadīth*s about this duty, see ibid., 35–45.

[48] Cook, *Commanding Right*, 50–67. [49] Ibid., 18. [50] Crone, *God's Rule*, 301.

wrong', acting as a link between the adjacent concept of '*umma*' and the core concept of 'caliph', moved away from the former and towards the latter, thereby decreasing its value as a means of the *umma*'s political participation in the caliph's affairs and effectively allowing '*umma*' to recede to the periphery.

Consultation and Oath of Fealty

The second and third links between '*umma*' and 'caliph' – *shūrá* and *bayʿa* – do not deal with the possibility of deposing or controlling a leader, but with choosing one, which is obviously also an important potential avenue of political participation for the *umma*. The pre-Islamic term[51] *shūrá* appears once in the Qurʾan (Q. 42:38: '[...] their affair being counsel (*shūrá*) between them [...]')[52] and there are two instances in which forms derived from the term appear (Q. 2:233: '[...] But if the couple desire by mutual consent and consultation (*tashāwur*) to wean, then it is no fault in them [...]' and Q. 3:159: '[...] take counsel with them (*shāwirhum*) in the affair [...]'). A more explicitly political example – and one that is directly relevant for this discussion – is the formation of a consultation council (*shūrá*) consisting of six prominent Muslim men by the second caliph, ʿUmar b. al-Khattab (r. 634–644), to decide on his successor.[53] Though less formally executed, his predecessor as caliph and the first Muslim leader after the Prophet himself, Abu Bakr (r. 632–634), is also said to have consulted leading Muslim men on the question of who should succeed him as the leader of the faithful.[54]

As such, the concept of *shūrá* seems to have provided the *umma* with a role in the selection of a new caliph, albeit a modest one in which only a limited number of Muslim men were involved and one that does not seem to have been adopted by many Muslim rulers since.[55] The participating role of the *umma* was expanded, however, through the much more commonly used ritual of *bayʿa*, the third link between the adjacent concept of '*umma*' and the core one of 'caliph'. The origin of this term is not entirely clear, but seems to refer to either the act of selling (Ar. *bāʿa-yabīʿu*) or the physical act of clasping someone's hand, both meant

51 C. E. Bosworth, 'Shūrā', in *Encyclopaedia of Islam: New Edition*, vol. 9, ed. C. E. Bosworth (Leiden: E.J. Brill, 1997), 504.
52 This *sūra* also derives its name from this term: Sūrat al-Shūrá.
53 M. J. Kister, 'Notes on an Account of the Shura Appointed by ʿUmar b. al-Khattab', *Journal of Semitic Studies* 9 (1964): 320–6; William Muir, *The Caliphate: Its Rise, Decline and Fall*, ed. T. H. Weir (Edinburgh: J. Grant, 1915[1891]), 193–7; Gernot Rotter, *Die Umayyaden und der zweite Bürgerkrieg (680–692)* (Wiesbaden: Deutsche Morgenländische Gesellschaft, 1982), 7–16.
54 Watt, *Islamic Thought*, 35.
55 Bosworth et al., 'Shūrā', 505.

as an oath of fealty to another person.[56] Early believers are said to have pledged allegiance to the Prophet Muhammad this way and it is probably in reference to such an event that Q. 48:18 states: 'God was well pleased with the believers when they were swearing fealty to thee (*yubāyiʿūnaka*) under the tree [...].' Other forms related to *bayʿa* also occur in the Qurʾan, although there is no mention of the actual term itself.[57]

The *bayʿa* as an oath of fealty was applied to the caliphs after the death of the Prophet.[58] Interestingly, the *bayʿa* seems to have denoted a contractual relationship between the ruler and the ruled that implied that the caliph perform his duties as a leader and that the person pledging fealty be obedient to him. This, like *shūrá*, suggests that the *umma* played an active role in choosing (or at least approving) the caliph. As time went by, however, the caliph's side of the bargain – performing his duties as a ruler – was gradually lost and although the *bayʿa* remained a contract in theory, in practice it increasingly became a one-sided pledge of fealty only.[59] As such, in the work of important writers on Islamic political thought such as al-Mawardi (974–1058) the *bayʿa* became merely a stamp of approval for the caliph who happened to be in power at the time.[60] This even applied to rulers who had, in fact, not been chosen at all but had simply been designated by their predecessors to succeed them[61] or – particularly in the writings of Ibn Jamaʿa (1241–1333) – had usurped power through a military coup.[62]

The application of the *bayʿa* thus came to favour the caliph by absolving him of his duties while retaining the allegiance owed to him by the *umma*. The same applied to the people who were involved in actually pledging allegiance to the caliph. *Bayʿa* maintained its ineliminable feature – that fealty be pledged – and one quasi-contingent feature – the object of fealty (i.e. the caliph) – also remained the same. The other quasi-contingent feature of the term – the ones pledging fealty – changed, however. At first, the *bayʿa* seems to have been split up into two separate rituals: a private one (*bayʿa khāṣṣa*) to the caliph by a limited number of dignitaries, followed by a public oath of fealty (*bayʿa ʿāmma*) by Muslims in general

[56] Ella Landau-Tasseron, *The Religious Foundations of Political Allegiance: A Study of Bayʿa in Pre-modern Islam*, Research Monographs on the Muslim World 2, no. 4 (Washington, DC: Hudson Institute, 2010), 1; E. Tyan, 'Bayʿa', in *Encyclopaedia of Islam: New Edition*, vol. 1, ed. H. A. R. Gibb, J. H. Kramers, E. Lévi-Provençal, J. Schacht, B. Lewis and Ch. Pellat (Leiden: E.J. Brill, 1986 [1960]), 1113.

[57] Landau-Tasseron, *Religious Foundations*, 5–6.

[58] Roy P. Mottahedeh, *Loyalty and Leadership in an Early Islamic Society* (Princeton, NJ: Princeton University Press, 1980), 50–1.

[59] Landau-Tasseron, *Religious Foundations*, 10–14.

[60] Lambton, *State*, 90.

[61] Crone, *God's Rule*, 227; Lambton, *State*, 141; Rosenthal, *Political Thought*, 30.

[62] Lambton, *State*, 141–2.

to show the *umma*'s support for the new ruler.[63] The public aspect of the oath of fealty seems to have declined in importance, however, leading to a situation in which only a small number of Muslims pledged fealty to the caliph. This means that this quasi-contingent feature of *bayʿa* – the ones pledging fealty – changed from (significant parts of) the *umma* to a limited group of leading Muslim dignitaries. Similarly, while maintaining the ineliminable feature of *shūrá* (i.e. that there be consultation), one of its quasi-contingent features – the ones being consulted – was also limited to a small number of dignitaries.

Yet who were these dignitaries being consulted and pledging fealty? According to some, they were members of an elite group of people,[64] mostly referred to by the words 'the people of loosening and binding' (*ahl al-ḥall wa-l-ʿaqd*), denoting a group of local political leaders and religious scholars, possibly also varying depending on the circumstances.[65] According to some scholars, these people should have justice (*ʿadāla* or *ʿadl*), (religious) learning or knowledge (*ʿilm*) and the necessary judgement and wisdom.[66] Still, even in cases in which the *ahl al-ḥall wa-l-ʿaqd* were actually involved in the election (*ikhtiyār*) of the caliph, rather than merely pledging fealty to the candidate who had been chosen for them,[67] their role was sometimes limited. Some classical scholars of Islamic political thought deemed the *bayʿa* valid even if a single member of the *ahl al-ḥall wa-l-ʿaqd* performed it.[68] In such cases, the quasi-contingent feature of the ones pledging fealty was further limited to be even less representative of the *umma*.[69]

Obedience

All of this resulted in a situation in which the link between the core concept of 'caliph' and the adjacent concept of '*umma*' became ever weaker. This, in turn, meant that the political participation of the *umma* decreased and that its relationship with the caliph was increasingly characterised as one of obedience (*ṭāʿa*), the fourth link between 'caliph' and

63 Landau-Tasseron, *Religious Foundations*, 9; Rosenthal, *Political Thought*, 31; Tyan, 'Bayʿa', 1113.

64 Black, *History*, 29. For more on the class differences between the 'distinguished' (*khawāṣṣ*) and the 'commoners' (*al-ʿawāmm*) and other divisions, see Mottahedeh, *Loyalty*, 120–9.

65 Black, *History*, 103; Crone, *God's Rule*, 227–8; Lambton, *State*, 18.

66 Lambton, *State*, 89. 67 Ibid., 114.

68 Black, *History*, 85; Lambton, *State*, 73–4, 105.

69 This is further confirmed by the dim view several classical Muslim scholars took of democracy. Like the Greek philosophers (e.g. Plato and Aristotle) through whose work they got to know it, they rejected this system of governance. See Crone, *God's Rule*, 279–81.

'*umma*'. As Afsaruddin writes: '[T]umultuous times [of war and civil strife] predisposed many of the scholars of this [late Abbasid] period to focus primarily on the ability of the leader to maintain law and order at all times by curbing internal political rebellion and warding off external threats.'[70] This predisposition expressed itself in the increasingly pro-caliph attitude to *al-amr bi-l-maʿrūf wa-l-nahy ʿan al-munkar*, *shūrá* and *bayʿa* at the expense of the *umma*'s role in all of these, as we saw above, and the same applied to *ṭāʿa*. Increasing emphasis was put on the necessity of obeying the caliph.[71] Whereas in early Islam *ṭāʿa* used to be seen as not applicable to caliphs who acted contrary to the *sharīʿa*, this changed into almost unconditional obedience that only became invalid if the caliph became an unbeliever (*kāfir*, pl. *kuffār*).[72]

A scenario in which the caliph openly and noticeably abandoned Islam was not only highly unlikely, but even if such a scenario did unfold, there would still not be any procedure to depose the ruler, as we saw above. While Muslim scholars have pointed to Q. 4:59 ('O believers, obey God (*aṭīʿū llāh*), and obey the Messenger (*aṭīʿū l-rasūl*) and those in authority among you (*ūlī l-amr minkum*) [. . .]') as justification for their emphasis on *ṭāʿa*, it is likely that their fear of civil strife and the ensuing disunity of the *umma* were more decisive in their willingness to accord so much power and obedience to the caliph. As such, they concluded that even tyrannical and unjust caliphs must be obeyed.[73] This means that – while maintaining *ṭāʿa*'s ineliminable feature (that someone be obeyed) – one of the term's quasi-contingent features (the person obeyed) is decoupled from the *sharīʿa*, whereas its other main quasi-contingent feature (the ones obeying) remains the same. This, in turn, resulted in the core concept of 'caliph' becoming even more associated with the adjacent concept of '*sulṭa*', which caused '*umma*' – just like '*sharīʿa*' – to be pushed to the periphery. This process underlined the *sulṭa*-centred approach that we saw before, but this time it did not come at the expense of the *sharīʿa*, but of the *umma*.

Rida on Political Participation

The lopsided situation described above was the one encountered by nineteenth- and twentieth-century reformers like Rida. With regard to the deposition of a caliph, Rida follows classical thinking by pointing out that – theoretically speaking – there is a right to depose an unjust ruler, but

70 Afsaruddin, 'Loyalty', 368. 71 Black, *History*, 18–21; Lambton, *State*, 19–20.
72 Black, *History*, 84, 104; Rosenthal, *Political Thought*, 44.
73 Black, *History*, 104, 143–4; Crone, *God's Rule*, 155–6, 229–30.

that this only works in an ideal caliphate, not one that is tyrannical and oppressive.[74] He is more willing to show his reformist side with regard to *shūrá*. Citing the Prophet Muhammad, Abu Bakr and ʿUmar as examples and referring to the Qurʾanic verses on *shūrá* mentioned earlier,[75] but unlike what seems to have been the trend in the various Muslim empires, Rida wants to reinstate the principle of consultation between the ruler and the ruled.[76] This should apply to all matters 'on which there is no text from God and his messenger and no consensus (*ijmāʿ*)'.[77]

Rida's attempt to get the *umma* more involved can also be seen in his writings on *bayʿa*. Referring to early Islamic times again, he states that the oath of fealty started out as a broad-based pledge of allegiance from the community, not just a small group of people. In reference to Abu Bakr's appointment of ʿUmar as second caliph, he states that 'the imamate was not concluded through [Abu Bakr's] *bayʿa* alone (*bi-mubāyaʿatihi waḥdahu*); on the contrary, [it was done] through the *bayʿa* of his community (*bi-mubāyaʿat al-jamāʿa lahu*)'.[78] Rida does not just get the *umma* to participate more in this way, however, but also stresses the contractual nature of the *bayʿa* by pointing out that – in early Islamic times – the oath of fealty was conditioned upon both the rulers and the ruled living up to their duties, which included that the ruler should govern according to Islam.[79] It is also on this condition – ruling on the basis of the *sharīʿa* – that Muslims should be obedient to their rulers. Rida thus explicitly ties *ṭāʿa* to the application of Islamic law by the ruler.[80]

Through his treatment of *shūrá*, *bayʿa* and *ṭāʿa*,[81] Rida thus tries to bring back the role of the *umma* in the relevant quasi-contingent features of *shūrá* (the ones being consulted) and *bayʿa* (the ones pledging fealty), while re-coupling the *sharīʿa* with *ṭāʿa*'s relevant quasi-contingent feature (the person obeyed). As such, he decontests their meaning by pulling back both '*sharīʿa*' and '*umma*' from the peripheral position that they fell into through the centuries and 'restoring' them to the positions adjacent to the core concept of 'caliph' (or 'ruler') he feels they deserve. Still, there are limits to the role Rida gives to the *umma*. Like his scholarly predecessors, Rida regularly uses the term *ahl al-ḥall wa-l-ʿaqd*. While he broadens the meaning of this term to include people who are also knowledgeable in, for instance, international law,[82] it is unclear how these people come to represent the *umma* as a whole. While Rida suggests that parliaments

[74] Enayat, *Modern Thought*, 71–2; Riḍā, *Al-Khilāfa*, 38–47, especially 40.
[75] Riḍā, *Al-Khilāfa*, 31–2. [76] Enayat, *Modern Thought*, 74. [77] Riḍā, *Al-Khilāfa*, 30.
[78] Ibid., 11–15. The quotation is on p. 13. [79] Ibid., 24–30, 36. [80] Ibid., 27.
[81] The first link between 'caliph' and '*umma*' distinguished above ('commanding right and forbidding wrong') is not treated extensively in Riḍā's book on the caliphate.
[82] Riḍā, *Al-Khilāfa*, 16.

could fulfil the role of the *ahl al-ḥall wa-l-ʿaqd*,[83] he seems to shy away from ideas of popular sovereignty.[84] This, as we will see later on, is an issue that members of the Muslim Brotherhood would tackle.[85]

Societal Rights and Freedoms

When the empires of the Umayyads (661–750), the aforementioned Abbasids and other dynasties rose and fell in the Muslim world, the ideas discussed above were not just applied to politics, but also to society. This included areas in which the majority of people were initially not adherents to Islam, but mostly Jews and Christians of various types. The *sharīʿa*, being part and parcel of the new Muslim rule that came about from the seventh century on, was also applied to these people and developed in the context of their presence. In this section, we will look at what main Sunni Islamic points of view have developed with regard to the subjects of religious minority rights, women's rights and civil liberties.[86]

Religious Minority Rights

Muslims have had to deal with non-Muslims[87] from the very beginning of Islam. Tradition has it that Islam came into existence in Mecca, a town dominated by polytheists but also populated by some Christians. After the *hijra* to Medina in 622, the Prophet encountered various Jewish tribes. Unsurprisingly, these contacts are reflected in the text of the Qurʾan as well as in Muslim stories about the life of the Prophet Muhammad. Both provide modern believers with tools to justify seeing ties with especially Jews and Christians as either part of a polemical and conflictual

83 Ibid., 59. 84 Black, *History*, 316.

85 Although Anjum's book only belatedly came to my attention, it is nevertheless remarkable to read how he describes not only the decline of the role of the *umma* in the Muslim empires throughout the Middle Ages, but also how the scholar Ibn Taymiyya (1263–1328) responded to this trend by trying to bring the *umma* back into politics in a way that is quite similar to reform efforts by Riḍā and others. See Anjum, *Politics*, 107–36, 229–65.

86 In discussions on contentious issues such as the ones described in this chapter, it is tempting to apply modern-day standards (in all their variety) to different time periods and different contexts, particularly since ideas formulated as 'women's rights' are rather modern themselves. My intention is not, however, to measure mediaeval Muslims by today's standards and to see where they do well or fall short. In fact, it is not my intention to express any opinion on this, but merely to distinguish the texts, concepts and positions that are relevant for the debates on these issues, on which the Jordanian Muslim Brotherhood builds.

87 The term 'non-Muslims' is used here to refer to Jews and Christians. Although the Prophet encountered polytheists, too, these no longer have a relevance for the situation in Jordan and, in any case, differed from Jews and Christians because they – unlike those two groups – were mostly not seen as 'people of the Book' (*ahl al-kitāb*).

relationship that started with Muhammad and continues to this day or as characterised by peace and equality.

In Medina, the Prophet is said to have encountered three major Jewish tribes, the Banu Qaynuqaʿ, the Banu l-Nadir and the Banu Qurayza, all of whom he eventually defeated. Given the fact that Muslim accounts relate that Muhammad had some 600–900 Jews of the latter tribe killed, it is tempting to conclude that Muslim–Jewish relations were quite bad and there are, indeed, more indications of this. The Prophet continued to fight the Jews at the oasis of Khaybar in the Arabian Peninsula, eventually defeating them as well.[88] This attitude also seems to be reflected in the Qurʾan, where several verses appear to refer to Muhammad's relations with both Jews and Christians. Q. 5:51, for instance, says: 'Oh believers, take not Jews and Christians as friends (*awliyāʾ*); they are friends of each other. Whoso of you makes them his friends is one of them. God guides not the people of the evildoers.' The Qurʾan even seems to distinguish between non-Muslim religions by indicating in Q. 5:82: 'Thou wilt surely find the most hostile of men to the believers are the Jews and the idolaters; and thou wilt surely find the nearest of them in love to the believers are those who say "We are Christians" [. . .].'[89]

Jews and Christians were often referred to as *ahl al-kitāb* (the people of the Book), a reference to the idea that they – like Muhammad, but unlike other religious groups – had received a revelation from God through earlier prophets, or *ahl al-dhimma* (the people of protection).[90] This latter term is most relevant to us since it formed an important part of how Muslim scholars would assess non-Muslims' positions in Muslim societies thereafter. The *dhimma* was essentially a contract between the Prophet (and later Muslim leaders) and a group of non-Muslims in which the former agreed to protect the latter, for which the latter would pay the former and also submit to his rule.[91] This payment or poll tax became known as the *jizya*, referred to once in the Qurʾan (Q. 9:29, see below) and paid by Jews and Christians and sometimes other groups included in the *ahl al-dhimma*.[92]

88 Norman A. Stillman, *The Jews of Arab Lands: A History and Source Book* (Philadelphia, PA, and New York: Jewish Publication Society of America, 1979), 3–19.

89 Bernard Lewis, *The Jews of Islam* (Princeton, NJ: Princeton University Press, 2014 [1984]), 10–14.

90 On the classification of various types of non-Muslims by Muslims, see Yohanan Friedmann, *Tolerance and Coercion in Islam: Interfaith Relations in the Muslim Tradition* (Cambridge: Cambridge University Press, 2003), 54–86.

91 Lewis, *Jews*, 21; Rachel M. Scott, *The Challenge of Political Islam: Non-Muslims and the Egyptian State* (Stanford, CA: Stanford University Press, 2010), 16–17.

92 Mark R. Cohen, *Under Crescent & Cross: The Jews in the Middle Ages* (Princeton, NJ: Princeton University Press, 2008 [1994]), 56; Stillman, *Jews*, 19–20.

The description above has led some, like Watt, to conclude that a member of the *ahl al-dhimma* was 'a second-class citizen'.[93] In such a reading, the *jizya* was levied to punish non-Muslims for their unbelief[94] or to humiliate them.[95] The latter is said to be based on Q. 9:29, which states:

> Fight against those who believe not in God and the Last Day and do not forbid what God and His Messenger have forbidden – such men as practise not the religion of truth, being of those who have been given the Book – until they pay the tribute (*jizya*) out of hand and have been humbled (*wa-hum ṣāghirūna*).

Yet the *jizya* has also been described as mere protection money paid for the security that non-Muslims enjoyed under Muslim rule[96] and, more specifically, has been tied to the fact that they did not participate in Muslims' jihad on behalf of the caliphate, which was waged against non-Muslim peoples with which Jews and Christians might sympathise.[97]

In short, the interpretation of what the *dhimma* and the *jizya* meant differs. This difference can also be seen in how non-Muslims were treated after the death of the Prophet. One document that has been of great importance with regard to the Muslim treatment of non-Muslims is the so-called Pact of ʿUmar, a document that is ascribed to the second caliph, ʿUmar b. al-Khattab, but that probably reflects developments that occurred later. The document takes the form of a letter from Syrian Christians who wrote to ʿUmar to indicate their willingness to submit to his rule and the conditions they attach to that submission.[98] The actual conditions mentioned in the Pact of ʿUmar include that no new houses of worship may be built, nor may existing ones be repaired; there may be no public displays of religion other than Islam in order to keep non-Muslims humbled; there may be no conversions to any religion except for Islam; non-Muslims must rise in the presence of Muslims when the latter take a seat; they must not ride horses or carry arms; non-Muslims must construct lower houses than Muslims; and they should distinguish themselves in their clothing so as not to resemble Muslims.[99]

Although these stipulations seem clear and also appear to reflect a more polemical reading of the Qurʾanic verses and the life of Muhammad, the actual application of such rules differed greatly from time to time and from caliph to caliph. Depending on the piety of the ruler, the political

[93] Watt, *Islamic Thought*, 51. [94] Scott, *Challenge*, 22.
[95] Cohen, *Crescent*, 69; Lewis, *Jews*, 14; Scott, *Challenge*, 22.
[96] Cohen, *Crescent*, 69, 70, 72; Scott, *Challenge*, 21. [97] Scott, *Challenge*, 17.
[98] Cohen, *Crescent*, 54–8; Lewis, *Jews*, 24–5. The dating and formation of the document is discussed in Milka Levy-Rubin, *Non-Muslims in the Early Islamic Empire: From Surrender to Coexistence* (Cambridge: Cambridge University Press, 2011), 60–2.
[99] Cohen, *Crescent*, 58–62.

circumstances and the size of the minority communities living in certain areas, rulers applied the stipulations from the Pact of ʿUmar selectively and with varying zeal.[100] This also applies to some of the less drastic measures taken against non-Muslims. While some expressions used for non-Muslims clearly appeared to be signs of contempt ('apes' for Jews and 'pigs' for Christians),[101] some measures – such as the stipulation that Jews and Christians need to look and dress differently from Muslims – need not be seen as hostile, but merely as attempts to distinguish between religious communities. This idea may have sprung from a desire to stress one's own identity and to show it as distinct from others, although in some instances it does appear to have been meant to underline non-Muslims' supposed inferiority.[102]

The question of how Muslims should deal with Jews and Christians becomes even more complicated when some other factors are taken into account, the most important of which is probably the so-called Constitution of Medina. While the relations between the Prophet and the Jews of Medina were sometimes conflictual, this was not always the case. Somewhere during the later years of Muhammad's stay in Medina (probably after 627), the Prophet is said to have drawn up a document that allocated rights and duties to both the Muslims and the Jews living there. This document, which later became known as the Constitution of Medina, distinguishes between the two religious groups, but also allows Jews to keep their religion and generally deals with them as equal partners.[103]

The Constitution of Medina could, in fact, be viewed as part of a wider context of tolerance towards non-Muslims. This context is strongly informed by Q. 2:256, which states: 'No compulsion (*ikrāha*) is there in religion [. . .].' Scholars disagreed on whether this verse should be read as a command or as a mere description of reality (i.e. that it is impossible to force people to believe something in their hearts). They also differed over whether this verse was abrogated by later verses that are more hostile towards non-Muslims, was not abrogated at all or perhaps abrogated such hostile verses itself.[104] In any case, both the Constitution of Medina and Q. 2:256 may suggest that it is not so much the religion of Jews and Christians that is problematic to Muslims, but their societal and political

[100] Levy-Rubin, *Non-Muslims*, 99–112; Scott, *Challenge*, 22–8; Stillman, *Jews*, 22–107.
[101] Lewis, *Jews*, 33. [102] Ibid., 34–6.
[103] Watt, *Islamic Thought*, 4–6, 130–4. Detailed studies of this document include Saïd Amir Arjomand, 'The Constitution of Medina: A Sociolegal Interpretation of Muhammad's Acts of Foundation of the *Umma*', *International Journal of Middle East Studies* 41, no. 4 (2009): 555–75; Uri Rubin, 'The "Constitution of Medina": Some Notes', *Studia Islamica* 62 (1985): 5–23.
[104] Friedmann, *Tolerance*, 100–6.

behaviour. This could also partly explain why relatively little violence has been used against non-Muslims, particularly against Jews, throughout classical Islamic history.[105]

Although Muslim views on non-Muslims are difficult to pinpoint, they can still be put in Freeden's terms if we return to two of the concepts adjacent to the core concept of 'caliph': '*sharīʿa*' and '*umma*'. It would be incorrect to state that the Muslim positions hostile towards non-Muslims are solely focussed on the *sharīʿa* and that those tolerant of Jews and Christians only rely on the wishes of the *umma*. One could say, however, that the former group tends to view the *umma* through the prism of the *sharīʿa* or, to put it differently, as a community to whom – first and foremost – Islamic law should be applied. Partly as a result of this, stipulations such as those from the Pact of ʿUmar were applied to Jews and Christians.

The more tolerant group, by contrast, sees the *sharīʿa* through the lens of the interests of the *umma*, which causes it to tone down the measures historically taken against non-Muslims and revert to the more ambiguous examples of the Qurʾan and the Prophet Muhammad. While both adjacent concepts of '*sharīʿa*' and '*umma*' are important to both groups, it is clear that the more hostile group favours the former over the latter, while the more tolerant group sees things the other way round. Although this is a very rudimentary sketch, one can already see the outlines of the *sharīʿa*-centred and *umma*-centred approaches mentioned earlier, which would become clearer in the hands of the Muslim Brotherhood, as we will see later on.[106]

Women's Rights

A major difference between religious minority rights and those of Muslim women is that the latter group is clearly dealt with as part of the *umma*. As such, women are also implicitly viewed as sharing the beliefs of other Muslims and therefore as supporting the tenets of the *sharīʿa*. The Qurʾan seemingly speaks of men and women in the same manner several times, perhaps suggesting that they (should) enjoy equal rights. Examples of these include Q. 3:195, which states: 'And their Lord answers them: "I waste not the labour of any that labours among you, be you male or

105 Cohen, *Crescent*, 163–9; Lewis, *Jews*, 46.
106 The *umma*-centred approach, as described here, presumes that Jews and Christians, while perhaps not part of the *umma* itself, are certainly tied to the *umma* and are seen as people whose interests should not be completely divorced from those of the Muslim community. This dimension is less clear in what we have seen so far, but will become clearer in the Jordanian Muslim Brotherhood's discourse.

female – the one of you is as the other["].'[107] In matters of chastity, men and women are both told to '[...] cast down their eyes and guard their private parts [...]' (Q. 24:30, 31), suggesting that both have an equal role to play in this respect.

At the same time, the Qur'an is also clear about the differences between men and women, sometimes even using words that may easily be interpreted as suggesting inequality. In the context of divorce, for example, Q. 2:228 states that '[...] women have such honourable rights as obligations, but their men have a degree above them (*li-l-rijāl ʿalayhinna daraja*). God is All-mighty, All-wise'. Similarly, with regard to inheritance, men are said to receive twice as much as women: 'God charges you, concerning your children: to the male the like of the portion of two females (*li-l-dhakar mithl ḥaẓẓ al-unthayayn*) [...]' (Q. 4:11). A similar wording is used in Q. 4:176.

However one reads such verses, it is clear that the texts cited have become part of the *sharīʿa* and its regulations with regard to the female half of the *umma*. In classical legal writings on rights for women, the latter are often portrayed as responsible for procreation within marriage and raising a family. Probably inspired by verses such as Q. 2:223 ('Your women are a tillage for you; so come unto your tillage as you wish, and forward for your souls [...]') and Q. 4:34 ('Men are the managers (*qawwāmūn*) of the affairs of women [...]'), Muslim scholars deal with husbands as responsible for maintenance of the family and wives as obedient. As Tucker points out, these mutual responsibilities have not always been explained in an equal way, but have sometimes emphasised the wife's duties to her husband to deserve his maintenance without paying much attention to the husband's responsibilities to his wife.[108]

Perhaps partly as a result of scholarly bias in favour of men, the obedience of the wife was made central to a good Muslim marriage by many *ʿulamāʾ*. In practice, this entailed staying at home and not going out or receiving visitors without the husband's permission, for which there also appears to be some Qur'anic justification (Q. 33:33: 'Remain in your houses (*wa-qarna fī buyūtikunna*); and display not your finery, as did the pagans of old [...]'),[109] so that the husband was sure to have his wife for himself alone. Failure by the husband to maintain his wife could result in

107 Enayat, *Modern Thought*, 132.

108 Judith E. Tucker, *Women, Family, and Gender in Islamic Law* (Cambridge: Cambridge University Press, 2008), 53.

109 The preceding verse strongly suggests that these words are directed at the wives of the Prophet only. For more on the distinction between the rights of the Prophet's wives and Muslim women in general, see Harald Motzki, 'Das Kopftuch – ein Symbol wofür?', *Religion, Staat, Gesellschaft: Zeitschrift für Glaubensformen und Weltanschauungen* 5, no. 2 (2004): 175–201.

his wife refusing to have sex with him and could, according to some, also be grounds for divorce. The wife's disobedience could result in various sanctions, including physical punishment, for which there also seems to be Qur'anic evidence (Q. 4:34): '[...] And those you fear may be rebellious admonish; banish them to their couches and beat them (*wa-ḍribūhunna*). If they then obey you, look not for any way against them; God is All-high, All-great.'[110]

While scholars sometimes had quite different views on how to interpret texts such as those mentioned above as well as women's rights in general,[111] these Qur'anic verses did shape their views in the sense that they could not just ignore them but had to deal with them somehow. The same applies to other relevant questions regarding women's rights, such as the prohibition of gender-mixing (*ikhtilāṭ*) between unrelated people. Although this was apparently only a minor issue in classical Islamic legal discussions,[112] it is important to the Jordanian Muslim Brotherhood and therefore must be dealt with here. There are several *ḥadīth*s that are important in this respect, including the Prophet's statement that 'I have not left after me a temptation more harmful to men (*fitna aḍarra ʿalá l-rijāl*) than women'.[113] Statements such as these, in combination with Qur'anic verses like Q. 33:53 ('[...] And when you ask [the Prophet's] wives for any object, ask them from behind a curtain; that is cleaner for your hearts and theirs [...]'), suggest that women may act as a temptation for men and, as such, should be separated from men so as to keep unwanted sexual attention at bay.[114]

The undesirability of having unrelated men and women mix could be seen as another reason to keep women indoors and prevent them from going out without their husbands' permission. This also has practical consequences with regard to appearance and religious rituals. It means that women have to cover the lust-inducing parts of their bodies (*ʿawra*), the exact meaning of which depends on the school of Islamic law, are not compelled to go to Friday prayers in the mosque and should travel to perform the *ḥajj* (pilgrimage to Mecca) only under the supervision of a close male relative acting as a guardian (*maḥram*).[115] All of this means

110 Tucker, *Women*, 53–6.
111 Crone, *God's Rule*, 348–50; Nelly Lahoud, *Political Thought in Islam: A Study in Intellectual Boundaries* (London and New York: Routledge, 2005), 119–22.
112 Tucker, *Women*, 175.
113 *Ṣaḥīḥ al-Bukhārī*, book 62 ('Kitāb al-Nikāḥ'), *bāb* 18 ('Mā Ittaqá min Shuʾūm al-Marʾa wa-Qawl Taʿāla Inna min Azwājikum wa-Awlādikum ʿAduwwan Lakum'), no. 33.
114 For more *ḥadīth*s and Qur'ānic verses about this subject, see Joas Wagemakers, 'Salafi Scholarly Views on Gender-Mixing (*Ikhtilāṭ*) in Saudi Arabia', *Orient* 57, no. 2 (2016): 42–5.
115 Tucker, *Women*, 177–82.

that women could be confined to their homes and that their freedom was largely dependent on the permission they got from their fathers, brothers and, later, husbands. Still, some scholars allowed women to perform public duties, such as acting as judges (presumably only among other women) in civil matters (but not criminal cases), although these appear to be exceptions.[116]

The subject of women's rights as described above is a topic that leads us back to the two adjacent concepts of '*sharīʿa*' and '*umma*'. As discussed before, these can only be in perfect harmony at all times if the former – like the latter – is flexible and subject to change. If not, then the one has to take precedence over the other. This is not the impression one gets from reading about women's rights, however, presumably because Muslim women are assumed to agree with the *sharīʿa* and a conflict between Islamic law and the female half of the *umma* simply does not seem to occur to the scholars writing about this. As time went by, however, the idea that a perfect balance between a (possibly reformed but) rigid and inflexible *sharīʿa* and the ever-changing *umma* could not be maintained did take hold among some Muslim thinkers, including members of the Jordanian Muslim Brotherhood.

Civil Liberties

In the section on commanding right and forbidding wrong, we saw that the caliphate monopolised much of this duty by appointing a censor to control people's behaviour according to the *sharīʿa* and that the *umma* itself also had a limited role in correcting the actions of other Muslims. Since this duty clearly went further than arresting individuals for what most people would consider actual crimes, it is interesting to look at what room this left for what we now refer to as civil liberties: aspects of personal freedom that the state cannot interfere with. Such freedoms can include many things, such as the right to own property, freedom of assembly and being entitled to a fair trial, but this section concentrates on two aspects that are especially important with regard to the Muslim Brotherhood: freedom of speech and the freedom to leave Islam.

It is clear that the caliphate was expected to play a role in protecting and maintaining the *sharīʿa* in the Muslim empire and, as such, was responsible for the preservation of the religion (*ḥifẓ al-dīn*). In practice, this entailed ensuring that Muslims adhered to the norms of Islamic law and that heretics and the like were repressed, although active persecution of such people seems to have been rare.[117] Still, certain limits to what we

[116] Crone, *God's Rule*, 350. [117] Black, *History*, 156; Crone, *God's Rule*, 303–4.

now know as freedom of speech must have applied. What were the limits to this and how were they justified by scholars? As with other issues dealt with in this chapter, no easy answer can be given to this question.

The ambiguity on this issue starts with the Qurʾan and the life of the Prophet, where evidence can be found for multiple points of view with regard to freedom of speech, specifically as it pertains to insulting Islam. The latter is referred to several times in the Qurʾan, like in Q. 6:108 ('Abuse not (*wa-lā tasubbū*) those to whom they pray, apart from God, or they will abuse (*fa-yasubbū*) God in revenge without knowledge [. . .]') and Q. 33:57 ('Those who hurt (*yuʾdhūna*) God and His Messenger – them God has cursed in the present world and the world to come, and has prepared for them a humbling chastisement'). Irrespective of whether 'abuse' (*sabb*) or 'hurt' (*īdhāʾ*) is used, these verses appear to show that insulting God or the Prophet is seen as wrong. The punishment for this, however, is less clear. Q. 5:33–4 states that

> This is the recompense of those who fight (*yuḥāribūna*) against God and His Messenger, and hasten about the earth and do corruption there (*wa-yasʿawna fī l-arḍ fasādan*): they shall be slaughtered, or crucified, or their hands and feet shall alternately be struck off, or they shall be banished from the land. That is a degradation for them in this world; and in the world to come awaits them a mighty chastisement except for such as repent, before you have power over them. So know you that God is All-forgiving, All-compassionate.

While these verses do not explicitly say anything about insulting Islam in any way, scholars have apparently applied the punishments mentioned in them to those who insult God, the Prophet or Islam as well.[118]

This scholarly treatment of those who insult or blaspheme Islam seems to be confirmed by what the Prophet himself did when he was confronted with blasphemers. According to some Muslim scholars, Muhammad and his companions had several people put to death for ridiculing, vilifying or satirising him or for creating doubts about his position as a prophet, suggesting this was as serious as fighting Islam militarily.[119] While legal scholars debated whether or not the culprit should be given the chance to repent, they did agree that vilifying the Prophet (and, presumably, God) was a sin punishable by death.[120] This applied to Muslims who insulted Islam, but to a lesser extent also to non-Muslims, although the actual application of such punishment was uncommon.[121]

[118] Siraj Khan, 'Blasphemy against the Prophet', in *Muhammad in History, Thought and Culture: An Encyclopedia of the Prophet*, ed. Coeli Fitzpatrick and Adam H. Walker (Santa Barbara, CA: ABC-CLIO, 2014), 59–60.

[119] Friedmann, *Tolerance*, 149–51. [120] Ibid., 151–2; Khan, 'Blasphemy', 63–7.

[121] Khan, 'Blasphemy', 62; Lewis, *Jews*, 39–40.

Yet there is also a different way of reading the texts cited above, leading to rather different conclusions about freedom of speech in Islam and the punishment for insulting the religion. Several academics have pointed out that some Muslim scholars did not believe the death penalty should be applied to those who blasphemed Islam, but only to those who had done so in cases in which it was accompanied by hostility towards the Muslim polity or entailed the sowing of chaos in society. For such Muslim scholars, in other words, it was not the act of blasphemy as such that was punishable by death, but the public danger and civil strife that was caused by it.[122]

This argument is supported by the value attached to privacy in Islamic law, which suggests that certain things may be sinful but should not be punished as long as they have no negative public consequences. Several verses from the Qurʾan suggest that one should not enter people's houses without their knowledge or permission (Q. 2:189: '[. . .] It is not piety to come to the houses from the backs of them; but piety is to be godfearing; so come to the houses by their doors, and fear God [. . .]' and Q. 24:27: 'Oh believers, do not enter houses other than your houses until you first ask leave and salute the people thereof [. . .]') or spy on others (Q. 49:12: 'Oh believers, eschew much suspicion; some suspicion is a sin. And do not spy, neither backbite one another [. . .]').[123]

Similar ideas can be seen in stories about early Muslim leaders who advise against arresting or bothering people who may have sinned in private, but not in public. The best-known example of this is perhaps caliph ʿUmar's sneaking into a house, where he found the owner engaged in sinful behaviour. When ʿUmar reprimanded him, the man answered that he might have sinned, but that ʿUmar himself had done so in three ways: by spying on him, by not entering his house through the door and by failing to greet him, all of which are mentioned in the three Qurʾanic verses cited above. ʿUmar told the man to repent, but did not punish him.[124]

A different civil liberty, but one that is closely related to freedom of speech, is the freedom to abandon one's religion, in this case Islam. In the literature on blasphemy discussed above, insulting Islam is frequently mentioned in the context of apostasy (*ridda*) because of the belief that

122 Khan, 'Blasphemy', 64–7; Intisar A. Rabb, 'Negotiating Speech in Islamic Law and Politics: Flipped Traditions of Expression', in *Islamic Law and International Human Rights Law: Searching for Common Ground?*, ed. Anver M. Emon, Mark S. Ellis and Benjamin Glahn (Oxford: Oxford University Press, 2012), 158–62.
123 Cook, *Commanding Right*, 80–1.
124 Ibid., 81–2. For a more detailed discussion of the balance between forbidding wrong and respecting privacy, see ibid., 479–86.

only apostates (*murtaddūn*, sing. *murtadd*) would blaspheme the religion and, as such, should be punished as people who have abandoned Islam.[125] Apostates are, importantly, seen as more blameworthy than non-Muslims, precisely because they have already been Muslims but have left the religion, rather than never having been part of Islam at all.[126] It has been argued that such an issue was important to the budding *umma* after the death of the Prophet to strengthen the integrity of the Muslim community and keep it together when its survival was not assured.[127]

Whatever the case may be, the idea that apostasy is wrong and should be punished is mostly based on several *ḥadīth*s. Perhaps the most commonly cited one is the statement by the Prophet that 'Whoever changes his religion (*man baddala dīnahu*), kill him.'[128] Others seem to corroborate this, as in the statement of one companion of the Prophet who labels the execution of an apostate 'the judgement of God (*qaḍāʾ Allāh*)'[129] and Muhammad's own words, stating that 'the blood of no Muslim who professes that there is no god but God and that I am the messenger of God may be shed, except in three cases: a life for a life (*al-nafs bi-l-nafs*) [i.e. retribution for murder], the adulterer and the one who parts with his religion (*al-mufāriq li-dīnihi*), leaving the community (*al-tārik li-l-jamāʿa*).'[130]

The *ʿulamāʾ* have debated whether such texts mean that allowing an apostate to repent is mandatory or desirable and whether God would even accept such a repentance, on which they did not agree.[131] Another source of disagreement was what the words 'whoever changes his religion, kill him' actually meant. It seems obvious that whoever changes his religion to Islam should not be killed and that if a non-Muslim converts to another non-Muslim religion, this is not a problem since they remain non-Muslims. Yet such a conversion could also undo their status as protected people (*ahl al-dhimma*), making them unwanted in the lands of Islam, unavailable as marriage partners and ineligible to pay the *jizya*. Such

125 Friedmann, *Tolerance*, 151–2; Khan, 'Blasphemy', 63–4.
126 Friedmann, *Tolerance*, 123–4. 127 Ibid., 124–6.
128 *Ṣaḥīḥ al-Bukhārī*, book 52 ('Kitāb al-Jihād'), *bāb* 149 ('Lā Yuʿadhdhibu bi-ʿAdhāb Allāh'), no. 260. See also ibid., book 84 ('Kitāb Istatābat al-Murtaddīn wa-l-Muʿānidīn wa-Qitālihim'), *bāb* 2 ('Ḥukm al-Murtadd wa-l-Mutadda'), no. 57.
129 Ibid., book 84 ('Kitāb Istatābat al-Murtaddīn wa-l-Muʿānidīn wa-Qitālihim'), *bāb* 2 ('Ḥukm al-Murtadd wa-l-Mutadda'), no. 58.
130 Jonathan A. C. Brown, 'The Issue of Apostasy in Islam' (Yaqeen Institute, https://yaqeeninstitute.org/en/jonathan-brown/apostasy/, accessed 8 July 2017), 5 July 2017; Friedmann, *Tolerance*, 126–7. The *ḥadīth* can be found in *Ṣaḥīḥ Muslim*, book 28 ('Kitāb al-Qasāma wa-l-Muḥāribīn wa-l-Qiṣāṣ wa-l-Diyāt'), *bāb* 6 ('Mā Yubāḥu bihi Dam al-Muslim'), no. 1676.
131 Friedmann, *Tolerance*, 127–33.

consequences show that conversion in general was looked at in a more nuanced way than the actual words of this particular *ḥadīth* seem to suggest.[132]

The punishment for apostasy, according to the scholars, was very often said to be execution.[133] Yet what exactly was being punished here? While it appears as if a change of heart with regard to religion was enough to receive a death sentence, this may not have been the case in classical Islam. We have already seen that blasphemy might have only been a problem when done openly and publicly and the same may have been the case for apostasy. A change of religion, some scholars have pointed out, was not merely an inward change of heart in mediaeval Muslim lands, but – given that status was closely tied to religion – actually meant a change of community altogether, which is also what the last *ḥadīth* cited above ('leaving the community') suggests. Conversion, in this sense, may have amounted to something akin to treason and joining the enemy's side in a situation of conflict and war.[134] According to one academic scholar, it was this public, hostile and possibly treasonous change of loyalty, rather than just a change of faith, that Muhammad and the early caliphs punished by death, not conversion as such.[135]

As with religious minority rights and women's rights, classical Muslim scholars disagree about civil liberties. Like the issue of religious minorities, civil liberties prove to be a struggle between the two adjacent concepts of '*sharīʿa*' (applying the rules) and '*umma*' (looking out for the interests of society, particularly blasphemers and apostates). Whereas with women's rights there appeared to be little attempt to reconcile the *sharīʿa* with the dynamic *umma*, this is clearly different with regard to the question of civil liberties, where scholars have apparently been willing to (re)interpret *ḥadīth*s on the necessity of killing blasphemers and apostates in a way that accommodates civil liberties a bit more. As such, the subject of civil liberties appears to be one where the scholars have attempted not to privilege '*sharīʿa*' over '*umma*' or the other way round, but – by being flexible in their interpretation of the *sharīʿa* to make it compatible with a diverse *umma* – have allowed them both to maintain their position as concepts adjacent to the core concept of 'caliph'. In such a case, one can

132 Ibid., 146–8.

133 Brown, 'Issue'; Friedmann, *Tolerance*, 127–9; Rudolph Peters and Gert J. J. de Vries, 'Apostasy in Islam', *Die Welt des Islams* 17 (1977): 5–9.

134 Brown, 'Issue'; Jonathan A. C. Brown, *Misquoting Muhammad: The Challenge and Choices of Interpreting the Prophet's Legacy* (London: Oneworld, 2014), 187–8; Rabb, 'Negotiating Speech', 146–8.

135 Brown, 'Issue'.

speak of neither a *sharīʿa*-centred nor an *umma*-centred approach, but a balanced one.

Rida on Societal Rights and Freedoms

As we saw above, Rida's writings tried to decontest the contents of several terms by changing the meaning of the core concept of 'caliph' and linking others with both '*sharīʿa*' and '*umma*' again. With regard to societal rights and freedoms, it seems Rida continues this trend on the two issues that he has dealt with extensively, namely, religious minority rights and women's rights, but in different ways. As for religious minority rights, he – like some of his contemporaries[136] – mostly focussed on Christians. This was likely not a coincidence. While Rida dealt with Christianity in a way that reflected classical Islamic thought, disputing several tenets of the Christian religion,[137] he did not necessarily see Christians as enemies[138] but was aware of the Western 'Christian' colonial influence of his day and the Christian missionaries that had come to the Middle East.[139] As such, his views on Christianity were probably informed by what he saw as the interests of the *umma*, without losing sight of the *sharīʿa*, thereby – in a sense – applying the latter in the service of the former.

Rida's attitude towards Christians often remained highly polemical. This was far less the case with his views on women's rights. Being merely one of the reformist authors in the late nineteenth and early twentieth centuries who wrote about gender issues,[140] Rida argued in favour of seeing husbands and wives as equals,[141] although he did maintain that the husband ought to be the head of the family, but that this should be done in a consultative way, not an authoritarian one.[142] The words from Q. 2:228 that 'men have a degree above them' cited earlier are interpreted by Rida as referring to different natures men and women have.[143] He also states that forced marriages are wrong, that women are free to choose their partners and that '[fathers] do not have the right to force them to marry someone [their daughters] are not satisfied with'.[144] He similarly points out that while Q. 4:34, which appears to allow husbands to beat their wives, is part of the Qurʾan and therefore not in doubt, it is nevertheless

136 Umar Ryad, *Islamic Reformism and Christianity: A Critical Reading of the Works of Muḥammad Rashīd Riḍā and His Associates (1898–1935)* (Leiden: Brill, 2009), 243–63.
137 Ibid., 263–76; Simon A. Wood, *Christian Criticisms, Islamic Proofs: Rashīd Riḍā's Modernist Defense of Islam* (Oxford: Oneworld, 2008), 30–47.
138 Ryad, *Islamic Reformism*, 67–123.
139 Ibid., 125–74; Wood, *Christian Criticisms*, 17–23. 140 Tucker, *Women*, 65–77.
141 Muḥammad Rashīd Riḍā, *Ḥuqūq al-Nisāʾ fī l-Islām wa-Ḥaẓẓuhunna min al-Iṣlāḥ al-Muḥammadī al-ʿĀmm* (Beirut and Damascus: Al-Maktab al-Islāmī, 1984), 30–8.
142 Ibid., 39–42. 143 Ibid., 45. 144 Ibid., 24–8. The quotation is on p. 28.

better for a man to use his head than his hand to get his wife to obey him and also mentions several *ḥadīth*s that frown upon beating women.[145]

Rida also deals with other issues that are relevant to women's rights, such as divorce and polygamy,[146] that are less important for our later analysis of the Jordanian Muslim Brotherhood. All the more interesting is the issue of seclusion (*khalwa*) of women and men, which is directly relevant to the question of gender-mixing discussed above. Rida points to early Islamic examples of women who were involved in business and other professional activities and, as such, argues that today's Muslim women are allowed to do so as well.[147] This also applies, according to Rida, to activities such as engaging in commanding right and forbidding wrong and participating in the oath of fealty, which opens up the possibility of a political role for Muslim women.[148]

In short, Rida continues his earlier efforts of reformist decontestation and applies them to religious minority rights and women's rights. He does not do so by clearly subordinating '*sharīʿa*' to '*umma*' by simply allowing the wishes of the latter to decide everything and ignore certain texts, but by (re)interpreting some texts themselves in such a way that they concur with what he sees as the interests of the Muslim community. As such, he attempts to give equal weight to both '*sharīʿa*' and '*umma*', keeping them both equally adjacent to the core concept of 'caliph' without allowing either to become peripheral. The Muslim Brotherhood of Hasan al-Banna, who was personally so greatly influenced by Rida, followed him in this balancing act between a *sharīʿa*-centred approach and an *umma*-centred one, but the organisation's members also pushed their reformism in other directions, as we will see in Chapter 2.

[145] Ibid., 45–53. [146] Ibid., 60–145, 160–71. [147] Ibid., 181–2; Tucker, *Women*, 201.
[148] Riḍā, *Ḥuqūq*, 11–17.

2 The Early Muslim Brotherhood's Political Thought

The *sharīʿa*-centred and *umma*-centred approaches distinguished in Chapter 1 are labels for different strategies towards Islamic political thought. Such approaches are usually called 'fundamentalist' and 'modernist' in other studies.[1] While I do not necessarily disagree with these, in this book I prefer the labels of '*sharīʿa*-centred' and '*umma*-centred' (as well as 'balanced') for two reasons: firstly, my terms emanate from the Freedenesque, concept-focussed analysis of the trajectories of ideology that I employ here; secondly, a term like '*sharīʿa*-centred' describes exactly the type of development in political thought that seeks to emphasise Islamic law at the expense of other important elements of ideology, while 'fundamentalism' does not quite catch that.[2]

Both the *sharīʿa*-centred and the *umma*-centred approaches (as well as those that sought to balance the two) can be found among exponents of the very broad Islamic reformist movement of the late nineteenth and early twentieth centuries. Supporters of this movement had in common that they resisted what they saw as the rigid traditionalism of Sunni Islamic scholasticism, but otherwise consisted of a wide variety of scholars and thinkers. Indeed, Muhammad Rashid Rida himself developed from the more progressive reformer he was in his early years to a more conservative scholar supportive of Saudi Wahhabism towards the end of his life.[3] This diversity of reformist thought is also reflected in the early Muslim Brotherhood, which is the subject of this chapter.

The Muslim Brotherhood (including its branch in Jordan) has mostly been a layperson's organisation with a very broad message[4] and its founder, Hasan al-Banna, was rather vague and ambiguous about his exact

[1] See, for instance, Michael Cook, *Ancient Religions: Modern Politics: The Islamic Case in Comparative Perspective* (Princeton, NJ, and Oxford: Princeton University Press, 2014), 371–5; William E. Shepard, 'Islam and Ideology: Towards a Typology', *International Journal of Middle East Studies* 19 (1987): 307–36.

[2] People may call for the application of the *sharīʿa* in a liberating, emancipatory way that is quite different from what is usually meant by 'fundamentalism'.

[3] Hourani, *Arabic Thought*, 231–2. [4] Husaini, *Moslem Brethren*, 25; Lia, *Society*, 33–5.

beliefs.[5] As such, Muslims of all stripes could join it, including traditionalist Muslims, but also Islamists whose roots lay in the reformist trend mentioned above.[6] The breadth of the organisation is exemplified in al-Banna's famous statement that the Muslim Brotherhood is

> a Salafi call (*da'wa Salafiyya*) [. . .], a Sunni path (*ṭarīqa Sunniyya*) [. . .], a Sufi truth (*ḥaqīqa Ṣūfiyya*) [. . .], a political organisation (*hay'a siyāsiyya*) [. . .], a sports group (*jamā'a riyāḍiyya*) [. . .] a league of cultural knowledge (*rābiṭa 'ilmiyya thaqāfiyya*) [. . .], an economic company (*sharika iqtiṣādiyya*) [. . .] and a social idea (*fikra ijtimā'iyya* [. . .].[7]

This was no mere slogan.[8] Al-Banna was clearly a wide-ranging activist immersed in Sufism[9] and, as mentioned, had been strongly influenced by reformers like Rida and other scholars[10] who were later labelled 'Salafi'.[11] Al-Banna also made clear in his speeches and writings that he believed that 'the rulings and teaching of Islam (*aḥkām al-Islām wa-ta'līmahu*) are all-encompassing (*shāmila*), organising people's affairs in the world and the hereafter (*fī l-dunyā wa-l-ākhira*)'. As such, 'Islam is creed and worship (*'aqīda wa-'ibāda*), homeland and citizenship (*waṭan wa-jinsiyya*) as well as religion and state (*dīn wa-dawla*), spirituality and work (*rūḥāniyya wa-'amal*) and book and sword (*muṣḥaf wa-sayf*)'.[12]

Suffice it to say, the Muslim Brotherhood – in such a context of broad, Islam-based activism and ideological vagueness – was likely to attract a diverse group of activists and this is, indeed, precisely what happened. This chapter deals with the variety of thought among the thinkers of the early Muslim Brotherhood about the three subjects of the state, political participation and societal rights and freedoms in the period of the late 1920s to the late 1970s. As with Chapter 1, it is not my intention to give an exhaustive account of the Brotherhood's political thought throughout

5 Meijer, 'Muslim Brotherhood', 298–308.

6 The breadth of the organisation is also acknowledged by members of the Jordanian Muslim Brotherhood. Interviews with Jamīl Abū Bakr, Amman, 18 June 2012; 'Abd al-Laṭīf 'Arabiyyāt, Amman, 20 June 2012; Faraj Shalhūb, Amman, 21 June 2012.

7 Ḥasan al-Bannā, *Majmū'at Rasā'il al-Imām al-Shahīd Ḥasan al-Bannā* (N.p.: Dār al-Tawzī' wa-l-Nashr al-Islāmiyya, 1992), 122–3.

8 For an explanation of what al-Bannā meant by this statement, see ibid., but also Husaini, *Moslem Brethren*, 41–4.

9 Husaini, *Moslem Brethren*, 4, 9–11, 28–30; Lia, *Society*, 25–7.

10 Husaini, *Moslem Brethren*, 7, 30–1; Lia, *Society*, 29–30.

11 The movement or trend we now know as 'Salafism' is a far more textual, conservative movement than the reformist trend labelled 'Salafī' that Riḍā was part of. There is some debate as to whether the label 'Salafī' should even be applied to Riḍā and other reformers of his time. For more on this, see Henri Lauzière, *The Making of Salafism: Islamic Reform in the Twentieth Century* (New York: Columbia University Press, 2016), 4–19.

12 Al-Bannā, *Majmū'at*, 119.

that period, but simply to indicate what main stances can be discerned about the three issues mentioned among the major thinkers associated with the organisation. This is important because the ideological divisions in the Jordanian Muslim Brotherhood still run along the lines of *sharīʿa*-centred, *umma*-centred or balanced thinking and, as with classical Islamic political thought, have also been heavily influenced by the early Brotherhood's beliefs. As such, the ideological outlook of these three different trends has shaped the Jordanian Muslim Brotherhood's overall stance towards the subjects of the state, political participation and societal rights and freedoms dealt with in this chapter and all information below should be seen in this context.

The State

The early history of the Muslim Brotherhood in Egypt was one of intense turmoil: apart from regional developments that included the recent fall of the Ottoman Empire and the abolition of its caliphate, the country was still under British colonial influence and the conflict in Palestine between Zionist Jews and Palestinian Arabs was becoming increasingly violent as time went by. Given the fact that al-Banna was strongly anti-colonial and that the Muslim Brotherhood was (and remains) staunchly pro-Palestinian[13] – even participating in the 1948 war for Palestine[14] – we might expect al-Banna to harbour feelings of strong animosity towards the West. Although that is partly correct, al-Banna was simultaneously open to innovations and knowledge from the West, sometimes claiming that Western ideas squared perfectly well with Islam or even originated in the Muslim world.[15] As we will see in this chapter, the influence of colonialism and the West has been quite important in shaping the early Muslim Brotherhood's ideas.[16]

[13] El-Awaisi, *Muslim Brothers*, 21–131; Lia, *Society*, 235–47. Several members of the Jordanian Muslim Brotherhood have also written on the Brotherhood's early involvement in the Palestine question. See, for example, Ziyād Abū Ghanīma, *Al-Ḥaraka al-Islāmiyya wa-Qaḍiyyat Filasṭīn* (Amman: Dār al-Furqān li-l-Nashr wa-l-Tawzīʿ, 1989); ʿAwnī Jadwaʿ al-ʿUbaydī, *Jamāʿat al-Ikhwān al-Muslimīn fī l-Urdunn wa-Filasṭīn, 1945–1970: Ṣafaḥāt Tārkhīyya* (Amman: 1991), 14–33.

[14] El-Awaisi, *Muslim Brothers*, 135–210; al-ʿUbaydī, *Jamāʿat*, 53–66, 182–226.

[15] Lia, *Society*, 76–9.

[16] For an extensive treatment of the Brotherhood's ties with the West, see Martyn Frampton, *The Muslim Brotherhood and the West: A History of Enmity and Engagement* (Cambridge, MA, and London: Belknap/Harvard University Press, 2018). See also Alia Al Kadi, 'Between Foreign Policy and the *Umma*: The Muslim Brotherhood in Egypt and Jordan', *The Muslim World* 109 (2019): 240–60.

Hasan al-Banna

Unlike the aforementioned ʿAli ʿAbd al-Raziq and in line with Rida, al-Banna had a positive attitude towards the caliphate.[17] He labels the caliphate 'the symbol (*ramz*) of Islamic unity and the manifestation of connection (*maẓhar al-irtibāṭ*) between the communities (*umam*) of Islam' and claims it is 'the object (*manāṭ*) of many rulings in God's religion'. Al-Banna further states that it 'is the Muslims' duty to care about thinking about the matter of their caliphate'. As such, the Muslim Brothers 'make the idea of the caliphate and working for its return their top priority (*raʾs manāhijihim*)'.[18] This project, al-Banna claims, needs to be preceded by several steps, among them 'complete cultural, social and economic cooperation', which ultimately leads to a 'league of Islamic communities (*ʿaṣbat al-umam al-Islāmiyya*)'.[19] Because al-Banna does not mention *political* cooperation and suggests a caliphate that resembles the spiritual one Rida called for, it may well be the case that al-Banna was influenced by Rida in this respect.[20]

So al-Banna wanted a return to the caliphate (even if this was likely a different type of caliphate than the traditional one) and believed the Muslim Brotherhood should strive for this, but he also seems to have accepted the states of the Middle East as parts of this overarching caliphate. As such, much of al-Banna's writing on this topic was framed in terms of the Islamic state, not the caliphate. This appears to be another continuation of Rida by al-Banna, in which the latter adopts the former's transformation of the core concept of this Islamist ideology – 'caliph' – into 'ruler', a more suitable and concretely applicable concept for the twentieth century. This can also be seen in his reference to Islamic 'communities' (*umam*), rather than the single, overarching Muslim community (*umma*) that is ruled by the caliph. We saw this in the quotation above, but al-Banna makes this even clearer in his statement that 'every community of Islam (*kull umma min umam al-Islām*) has a general constitution (*dustūran ʿāmman*)'.[21] Such a statement not only acknowledges the presence of separate Muslim communities, but also that they are governed individually, rather than collectively by one Muslim ruler. The fact that al-Banna goes on to describe what kind of constitutions such communities should have suggests that he is not merely describing the

[17] Husaini, *Moslem Brethren*, 71. [18] Al-Bannā, *Majmūʿat*, 144.
[19] Ibid., 144–5. See also Phelps Harris, *Nationalism*, 162–3.
[20] See also Enayat, *Modern Thought*, 87, where he calls the Muslim Brotherhood's concept of the Islamic state 'an accentuated form of Rashīd Riḍā's'.
[21] Al-Bannā, *Majmūʿat*, 48.

reality of individual states, but has actually accepted them and is willing to realise his views on an Islamic state through them.[22]

Yet what did al-Banna's ideal Islamic state look like? According to al-Banna, 'the system of Islamic rule (*niẓām al-ḥukm al-Islāmī*)' is based on three principles (*qawāʿid*): 'the responsibility of the ruler (*masʾūliyyat al-ḥākim*), the unity of the *umma* and respecting its will'. While the latter will be dealt with in the next section, the first of these three principles is relevant now. Citing the Prophet ('each one of you is a shepherd (*rāʿin*) and each one of you is responsible for his [own] flock (*raʿiyya*)'),[23] al-Banna not only invokes two very old Islamic terms to refer to the ruler and the ruled,[24] but also shows that he does not ignore '*sulṭa*', one of the concepts adjacent to the core concept of 'caliph' (or, in his case, 'ruler'). He further underlines this by another *ḥadīth* that says: 'If you come to a country where there is no ruler (*sulṭān*), leave it.' This stems from the idea that 'true Islam (*al-Islām al-ḥanīf*) prescribes the government to be a basis of the social system (*al-niẓām al-ijtimāʿī*) that it brought to the people, so it does not establish chaos (*fawḍá*) and does not place the Muslim community (*al-jamāʿa al-Muslima*) [in a situation] without an imam'.[25]

The importance of having a ruler in order to prevent chaos can easily turn into an outsized appreciation of the leader's power at the expense of the other adjacent concepts ('*sharīʿa*' and '*umma*'), which is also what we saw in Chapter 1 with regard to Muslim empires. Al-Banna, however, seems to have been more hesitant in this regard, giving a major role to the *sharīʿa*, which – he insists – should not just be referred to in an article in the constitution, but should also be the guiding light for rulers.[26] To ensure this in a legal sense, the constitution itself should, al-Banna says, 'base its articles on the rulings of the Noble Qurʾan. The *umma* that says in the first article of its constitution that Islam is its official religion needs to found the rest of the articles on the basis of this [same] principle.'[27] Al-Banna, like Rida before him, thus tries to decontest the political meaning of '*sharīʿa*' by 'restoring' it as an adjacent concept to the core concept of 'caliph'/'ruler'.[28]

ʿAbd al-Qadir ʿAwda

Al-Banna did not express his views in a political vacuum. Apart from the regional factors already mentioned, the early Muslim Brotherhood was

[22] Ibid. [23] Ibid., 318. [24] See, for instance, Mottahedeh, *Loyalty*, 120–2.
[25] Al-Bannā, *Majmūʿat*, 317. [26] Ibid., 317. [27] Ibid., 48.
[28] For a more detailed analysis of al-Bannā's ideas of an Islamic state, see Ahmad S. Moussalli, 'Ḥasan al-Bannā's Islamist Discourse on Constitutional Rule and Islamic State', *Journal of Islamic Studies* 4, no. 2 (1993): 164–73.

up against the Egyptian regime, which became increasingly suspicious of its ideas and activities. This climate of suspicion caused the Brotherhood to found the Secret Apparatus (al-Jihāz al-Sirrī) to protect it from regime repression, but some of its members also actively used violence against the state, probably against the wishes of al-Banna himself, who seemed to have lost control of them. In the period 1948–1949, the Muslim Brotherhood was dissolved, al-Banna was arrested and, after his release, was even assassinated, probably by the regime, on 12 February 1949. This, in turn, led the regime to take extra security measures and arrest even more members of the Muslim Brotherhood.[29]

Only three years after al-Banna's assassination, a group of so-called Free Officers, officially led by General Muhammad Najib but really commanded by Colonel Nasser, staged a military coup and took control in 1952. The Free Officers had maintained close contact with several Muslim Brothers, hoping to use their popular power base to control the streets once their revolution got under way and to spread their legitimacy once they were in power. The Muslim Brotherhood, for its part, saw in the revolution the first step towards replacing the old regime with an Islamic government. This was not to be, however. As time went by, it became increasingly clear that the new regime was trying to use the Brotherhood to propagate its own pan-Arab, socialist solutions rather than to move in the direction of an Islamic state. As a result, the Brotherhood became more and more critical of the military rulers and the latter increasingly saw the organisation as a liability that they needed to suppress. When, in 1954, one member of the Brotherhood's Secret Apparatus tried to assassinate Nasser, the latter saw his chance to push back against the Muslim Brotherhood. Consequently, the regime cracked down on the organisation and imprisoned or executed many of its members in the decade or so that followed.[30]

One of the Muslim Brothers who was executed after the failed attempt on Nasser's life was the judge and prominent Islamist legal scholar ʿAbd al-Qadir ʿAwda (1906–1954). Like al-Banna, ʿAwda deals with the caliphate in his writings and, under the subheading '*al-khilāfa aw al-imāma al-ʿuẓmá*' (the caliphate or the greatest imamate; the exact title of Rida's book on the subject), states that the caliph has two duties (*waẓīfatān*):

[29] Mitchell, *Society*, 58–72.
[30] John Calvert, *Sayyid Qutb and the Origins of Radical Islamism* (London: Hurst & Co., 2010), 179–95; Carré and Seurat, *Frères*, 49–79; Adnan A. Musallam, *From Secularism to Jihad: Sayyid Qutb and the Foundation of Radical Islamism* (Westport, CT: Praeger Publishers, 2005), 137–50; Phelps Harris, *Nationalism*, 195–225; James Toth, *Sayyid Qutb: The Life and Legacy of a Radical Islamic Intellectual* (Oxford: Oxford University Press, 2013), 76–91; Zollner, *Muslim Brotherhood*, 25–48.

'Firstly, to establish the Islamic religion and execute its rulings (*tanfīdh aḥkāmihi*); and secondly, setting the policy of the state (*siyāsat al-dawla*) within the limits that Islam has drawn (*fī l-ḥudūd allatī rasamahā l-Islām*).'[31] ʿAwda goes on to state that setting up a caliphate is a duty incumbent upon Muslims, both from a religious and from a rational point of view,[32] and he lists the conditions a person must fulfil to be seen as eligible for the position of caliph.[33]

ʿAwda's discussion of the caliphate suggests that he wants it back, but he actually uses the term 'caliph' rather loosely. He claims that old terms like 'kingship (*mulk*), caliphate (*khilāfa*) and emirate (*imāra*)' can be compared with modern terms like 'president of a republic (*raʾīs jumhūriyya*)'. The difference, ʿAwda states, is just the name[34] and when the older terms are used in the Qurʾan, what is meant is 'just leadership (*al-riʾāsa*) in its general sense (*bi-maʿnāhā l-ʿāmm*). No indication is intended with regard to a specific system of governance (*niẓām muʿayyan min anẓimat al-ḥukm*).'[35] The term 'greatest imamate' (*al-imāma al-ʿuẓmá*) was merely coined, ʿAwda writes, to distinguish the imamate of the caliph-imam from the imams leading prayers in mosques.[36]

All of this entails that ʿAwda does not attach much value to the term 'caliph' itself and his use of that word should thus be read in the context of the above. While this suggests that ʿAwda, like Rida and al-Banna before him, is keen on moving away from 'caliph' as a core concept of Islamist ideology and replacing it with the more general 'ruler', he simultaneously – and unlike ʿAbd al-Raziq – sees the latter term as equally invested with religious significance. To ʿAwda, this goes all the way back to God's creation of the world, which he placed in the service of human beings in order for them to rule over it and to live with each other harmoniously.[37] As such, ʿAwda claims, God is the possessor of creation and while he has given it to human beings to take care of, this has to happen within certain limits because of the fact that they do not own creation, but only manage it temporarily.[38]

Because of this relationship, the ultimate judgement does not lie with human beings, but with God. ʿAwda mentions Qurʾanic verses such as Q. 28:70 ('[. . .] His too is the judgement (*al-ḥukm*), and unto Him you shall be returned') and Q. 2:213 ('[. . .] He sent down with [the Prophets] the Book with the truth (*al-kitāb bi-l-ḥaqq*), that He might decide between the people touching their differences') to indicate that 'God has revealed

31 ʿAbd al-Qādir ʿAwda, *Al-Islām wa-Awḍāʿunā al-Siyāsiyya* (n.p.: n.d.), 92.
32 Ibid., 94–101. 33 Ibid., 101–9. 34 Ibid., 86–7. The quotation is on p. 86.
35 ʿAbd al-Qādir ʿAwda, *Al-Māl wa-l-Ḥukm fī l-Islām* (Dammam and Riyadh: al-Dār al-Saʿūdiyya li-l-Nashr wa-l-Tawzīʿ, 1984 [1951]), 117.
36 Ibid., 121. 37 Ibid., 13–19. 38 Ibid., 47–82.

the Qur'an to his Prophet Muhammad [...] in order for it to be the constitution of humanity (*dustūr al-bashariyya*) and its highest law (*wa-qānūnahā al-aʿlá*)'.[39] As this statement suggests, ʿAwda believes that God's judgement should not just be applied to Muslims' daily lives, but also to politics, which, he writes, is 'part of the nature of Islam (*min ṭabīʿat al-Islām*)'.[40] Echoing al-Banna, he states that Islam is an 'all-encompassing, precise system (*niẓāman daqīqan shāmilan*)'[41] of which the state is very much part.[42] As such, ʿAwda believes that the Muslim ruler – whatever term one uses for him – is acting on God's behalf, enforcing his rule and therefore of great religious significance.

If God's rule is so important and it also applies to politics, ʿAwda states, then Muslims must set up governments that apply God's rule. This includes having people pay alms (*zakāt*) and enforcing prayer (*ṣalāt*),[43] but it generally refers to the application of the *sharīʿa*. Islamic law is superior to non-Islamic law, ʿAwda states, because the success of a law is decided by two factors: the spiritual component, by which ʿAwda means the extent to which a law concurs and resonates with the views of the people who have to abide by it; and the component of commitment, which indicates that a law should be enforced in the form of punishment of those who break it. ʿAwda maintains that, unlike human (Western) laws, the *sharīʿa* is ideal from this perspective because it concurs with the Islamic tradition shared by Muslims (the spiritual component) and is enforced against people (the component of commitment) in an unchanging form, irrespective of their wishes.[44]

ʿAwda's view of the *sharīʿa* suggests that in an Islamic state not just ordinary Muslims but also rulers must abide by Islamic regulations. ʿAwda not only limits rulers in their mandate with regard to legislative issues,[45] but also states that rulers should not apply any laws that do not concur with the *sharīʿa*. If they do, however, then Muslims should ignore them.[46] Thus, although ʿAwda clearly takes the rights of rulers into account,[47] it is clear that, like Rida and al-Banna before him, he tries to decontest the adjacent concept of '*sharīʿa*' by giving it more authority and he does so at the expense of '*sulṭa*' in a way that tries to reverse a development that occurred in classical Islamic political thought.

Yet ʿAwda clearly goes further than his two predecessors, since he explicitly condemns the Egyptian state for applying non-Islamic, colonial-era laws, neglecting Islam and actively persecuting those who call for that religion's application, despite the fact that Egypt is a Muslim

[39] Ibid., 88–9. The quotation of ʿAwda's own words is on p. 89. [40] Ibid., 92.
[41] Ibid., 93. [42] Ibid., 99–103. [43] Ibid., 109.
[44] ʿAbd al-Qādir ʿAwda, *Al-Islām wa-Awḍāʿunā al-Qānūniyya* (n.p.: 1967 [1951]), 36–40.
[45] Ibid., 61. [46] Ibid., 57. [47] ʿAwda, *Al-Islām wa-Awḍāʿunā al-Siyāsiyya*, 188–94.

country.[48] While ʿAwda acknowledges that the rulers are not the only ones responsible for the alleged decline of Islam in Egypt, he does hold them most responsible, precisely because they enforce the laws.[49] Citing Q. 5:44 ('[. . .] Whoso judges not according to what God has sent down – they are the unbelievers'),[50] ʿAwda states that 'whoso judges not according to what God has sent down or appeals to something other than his *sharīʿa*, he is an unbeliever in whose heart there is not [even] an atom of Islam (*laysa fī qalbihi dharra min al-Islām*), even if he calls himself a Muslim'.[51]

Thus, while ʿAwda does not relegate '*sulṭa*' to a position peripheral to the core concept of 'ruler', he unmistakeably privileges '*sharīʿa*' over the power of the Egyptian rulers of his day. His actual judgement over these rulers, however, remains vague, allowing for the possibility that they are not consciously ruling by non-Islamic laws[52] or are entirely ignorant of the duty to do so.[53] In other words, for all his emphasis on the necessity of applying Islamic law, ʿAwda does not go quite so far as to apply *takfīr* (excommunication) to Egypt's rulers and call for jihad against them. This conclusion would be drawn after him.

Sayyid Qutb

A second and far more famous Muslim Brother who was imprisoned and eventually executed during the Nasser years was Sayyid Qutb (1906–1966). Arrested several times since 1954, Qutb wrote or rewrote some of his best-known works while in jail and was most likely radicalised through the events that took place in Egypt when he was imprisoned and through the torture that he had to endure there, which is likely to have reinforced his negative views of the Egyptian state.[54] Qutb clearly went further than al-Banna and even ʿAwda, however, not only with regard to his assessment of the Egyptian state, but also concerning his more radical path towards a solution to this problem.[55]

48 ʿAwda, *Al-Islām wa-Awḍāʿunā al-Qānūniyya*, 67–77.
49 ʿAwda, *Al-Islām wa-Awḍāʿunā al-Siyāsiyya*, 218–22.
50 See also ʿAwda, *Al-Māl*, 90–1. For an extensive study of this verse, see Mark S. Wagner, '*Ḥukm bi-mā anzala'llāh*: The Forgotten Prehistory of an Islamist Slogan', *Journal of Qurʾanic Studies* 18, no. 1 (2016): 117–43.
51 ʿAwda, *Al-Islām wa-Awḍāʿunā al-Qānūniyya*, 72.
52 ʿAwda, *Al-Māl*, 91–2.
53 ʿAwda, *Al-Islām wa-Awḍāʿunā al-Qānūniyya*, 147–54.
54 Calvert, *Sayyid*, 197–227; Emmanuel Sivan, *Radical Islam: Medieval Theology and Modern Politics* (New Haven, CT, and London: Yale University Press, 1985), 89–90; Toth, *Sayyid*, 79–91; Zollner, *Muslim Brotherhood*, 50–63.
55 Yet see also Ana Belén Soage, 'Ḥasan al-Bannā and Sayyid Quṭb: Continuity or Rupture?', *The Muslim World* 99 (2009): 294–311.

Like ʿAwda, Qutb sees Egypt as a country in crisis because of the supposedly un-Islamic situation it is in. While ʿAwda was quite clear in ascribing this to the non-Islamic laws that Egypt was governed by, Qutb's reasoning is somewhat different. As has been discussed extensively elsewhere, Qutb refers to Egyptian society by the term '*jāhiliyya*', a word usually reserved for the so-called pre-Islamic period of ignorance.[56] While it is not entirely clear from whom Qutb got this term[57] or what he meant by it exactly – were Egyptians non-Muslims in his view or merely ignorant of their faith?[58] – it is obvious that Qutb felt that there was something seriously wrong with Egyptian society because people did not follow Islam properly.[59] As such, '*jāhiliyya*' acts as a peripheral concept that influences Qutb's decontestation of the adjacent concept of '*umma*'.

Unlike other scholars dealt with above, Qutb does not seem to have been very interested in whether the core concept of Islamist ideology was 'caliph' or the more general 'ruler'.[60] Yet he is all the more adamant in his conviction that the solution to the crisis of modern-day *jāhiliyya* is 'the Islamic system (*al-niẓām al-Islāmī*)'. The latter is based on 'the unity of humanity (*waḥdat al-insāniyya*)' and on

> the idea that Islam is the general global system (*al-niẓām al-ʿālamī al-ʿāmm*), which is the only system God accepts from anyone (*alladhī lā yaqbalu llāh min aḥad niẓāman ghayrahu*) because he does not accept a religion other than Islam (*dīnan illā l-Islām*) from anyone. The religion – in the Islamic understanding – is the general system that governs life (*yaḥkumu l-ḥayāt*).[61]

Qutb maintains that the person responsible for upholding Islam in society is the ruler and that he should only be seen as such as long as he implements the religion. Moreover, while this ruler is positioned above the rest of the *umma*, his power is kept in check by Islam, he is simultaneously a servant of God and he does not enjoy any special status or privileges other than his position of power.[62]

So like ʿAwda before him, Qutb does not ignore the adjacent concept of '*sulṭa*', but does set the condition that the ruler enjoying power must uphold Islam, thereby implicitly subjugating '*sulṭa*' to '*sharīʿa*', just as other reformers had done. In order to understand why the ruler is supposed to do this, we must make a slight detour to include the Indian/Pakistani Islamist scholar Abu l-Aʿla Mawdudi (1903–1979) in our

56 For more on the origins of *jāhiliyya*, see Sayyed Khatab, *The Political Thought of Sayyid Qutb: The Theory of Jahiliyyah* (London and New York: Routledge, 2006), 14–43.
57 Ibid., 5–9, 59. 58 Ibid., 70–2. 59 Ibid., 59–171. 60 Toth, *Sayyid*, 197.
61 Sayyid Quṭb, *Al-ʿAdāla al-Ijtimāʿiyya fī l-Islām*, 27th ed. (Cairo: Dār al-Shurūq, 2009), 78.
62 Toth, *Sayyid*, 193–4.

discussion.[63] Although Mawdudi was not a member of the Muslim Brotherhood, he did try to achieve similar things in India/Pakistan with his Jamaat-i-Islami party, which he founded in 1941.[64] He was also of the same generation as al-Banna, ʿAwda and Qutb and, most importantly, is said to have been of great influence to the latter.[65]

Mawdudi, despite mentioning the caliphate a lot, seems to have been more concerned with applying Islam in a modern state.[66] His reason for doing so was that he believed, like other reformers we saw above, that Islam was an all-encompassing system that necessarily included the state.[67] Mawdudi's approach to the Islamic state starts with the concept of *tawḥīd* (the unity of God), which is central to Islam and – in its most basic form – is expressed by Muslims through the first part of the confession of faith (*shahāda*), which states that 'there is no god but God'. Mawdudi interprets some words used in the Qurʾan to refer to God (*rabb* (lord) and *ilāh* (god)) to have legislative meaning, too, and believes that the problems people have derive at least partly from the fact that they have followed other 'gods' (laws, political parties, ideologies, etc.) than God. As such, Mawdudi interprets *tawḥīd* as implying that God ought to be absolutely sovereign in legislation. This divine sovereignty (*ḥākimiyya*),[68] expressed primarily through the application of the *sharīʿa*,[69] is central to Mawdudi's ideas on the Islamic state.[70]

While it is difficult to disentangle Mawdudi's influence on Qutb and Qutb's influence on Mawdudi, it is likely that the latter's use of *ḥākimiyya*[71]

63 For general analyses of Mawdudi and his ideology, see Charles J. Adams, 'The Ideology of Mawlana Mawdudi', in *South Asian Politics and Religion*, ed. Donald Eugene Smith (Princeton, NJ: Princeton University Press, 1966), 371–97; Seyyed Vali Reza Nasr, *Mawdudi & the Making of Islamic Revivalism* (Oxford: Oxford University Press, 1996).

64 Seyyed Vali Reza Nasr, 'Mawdudi and the Jamaʿat-i Islami: The Origins, Theory and Practice of Islamic Revivalism', in *Pioneers of Islamic Revival*, ed. Ali Rahnema (London and New York: Zed Books, 2005), 111–21.

65 Musallam, *Secularism*, 150–3. He is also cited or discussed in the Jordanian Muslim Brotherhood's newspapers sometimes. See, for instance, Abū l-Aʿlá al-Mawdūdī [*sic*], 'Asbāb ʿUbūdiyyatinā 3', *Al-Kifāḥ al-Islāmī*, 8 February 1957, 4; ʿAbdallāh al-ʿAqīl, 'Al-Mufakkir al-ʿAllāma Abū l-Aʿlá al-Mawdūdī [*sic*]', *Al-Sabīl*, 23–29 December 1997, 13.

66 Nasr, *Mawdudi*, 80.

67 Charles J. Adams, 'Mawdudi and the Islamic State', in *Voices of Resurgent Islam*, ed. John L. Esposito (Oxford: Oxford University Press, 1983), 113–14.

68 For a critical treatment of Mawdudi's use of this concept, see Asma Afsaruddin, 'Theologizing about Democracy: A Critical Appraisal of Mawdudi's Thought', in *Islam, the State, and Political Authority: Medieval Issues and Modern Concerns*, ed. Asma Afsaruddin (New York: Palgrave Macmillan, 2011), 139–41.

69 For more on this, see Afsaruddin, 'Theologizing', 144–7.

70 Adams, 'Mawdudi', 115–16; Afsaruddin, 'Theologizing', 132–3; Lahoud, *Political Thought*, 52–3; Nasr, *Mawdudi*, 89.

71 For a linguistic analysis of this term, see Sayyed Khatab, *The Power of Sovereignty: The Political and Ideological Philosophy of Sayyid Qutb* (London and New York: Routledge, 2006), 15–19.

reinforced the Egyptian thinker's own ideas on this subject.[72] Qutb does, indeed, apply the concept in a way that is very similar to Mawdudi[73] and equally derives it from a legislative interpretation of *tawḥīd*.[74] Qutb explains his use of *ḥākimiyya* – which acts as a peripheral concept flavouring his views on '*sharīʿa*' as adjacent to 'caliph'/'ruler', at the expense of '*sulṭa*' – by stating that

> the theory of governance in Islam (*naẓariyyat al-ḥukm fī l-Islām*) is based on the foundation of the *shahāda* that there is no god but God. When it was decided that the divinity (*ulūhiyya*) belongs to God alone (*li-llāh waḥdahu*) through this *shahāda*, it was decided through it that the sovereignty in the life of people (*al-ḥākimiyya fī ḥayāt al-bashar*) [also] belongs to God alone.[75]

The belief that there is no god but God thus entails that he is also sovereign in legislation, which means that 'the *sharīʿa* of God stands alone in this [system] through the wholesale (*jumlatan wa-tafṣīlan*) domination of the lives of the people (*bi-l-haymana ʿalá ḥayāt al-nās*)'.[76] Like ʿAwda, Qutb shows he is aware that this was not the case in Egypt at the time. Unlike ʿAwda, however, Qutb calls for the formation of a vanguard (*ṭalīʿa*) of Muslims who should wage jihad against the forces of *jāhiliyya* to restore the divine *ḥākimiyya*, which is not limited to non-violent forms of struggle, but includes actual fighting.[77] Given Qutb's belief in these forces' importance in the state's legislation, he not only decontests '*sharīʿa*' as adjacent to the core concept of 'caliph'/'ruler', but also implies that an armed revolution should be waged against the Egyptian state.[78]

Hasan al-Hudaybi

A third member of the Muslim Brotherhood arrested – but not executed – during Nasser's presidency was the judge and second General Guide

[72] Calvert, *Sayyid*, 214.
[73] Ibid., 214–17; Khatab, *Power*, 8; Lahoud, *Political Thought*, 52–4; Toth, *Sayyid*, 137–43.
[74] Khatab, *Power*, 19–26; Ahmad S. Moussalli, *Radical Islamic Fundamentalism: The Ideological and Political Discourse of Sayyid Quṭb* (Beirut: American University of Beirut, 1992), 149–72.
[75] Quṭb, *Al-ʿAdāla*, 80. [76] Ibid., 182.
[77] Calvert, *Sayyid*, 221–7; Toth, *Sayyid*, 143–57. For more on such views among other Muslim Brothers, see Uriya Shavit, 'The Muslim Brothers' Conception of Armed Insurrection against an Unjust Regime', *Middle Eastern Studies* 51, no. 4 (2015): 606–11. For Quṭb's own writings on this point, see Sayyid Quṭb, *Maʿālim fī l-Ṭarīq*, 6th ed. (Beirut and Cairo: Dār al-Shurūq, 1979), 55–82.
[78] Yvonne Yazbeck Haddad, 'The Qurʾanic Justification for an Islamic Revolution: The View of Sayyid Quṭb', *Middle East Journal* 37, no. 1 (1983): 26–8. This explanation is disputed by some members of the Jordanian Muslim Brotherhood, however. See, for example, Sayyid Quṭb, *Maʿālim fī l-Ṭarīq: Dirāsa wa-Taḥqīq*, ed. Ṣalāḥ ʿAbd al-Fattāḥ al-Khālidī (Amman: Dār ʿAmmār, 2009). There are a number of books like this trying to defang some of Quṭb's work, but dealing with this would require a separate publication.

(Murshid ʿĀmm) after al-Banna, Hasan al-Hudaybi (1891–1973), in the period between 1951, when the Brotherhood was reinstated in Egypt, and 1973. Because of his close connections with the Egyptian regime and his moderate views, al-Hudaybi can be described as a compromise candidate for the Muslim Brotherhood, which apparently wanted a new leader who was uncontroversial from the regime's point of view. Al-Hudaybi still had to cope with the ideological diversity within the organisation, however, which was not always easy. While al-Banna had mostly been able to keep the Brothers' infighting to a minimum, al-Hudaybi had to deal with a radicalised wing within the organisation that followed Qutb's ideas.[79]

To counter the Muslim Brotherhood views considered too radical – including especially Qutb's – al-Hudaybi and others circulated writings while in prison that refuted those advocating violence against the state and favoured gradual political reform rather than revolution.[80] This eventually resulted in the book *Duʿat La Qudat* (Preachers, Not Judges), which is ascribed to al-Hudaybi, but was most likely not written by him,[81] and which was published several years after his death, in 1977.[82] As Zollner has pointed out, the work proved to be the link between al-Hudaybi's generation and the later Brotherhood in the 1970s[83] and, perhaps more importantly, its ideas have become an important part of the organisation's ideology.[84]

Unlike the other Muslim Brothers analysed so far, al-Hudaybi, when discussing issues of politics, strongly relies on the classical tradition of the caliphate analysed in Chapter 1.[85] This is not only apparent from the fact that he cites mediaeval scholars, but also from the strong emphasis he places on the importance of the ruler's power.[86] This sets him apart from al-Banna, ʿAwda and Qutb who – while acknowledging the need for a powerful ruler – put less stress on the adjacent concept of '*sulṭa*' because they want to 'restore' the adjacent concept of '*sharīʿa*' at the expense of the ruler's power. Al-Hudaybi's approach expresses itself in a (by that time entirely theoretical) discussion on the exact requirements of the caliph[87] and, most importantly, in strongly associating the Islamic state

[79] Husaini, *Moslem Brethren*, 13–19; Mitchell, *Society*, 84–162; Phelps Harris, *Nationalism*, 185–94; Zollner, *Muslim Brotherhood*, 16–25.

[80] Barbara H. E. Zollner, 'Prison Talk: The Muslim Brotherhood's Internal Struggle during Gamal Abdel Nasser's Persecution, 1954 to 1971', *International Journal of Middle East Studies* 39, no. 3 (2007): 416–21.

[81] Zollner, *Muslim Brotherhood*, 64–71; Barbara H. E. Zollner, 'Opening to Reform: Hasan al-Hudaybi's Legacy', in *The Muslim Brotherhood in Europe*, ed. Roel Meijer and Edwin Bakker (London: Hurst & Co., 2012), 285–9; Zollner, 'Prison Talk', 421–4.

[82] Ḥasan al-Huḍaybī, *Duʿāt Lā Quḍāt* (Cairo: Dār al-Tawzīʿ wa-l-Nashr al-Islāmiyya, 1977).

[83] Zollner, 'Opening', 285. [84] Zollner, 'Prison Talk', 426.

[85] Zollner, *Muslim Brotherhood*, 111. [86] Ibid., 117–20. [87] Ibid., 120–1.

with the ruler or, as he calls him, 'the rightful leader (*imām al-ḥaqq*)'. Al-Hudaybi does not so much view the *sharīʿa* as a necessary prerequisite of an Islamic state, but rather the ruler who is responsible for its implementation, for which

> there needs to be planning (*tadbīr*), organisation (*tanẓīm*) and direction (*tawjīh*). This can only be pursued through a general power (*sulṭa ʿāmma*) whose will is above individual wills (*irāda fawqa l-irādāt al-fardiyya*). [. . .] This is the power of the imamate (*sulṭat al-imāma*).[88]

In fact, in al-Hudaybi's view the entanglement between the Islamic state and the ruler is so great that he names the relevant chapter 'the Islamic government or the rightful leader', practically equating the two. As Zollner points out, '[al-Hudaybi] does not even consider the possibility of an Islamic state without the leadership of the *imam al-haqq*'.[89]

Given the fact that Qutb employs the term '*ḥākimiyya*' to point out that God should be sovereign in Muslim states but that this is not the case in Egypt because of the country's laws and rulers, one may expect al-Hudaybi to resist this anti-establishmentarian interpretation. Indeed, he does. Al-Hudaybi points out that '*ḥākimiyya*' is not found in the Qurʾan and states that 'we have no need, after God's book and the *ḥadīth*s of the Messenger [. . .], to cling to any technical terms that fallible human beings implement'.[90] To be sure, al-Hudaybi makes it quite clear that he wants the *sharīʿa* to be implemented.[91] He objects, however, to the use of '*ḥākimiyya*', particularly when used to accuse others – who may be merely ignorant of certain aspects of the *sharīʿa* – of unbelief when they are Muslims in his view.[92] In the writings of Qutb – who al-Hudaybi never mentions by name but who is clearly on his mind – this leads to revolution, which al-Hudaybi is highly sceptical of.[93]

In his decontestation of the concepts involved, al-Hudaybi thus emphasises both the adjacent concepts of '*sharīʿa*' and – unlike his predecessors – '*sulṭa*'. This may have been a result of his close ties with the regime of his time, but should probably also be read in the context of his conflict with the radical followers of Qutb, whom he clearly saw as a danger and whom he wanted to stop. Precisely because Qutb seemed to be calling for a violent revolution against the rulers of his time, al-Hudaybi's emphasis on '*sulṭa*' and, implicitly, on the legitimacy of the rulers was therefore perhaps not surprising. Before we can draw conclusions on whether any of these Muslim Brothers were '*sharīʿa*-centred', '*umma*-centred' or

[88] Al-Huḍaybī, *Duʿāt*, 183. [89] Zollner, *Muslim Brotherhood*, 117.
[90] Al-Hudaybī, *Duʿāt*, 91–3. The quotation is on p. 93. [91] Ibid., 97–109.
[92] Ibid., 109–13. [93] Shavit, 'Muslim Brothers' Conception', 607–8.

'balanced' in their approach to Islamist ideology, however, we first need to look at the early Muslim Brotherhood's views on political participation.

Political Participation

The previous section saw various members of the Muslim Brotherhood in Egypt respond differently to the challenges of their time, mostly by contesting the '*sulṭa*-centred' approach that was the result of centuries of encroaching caliphal power and the scholarly justifications of this and by decontesting the political value of '*sharīʿa*'. Yet '*sharīʿa*' was only one concept adjacent to the core concept of 'caliph'/'ruler'; '*sulṭa*' and – most importantly for this section – '*umma*' were the others. As we will see below, the increased value of '*sharīʿa*' in the writings of the early Muslim Brotherhood also had an impact on '*umma*' and, more precisely, on the four different links between that concept and 'caliph'/'ruler' that we saw in Chapter 1.

Commanding Right and Forbidding Wrong

As we saw earlier, the first link between 'caliph'/'ruler' and '*umma*' – the duty to command right and forbid wrong – has an ineliminable feature (that right be commanded and wrong forbidden), but also has some quasi-contingent features (the person commanding/forbidding and the person being commanded/forbidden). Giving a different meaning to the latter can change the meaning of the link as a whole and change it from a Qurʾan-based means of confronting the ruler to an instrument in the hands of the ruler himself to impose order and morality on society, as Chapter 1 shows. Although not all prominent early Brotherhood thinkers expressed practical alternatives,[94] some were keen to give new meaning to the duty to command right and forbid wrong.

For al-Banna, it was clear that the *umma* had a role to play in politics. The idea that Islam was an all-encompassing system did not just mean that politics was included, but also that Muslims needed to be political.[95] He translated this into the idea that it was the *umma*'s job to hold the ruler accountable. The ruler should, according to al-Banna, work for the benefit of the people and if he went astray,[96] it was their duty to force him to return to some undefined form of just rule. Such reasoning gives the *umma* a say in the political affairs of a country, at least in

[94] See Cook, *Commanding Right*, 528–30, on Quṭb's views on this matter, for example.
[95] Lia, *Society*, 202.
[96] It is not clear whether going astray meant that the ruler started living a sinful life or that he was not acting in the interests of the people.

theory.[97] As such, the duty to command right and forbid wrong is, as Moussalli points out, translated 'into a formulation of public, legal, and political right to watch over the government'.[98] Al-Banna, then, decontests the quasi-contingent features of this duty by describing the *umma* as the one doing the commanding/forbidding and the rulers as the object of its actions.

A scholar who clearly agrees with al-Banna on this but takes it a step further is ʿAwda, who explicitly writes that 'it is imposed on the *umma* to supervise the rulers (*murāqabat al-ḥukkām*) and to correct them (*taqwīmahum*) according to what God has imposed on the *umma*, namely, to command right and forbid wrong'.[99] After mentioning the relevant Qurʾanic verses and *ḥadīth*s[100] that we also saw in Chapter 1, ʿAwda emphasises that this is not just the *umma*'s right, but really its duty and that it should be fulfilled by governments, groups and individuals. If rulers go astray, ʿAwda states, Muslims must not follow them in their disobedience to God, but must obey God instead.[101] Given that Muslim rulers are, ʿAwda claims, not doing their duty towards God and imposing un-Islamic laws, believers in any position of power should 'attack the laws (*yuhājima l-qawānīn*) and the situations that are contrary to Islam (*al-mukhālafa li-l-Islām*)'. Moreover, it is the duty of 'Muslims from the ends of the earth to cooperate [to change these laws] and smash them (*taḥṭīmihā*) with their hands'.[102] ʿAwda thus decontests the role of the *umma* to command right and forbid wrong by holding the supposedly un-Islamic rulers to account in a forceful and perhaps even violent way.

While al-Banna and ʿAwda both place commanding right and forbidding wrong in the hands of the *umma*, al-Hudaybi takes a different approach. He clearly acknowledges that the *umma* has a role to play, thereby – like al-Banna and ʿAwda – bringing '*umma*' back from the peripheral position that classical scholars had pushed it into.[103] He also draws the connection between *al-amr bi-l-maʿrūf wa-l-nahy ʿan al-munkar* and correcting rulers who transgress the *sharīʿa*.[104] Yet the logical conclusion of this that both al-Banna and ʿAwda draw – commanding right and forbidding wrong as a form of opposition to 'un-Islamic' rule – is clearly a bridge too far for al-Hudaybi. He not only wants this to be used as a last resort in order to avoid *fitna*,[105] but he also believes the motives for rulers' 'un-Islamic' leadership should be taken into account. Given that these are nearly impossible to determine, this means that al-Hudaybi

97 Lia, *Society*, 203. 98 Moussalli, 'Ḥasan', 171.
99 ʿAwda, *Al-Islām wa-Awḍāʿunā al-Siyāsiyya*, 179.
100 ʿAwda, *Al-Islām wa-Awḍāʿunā al-Qānūniyya*, 15–16. 101 Ibid., 17. 102 Ibid., 18.
103 Zollner, *Muslim Brotherhood*, 123. 104 Ibid., 136–7.
105 Zollner, 'Opening', 283–4.

leaves the theoretical possibility of *takfīr* of the rulers (and the subsequent deposition of them) intact, but basically excludes that eventuality in practice, just like classical Muslim scholars have done.[106] Al-Hudaybi thus decontests the quasi-contingent features of 'those who command/ forbid' and 'those who are commanded/forbidden' and ascribes them to, respectively, '*umma*' and the ruler's '*sulṭa*', but does so in such a way that it hardly differs from mediaeval practices.

Consultation and Oath of Fealty

The second link between 'caliph'/'ruler' and '*umma*' (*shūrá*), with its ineliminable feature (that there be consultation) and one of its quasi-contingent ones (the people consulted), changed drastically in mediaeval times. The same applies to the third link – *bayʿa* – whose ineliminable feature (fealty) remained, but one of whose quasi-contingent features (the ones pledging fealty) changed throughout the centuries. Both developments came at the expense of '*umma*'. Considering al-Banna's statement that 'we are politicians in the sense that we are interested in the affairs of the *umma*',[107] it is not surprising that the Brotherhood thinkers cited also take an interest in consultation and the oath of fealty.

As mentioned in this chapter's section on the state, al-Banna believes that Islamic rule is based on three principles, the first of which (the responsibility of the ruler) was dealt with above. Of the other two – the unity of the *umma* and respecting the will of the *umma* – the latter is of particular relevance here. He states that '[the ruler] must consult (*yushāwira*) [the *umma*] and respect its will' and subsequently cites the Qurʾanic verses and the example of caliph ʿUmar's *shūrá* we saw in Chapter 1.[108] This suggests that al-Banna believes the *umma* is, in effect, in control. Yet his words that immediately follow those cited above state that the ruler must 'take what is good (*al-ṣāliḥ*) from among their views',[109] meaning that consultation is not binding and that it is ultimately up to the ruler – not the *umma* – to decide.[110] The will of the *umma* as expressed through *shūrá*, moreover, is not just limited by what the person in power wants (*sulṭa*), but also by the *sharīʿa*. Echoing Rida, al-Banna states that if there is textual evidence for a certain position, that position must be implemented. *Ijtihād* only occurs when a matter is not definitive in the sources. This obviously leaves far less room for decision-making on the *umma*'s part and even the room that is left yields

106 Zollner, *Muslim Brotherhood*, 137. 107 Al-Bannā, *Majmūʿat*, 213.
108 Ibid., 319–21. The quotation is on p. 319. 109 Ibid., 319.
110 Tadros, *Muslim Brotherhood*, 62.

opinions from the *umma* from which the ruler gets to pick the ones he prefers.[111]

The respect for the will of the *umma* through *shūrá* is difficult to realise if one seeks to consult the entire Muslim community. This is where the *ahl al-ḥall wa-l-ʿaqd*, who can act as representatives of the *umma*, become relevant again. Like Rida, al-Banna broadens this group in comparison with what classical scholars did by also including – apart from Muslim legal scholars (*fuqahāʾ*) capable of *ijtihād* – 'the people of experience in general matters' and 'those who have a type of leadership (*qiyāda aw riʾāsa*) among the people, like heads of households and families, tribal sheikhs and leaders of groups'.[112] Al-Banna seems to go slightly further than Rida by acknowledging that the *ahl al-ḥall wa-l-ʿaqd* could be embodied by members of parliament,[113] but insists that those elected should only include 'the people of loosening and binding' and not others who merely want to represent the *umma*.[114] As such, al-Banna's decontestation of *shūrá* clearly connects its quasi-contingent feature of 'the people consulted' with the adjacent concept of '*umma*' in the form of an expanded *ahl al-ḥall wa-l-ʿaqd*, but simultaneously limits its significance by making it subservient to the adjacent concepts of '*sulṭa*' and '*sharīʿa*'.[115]

The approach to *shūrá* taken by ʿAwda begins by pointing out that the ruler is merely a first among equals.[116] ʿAwda further states that the caliph – like all other human beings – is a representative (*nāʾib*) of God, thereby echoing some classical scholars, and that 'his power (*sulṭānuhu*) is only based on his being nominated by the community'.[117] In fact, ʿAwda continues in reference to Q. 42:38, 'the mandate of the caliphate is only fulfilled through the election of the caliph by the community [...] because the Qurʾan compels Muslims that their affair is counsel (*shūrá*) between them'.[118] This, he maintains, 'confirms that the caliphate is nothing but a contract of nomination that is fulfilled between the community and the caliph'.[119] As such, ʿAwda claims, 'it is compulsory for the ruler to consult [people] in everything that touches upon the community. [...]

111 Ibid., 62–3.
112 Al-Bannā, *Majmūʿat*, 328. See also Mitchell, *Society*, 248; Tadros, *Muslim Brotherhood*, 60.
113 Al-Bannā, *Majmūʿat*, 321.
114 Tadros, *Muslim Brotherhood*, 60.
115 This attitude seems to be underlined by al-Bannā's dim view of political parties. See al-Bannā, *Majmūʿat*, 146–8, 165–9, 321–2, 326–7. This attitude seems to have been inspired more by the division and corruption in Egyptian political parties than by any strongly held ideological view, however. See Husaini, *Moslem Brethren*, 66–7; Mitchell, *Society*, 218–20; Lia, *Society*, 69, 203–5.
116 ʿAwda, *Al-Islām wa-Awḍāʿunā al-Siyāsiyya*, 132.
117 ʿAwda, *Al-Māl*, 122–3.
118 Ibid., 123; ʿAwda, *Al-Islām wa-Awḍāʿunā al-Siyāsiyya*, 129–30.
119 ʿAwda, *Al-Māl*, 124.

So the ruler does not have the right to impose his view in general matters'.[120] An Islamic government is therefore not theocratic, because 'it does not derive its power (*sulṭānuhā*) from God, but [...] from the community'.[121]

This appears to give the *umma* a substantial say in matters of state. Yet ʿAwda's views give less power to the *umma* than they seem to. This becomes clear when we look at ʿAwda's views on the *ahl al-ḥall wa-l-ʿaqd*, who turn out to be the members of the *umma* electing the ruler on their behalf, not the *umma* directly.[122] They should be people of justice, knowledge, informed opinion and wisdom[123] for whom there is no specific procedure of election, which may therefore be decided according to the time and place in which it happens,[124] although ʿAwda seems to restrict the number of people who can elect the *ahl al-ḥall wa-l-ʿaqd* to experts, particularly religious scholars.[125]

The importance of religion is further underlined by ʿAwda when he – like Rida and al-Banna – stresses that *shūrá* is limited by the *sharīʿa*, both in the sense that it only decides about things not clear from Islamic law already and in the sense that its conclusions may not go against the *sharīʿa*.[126] This is obvious, ʿAwda states, since the truth – represented by the *sharīʿa* – is uniform, leads only one way and must be obeyed.[127] ʿAwda acknowledges that this limits both the ruler and the ruled, but he sees this as an advantage that *shūrá* has over democracy, which is not ruled by the *sharīʿa*'s justice but by whatever rulers and people want.[128] Thus, ʿAwda's decontestation of '*umma*' through its 'restoration' to a place adjacent to the core concept of 'caliph'/'ruler' by connecting it to *shūrá*'s quasi-contingent feature of 'the people consulted' is real. Yet like al-Banna, ʿAwda restricts the *umma* but, unlike him, does not do so by privileging both '*sulṭa*' and '*sharīʿa*' as adjacent concepts. Instead, ʿAwda clearly sees '*sharīʿa*' as the most important adjacent concept.

The empowering of the *umma* on the one hand but limiting its mandate through the *sharīʿa* is also clear in Mawdudi's work, though in a different way. He, too, argues in favour of allowing the *umma* to be the consulted party in *shūrá* and, again, only with regard to issues not already settled by Islamic law, which severely limits the mandate of the *ahl al-ḥall wa-l-ʿaqd*.[129] A legislature in such a system is therefore not primarily

[120] Ibid., 115. [121] Ibid., 126. [122] ʿAwda, *Al-Islām wa-Awḍāʿunā al-Siyāsiyya*, 110.
[123] Ibid., 156. [124] Ibid., 155. [125] Tadros, *Muslim Brotherhood*, 61.
[126] ʿAwda, *Al-Islām wa-Awḍāʿunā al-Siyāsiyya*, 145–7; ʿAwda, *Al-Māl*, 116.
[127] ʿAwda, *Al-Māl*, 86–9.
[128] Ibid., 128–9. See also the views by Syrian Muslim Brothers on the issues of democracy, *shūrá* and the *ahl al-ḥall wa-l-ʿaqd* in Weismann, 'Democratic Fundamentalism?', 7–12.
[129] Afsaruddin, 'Theologizing', 135; Nasr, *Mawdudi*, 194–5.

intended to *make* laws, but to search the *sharīʿa* in order to *find* them.[130] Mawdudi refers to this system as 'theo-democracy': human rule under divine sovereignty.[131] Unlike ʿAwda, however, who acknowledges and even advocates the importance of the *sharīʿa* over the *umma*, Mawdudi seems to assume that the ruler's policies and the will of the people always concur with the *sharīʿa* because both the ruler and the *umma* are Muslims. The idea that this might lead to abuse by a ruler claiming God's mandate or that the will of the *umma* might clash with the provisions of the *sharīʿa* seems not to occur to him.[132]

Qutb's stance on *shūrá* is less complicated than Mawdudi's and more closely resembles ʿAwda's approach. Although Qutb recognises the 'popular' character of *shūrá* and even says that the members of a consultation council should be elected by neighbourhoods and small communities,[133] he states that the *umma* itself does not exist without an Islamic state. One may speak of 'Muslims' in the absence of such a state, but these cannot really be seen as a single *umma* without the application of the *sharīʿa* by the state.[134] It should therefore not come as a surprise that Qutb also insists that *shūrá* cannot exist outside the boundaries of the *sharīʿa*[135] and differs from democracy, which – because of the sovereignty it gives to the people – he considers an infringement on *ḥākimiyya*.[136] Like ʿAwda, Qutb thus decontests both '*umma*' and '*sharīʿa*' as adjacent to the core concept of 'caliph'/'ruler', but clearly sees the goals of the former as only realisable in the context of the latter.

The Muslim Brothers cited so far also write about *bayʿa*, although not as much as about *shūrá*.[137] In the case of ʿAwda, the oath of fealty should be seen in the context of the election of the ruler. He views the *bayʿa* as the final stage in a selection procedure of a caliph, a stage in which the members of the *shūrá* pledge fealty to him.[138] Although ʿAwda is certainly aware of the early Islamic use of *bayʿa*[139] and sees it as 'a contract between the caliph, on the one hand, and the people of considered opinion (*ūlū l-raʾy*; i.e. the *ahl al-ḥall wa-l-ʿaqd*) in the *umma*, on the other',[140] it should be borne in mind that he believes the latter's role should be strictly circumscribed by Islamic law, as we saw above. As such, his decontestation of *bayʿa* should not be seen as an endorsement of popular approval of

130 Adams, 'Mawdudi', 125. 131 Afsaruddin, 'Theologizing', 133–4.
132 Adams, 'Mawdudi', 117–19; Nasr, *Mawdudi*, 84–9. 133 Toth, *Sayyid*, 208.
134 Khatab, *Power*, 40–5. 135 Ibid., 8. 136 Ibid., 29–30; Toth, *Sayyid*, 176–7.
137 For more on the early Egyptian Brotherhood's application of *bayʿa*, see Landau-Tasseron, *Leadership*.
138 ʿAwda, *Al-Islām wa-Awḍāʿunā al-Siyāsiyya*, 166–9; Mitchell, *Society*, 247.
139 ʿAwda, *Al-Islām wa-Awḍāʿunā al-Siyāsiyya*, 110–16. 140 Ibid., 166.

the ruler, but as a *sharīʿa*-inspired effort to keep the leader's policies Islamic.

Al-Hudaybi also discusses *bayʿa* very briefly. While he – like ʿAwda – sees leadership in Islam as a contractual relationship between the ruler and the people,[141] the persons pledging fealty to the leader seem to be the *ahl al-ḥall wa-l-ʿaqd*, not the *umma*. Moreover, al-Hudaybi, citing Q. 2:286 ('God charges no soul save to its capacity [. . .]'), suggests that common people are incapable of making decisions on leadership.[142] This is underlined by his suggestion that getting the people involved in such activities is likely to lead to differences of opinion, conflicts and paralysis. To counter this and avoid *fitna*, a strong leader is needed who can maintain security, thereby allowing the religion to come to fruition.[143] Thus, as we saw above, al-Hudaybi's decontestation – unlike that of the other Muslim Brothers cited – does not so much bring '*umma*' back in as an adjacent concept to the central concept of 'caliph'/'ruler', but concentrates more on '*sharīʿa*' and '*sulṭa*'.

Obedience

The fourth link between '*umma*' and 'caliph'/'ruler' – *ṭāʿa* – is not something that the scholars of the early Muslim Brotherhood disagree on in principle; they just differ about the conditions under which it should be applied. ʿAwda certainly sees obedience as positive and clearly associates its quasi-contingent feature of 'the person obeyed' with the ruler, yet he unequivocally states that there is an even higher 'person' to obey, namely, God, and that he must always take precedence over any ruler. ʿAwda thus decontests *ṭāʿa* to the ruler as conditioned upon his adherence to the *sharīʿa*[144] and the same applies to Qutb.[145]

Al-Hudaybi, on the other hand, while not fundamentally disagreeing with this,[146] places an inordinate amount of emphasis on 'listening [to] and obeying (*al-samʿ wa-l-ṭāʿa*)' the ruler.[147] In addition to statements such as 'there is no meeting of words and unity of ranks (*lā ijtimāʿ li-l-kalima wa-lā waḥda li-l-ṣaff*) except with listening and obeying',[148] he also stresses that rulers have the duty to fight rebels.[149] While al-Hudaybi's emphasis on '*sulṭa*' as an adjacent concept to the core concept of 'caliph'/'ruler' should, as mentioned above, likely be seen in the context of his fear of Qutb-inspired civil strife, it is nevertheless striking how much his decontestation differs from those of his contemporaries.

141 Zollner, *Muslim Brotherhood*, 122. 142 Ibid., 126–7. 143 Ibid., 127.
144 ʿAwda, *Al-Islām wa-Awḍāʿunā al-Qānūniyya*, 14–15, 59–60.
145 Quṭb, *Al-ʿAdāla*, 81–2. 146 Al-Huḍaybī, *Duʿāt*, 45. 147 Ibid., 161–71, 184–91.
148 Ibid., 185. 149 Ibid., 186–90.

Having discussed the treatment of both '*sharīʿa*' and '*umma*' in the writings of several Muslim Brotherhood thinkers, we can now draw some tentative conclusions as to where they stand in the Islamist ideological spectrum. Mawdudi can be said to take a balanced approach between '*sharīʿa*' and '*umma*' as concepts adjacent to the core concept of 'caliph'/ 'ruler', not privileging either over the other too much, but simply assuming that they will not clash. Al-Banna, while more *sharīʿa*-centred than Mawdudi, and al-Hudaybi, though more *sulṭa*-centred than both others, can be said to do the same. ʿAwda and Qutb, however, clearly privilege '*sharīʿa*' over '*umma*' and, as such, may be labelled '*sharīʿa*-centred'. Both the balanced and the *sharīʿa*-centred approaches became more pronounced in later decades, including among members of the Jordanian Brotherhood, as we will see later. First, however, we must look at how the early Brothers' views on societal rights and freedoms fit into this.

Societal Rights and Freedoms

As has become abundantly clear so far, the *sharīʿa* is quite important to the Muslim Brotherhood. Its early ideologues believed that Islamic law should not only encompass the state, but society as well. In the words of ʿAwda:

> The social system in Islamic countries means the Islamic system because Islam governs every situation of the Muslim (*ḥarakāt al-Muslim wa-sakanātahu*), his acts (*afʿālahu*), his sayings (*aqwālahu*), his relations with others (*muʿāmalātahu*), his behaviour (*taṣarrufātahu*) and his ties with relatives, strangers, enemies and friends and it indicates his morals (*akhlāqahu*) and his way (*minhājahu*) to him in life.[150]

Qutb equally distinguishes between what he sees as *jāhilī* societies and Islamic ones and stresses that Islam should not be separated from society.[151]

Applying the *sharīʿa* to ever-changing societies is easier said than done, however. The *sharīʿa* – a term encompassing the totality of Islamic legal developments throughout the centuries – is not a rule book that one can open to find easy answers to practical questions in every situation. The early (lay) members of the Muslim Brotherhood realised this and were often sceptical of the learned scholarly tradition with its complicated discussions of legal niceties. Instead, they relied on the Qurʾan and the Sunna and preferred new and clear works that interpreted those sources in light of modern times. Using concepts such as *ijtihād* and the general

150 ʿAwda, *Al-Islām wa-Awḍāʿunā al-Qānūniyya*, 105.
151 Khatab, *Political Thought*, 118–19.

interest (*maṣlaḥa*) of the Muslim community to reform the legal corpus, the Brotherhood advocated a 'general' or 'flexible' approach to the *sharīʿa*.[152]

This flexibility is not applicable to all aspects of the *sharīʿa*, however, and neither is it equally shared by all early Muslim Brotherhood thinkers dealt with in this chapter. An oft-used distinction within the *sharīʿa* is that between *ʿibādāt* (acts of worship) and *muʿāmalāt* (relations with others). While the former are often seen as fixed, the latter can change. Al-Hudaybi clearly acknowledges this difference and treats the two categories differently.[153] Qutb, however, tends to blur the two, is sceptical of changing either[154] and believes that *ijtihād* can be used to change Islam, yet not so much to modernise it but to revert to the text of the Qurʾan.[155] This section deals with how early Muslim Brothers translated such diverging ideas on the *sharīʿa* to views on societal rights and freedoms.

Religious Minority Rights

The views of Jews and Christians held by the early Muslim Brothers should be seen in the context of the turbulent period the Middle East was going through in the 1920s–1970s. The conflict over Palestine was particularly important in determining perceptions of Jews, whom the early Muslim Brothers seem to have equated with Zionists, citing both contemporary politics and some of the Qurʾanic verses we saw in Chapter 1 to justify their deep distrust of them.[156] Despite the fact that the colonial period was a time during which major powers perceived to be Christian controlled substantial parts of the region, the Muslim Brothers appear to have been less generalising with regard to Christians, distinguishing between Western missionaries and the local Christian population.[157] Al-Banna cites Q. 60:8 ('God forbids you not, as regards those who have not fought you in religion's cause, nor expelled you from your habitations, that you should be kindly to them, and act justly towards them; surely God loves the just') to justify tolerance of Christians and quotes verses on pre-Islamic prophets to stress the links between Christians and Muslims.[158] This attitude of tolerance seems to have translated into actual practice with al-Banna, during whose leadership several Coptic Christians were members of the Brotherhood.[159]

152 Mitchell, *Society*, 237–9. 153 Zollner, *Muslim Brotherhood*, 103–6.
154 Toth, *Sayyid*, 98–9, 203–4. 155 Ibid., 199–203, 204–6.
156 El-Awaisi, *Muslim Brothers*, 7–8. 157 Mitchell, *Society*, 224–31.
158 Al-Bannā, *Majmūʿat*, 285–6.
159 El-Awaisi, *Muslim Brothers*, 6–7; Husaini, *Moslem Brethren*, 70.

Although al-Banna shows tolerance to Egyptian Christians, he appears to have seen them as a tolerated minority in the mould of the classical *dhimma*, but not as anything more than that.[160] ʿAwda goes further, however, and states that there is complete equality between people, individuals, communities, races and ethnicities, quoting Q. 49:13 ('Oh mankind, We have [. . .] appointed you races and tribes, that you may know one another [. . .]') to make his case, and maintains that there is complete justice for all in Islam.[161] This emphasis on equality seems to be aimed at serving the people's interests first and foremost, yet it is important to understand the context in which ʿAwda makes these claims. He explicitly states, for example, that there is equality between Muslims and *dhimmīs*,[162] thus also linking this to the Islamic legal concept of *dhimma*. He also states that both Muslims and *dhimmīs* have Islamic citizenship (*jinsiyya Islāmiyya*) in the abode of Islam (*dār al-Islām*)[163] and that the only difference that counts is piety.[164] In other words, in ʿAwda's *sharīʿa*-centred approach, non-Muslims' position is decontested not as that of full stakeholders, but as that of a protected, tolerated and equal minority in the context of an Islamic state whose religious ideology they do not subscribe to.

A consequence of seeing non-Muslims as merely a tolerated minority is that their political rights are limited. This is perhaps clearest with Mawdudi. Informed by relations with India and the perceived need to distinguish Pakistan as Muslim,[165] he not only excludes *dhimmīs* as full citizens of the Pakistani state, but also believes they should not have a say in the politics of that country.[166] Qutb, too, endorses the idea of complete equality between Muslims and non-Muslims and also believes the latter should be free to practise their religions, but nevertheless maintains that they should pay the *jizya* to avoid military service in an Islamic state.[167] He also clearly sees Jews and Christians as adhering to religions inferior to Islam,[168] portrays Jews as untrustworthy from the days of Muhammad to his own time[169] and speaks of non-Muslims as the enemies of Islam.[170]

[160] For more on al-Bannā's rudimentary views on citizenship, see Roel Meijer, 'The Political, Politics, and Political Citizenship in Modern Islam', in *The Middle East in Transition: The Centrality of Citizenship*, ed. Nils A. Butenschon and Roel Meijer (Cheltenham: Edward Elgar Publishing, 2018), 186–9.
[161] ʿAwda, *Al-Islām wa-Awḍāʿunā al-Qānūniyya*, 106–8.
[162] ʿAwda, *Al-Islām wa-Awḍāʿunā al-Siyāsiyya*, 196. [163] Ibid., 207.
[164] ʿAwda, *Al-Islām wa-Awḍāʿunā al-Qānūniyya*, 107. [165] Nasr, *Mawdudi*, 100–2.
[166] Adams, 'Mawdudi', 121–2; Afsaruddin, 'Theologizing', 137; Nasr, *Mawdudi*, 99–100.
[167] Khatab, *Power*, 62.
[168] Michael Ebstein, *In the Shadows of the Koran: Said* [*sic*] *Qutb's Views on Jews and Christians as Reflected in his Koran Commentary*, Research Monographs on the Muslim World 2, no. 4 (Washington, DC: Hudson Institute, 2009), 5–6.
[169] Toth, *Sayyid*, 280. [170] Ebstein, *Shadows*, 10–20.

While these views were, as mentioned, partly inspired by contemporary colonialism and conflict, Qutb also decontested the classical concept of *dhimma* as applicable to the position of non-Muslims in a state led by Islam in which they were a tolerated minority, not full citizens,[171] and, as such, his views on this issue confirm the *sharīʿa*-centredness of his approach.

Women's Rights

Just as early Muslim Brotherhood thinkers based their ideas about religious minorities on the *sharīʿa*, like classical scholars did, they also saw women's rights through the prism of Islamic law. While arguing that men and women are equal according to Islam, the early Brothers nevertheless criticised the supposedly overly permissive Western traditions of women's rights.[172] The reason for this is not that the Muslim Brotherhood believed that women are inferior to men, but that the latter have different mental and emotional attributes than women. As a result, early Muslim Brothers believed, men have to bear a greater responsibility, which explains why the Qurʾan distinguishes between the sexes,[173] as we saw in Chapter 1. The rules of the *sharīʿa* were therefore not seen as discriminatory, but in line with women's natural abilities and characteristics. It is in this spirit that early Muslim Brothers wanted to provide women with the limited, *sharīʿa*-based rights that they claimed cultural traditions have sometimes deprived them of.[174]

Advocating women's rights according to the *sharīʿa* sometimes meant repeating age-old rules with regard to women's duty to dress modestly or a generally dim view of divorce.[175] Still, in other areas the early Muslim Brotherhood used the text of the Qurʾan to change rules, such as with regard to polygamy, arguing that the Qurʾanic injunction to treat the maximum number of four wives equally (Q. 4:3) is quite unrealistic, thus effectively making the whole practice impossible.[176] The early Muslim Brotherhood was also slightly more flexible with regard to gender-mixing, allowing it when necessary.[177] This opened up the possibility for women to get an education and be employed, although it was seen as preferable for women to study subjects or do jobs that were supposedly in line with their nature, such as medicine.[178] The early Muslim

171 See also Meijer, 'Political', 189–92. 172 Mitchell, *Society*, 255.
173 Ibid.; Tadros, *Muslim Brotherhood*, 138. 174 Mitchell, *Society*, 254, 256.
175 Ibid., 256, 259. 176 Ibid., 258–9. See also Toth, *Sayyid*, 276, however.
177 Mitchell, *Society*, 256, 257; Tadros, *Muslim Brotherhood*, 140–1.
178 Mitchell, *Society*, 256–7; Phelps Harris, *Nationalism*, 167; Tadros, *Muslim Brotherhood*, 139, 141–2.

Brotherhood saw women's primary responsibility, however, as staying at home, where they could take care of family matters, such as raising children.[179] Politics was therefore not something that the early Brothers envisaged for Muslim women, at least not until society was purged of the 'corruption' that tainted it at the time.[180]

The views described above seem to have been held more or less across the board among Muslim Brothers, but the latter do not seem to have spent a great amount of time explaining them. An exception in this regard is the founder of the Syrian branch of the Muslim Brotherhood, Mustafa al-Siba'i (1915–1964),[181] who wrote an entire book on the subject entitled *Al-Mar'a bayna l-Fiqh wa-l-Qanun* (The Woman between [Islamic] Jurisprudence and the Law).[182] Al-Siba'i starts his book by stating that

> I cannot imagine a man being aggressive towards a woman because the woman is his mother, his wife, his daughter, his sister or his relative. So how can one imagine man to be aggressive towards his mother, his wife, his daughter or his sister, for example? If he wants to prevent her from doing some things, that is because through that he wants [to act in] her interest (*maṣlaḥatahā*) before anything [else] and then the interest of society after that.[183]

This quotation exemplifies al-Siba'i's attitude towards women's rights (as well as those of other early Muslim Brothers): equality for women based on their best interests, which are obviously represented by the *sharīʿa*. As such, al-Siba'i favourably compares women's rights in Islam with those in ancient cultures and other religions, where women were often subjected to the whims of earthly men, rather than the supposedly divine justice found in the *sharīʿa*.[184] He similarly finds the *sharīʿa* to be in people's best interests, practical and superior to Western practices with regard to marriage rights,[185] polygamy[186] and divorce.[187]

More relevant with regard to the Jordanian Muslim Brotherhood's views are issues such as gender-mixing. Al-Siba'i acknowledges that *ikhtilāṭ* was not uncommon in 'our societies' because of the influence of the 'customs of the Westerners (*ʿādāt al-Gharbiyyīn*) in everything'. Yet it

[179] Mitchell, *Society*, 257; Phelps Harris, *Nationalism*, 167; Tadros, *Muslim Brotherhood*, 138; Toth, *Sayyid*, 275. See also al-Bannā, *Majmūʿat*, 373–5.
[180] Mitchell, *Society*, 257–8; Tadros, *Muslim Brotherhood*, 147–8.
[181] For more on al-Sibāʿī and his role in the Syrian Muslim Brotherhood, see Lefèvre, *Ashes*, 23–40; Reissner, *Ideologie*, 121–6.
[182] Muṣṭafá al-Sibāʿī, *Al-Marʾa bayna l-Fiqh wa-l-Qānūn*, 7th ed. (Beirut: Dār al-Warrāq, 1999).
[183] Ibid., 9. [184] Ibid., 13–38. [185] Ibid., 49–59. [186] Ibid., 60–98.
[187] Ibid., 99–118.

is, he states, forbidden in Islam and opens the door to *fitna*.[188] Gender-mixing and the resulting adultery were also, al-Sibaʿi writes, among the main reasons why the Greek and Roman civilisations fell and, he states, even twentieth-century intellectuals from European countries are beginning to see the drawbacks of *ikhtilāṭ*, thereby buttressing his case against the practice.[189] This should not stop girls and women from getting a good education, however, which al-Sibaʿi argues strongly in favour of,[190] as long as they sit separately in class.[191]

Similar restrictions apply to women working outside the home: arguing against alleged Western practices of making seventeen-year-old girls fend for themselves, al-Sibaʿi states that women may work, but only if they adhere to the rules of the *sharīʿa*.[192] It is clear, however, that al-Sibaʿi sees the home as the natural place for a woman and even blames broken homes, moral decay and economic recessions on working women.[193] He claims people have to choose between the Western philosophy about women and the Islamic one, which respects 'the dignity of the woman and frees her to pursue her societal mission as a wife and a mother'.[194] Al-Sibaʿi essentially holds the same views with regard to women in politics. While he states that there are no texts that forbid women to participate in politics (either by voting or by becoming a member of parliament), it is probably best if they do not engage in such practices because it may lead to sinful behaviour and will divert their attention away from their primary interest: raising a family. Al-Sibaʿi therefore encourages men to take care of this, so that there is no need for women in politics.[195] Thus, al-Sibaʿi (as well as other Muslim Brothers) calls for the *sharīʿa* to be adopted with regard to women's rights, overriding the supposedly Western-influenced views of the *umma*. As such, al-Sibaʿi and the other Brothers take a clearly *sharīʿa*-centred approach on this issue.

Civil Liberties

In classical Islam, as we saw in Chapter 1, two clearly diverging trends with regard to civil liberties could be discerned: a *sharīʿa*-centred one that stressed the application of the rules of the *sharīʿa* and a balanced one that sought to align the interests of the *umma* with a reinterpreted form of Islamic law. As mentioned, some academics ascribed the use of punishments for blasphemy or apostasy to the insecurity of the community and the need to set up strict boundaries as a result thereof. It may be because

188 Ibid., 149. 189 Ibid., 149–53. 190 Ibid., 133. 191 Ibid., 148. 192 Ibid., 137.
193 Ibid., 138, 140, 154. 194 Ibid., 148. 195 Ibid., 121–7, 134–6.

the *umma* found itself in perceivably similar circumstances under Western colonial rule that the early Muslim Brothers seem to have adopted the *sharīʿa*-centred trend in the little they wrote about the subject. Mitchell quotes a 1950s Brotherhood magazine stating that when Western armies came to Egypt, they brought good things, such as schools and sciences, but also their 'wine, women, and sin'.[196] Given the Brotherhood's beliefs that societal rights and freedoms should generally also be decided by the *sharīʿa*, the organisation felt that practices such as adultery, drinking and gambling should be outlawed[197] and that freedom of expression and freedom of worship – though certainly allowed – should also be restricted so as not to violate the *sharīʿa*.[198]

It is in this context that early Muslim Brotherhood discourse on this subject should be seen. ʿAwda, for example, spends several pages extolling the freedoms that Islam has provided human beings with, distinguishing – among others – freedom of speech (*ḥurriyyat al-qawl*) and freedom of belief (*ḥurriyyat al-iʿtiqād*).[199] He also explicitly states that '[t]he Islamic *sharīʿa* has made freedom of speech a right for every human being', but also mentions that this freedom 'is not absolute. It is limited in that no things can be written or said that go against the texts and the spirit of the *sharīʿa* (*khārijan ʿalá nuṣūṣ al-sharīʿa wa-rūḥihā*).'[200] With regard to freedom of religion, ʿAwda cites the words 'no compulsion is there in religion' from Q. 2:256 and states that 'people need to respect the right of the other to believe what he wants',[201] but does not talk about the right to leave Islam.

Mawdudi equally states that individual expressions should be curtailed by the sovereignty of God as expressed by the *sharīʿa*.[202] Just like with the application of Islamic law on a state level, Mawdudi seems convinced that in an ideological state such as the one he wants this is not in contradiction to the will of the *umma*. Precisely because the state and its society have Islamic underpinnings, its inhabitants surrender to God's will voluntarily, Mawdudi believes.[203] In fact, Qutb maintains that true freedom can only be found under God's rule, not that of human beings. In an Islamic state, people are therefore truly liberated, while those living in *jāhilī* societies remain enslaved to earthly authorities.[204]

The Muslim Brotherhood's views on societal rights and freedoms were thus generally decontested in a way that underlines the *sharīʿa*-centredness

[196] Mitchell, *Society*, 223. [197] Husaini, *Moslem Brethren*, 64.
[198] Mitchell, *Society*, 249.
[199] ʿAwda, *Al-Islām wa-Awḍāʿunā al-Qānūniyya*, 108–11; ʿAwda, *Al-Islām wa-Awḍāʿunā al-Siyāsiyya*, 197–200.
[200] ʿAwda, *Al-Islām wa-Awḍāʿunā al-Siyāsiyya*, 199. [201] Ibid., 198.
[202] Nasr, *Mawdudi*, 90. [203] Adams, 'Mawdudi', 120. [204] Toth, *Sayyid*, 209–10.

of some of its prominent early thinkers because they argued that these rights and freedoms should be derived from the *sharīʿa*. 'Restoring' the concept of '*sharīʿa*' to a position adjacent to the central concept of 'caliph'/ 'ruler' did not come at the expense of the adjacent concept of '*sulṭa*', however, like some of the Brotherhood's views on the state, but of the '*umma*', particularly if it had been influenced by outside forces like the West. As such, just like arguing in favour of an Islamic state could easily be seen as liberation from (often oppressive) human rule, pushing for the adoption of the *sharīʿa* in society could be construed as freeing the *umma* from Western domination. Before we look at the extent to which the Jordanian Muslim Brotherhood has (dis)continued this and other lines of thinking, we must first turn to the history of the kingdom's branch of the organisation to see in what political context it operates.

3 The Muslim Brotherhood's Behaviour in the Jordanian Context

Besides the historical, theoretical context that we saw in Chapters 1 and 2, the political, practical context of the Kingdom of Jordan is also of great importance to the development of the Muslim Brotherhood because it directly shapes, confronts and limits the ideas, opportunities and influence of the organisation. Moreover, it is in this context that the Brotherhood is included in or excluded from the political system and their ideological moderation or radicalisation also plays out here. Thus, to understand the extent to which the Jordanian regime's policies vis-à-vis the Brotherhood have affected the organisation's ideological development in a *sharī'a*-centred, *umma*-centred or balanced direction – i.e. to test the 'inclusion-moderation' thesis – we must first know more about the regime's policies towards the Brotherhood.

This chapter delves into this issue by dividing the history of the Muslim Brotherhood's behaviour in Jordan into three different periods: 1946–1989, during which relations with the regime were mostly good and characterised by cooperation; 1989–1999, when the regime and the Brotherhood had less need for each other and the latter began to contest the former's power; and 1999–2016, during which both parties took a more confrontational approach, with the regime eventually subjugating the Brotherhood to its will. Because the next three chapters are dedicated to the Muslim Brotherhood's ideological moderation or radicalisation in the context of Jordanian politics and society, this chapter will focus on the group's behaviour and the regime's inclusion or repression of the organisation.

Cooperation: 1946–1989

The history of the area now known as Jordan goes back thousands of years and various empires have settled there, the last of which was the Ottoman Empire. Although Muslims had already conquered and settled part of present-day Jordan in the seventh century, the Ottomans gained control of the area in 1516.[1] Their rule was mostly flexible and seems to have taken local rules and customs into account. Even so, the Ottomans sometimes reached the limits of what the local population was willing to put up with from what was essentially foreign rule and a revolt even broke out in the southern city of al-Karak in 1910.[2] This revolt came in the midst of growing resistance against Ottoman rule throughout the region, partly as a result of increasing feelings of Arab nationalism. This gained a boost during the First World War, when the Ottoman Empire sided with the Triple Alliance of Germany, Austria-Hungary and Italy and lost the war with them, as well. During these years, the emir of Mecca, Husayn b. ʿAli (c. 1853–1931), struck a deal with the British: Husayn and his sons would help Great Britain fight the Ottomans and gain Arab independence in return.[3] In practice, this meant that Husayn's son ʿAbdallah, who considered the area now known as Jordan a mere 'consolation prize' in comparison with Iraq and Syria,[4] was made ruler of that country, where he was installed as emir of Transjordan in 1921.[5]

Losing Ottoman control over Transjordan meant gaining British dominance. Although the country was nominally ruled by ʿAbdallah, the British were the ones propping up his leadership and steering it into the direction they wanted, which was formally concluded in the Anglo-Jordanian agreement of 1928.[6] There was opposition to this agreement from within the country, but the British cooperated with ʿAbdallah to keep this at bay.[7] Part of the opposition in Transjordan came from the local tribes. ʿAbdallah had been quite successful in bringing these under his control,[8] but not all of them were willing to fully accept his

1 Kamal Salibi, *The Modern History of Jordan* (London and New York: I.B. Tauris, 2006 [1993]), 16–26.

2 Eugene L. Rogan, 'Bringing the State Back: The Limits to Ottoman Rule in Jordan, 1840–1910', in *Village, Steppe and State: The Social Origins of Modern Jordan*, ed. Eugene L. Rogan and Tariq Tell (London and New York: British Academic Press, 1994), 32–57; Eugene L. Rogan, *Frontiers of the State in the Late Ottoman Empire* (Cambridge: Cambridge University Press, 1999), 184–217. For more on the independence of al-Karak and its later integration in the Kingdom of Jordan, see Peter Gubser, *Politics and Change in Al-Karak, Jordan* (Oxford: Oxford University Press, 1973).

3 For an in-depth account of Arab nationalism and how this contributed to the formation of the modern Middle East, see George Antonius, *The Arab Awakening* (New York: Capricorn Books, 1965 [1946]), especially 125–242.

4 Philip Robins, *A History of Jordan* (Cambridge: Cambridge University Press, 2004), 16–19.

5 Mary C. Wilson, *King Abdullah, Britain and the Making of Jordan* (Cambridge: Cambridge University Press, 1987), 39–53.

6 Naseer H. Aruri, *Jordan: A Study in Political Development (1921–1965)* (The Hague: Martinus Nijhoff, 1972), 75–8.

7 Ibid., 78–87.

8 Yoav Alon, *The Making of Jordan: Tribes, Colonialism and the Modern State* (London and New York: I.B. Tauris, 2007), 40–6.

rule.[9] With the help of the British, however, he managed to remain in power, partly through the work done by John Bagot Glubb, a British colonial army officer who was installed as chief of staff of the Transjordanian army in 1936.[10] In this position, he incorporated tribal forces into the army, thereby laying the basis for a loyal relationship between the tribes and the ruling family that continues to this day.[11] Indeed, the army still remains heavily populated by tribal Jordanians and is strongly tied to the regime and, more specifically, the king.[12]

The Regime and the Muslim Brotherhood: The Beginning of a Relationship

Apart from the legitimacy derived from the regime's Arab nationalism and its role in the Arab Revolt of 1916, as well as the status the emir had acquired among local tribes, ʿAbdallah also relied on Islam to buttress his rule. This was partly seen in his descendance from the Prophet Muhammad's Hashim clan – hence Jordan's official name, 'Hashimite Kingdom of Jordan' – but also in measures taken to ensure, for example, that women dressed according to Islamic norms when leaving their houses. As such, some observers have labelled Jordan's system one of 'conservative secularism'. This term refers to the idea that Jordan is a secular (not an Islamic) state in the sense that the *sharīʿa* is not the law of the land, but a country that is nevertheless conservative because of the Islamic influence reflected in its constitution, politics, culture and society.[13]

The conservative and Islamic culture in (Trans)Jordan later expressed itself in the founding of various religious institutes,[14] but also in allowing Islamic activism of various types, such as the controversial Hizb al-Tahrir al-Islami, an organisation that strives for the resurrection of the caliphate.[15] It is in this context that a merchant from the town of al-Salt, ʿAbd al-Latif Abu Qura (d. 1967), founded the Transjordanian branch of the Muslim

[9] For an example of a tribal shaykh who had to deal with the rulers of Jordan, see Yoav Alon, *The Shaykh of Shaykhs: Mithqal al-Fayiz and Tribal Leadership in Modern Jordan* (Stanford, CA: Stanford University Press, 2016).

[10] Aruri, *Jordan*, 27–32.

[11] For an excellent example of how tribal culture plays a major role in Jordanian culture and politics, see Andrew Shryock, *Nationalism and the Genealogical Imagination: Oral History and Textual Authority in Tribal Jordan* (Berkeley, CA, Los Angeles and London: University of California Press, 1997).

[12] Beverley Milton-Edwards and Peter Hinchcliffe, *Jordan: A Hashemite Legacy* (London and New York: Routledge, 2001), 37.

[13] Muḥammad Abū Rummān and Ḥasan Abū Haniyya, *Al-Ḥall al-Islāmī fī l-Urdunn: Al-Islāmiyyūn wa-l-Dawla wa-Rihānāt al-Dīmuqrāṭiyya wa-l-Amn* (Amman: Friedrich Ebert Stiftung, 2012), 23–7.

[14] Ibid., 38–53. [15] Ibid., 397–423.

Brotherhood in 1945.[16] Strongly influenced by Hasan al-Banna and the Egyptian Brotherhood, Abu Qura wanted to aid the fight against the Zionists in neighbouring Palestine, but founded the organisation on the basis of a cultural and social agenda of Islamic education and preaching.[17]

Given the emphasis that Emir ʿAbdallah placed on Islam, it was perhaps not surprising that he supported the founding of the Muslim Brotherhood in Transjordan. When the organisation asked ʿAbdallah whether they could set up a branch of the Brotherhood, the High Council of Ministers decided to give them official permission and allowed the opening of the organisation's headquarters under the guidance of the emir. As such, the Muslim Brotherhood in Transjordan was officially established in the same year the country became independent and ʿAbdallah became king: 1946.[18] Knowing that the Brotherhood disagreed with some of his policies – especially his friendly ties with Zionist leaders (see below) – ʿAbdallah gave his permission with the understanding that the organisation would be religious – not political – in nature. He believed the Brotherhood could act as a counterweight to communist and other political groups more hostile to his rule, but nevertheless remained suspicious of its activities and kept a close watch on it, although relations between them remained mostly cordial and without much interference from the regime's side.[19]

The Brotherhood, for its part, seems to have been aware of its ambiguous relationship with ʿAbdallah, despite his ultimate willingness to tolerate the organisation. While some seem to ascribe the king's permission to his religious personality[20] or stress his support for the organisation,[21] others clearly realise that the monarchy – despite its faults – was far preferable to alternatives in the region.[22] This pragmatic approach and the Brothers' limited, non-political agenda at the time allowed them to overlook their differences with the king on the question

[16] Al-ʿUbaydī, *Jamāʿat*, 34–7. For more on the life of Abū Qūra from the perspective of sympathetic Muslim Brothers, see Yūsuf al-ʿAẓm, 'Al-Ḥāj ʿAbd al-Laṭīf Abū Qūra Kamā ʿAraftuhu', *Al-Sabīl*, 17–23 October 1995, 2; ʿAwnī Jadwaʿ al-ʿUbaydī, *Ṣafaḥāt min Ḥayāt al-Ḥāj ʿAbd al-Laṭīf Abū Qūra, Muʾassis Jamāʿat al-Ikhwān al-Muslimīn fī l-Urdunn* (Amman: Markaz Dirāsāt wa-Abḥāth al-ʿAmal al-Islāmī, 1992).

[17] Boulby, *Muslim Brotherhood*, 39–46. For more on how the Brotherhood contributed to the development of an Islamic identity in Jordan, see Daniel Atzori, *Islamism and Globalisation in Jordan: The Muslim Brotherhood's Quest for Hegemony* (London and New York: Routledge, 2015), 82–145.

[18] Ibrāhīm Gharāyiba, *Jamāʿat al-Ikhwān al-Muslimīn fī l-Urdunn, 1946–1996* (Amman: Markaz al-Urdunn al-Jadīd li-l-Dirāsāt and Dār Sindbād li-l-Nashr, 1997), 47.

[19] Abū Rummān and Abū Haniyya, *Al-Ḥall*, 65–7; Boulby, *Muslim Brotherhood*, 46–7.

[20] Al-ʿUbaydī, *Jamāʿat*, 38–41.

[21] Bassām ʿAlī al-ʿUmūsh, *Maḥaṭṭāt fī Tārīkh Jamāʿat al-Ikhwān al-Muslimīn fī l-Urdunn* (Amman: al-Akādīmiyyūn li-l-Nashr wa-l-Tawzīʿ, 2008), 10–13. Interview with Bassām al-ʿUmūsh, Amman, 30 January 2013.

[22] Rosefsky Wickham, *Muslim Brotherhood*, 197–8.

of Palestine and enabled them to function as a charitable organisation engaging in cultural and social activities in relative freedom.[23]

Consolidating the relationship between the regime and the Muslim Brotherhood was the presence of the Palestinian branch of the same organisation. Founded in 1946 in Jerusalem and spread throughout Palestine in the years immediately after,[24] the Palestinian Brotherhood joined other branches of the organisation in the war over Palestine in 1948.[25] After that war, one part of Palestine – the West Bank – became part of Transjordan in 1949 and was even annexed by the kingdom in 1950, making its inhabitants citizens of what was now named 'Jordan'.[26] Like its Jordanian counterpart, the Palestinian Muslim Brotherhood was allowed to be active in cultural and social work in the territories under Jordanian control.[27] As a result, the Palestinian Muslim Brotherhood quickly established close ties with the Jordanian branch and thereby became part of the same pragmatic and unwritten understanding with King ʿAbdallah.[28]

Both the Muslim Brotherhood and the Jordanian monarchy changed in the 1950s. The Brotherhood, firstly, was officially registered as an Islamic group (rather than merely a charitable association) in 1953, which opened up the possibility of engaging in other activities, including political ones.[29] This change of character was strongly related to a new leadership that had emerged in the Brotherhood's ranks. The incorporation of the West Bank, with its 460,000 inhabitants, as well as the influx of another 350,000 mostly urban and politicised Palestinian refugees who came to Jordan after the 1948–1949 war for Palestine, drastically changed Jordan, which until then had largely been a rural, nomadic country. Their presence and politicisation stimulated the emergence of a younger generation of Jordanian, mostly educated and professional Muslim Brothers who were more interested in political issues – particularly the Palestinian question – and criticised Abu Qura for his unwillingness to tackle them. As a result, Abu Qura resigned as leader of the Brotherhood in 1953[30] and was succeeded by Muhammad ʿAbd al-Rahman Khalifa (1919–2006),[31] a prominent member of the new generation of Muslim Brothers.[32] The monarchy, secondly, changed as well

[23] Boulby, *Muslim Brotherhood*, 47–8.
[24] Shadid, 'Muslim Brotherhood', 659; al-ʿUbaydī, *Jamāʿat*, 48.
[25] Abu-Amr, *Islamic Fundamentalism*, 2. [26] Ibid., 4.
[27] Ibid.; Shadid, 'Muslim Brotherhood', 660–1.
[28] Caridi, *Hamas*, 45–7; Milton-Edwards, *Islamic Politics*, 57–9.
[29] Abū Rummān and Abū Haniyya, *Al-Ḥall*, 67.
[30] Al-ʿUbaydī, *Jamāʿat*, 105; al-ʿUmūsh, *Maḥaṭṭāt*, 9.
[31] For more on Khalīfa, see Bakr Muḥammad al-Budūr, *Al-Tajriba al-Niyābiyya li-l-Ḥaraka al-Islāmiyya fī l-Urdunn, 1989–2007* (Amman: Dār al-Maʾmūn li-l-Nashr wa-l-Tawzīʿ, 2011), 39–41.
[32] Boulby, *Muslim Brotherhood*, 50–4.

when King ʿAbdallah was assassinated in Jerusalem in 1951, at which time he was succeeded by his son Talal and, in 1953, by the latter's son Husayn (r. 1953–1999).[33]

Siding with the Regime in Times of Trouble

Despite the change of leadership in the Muslim Brotherhood and the more politicised approach that the organisation took, the relationship with the Jordanian monarchy did not fundamentally change under King Husayn. The reason for this was that the Brotherhood focussed its political rhetoric mostly on the Palestinian question and Western influence in the region, not internal issues that directly affected the king's power. While they were at odds with King Husayn on these two foreign affairs, those who most fiercely championed pro-Palestinian and anti-Western views in the region were leftist pan-Arabists like Egyptian President Nasser, who – as we saw in Chapter 2 – had cracked down on the Brotherhood in Egypt and was therefore the organisation's sworn enemy. Thus, the Brotherhood's pragmatism again dictated that they should accept Hashimite rule because the alternative was bound to be much worse.[34] Moreover, the king also took some foreign-policy decisions the Brotherhood applauded, causing it to side with the regime in times of trouble, sometimes in opposition to the leftist, pro-Nasserist forces they both opposed.[35]

The first of these decisions involved the so-called Baghdad Pact, also known as the Middle East Treaty Organisation (METO) and, later, as the Central Treaty Organisation (CENTO), which was formed in 1955 to contain Soviet influence in the region. Given that President Nasser had already portrayed Jordan as less than fully Arab because of its ties with the British (among other things), joining the British- and American-led Baghdad Pact would only confirm this perception in the eyes of many. As such, Egyptian rhetoric steered Jordanian policy in this respect and the regime ultimately refused to join the Baghdad Pact.[36] This refusal squared not only with popular

[33] Wilson, *King Abdullah*, 207–15. [34] Boulby, *Muslim Brotherhood*, 55–6.

[35] See also Joas Wagemakers, 'Foreign Policy as Protection: The Jordanian Muslim Brotherhood as a Political Minority during the Cold War', in *Muted Minorities: Ethnic, Religious and Political Groups in (Trans)Jordan, 1921–2016*, ed. Idir Ouahes and Paolo Maggiolini (London: Palgrave, forthcoming).

[36] Aruri, *Jordan*, 120–8; Douglas Little, 'A Puppet in Search of a Puppeteer? The United States, King Hussein, and Jordan, 1953–1970', *The International History Review* 17, no. 3 (1995): 518–21; Marc Lynch, *State Interests and Public Spheres: The International Politics of Jordan's Identity* (New York: Columbia University Press, 1999), 25.

Jordanian sentiment about this 'imperialist' treaty,[37] but also with the Brotherhood's views about British influence.[38] The same applied to the Eisenhower Doctrine, an anti-communist policy statement by the then-President of the United States, Dwight D. Eisenhower, formulated in 1957. Despite the Jordanian regime's enmity to communism, King Husayn refused to accept the doctrine,[39] which was – again – applauded by the Muslim Brotherhood.[40]

The second decision that King Husayn made that was strongly supported by the Muslim Brotherhood did not involve keeping outside British influence at bay, but ridding the country itself of the last vestiges of colonial impact. From the days of Emir (and later King) ʿAbdallah, the British had had great financial, military and political influence.[41] Perhaps the most conspicuous expression of this influence was the continued presence of the aforementioned John Bagot Glubb, also known as Glubb Pasha, as chief of staff of the Jordanian army. King Husayn – who had come under enormous popular and regional pressure for his support for the Baghdad Pact, even if he ultimately refused to join it – probably felt he had to take serious action to re-establish his credentials as a leader independent of foreign powers and win back people's favour.[42] Stimulated by this pressure and egged on by a growing group of nationalist officers who wanted the Arabisation of the military, the king decided to fire Glubb from the army and ordered him to leave the country in 1956.[43] This decision, again, was supported by the Muslim Brotherhood.[44]

The third decision King Husayn took was related to an event that was perhaps a natural result of what came before. As mentioned, the pro-Palestinian, anti-Western and pan-Arabist message coming from Nasser's Egypt was popular in Jordan. Despite King Husayn's decision to refrain from joining international coalitions and to dismiss Glubb, he was still seen as a puppet of the West by some, particularly given the fact that the United States had more or less replaced Great Britain as the Jordanian regime's benefactor.[45] As a result, a group of Nasserist Jordanian soldiers wanted to stage a coup against King Husayn's

[37] Al-ʿUbaydī, *Jamāʿat*, 161–2; al-ʿUmūsh, *Maḥaṭṭāt*, 105.

[38] Muḥammad ʿAbd al-Qādir Abū Fāris, *Ṣafaḥāt min al-Tārīkh al-Siyāsī li-l-Ikhwān al-Muslimīn fī l-Urdunn* (Amman: Dār al-Furqān, 2000), 29–30.

[39] Uriel Dann, *King Hussein and the Challenge of Arab Radicalism: Jordan, 1955–1967* (Oxford: Oxford University Press, 1989), 46–7. See also Aruri, *Jordan*, 139–46; Little, 'Puppet', 523–5.

[40] Abū Fāris, *Ṣafaḥāt*, 31–3. [41] Aruri, *Jordan*, 25–32, 75–8, 81–8. [42] Ibid., 128–31.

[43] Joseph A. Massad, *Colonial Effects: The Making of National Identity in Jordan* (New York: Columbia University Press, 2001), 178–85.

[44] Al-ʿUmūsh, *Maḥaṭṭāt*, 28. [45] Aruri, *Jordan*, 145–6.

regime in April 1957. The coup was foiled by supporters of the regime,[46] however, and King Husayn emerged much stronger.[47] As before, the Muslim Brothers, who – in the words of one observer – 'hated Abdel Nasser more than they did Hussein',[48] supported the regime.[49]

To understand the fourth major decision that King Husayn took that consolidated his relationship with the Brotherhood, it is necessary to return briefly to the Palestinian question. As mentioned, King ʿAbdallah had maintained cordial relations with several Zionist leaders and he had even negotiated with them over a solution to the Palestinian question when that was seen as treasonous by many in the region.[50] King ʿAbdallah's interest in the Palestinian question was motivated by several factors, among them his wish to become the leader of the Arab world and incorporate Palestine into his own kingdom,[51] but the religious significance of the holy city of Jerusalem – of which the Jordanian king remains the custodian to this day – also played a role.[52] As such, the Palestinian question was of great importance to the Jordanian regime, which only increased when hundreds of thousands of Palestinians were incorporated into Jordan, as we saw above.[53]

This presence of so many Palestinians in Jordan inevitably led to discussions about the country's identity, particularly after 1967, when Jordan lost the West Bank to Israel in the June war of that year and even more Palestinians fled to the kingdom.[54] Among some tribal Jordanians, who often tend to view Jordan as the country of nomadic descendants of

46 For more on the role of the military in upholding the monarchy, see P. J. Vatikiotis, *Politics and the Military in Jordan: A Study of the Arab Legion, 1921–1957* (London: Frank Cass, 1967), 118–36.

47 Dann, *King Hussein*, 55–67.

48 Ibid., 39. See also Boulby, *Muslim Brotherhood*, 58–61.

49 Abū Fāris, *Ṣafaḥāt*, 37–41; Moaddel, *Jordanian Exceptionalism*, 104–5; Rosefsky Wickham, *Muslim Brotherhood*, 197; al-ʿUmūsh, *Maḥaṭṭāt*, 44–51.

50 For a detailed account of King ʿAbdallāh's relations with Zionist leaders, see Avi Shlaim, *The Politics of Partition: King Abdullah, the Zionists, and Palestine, 1921–1951* (Oxford: Oxford University Press, 1998 [1988]).

51 Kimberley Katz, *Jordanian Jerusalem: Holy Places and National Spaces* (Gainesville, FL: University of Florida Press, 2005), 54.

52 Ibid., 118–36, 144–50.

53 For more on the Palestinians in Jordan and how the regime has acted towards them and the Palestinian question, see Adnan Abu-Odeh, *Jordanians, Palestinians & the Hashemite Kingdom in the Middle East Peace Process* (Washington, DC: United States Institute of Peace, 1999); Sami Al-Khazendar, *Jordan and the Palestine Question: The Role of Islamic and Left Forces in Foreign Policy-Making* (Reading, UK: Ithaca Press, 1997); Shaul Mishal, *West Bank/East Bank: The Palestinians in Jordan, 1949–1967* (New Haven, CT, and London: Yale University Press, 1978).

54 Lynch, *State Interests*, 71–139; Curtis R. Ryan, '"We Are All Jordan" . . . But Who Is We?', *Middle East Report Online* (www.merip.org/mero/mero071310, accessed 2 November 2018), 13 July 2010.

Bedouins hailing from the Arabian Peninsula, the Palestinians are not just seen as foreign interlopers, but also as peasants who deserve no real place in Jordan.[55] This impression was underlined when Palestinian militant organisations set up shop in the kingdom and thereby not only invited Israeli attacks on Jordanian soil, but also became increasingly assertive towards the regime, going so far as to claim authority over parts of the country. This, in turn, led to a Jordanian crack-down on Palestinian militants in what has become known as Black September in 1970, killing thousands of Palestinians and effectively ending the Palestinian militants' presence in Jordan.[56] Despite the pro-Palestinian tendencies of the Brotherhood, the organisation once again – and in opposition to both its own and the king's leftist enemies – supported the regime in its clamp-down.[57]

Muslim Brotherhood Activities before 1989

The relationship described above is one of cooperation based on interests. The Muslim Brotherhood clearly understood that its interests lay with the regime, although its views sometimes also really coincided with those of the king. This does not mean that there was never friction between the two sides and members of the Brotherhood were sometimes arrested because of criticism of the regime.[58] In general, however, the regime refrained from attacking the organisation during this period and left it to build its own organisational structure. This was interesting because the Brotherhood in Jordan officially remained subordinate to the organisation's main branch in Egypt, although the local Jordanian branch has elected its own leader since the 1950s and functioned autonomously.[59] The leader of the Jordanian Muslim Brotherhood is known as the General Controller (al-Murāqib al-ʿĀmm),[60] who heads the Executive Council, which functions as the government of the organisation. The General Controller is elected by the Shūrá Council (the Brotherhood's parliament, as it were), whose members are, in turn, chosen by the members of

[55] Shryock, *Nationalism*, 58–9, 74, 306. See also Laurie Brand, 'Palestinians and Jordanians: A Crisis of Identity', *Journal of Palestine Studies* 24, no. 4 (1995): 46–61; Schirin Fathi, *Jordan: An Invented Nation? Tribe-State Dynamics and the Formation of National Identity* (Hamburg: Deutsches Orient-Institut, 1994), 210–21; Mishal, *West Bank*, 74–91; Curtis R. Ryan, *Jordan and the Arab Uprisings: Regime Survival and Politics Beyond the State* (New York: Columbia University Press, 2018), 90–113.

[56] Abu-Odeh, *Jordanians*, 169–92. [57] Abū Rummān and Abū Haniyya, *Al-Ḥall*, 33.

[58] Ibid., 69.

[59] Boulby, *Muslim Brotherhood*, 73; Moaddel, *Jordanian Exceptionalism*, 99.

[60] This title should not be confused with the Egyptian General Guide (al-Murshid al-ʿĀmm), who is actually the head of the entire organisation.

the organisation as a whole.[61] The latter are organised in cells referred to as *usar* (families; sing. *usra*) spread throughout the country, from which they recruit others.[62]

The recruitment of new members is partly done through personal contacts, but also through the Brotherhood's network of social and charitable activities, which was the organisation's primary concern during the period discussed in this section. These social activities have consisted of Muslim Brotherhood schools and scout clubs, although the organisation has also tried to influence the curriculum of state schools.[63] The Brotherhood has been involved in professional associations and in mosques, as well.[64] Its most important framework for social and charitable activities, however, is the Islamic Centre Association (Jamʿiyyat al-Markaz al-Islāmī), which is an umbrella organisation for a host of activities, including schools and charities.[65] Founded in 1963, the Islamic Centre Association has various branches across Jordan[66] and enjoyed a certain organisational autonomy within Muslim Brotherhood circles in the period analysed here.[67] It also controls a hospital in Jordan, the Islamic Hospital in Amman, which was founded in 1982.[68] Through this hospital and its many other activities, the Islamic Centre Association has helped hundreds of thousands of poor and otherwise needy Jordanians.[69]

While the Muslim Brotherhood developed these different associations, it also developed into other directions. One of these was military activity. With the rise of militant Palestinian groups and the military bases they established on Jordanian soil after 1967, some members of the Muslim Brotherhood were eager to assist them, train alongside them and commit

[61] Boulby, *Muslim Brotherhood*, 77; Moaddel, *Jordanian Exceptionalism*, 100–1; Tal, *Radical Islam*, 188–91.

[62] Boulby, *Muslim Brotherhood*, 74–7. [63] Ibid., 80–8. [64] Ibid., 87–90.

[65] Janine A. Clark, *Islam, Charity, and Activism: Middle-Class Networks and Social Welfare in Egypt, Jordan, and Yemen* (Bloomington and Indianapolis, IN: Indiana University Press, 2004), 82–3, 91–114. For more on Jordanian Islamist social and charitable activities in general, see Gharāyiba, *Jamāʿat*, 169–85; Egbert Harmsen, *Islam, Civil Society and Social Work: Muslim Voluntary Welfare Associations in Jordan between Patronage and Empowerment* (Amsterdam: Amsterdam University Press, 2008); Dietrich Jung and Marie Juul Petersen, '"We Think That This Job Pleases Allah": Islamic Charity, Social Order, and the Construction of Modern Muslim Selfhoods in Jordan', *International Journal of Middle East Studies* 46 (2014): 285–306.

[66] Escobar Stemmann, 'Crossroads', 65–6.

[67] Janine A. Clark, 'Patronage, Prestige, and Power: The Islamic Center Charity Society's Political Role within the Muslim Brotherhood', in *Islamist Politics in the Middle East: Movements and Change*, ed. Samer S. Shehata (London and New York: Routledge, 2012), 73–80.

[68] Ibid., 74.

[69] Similar but smaller Islamist associations were also founded in this period, such as the al-ʿUrwa al-Wuthqá Association, founded by the Brotherhood's first General Controller, ʿAbd al-Laṭīf Abū Qūra. See al-ʿUbaydī, *Jamāʿat*, 167–8.

attacks on Israel with them.[70] As a result, they made a deal with Palestinian leader Yasir ʿArafat (1929–2004) to cooperate with the Palestinian militant Fatah organisation to realise these goals. As a result, they set up several bases, together with Islamists from other countries, and even engaged in attacks on Israeli targets.[71] One Muslim Brother involved in these operations at the time was ʿAbdallah ʿAzzam (1941–1989),[72] a Palestinian who went on to lead the so-called Afghan Arabs: the Arabs who went to Afghanistan between 1979 and 1989 to fight the Soviet military occupation of that country and later formed part of the basis for Osama bin Laden's (1957–2011) al-Qaʿida organisation.[73] Others, however, later moved into Jordanian politics, thereby underlining the fact that participating in jihad against Israel need not mean that one was destined for a career in militancy. The training and attacks stopped altogether, however, when the Jordanian regime threw out the Palestinian militants and stopped their activities in 1970.[74]

The social, cultural and military activities that the Muslim Brotherhood was allowed to engage in could be seen as room provided by the regime as a reward for the organisation's support for the monarchy at crucial moments in Jordan's history. The popularity of these activities and the ties with the people they provided the Brotherhood with also partly explained the organisation's success in the electoral sphere.[75] In the 1950s, when the Nasser regime was repressing the Muslim Brotherhood in Egypt, Jordan allowed its own branch of the organisation to participate in elections. In the parliamentary elections of 1951 and 1954, this was done through independent candidates supported by the Brotherhood,[76] but the organisation participated under its own name in the elections of 1956, when it won four seats (out of forty). Its parliamentarians included prominent members, such as the aforementioned General Controller Muhammad ʿAbd al-Rahman Khalifa and long-time Member of Parliament for the Muslim Brotherhood Yusuf al-ʿAzm (1931–2007).[77]

In 1957, when the regime decided to disband all political parties[78] in response to the attempted coup, the Muslim Brotherhood – given that,

[70] Abū Rummān and Abū Haniyya, *Al-Ḥall*, 69.
[71] Gharāyiba, *Jamāʿat*, 77–9; al-ʿUmūsh, *Maḥaṭṭāt*, 66–73.
[72] Thomas Hegghammer, '‘Abdallāh ʿAzzām and Palestine', *Die Welt des Islams* 53, nos. 3–4 (2013): 367–76; Jed Lea-Henry, 'The Life and Death of Abdullah Azzam', *Middle East Policy* 25, no. 1 (2018): 67; al-ʿUmūsh, *Maḥaṭṭāt*, 66, footnote 1.
[73] For more on ʿAbdallāh ʿAzzām, see Hegghammer, '‘Abdallāh', 353–87.
[74] Abū Rummān and Abū Haniyya, *Al-Ḥall*, 69; Hegghammer, '‘Abdallāh', 374–5.
[75] Clark, *Islam*, 87–9. [76] Al-Budūr, *Al-Tajriba*, 35.
[77] Ibid., 35–51; al-ʿUbaydī, *Jamāʿat*, 78–80.
[78] For more on the different political parties in Jordan in the 1950s, see Aruri, *Jordan*, 78–80, 93–101; Ellen M. Lust-Okar, 'The Decline of Jordanian Political Parties: Myth or Reality?', *International Journal of Middle East Studies* 33 (2001): 545–69.

strictly speaking, it was not a political party but also involved in social activities – was the only one allowed to remain.[79] This further underlined the Brotherhood's relationship with the regime, as did its being allowed to participate in Jordan's government. Although it was controversial among some Brothers,[80] a prominent member of the organisation, Ishaq Farhan (1934–2018), was Minister of Education in several governments in the 1970s, which Clark links directly to the Brotherhood's support for the monarchy during Black September.[81] Another veteran member of the Brotherhood, ʿAbd al-Latif ʿArabiyyat (1933–2019), also held several important educational posts in the 1980s.[82]

The space given to the Muslim Brotherhood in the 1950s–1980s suggests that the regime reciprocated the support it got from the organisation and this was, indeed, the case. Still, just as the Muslim Brotherhood gave its support to the regime because that was where its interests lay, just so the regime dealt with the organisation based on its own interests. This became quite clear in the 1980s when, in an attempt to oppose the Syrian regime (and its Iranian backers), King Husayn allowed the Jordanian Brothers to support and train their Syrian counterparts against the regime in Damascus and clearly took the Brothers' side.[83] When, a few years later, he tried to improve relations with Syria, however, he did so at the Muslim Brotherhood's expense by repressing them.[84] This included arresting hundreds of Brothers, closely monitoring their actions and limiting their freedom to organise and demonstrate.[85] These measures were not only a break with earlier policy towards the Muslim Brotherhood, but they also represented the beginning of a new and more polemical relationship between the regime and the Brotherhood that started in 1989.

Contestation: 1989–1999

Since the war of 1967, in which the kingdom lost the West Bank to Israel, the Jordanian regime had suspended elections because it lost part of the territory it viewed as its own and would not have elections with some of its land under foreign occupation. Although the regime had got rid of its major enemies in the 1950s (Great Britain, Nasserists) and the 1970s

79 Lust-Okar, 'Decline', 558. 80 Brown, *Victory*, 97. 81 Clark, *Islam*, 87.
82 Rosefsky Wickham, *Muslim Brotherhood*, 198.
83 Robert B. Satloff, *Troubles on the East Bank: Challenges to the Domestic Stability of Jordan* (New York, Westport, CT, and London: Praeger/Washington, DC: The Center for Strategic and International Studies at Georgetown University, 1986), 40–8.
84 Abū Rummān and Abū Haniyya, *Al-Ḥall*, 72; Satloff, *Troubles*, 55–8.
85 Lawrence Tal, 'Dealing with Radical Islam: The Case of Jordan', *Survival* 37, no. 3 (1995): 143.

(Palestinian militants), the years that followed were by no means quiet. Regionally, the Islamic Revolution had taken place in Iran in 1979, the subsequent war between the new Islamic Republic of Iran and its neighbour Iraq started in 1980 and lasted until 1988 and the Palestinian uprising (*intifāḍa*) against Israeli occupation broke out in 1987.[86]

Locally, economic problems presented themselves. The 1970s had witnessed an enormous increase in wealth in the Gulf as a result of rising oil prices, leading to many job opportunities in the oil industry for Jordanians (and remittances for the people back home) and financial aid for the kingdom as well. As a result of the decline in oil prices in the 1980s, both the job opportunities (and the resulting remittances) and the aid from the Gulf declined sharply, causing serious economic problems in Jordan. In response, the regime agreed to a structural adjustment programme suggested by the International Monetary Fund (IMF) in return for loans, but the economic reforms this entailed led to higher taxes and lower subsidies, causing prices to rise. This, in turn, caused a number of riots and demonstrations during which especially people from tribal areas – traditionally a pillar of support for the regime – called for an end to the economic reforms.[87] In this context, the regime embarked upon a policy of political liberalisation that profoundly changed its relationship with the Muslim Brotherhood.

The Regime Thwarts the Brotherhood's Electoral Success

The political liberalisation that King Husayn started expressed itself most importantly in parliamentary elections in Jordan in 1989, the first in over twenty years.[88] This course of action had been facilitated by the king's earlier decision to sever ties with the Israeli-occupied West Bank in 1988,

[86] Al-Budūr, *Al-Tajriba*, 51–5.

[87] Anne Marie Baylouny, 'Militarizing Welfare: Neo-liberalism and Jordanian Policy', *Middle East Journal* 62, no. 2 (2008): 291–3; Rex Brynen, 'Economic Crisis and Post-rentier Democratization in the Arab World: The Case of Jordan', *Canadian Journal of Political Science/Revue canadienne de science politique* 25, no. 1 (1992): 83–93; Anne Mariel Peters and Pete W. Moore, 'Beyond Boom and Bust: External Rents, Durable Authoritarianism, and Institutional Adaptation in the Hashemite Kingdom of Jordan', *Studies in Comparative International Developments* 44 (2009): 270–4; Kathrine Rath, 'The Process of Democratization in Jordan', *Middle Eastern Studies* 30, no. 3 (1994): 536–40; Curtis R. Ryan, *Jordan in Transition: From Hussein to Abdullah* (Boulder, CO: Lynne Rienner, 2002), 52–3; Curtis R. Ryan, 'Peace, Bread and Riots: Jordan and the International Monetary Fund', *Middle East Policy* 6, no. 2 (1998): 55–7; Hamed El-Said and Jane Harrigan, 'Economic Reform, Social Welfare, and Instability: Jordan, Egypt, Morocco, and Tunisia, 1983–2004', *Middle East Journal* 68, no. 1 (2014): 101–5.

[88] Kamel S. Abu Jaber and Schirin H. Fathi, 'The 1989 Jordanian Parliamentary Elections', *Orient: Deutsche Zeitschrift für den modernen Orient* 31, no. 1 (1990): 67–86; Curtis

which meant that Palestinians living there could no longer vote in Jordan and elections could therefore be held without any part of the country being under occupation.[89] The elections were intended to accommodate the protesters' wishes and to channel the anger and frustration over the economic reforms into the more manageable form of a parliament, so as to avoid a source of instability in Jordan.[90] During these elections, the Muslim Brotherhood managed to win twenty-two seats (out of eighty in total), with another twelve seats won by independent Islamists.[91] Some serious attempts at real reform were made. Perhaps the most important of these was the National Charter (al-Mīthāq al-Waṭanī), an attempt to rewrite the social contract between the regime and the people[92] whose development the Muslim Brotherhood was also allowed to participate in.[93]

Significantly, the Brotherhood was also asked to take part in the government of Prime Minister Mudar Badran in 1991, perhaps as a result of its important role in the popular demonstrations against the American-led invasion of Iraq in 1990, after which the regime may have felt it could not ignore the Brotherhood.[94] Although its participation in government was short-lived (lasting only six months), it did give the organisation five ministerial posts that allowed the Brotherhood to work towards a greater role of Islam in the country (Education, Health, Justice, Social Development and Religious Endowments (*awqāf*)).[95] Moreover, the aforementioned Brotherhood-member ʿAbd al-Latif ʿArabiyyat was

R. Ryan, 'Jordan and the Rise and Fall of the Arab Cooperation Council', *Middle East Journal* 52, no. 3 (1998): 393–4.

89 Lynch, *State*, 81–99.

90 Ranjit Singh, 'Liberalisation or Democratisation? The Limits of Political Reform and Civil Society in Jordan', in *Jordan in Transition: 1990–2000*, ed. George Joffé (London: Hurst & Co., 2002), 75–82.

91 Boulby, *Muslim Brotherhood*, 102–14; Hanna Y. Freij and Leonard C. Robinson, 'Liberalization, the Islamists, and the Stability of the Arab State: Jordan as a Case Study', *The Muslim World* 86, no. 1 (1996): 10; Curtis R. Ryan, 'Elections and Parliamentary Democratization in Jordan', *Democratization* 5, no. 4 (1998): 177–80.

92 Renate Dieterich, 'The Weakness of the Ruled Is the Strength of the Ruler: The Role of the Opposition in Contemporary Jordan', in *Jordan in Transition: 1990–2000*, ed. George Joffé (London: Hurst & Co., 2002), 131–2; Moaddel, *Jordanian Exceptionalism*, 110–11; Glenn E. Robinson, 'Defensive Democratization in Jordan', *International Journal of Middle East Studies* 30, no. 3 (1998): 393–4; Avi Shlaim, *Lion of Jordan: The Life of King Hussein in War and Peace* (New York: Alfred A. Knopf, 2008), 483–4. For the National Charter's complete text, see Moaddel, *Jordanian Exceptionalism*, 159–90.

93 Hamid, *Temptations*, 81–2; Moaddel, *Jordanian Exceptionalism*, 122–4.

94 Beverley Milton-Edwards, 'A Temporary Alliance with the Crown: The Islamic Response in Jordan', in *Islamic Fundamentalisms and the Gulf Crisis*, ed. James Piscatori (Chicago, IL: American Academy of Arts and Sciences, 1991), 88–106.

95 Abū Rummān and Abū Haniyya, *Al-Ḥall*, 73–4; Boulby, *Muslim Brotherhood*, 141–5; Ryan, *Jordan in Transition*, 24–5.

made Speaker of Jordan's parliament.[96] During its time in government, as well as in the two years in parliament directly prior to this, the group unsuccessfully tried to impose the *sharīʿa* in various ways.[97] This seems to have been partly the result of an explicitly Islamist ideology held by the group at the time, but also of politically naive and inexperienced behaviour, rather than merely an attempt to exploit the space it had been given to pursue a strictly Islamist agenda. In any case, it showed that the Muslim Brotherhood was willing to contribute to governing the country.[98]

This situation of allowing the Brotherhood to participate in government was exceptional, however, and the early 1990s also showed signs of repression of the organisation. The regime monitored the Brotherhood closely and banned its newspaper *Al-Ribat* several times in 1992, apparently because it had expressed views the regime did not like.[99] It also took other measures that impacted the Muslim Brotherhood. Perhaps the most lasting of these was the political parties law of 1992, which allowed political parties to be founded and also stated that they could not have organisational ties to bodies outside Jordan. This not only hampered pan-Arab parties, but also the Muslim Brotherhood, which obviously had connections with the other branches of the organisation, including – perhaps most importantly – the Palestinian one.[100]

To counter this problem, the Muslim Brotherhood set up a political party apart from its own organisation and entirely Jordanian, the Islamic Action Front (IAF; Jabhat al-ʿAmal al-Islāmī), in 1992.[101] Although the IAF had an organisational structure that was similar to the Brotherhood's,[102] the latter nevertheless considered it wise to distinguish between itself and the party.[103] This was not only because the

[96] Ryan, *Jordan in Transition*, 24. [97] Hamid, *Temptations*, 78–80.

[98] The names of the Brotherhood's ministers were ʿAbdallāh ʿAkāyila (Education), ʿAdnān Jaljūlī (Health), Mājid Khalīfa (Justice), Yūsuf al-ʿAẓm (Social Development) and Ibrāhīm al-Kīlānī (Religious Endowments). Two other non-Brotherhood Islamists also became ministers, namely, Jamāl Sarāyira (Communications) and Muḥammad al-ʿAlāwina (Agriculture). See Sabah El-Said, *Between Pragmatism and Ideology: The Muslim Brotherhood in Jordan, 1989–1994* (Washington, DC: Washington Institute for Near East Policy (WINEP), 1995), 2.

[99] Boulby, *Muslim Brotherhood*, 147–8.

[100] Robinson, 'Defensive Democratization', 395.

[101] For a description by the IAF itself on how its political party was founded, see *Al-Amāna al-ʿĀmma li-Ḥizb Jabhat al-ʿAmal al-Islāmī* (Amman: al-Muʾtamar al-ʿĀmm li-Ḥizb Jabhat al-ʿAmal al-Islāmī, 2002), 11–20.

[102] Ḥasan Abū Haniyya, *Al-Marʾa wa-l-Siyāsa min Manẓūr al-Ḥarakāt al-Islāmiyya fī l-Urdunn* (Amman: Friedrich Ebert Stiftung, 2008), 62; Gharāyiba, *Jamāʿat*, 138–49.

[103] For information on the background of IAF members, see Hamed El-Said and James E. Rauch, 'Education, Political Participation, and Islamist Parties: The Case of Jordan's Islamic Action Front', *Middle East Journal* 69, no. 1 (2015): 51–73. For the popularity and affiliation with the IAF among Jordanians, see Moaddel, *Jordanian Exceptionalism*, 115–22.

Brotherhood – with its foreign ties – could not participate in elections itself, but also because it wanted to establish a division of labour between the Brotherhood (religious, social, cultural and charitable work) and the IAF (political participation) and to protect the Brotherhood from a potential shut-down of political parties. If the latter ever happened, the Muslim Brotherhood itself could continue unabated.[104] The organisation's influence on the IAF was nevertheless substantial,[105] which seems to have remained that way, although the two were officially separated in 1994.[106]

The political parties law was not the only measure taken by the regime in the early 1990s, however. Indeed, it became clear that the entire process of liberalisation and democratisation in this period was embarked upon not to widen and deepen freedom and democracy in Jordan, but to channel discontent into manageable forms, thereby in effect consolidating the power of the regime.[107] Some of the measures taken to facilitate this process were specifically aimed at limiting the influence of the Muslim Brotherhood. Unhappy with the organisation's electoral success in 1989 and its oppositional behaviour in parliament, the regime changed the electoral law from one in which citizens could vote for as many candidates as there were seats available in their constituency to one in which people could only cast one vote in 1993.[108] Although this is portrayed as innocuous by the regime,[109] the latter (correctly) believed that this would cause Jordanians to vote for tribal representatives, rather than parties such as the IAF.[110]

The regime also engaged in reallocating seats to rural areas, where the more pro-regime tribal Jordanians lived, at the expense of urban areas, where the Muslim Brotherhood found much of its support.[111] Moreover, there was disappointment about the organisation's apparent inability to

[104] Moaddel, *Jordanian Exceptionalism*, 143–4.

[105] Brown, *Victory*, 143–6; Gharāyiba, *Jamā'at*, 145–9; Shadi Hamid, 'The Islamic Action Front in Jordan', in *The Oxford Handbook of Islam and Politics*, ed. John L. Esposito and Emad el-Din Shahin (Oxford: Oxford University Press, 2013), 546.

[106] El-Said, *Pragmatism*, 3.

[107] Russel E. Lucas, 'Deliberalization in Jordan', *Journal of Democracy* 14, no. 1 (2003): 138–9; Robinson, 'Defensive Democratization', 387–410.

[108] Hamid, *Temptations*, 103–4.

[109] Interview with an official at the Jordanian Royal Court who preferred to remain anonymous, Amman, 19 June 2012.

[110] Abū Rummān and Abū Haniyya, *Al-Ḥall*, 74; Abla M. Amawi, 'The 1993 Elections in Jordan', *Arab Studies Quarterly* 16, no. 3 (1994): 16; Frédéric Charillon and Alain Mouftard, 'Jordanie: Les élections du 8 novembre 1993 et le processus de paix', *Monde arabe/Maghreb-Machrek*, no. 144 (1994): 45–6; Hamid, *Temptations*, 103–4; Ryan, *Jordan in Transition*, 26.

[111] Amawi, '1993 Elections', 16–17; Ryan, *Jordan in Transition*, 27; Schwedler, 'Paradox', 28.

use its parliamentary presence to make a meaningful change to the economic situation in the country. Furthermore, some Jordanians resented the fact that the Brotherhood's fervent opposition to the Western attacks on Iraq after that country's invasion of Kuwait in 1990 and its strong support for the regime's rejection of participating in the US-led coalition against Iraq had contributed to the presence of sanctions against Jordan.[112]

As a result of all this, the Muslim Brotherhood – now participating through the IAF – lost six seats in the parliamentary elections of 1993. Instead of the twenty-two seats they won in 1989, they now only had sixteen, while independent Islamists won another six seats (as opposed to twelve in 1989).[113] The Muslim Brotherhood had already accused the regime of limiting its campaign rallies before the elections[114] and the number of votes cast for the IAF was, as it turned out, slightly higher than in 1989. It therefore seemed highly likely that it was the regime's measures against the Muslim Brotherhood – especially the new voting law, which the Brotherhood and other parties had rejected[115] – that caused the IAF to do significantly worse than the Islamists had done four years earlier.[116]

The Relationship between the Regime and the Brotherhood Deteriorates

The 1993 parliamentary elections thus epitomised the way the regime had thwarted the Muslim Brotherhood's earlier electoral success. Meanwhile, there were also significant developments with regard to foreign affairs. After the Gulf War in 1990–1991, the Middle East seemed ripe for change and a peace conference was held in Madrid in 1991 to discuss an end to the Arab–Israeli conflict. Moreover, Israelis and Palestinians had secretly conducted negotiations in Oslo, which resulted in the so-called Oslo Accords between Israel and the Palestine Liberation Organisation (PLO) in 1993. This was followed by a peace agreement

[112] Freij and Robinson, 'Liberalization', 17; Beverley Milton-Edwards, 'Façade Democracy in Jordan', *British Journal of Middle Eastern Studies* 20, no. 2 (1993): 198; Morten Valbjørn, 'Post-democratization Lessons from the Jordanian "Success Story"', *Foreign Policy* (https://foreignpolicy.com/2010/06/16/post-democratization-lessons-from-the-jordanian-success-story/#; accessed 12 December 2019), 16 June 2010.

[113] Hamid, *Temptations*, 104; Ryan, 'Elections', 182; Ryan, *Jordan in Transition*, 27.

[114] Yāsir Abū Hilāla, 'Hal Tafqidu l-Ḥukūma Ḥiyādahā fī l-Intikhābāt al-Qādima?', *Al-Sabīl*, 19–26 October 1993, 3.

[115] Al-Budūr, *Al-Tajriba*, 98–9.

[116] Ibid., 108–11; Hamid, *Temptations*, 104–5; Ryan, 'Elections', 182; Ryan, *Jordan in Transition*, 27–8.

between Israel and Jordan – often dubbed the 'Wadi ʿAraba Agreement' – named after the valley between the two countries.[117]

The Muslim Brotherhood, which, as we saw before, had long been staunchly pro-Palestinian and critical of the Jordanian monarchy's ties with Israel, was strongly against the peace agreement[118] and the IAF, along with other opposition parties, voted against it in parliament.[119] The Muslim Brotherhood also spoke out in favour of the suicide bombings that Hamas was using against Israeli civilians in the mid-1990s,[120] actively resisted the normalisation of relations with Israel[121] (and joined the Higher Committee for the Coordination of National Opposition Parties, founded to oppose normalisation)[122] and refused to attend the signing ceremony.[123]

The Muslim Brotherhood and the IAF were certainly not alone in their opposition to the peace agreement between Israel and Jordan. Not only did other opposition parties reject the accord as well, but the treaty had little popular support in general. Moreover, the expected (and promised) peace dividend from increased tourism, trade and economic development never really materialised because of existing business interests, trade obstacles and bureaucratic problems. As such, from the Jordanian side, the peace treaty mostly remained a regime affair.[124] Moreover, the king's staunch support for the agreement with Israel coupled with the strong popular opposition against it resulted in the stifling of dissent by any who expressed criticism of the treaty or of the regime's policy towards Israel. This way, the peace agreement had an adverse effect on the process of liberalisation that had begun in 1989.[125]

The relations between the regime and the Muslim Brotherhood with regard to the Palestinian question were complicated further by the presence of the Palestinian Hamas in Jordan. Founded in 1987 soon after the start of the Palestinian uprising, Hamas had more or less become the Palestinian branch of the Muslim Brotherhood and, as such, was closely tied to the Jordanian Brotherhood, but cooperation and solidarity between them could only go as far as the regime allowed it to.[126] The regime itself was sceptical of Hamas's presence – particularly given its own peace agreement with Israel and Hamas's violent opposition to the Oslo Accords – but sometimes did help the group, such as in 1997, when

117 Shlaim, *Lion*, 539–53. 118 Abū Fāris, *Ṣafaḥāt*, 66–89.
119 Ryan, *Jordan in Transition*, 29. 120 Abū Fāris, *Ṣafaḥāt*, 90. 121 Ibid., 91–4.
122 Clark, 'Conditions', 539–60. 123 Al-Budūr, *Al-Tajriba*, 122–3.
124 Shlaim, *Lion*, 555–7.
125 Laurie A. Brand, 'The Effects of the Peace Process on Political Liberalization in Jordan', *Journal of Palestine Studies* 28, no. 2 (1999): 59–64.
126 Abū Rummān and Abū Haniyya, *Al-Ḥall*, 196–207; Milton-Edwards, *Muslim Brotherhood*, 92–3.

Israeli agents tried to poison the organisation's representative in Jordan, Khalid Mash'al, close to his office in Amman. Embarrassed by this incident on Jordanian territory, King Husayn not only demanded – and got – Israel to provide the antidote to the poison used against Mash'al, thereby saving the latter's life, but he also arranged for one of Hamas's founders, Ahmad Yasin, to be released from Israeli prison. This led to a temporary upsurge in popularity for Hamas in Jordan, but its relations with King Husayn – probably loth to allow a popular and militant Palestinian organisation on Jordanian soil again, after his bad experiences with this in the 1960s and 1970s – deteriorated quickly thereafter.[127]

In this context of thwarted electoral success, peace with Israel and increasing efforts by the regime to limit freedom of expression and the press, the Muslim Brotherhood – under the leadership of 'Abd al-Majid Dhunaybat, who replaced Muhammad 'Abd al-Rahman Khalifa as General Controller in 1994 – decided to boycott the parliamentary elections of 1997. While some independent Islamists did run for office and managed to retain their six seats in parliament, the IAF was no longer represented there and had to continue its activities outside the realm of formal politics now.[128] This meant that the Muslim Brotherhood, after getting off to a successful start in 1989, had basically been reduced to the status it had before that year: under pressure and without a parliamentary presence.

Confrontation: 1999–2016

The year 1999 was a turning point in the history of the relationship between the Jordanian regime and the Muslim Brotherhood. On 7 February of that year, King Husayn died of cancer and was succeeded by his son 'Abdallah II (b. 1962). The latter had spent much of his life in Great Britain and the United States. Even his time in Jordan was mostly spent in the military and, as such, he was clearly less familiar with local politics (including its Islamist manifestations) than his father. It quickly became clear that King Husayn's approach of strong relations with the Muslim Brotherhood – though beset by periods of repression – would not be continued by the new king.[129]

[127] Abū Rummān and Abū Haniyya, *Al-Ḥall*, 164–96; Tal, *Radical Islam*, 222–6.

[128] Hamid, *Temptations*, 109–10; Ryan, 'Elections', 183–93; Ryan, *Jordan in Transition*, 30–40.

[129] Milton-Edwards, *Muslim Brotherhood*, 95; interview with Zakī Banī Irshīd, Amman, 13 June 2012.

Securitising the Muslim Brotherhood

The new policy by King ʿAbdallah II was not just implemented because of the king's background, but also because of the increasing concerns about the presence of Hamas in Jordan.[130] Unlike his predecessors, the new king was unimpeded by any dreams of controlling the West Bank and, as such, was less attuned to the idea of Palestinians as an internal Jordanian issue and he expelled Hamas's leadership in 1999.[131] Although there was some understanding within the Brotherhood for the idea that the king was merely implementing the law that no representatives of foreign organisations could reside in Jordan,[132] the Muslim Brotherhood as a whole rejected this decision. Tensions increased when the regime stated that Hamas had infiltrated the Jordanian Brotherhood and, as such, sought to provoke confrontations similar to those that preceded Black September in 1970.[133] That the regime saw Islamists as a threat (or was at least willing to treat them as such) became even clearer when, after the start of the al-Aqsa Intifada by the Palestinians in 2000, an unauthorised anti-Israel demonstration in which the Muslim Brotherhood participated was met with unprecedented force from the security services in 2001.[134]

Whereas the Muslim Brotherhood had turned from a social issue into a political one under King Husayn's reign, the organisation came to be seen as a security issue by King ʿAbdallah II.[135] This securitisation of the Brotherhood was probably strengthened with the terrorist attacks in the United States on 11 September 2001. Although King ʿAbdallah II was not uncritical towards the US-led 'War on Terror' launched by then-President George W. Bush after the attacks, he did provide full support for the American government.[136] Given the fact that the attacks in the United States had been perpetrated by Islamists – even if they were radically different from the Muslim Brotherhood – did not help the Jordanian organisation's reputation either. This was underlined when the Brotherhood expressed strong criticism of the presence of American troops on Jordanian soil during the controversial war on Iraq that was launched in 2003, which entailed an implicit critique of the Jordanian regime itself, too.[137]

[130] Abū Rummān and Abū Haniyya, *Al-Ḥall*, 34. [131] Ibid., 75.
[132] Al-ʿUmūsh, *Maḥaṭṭāt*, 265–6.
[133] Randa Habib, *Hussein and Abdullah: Inside the Jordanian Royal Family*, trans. Miranda Tell (London: Saqi, 2010), 201–3.
[134] Ibid., 203–4. [135] Abū Rummān and Abū Haniyya, *Al-Ḥall*, 75.
[136] King Abdullah II of Jordan, *Our Last Best Chance: The Pursuit of Peace in a Time of Peril* (London: Viking, 2011), 197–9.
[137] Habib, *Hussein*, 204–5.

In this context of the Palestinian uprising, the terrorist attacks in the United States and the impending war in Iraq, the Jordanian regime became increasingly repressive. A flurry of new (temporary) laws was adopted to stifle dissent, prevent demonstrations and limit the freedom of the press. As Schwedler has pointed out, the regime wanted to escape the sanctions that were imposed on it for not supporting the US-led coalition against Iraq during the previous Gulf War, on the one hand, yet also avoid the backlash from voters who would resent Jordanian support for the United States' attack on Iraq, on the other. The regime's solution to this was to support the Western coalition against Iraq and, ostensibly for security reasons, to postpone the elections, which had been scheduled for 2001.[138]

Meanwhile, the Muslim Brotherhood and the IAF also began showing signs of internal fissures. As we saw above, some Islamists ran as independents in the parliamentary elections of 1997, despite the IAF's boycott in that year. This willingness to break ranks with the party on the issue of parliamentary participation manifested itself more clearly with the founding of the Islamic Centre Party (Ḥizb al-Wasaṭ al-Islāmī) in 2001.[139] Started by independent Islamists as well as disaffected members of the IAF, the Islamic Centre Party disagreed with the IAF and the Muslim Brotherhood on a host of issues, including its relations with the regime.[140]

While conditions in Jordan were similar for the Muslim Brotherhood to what they were in 1997 (or worse), the IAF nevertheless decided to participate in the elections when they eventually did take place in 2003.[141] Some Brothers were convinced that their lack of parliamentary presence had not helped and the vast majority of the organisation's members supported participating in the elections this time.[142] Perhaps the Brotherhood also wanted to give King ʿAbdallah II a chance, rather than boycotting the first elections under his reign.[143] In any case, the IAF participated in the elections (for an increased total of 104 seats) with 30 candidates, of whom 17 won (including a woman, Hayat al-Musaymi).[144] Five independent Islamists managed to win seats, as well.[145] The

[138] Jillian Schwedler, 'Don't Blink: Jordan's Democratic Opening and Closing', *Middle East Report Online* (www.merip.org/mero/mero070302, accessed 12 January 2017), 3 July 2002.

[139] Abū Rummān and Abū Haniyya, *Al-Ḥall*, 36–7.

[140] Rosefsky Wickham, *Muslim Brotherhood*, 214–18.

[141] Muḥammad al-Najjār, 'Al-Ḥaraka al-Islāmiyya Tuʿlinu l-Mushāraka fī l-Intikhābāt al-Niyābiyya al-Qādima', *Al-Sabīl*, 29 April–5 May 2003, 7.

[142] Hamid, *Temptations*, 130. [143] Al-Budūr, *Al-Tajriba*, 132. [144] Ibid., 145–9.

[145] Curtis R. Ryan and Jillian Schwedler, 'Return to Democratization or New Hybrid Regime? The 2003 Elections in Jordan', *Middle East Report* 11, no. 2 (2004): 146.

Brotherhood's ʿAbd al-Latif ʿArabiyyat indicated that the electoral law remained an obstacle, but nevertheless expressed his satisfaction with the results.[146] Indeed, in almost all the districts in which it competed, the IAF had managed to get more votes than in 1993.[147]

Despite the good results for the IAF in the 2003 parliamentary elections, it turned out that there was little reason for the party to celebrate. Not only did dissent remain – several members of the IAF were dismissed after the elections because they had disagreed with their nomination[148] – but the regime also took new measures against the Brotherhood. It adopted a new political parties law that prohibited organisations to use mosques, professional associations or sports clubs for campaigning or other party activities. Recruiting or campaigning at educational institutes was also limited.[149] For an organisation like the IAF, which – through its links with the Muslim Brotherhood – relied on its network of social, cultural and religious facilities and institutes to mobilise supporters and reach new voters, this was obviously a blow.

The Brotherhood, despite all this, remained committed to making its political participation work. Several years after the elections, in 2006, the organisation held internal elections.[150] The General Controller, ʿAbd al-Majid Dhunaybat, indicated that he would not seek re-election[151] and was replaced by Salim al-Falahat, with Jamil Abu Bakr elected his deputy.[152] Since neither was known for his uncompromising views or radical stance towards the regime, the repression did not seem to have much radicalising effect on the Muslim Brotherhood in that respect.[153] One notable exception to this rule was the new Secretary General of the IAF, Zaki Bani Irshid.[154] Elected to that position in 2006, Bani Irshid was known to represent a less accommodating part of the organisation.[155]

146 ʿAbdallāh al-Majālī, 'Dr. ʿArabiyyāt: Natāʾij al-Jabha Jayyida wa-Hiya Tuʾakkidu anna l-Shaʿb al-Urdunnī maʿa l-Ḥaraka al-Islāmiyya Yuʾayyiduhā wa-Yaqifu Maʿahā', *Al-Sabīl*, 24–30 June 2003, 7.

147 Jihād Abū l-ʿĪs, 'Qirāʾa Raqmiyya fī Natāʾij al-Ḥaraka al-Islāmiyya fī l-Intikhābāt', *Al-Sabīl*, 24–30 June 2003, 9.

148 'Al-Jabha Tafṣilu (5) Aʿḍāʾ Khālafū Qarārahā bi-Shaʾn al-Tarshīḥ li-l-Intikhābāt al-Niyābiyya', *Al-Sabīl*, 10–16 June 2003, 6.

149 Hamid, *Temptations*, 134.

150 Ayman Faḍīlāt, 'Jabhat al-ʿAmal al-Islāmī Tantakhibu Majlis Shūrá l-Ḥizb al-Shahr al-Qādim', *Al-Sabīl*, 17–23 January 2006, 4.

151 'Al-Dhunaybāt: Yaʿtadhiru ʿan al-Tarshīḥ li-Mawqiʿ al-Murāqib al-ʿĀmm li-l-Ikhwān al-Muslimīn', *Al-Sabīl*, 28 February–6 March 2006, 1.

152 Ayman Faḍīlāt, 'Al-Falāḥāt Murāqiban ʿĀmman li-l-Ikhwān wa-Abū Bakr Naʾiban lahu bi-l-Tazkiya', *Al-Sabīl*, 7–13 March 2006, 1.

153 Hamid, *Temptations*, 134.

154 'Farʿ Jabhat al-ʿAmal al-Islāmī fī l-Zarqāʾ Yuqīmu Ḥafl Istiqbāl li-Banī Irshīd', *Al-Sabīl*, 28 March–4 April 2006, 10.

155 Markaz Ḥimāyat wa-Ḥurriyyat al-Ṣaḥafiyyīn, *Qamʿ*, 254, footnote 67.

Such men became increasingly common in the Brotherhood's and IAF's leadership after 2006.

Repressing the Muslim Brotherhood

As mentioned, King ʿAbdallah II tended to view the Muslim Brotherhood through the prism of security, rather than politics. Although the organisation was not revolutionary or a military threat to the regime, this does not mean that there were no other challenges to Jordanian security and stability in the 2000s. After the terrorist attacks in America in 2001 and the start of the war in Iraq in 2003, the Jordanian security services arrested an increasing number of people for their alleged involvement in several terrorism-related incidents.[156] The latter culminated in the hotel bombings in Amman on 9 November 2005, when several foreign radical Islamists, through suicide attacks, killed dozens and injured many more in three of the capital's most prominent hotels.[157]

The hotel bombings were directed by the leader of al-Qaʿida in Iraq, the Jordanian Abu Musʿab al-Zarqawi (1966–2006), and were thus not linked to the Muslim Brotherhood in any way. This changed when al-Zarqawi was killed in Iraq in June 2006 and four members of parliament for the IAF went to his wake to offer their condolences to his family. Given that al-Zarqawi was responsible for the hotel bombings, the regime arrested all four[158] and two of them were later even given prison sentences.[159] Apparently, some of the families of the victims had complained about their presence at the wake and the court sentenced ʿAli Abu l-Sukkar to eighteen months in prison and a $282 fine, while Muhammad Abu Faris – who had also referred to al-Zarqawi as a 'martyr' (*shahīd*) in an interview – was sentenced to two years' imprisonment and a $563 fine.[160]

Given the security situation in Jordan at the time, these prison sentences may appear to have been inspired by the idea that members of the IAF sympathised with al-Zarqawi's radical ideas and terrorism and that their imprisonment was therefore somehow justified. Given the fact,

156 International Crisis Group (ICG), *Jordan's 9/11: Dealing with Jihadi Islamism*, Middle East Report no. 47 (Amman and Brussels: ICG, 2005), 12.

157 Ibid., 1–2.

158 Ayman Faḍīlāt, 'Al-Ḥukūma Taʿtaqilu Arbaʿa min Nuwwāb Jabhat al-ʿAmal [al-Islāmī]', *Al-Sabīl*, 13–19 June 2006, 8. Apart from ʿAlī Abū l-Sukkar and Muḥammad Abū Fāris, Jaʿfar al-Ḥūrānī and Ibrāhīm al-Mashūkhī were also arrested, but not imprisoned.

159 Abū Rummān and Abū Haniyya, *Al-Ḥall*, 77.

160 Jihād Abū l-ʿĪs, 'Amn al-Dawla Taḥkumu bi-l-Sijn ʿĀmmayn ʿalá "Abū Fāris" wa-ʿĀmm wa-Niṣf ʿalá "Abū l-Sukkar"', *Al-Sabīl*, 8–14 August 2006, 4; Habib, *Hussein*, 206.

however, that al-Zarqawi was from a major Jordanian tribe – the Bani Hasan – and that local politicians may have felt the need to show their respects to a family from their constituency, the presence of IAF members at the wake may have amounted to nothing more than a courtesy call. Moreover, any sympathy IAF members may have had for al-Zarqawi could simply have been rooted in his armed resistance against American troops in neighbouring Iraq, which was certainly shared by other Jordanians, rather than his terrorist acts in Iraq and Jordan.[161]

In fact, the imprisonment of two IAF members for such a long time was unprecedented and, given the fact that eleven non-Islamist members of parliament were also present at the wake without action being taken against them, should probably be seen as disproportionately taking on the Muslim Brotherhood.[162] The government apparently also forbade the families of the arrested men[163] as well as the Brotherhood's leadership[164] to visit them in prison. The Muslim Brotherhood's General Controller, meanwhile, denied that his organisation had anything to do with al-Zarqawi's radical ideas, did not feel it had made a mistake and – while open to dialogue with the government – would not apologise for anything.[165] The matter was worsened for the Brotherhood by the fact that the two imprisoned men were parliamentarians: in the end, their membership of parliament was revoked,[166] although they themselves continued to insist that they remained representatives of the people.[167]

The idea that the regime was targeting the Muslim Brotherhood was confirmed in the weeks after the affair of al-Zarqawi's wake. The actions of the four IAF members sparked pro-government demonstrations in support of the victims of the hotel bombings in 2005. In this context of popular anti-IAF sentiment, the regime probably decided that the time was right to take action against the aforementioned Islamic Centre Association, which had long been a central platform of charitable

161 Interview with Shadi Hamid, Amman, 11 August 2008.
162 Hamid, 'Islamic Action Front', 548.
163 Tāmir al-Ṣamādī, 'Al-Ḥukūma Tuḥarrimu ʿĀʾilāt Nuwwāb al-Shaʿb min Ziyāratihim fī l-Jifr', *Al-Sabīl*, 20–26 June 2006, 8.
164 Ayman al-Faḍīlāt, 'Manʿ Qiyādat al-Ḥaraka al-Islāmiyya min Ziyārat "Abū Fāris" wa-"Abū l-Sukkar" fī Sijn Qafqafā', *Al-Sabīl*, 12–18 September 2006, 1.
165 Ayman al-Faḍīlāt and ʿAlāʾ ʿAwwād, 'Al-Falāḥāt: Lā Najidu Khaṭaʾ Irtakabathu l-Ḥaraka al-Islāmiyya li-Naʿtadhiru ʿanhu', *Al-Sabīl*, 4–10 July 2006, 7.
166 Ayman al-Faḍīlāt, 'Jadl Qānūnī Ḥawla Mushārakat al-Nāʾibayn al-Muʿtaqilayn "Abū Fāris" wa-"Abū l-Sukkar" fī l-Dawra al-Istithnāʾiyya li-Majlis al-Nuwwāb', *Al-Sabīl*, 15–21 August 2006, 9; Ayman al-Faḍīlāt, 'Al-Majlis al-ʿĀlī li-Tafsīr al-Dustūr Yaqḍī bi-ʿAdam al-Ḥāja li-Taṣwīt al-Nuwwāb ʿalá Isqāṭ ʿUḍwiyyat "Abū Fāris" wa-"Abū l-Sukkar" li-annahā Saqaṭat Ḥukman', *Al-Sabīl*, 5–11 September 2006, 8.
167 Ayman al-Faḍīlāt, 'Abū Fāris wa-Abū l-Sukkar Yuṣirrāni ʿalá annahumā Mā Zālā Nāʾibayn wa-Lam Tasquṭu ʿUḍwiyyatahumā', *Al-Sabīl*, 3–9 October 2006, 5.

activities for the Muslim Brotherhood.[168] Under the guise of accusations of financial violations, the regime dismissed the members of the Islamic Centre Association's board and replaced them with new ones, essentially taking over the association.[169]

Although the Muslim Brotherhood dismissed the allegations as false or minor, it was willing to meet with the prime minister and issued a statement afterwards in which it expressed its rejection of terrorism and radical Islamist beliefs, its commitment to the constitution and its loyalty to the king. Some Muslim Brothers interpreted this as a capitulation to the regime in response to the latter's take-over of the Islamic Centre Association and eighteen members (out of forty) of the Brotherhood's Consultation Council resigned in protest. Although they were eventually persuaded to rejoin, this episode did not just show the regime's unprecedented willingness to repress the Muslim Brotherhood and its affiliates, but also betrayed – once again – the divisions within the organisation.[170]

By the time new elections were organised in 2007, it was clear that the relationship between the regime and the Muslim Brotherhood had been thoroughly upset and that the latter was divided, unpopular (because of the al-Zarqawi affair) and crippled (because of repression, especially the take-over of the Islamic Centre Association). Although other factors, such as regime intervention and mistakes during the campaign,[171] could also be added, the IAF started the run-up to the elections at a disadvantage. It was therefore perhaps not surprising that the IAF won only 6 seats[172] (out of 110) in the parliamentary elections of 2007, which was the Brotherhood's worst electoral result since the 1950s.[173]

Just as the Jordanian regime had become increasingly intolerant towards the Muslim Brotherhood throughout the years, so had fewer compromising members of the organisation obtained prominent positions in its institutions. In 2008, after internal elections were held in the organisation, this trend was strengthened when Hammam Saʿid was chosen to be the Brotherhood's new General Controller. To be sure,

[168] Clark, 'Patronage', 73. [169] Ibid.; Hamid, *Temptations*, 135.

[170] Clark, 'Patronage', 77. This situation prevails until today. In 2014, for example, the head of the Islamic Centre Association, Jamīl Duhaysāt (a long-time member of the Brotherhood), stated that there is no relationship between the association and the Muslim Brotherhood. See Sāmī Maḥāsina, 'Al-Duhaysāt: Jamʿiyyatunā li-l-Urdunniyyīn Muslimīn wa-Masīḥiyyīn wa-lā ʿAlāqa li-l-Ikhwān bihā', *Al-ʿArab al-Yawm*, 10 September 2014, 2.

[171] Abu Rumman, *Muslim Brotherhood*, 27–32, 56–72; Abū Rummān and Abū Haniyya, *Al-Ḥall*, 111–17.

[172] For the names of the candidates, as well as the winners, see al-Budūr, *Al-Tajriba*, 167–71, 182–3.

[173] Abū Rummān and Abū Haniyya, *Al-Ḥall*, 110.

other prominent positions were still held by more pro-regime figures, but this was nevertheless significant.[174] It meant, for example, that the Brotherhood would be less likely to go along with the regime's plan to channel all opposition through the controllable parliament. Given the continued repression – not in the least through the still-present unfavourable election law – as well as the disappointing results in 2007, it was perhaps obvious that the Brotherhood would boycott the 2010 elections[175] again, which it did. Although there was internal disagreement over this boycott and the internal elections within the IAF earlier that year were also hotly contested,[176] the rejection of the ballot box in 2010 not only marked a sign of the Brotherhood's resistance to the state's policies, but also the beginning of a showdown with the regime.

Showdown

Soon after the elections were held in Jordan in 2010, a seemingly local event – a Tunisian street vendor set himself on fire to protest the treatment he had received from officials in December 2010 – set off a series of protests that not only overthrew the regime in Tunisia, but also led to revolts in other Arab countries in the years that followed. The 'Arab Spring', as this series of uprisings came to be called, did not lead to a revolt in Jordan, but it did not leave the kingdom untouched, either. Probably believing that this was the right time to demand change from the regime, many Jordanians – including members of the Muslim Brotherhood – took to the streets to protest for more reform.[177]

During this period, the Muslim Brotherhood took a confrontational approach, continuing to demand reform, attending or organising demonstrations and sometimes striking a seemingly defiant tone. This attitude was strengthened when a Muslim Brother – Muhammad Mursi – was elected president in Egypt in 2012 and the Egyptian branch of the organisation won a large number of seats in the country's parliament. Buoyed by this, the Jordanian Brotherhood continued to be involved in

174 '"Shūrá l-Ikhwān" Yantakhibu Murāqiban ʿĀmman wa-Raʾīs Majlis al-Shūrá wa-Aʿḍāʾ al-Maktab al-Tanfīdh', *Al-Sabīl*, 6–12 May 2008, 1.

175 For more on these elections, see Ellen Lust and Sami Hourani, 'Jordan Votes: Election or Selection?', *Journal of Democracy* 22, no. 2 (2011): 119–29.

176 Jillian Schwedler, 'Jordan's Islamists Lose Faith in Moderation', *Foreign Policy* (https://foreignpolicy.com/2010/06/30/jordans-islamists-lose-faith-in-moderation/#; accessed 3 December 2019), 30 June 2010.

177 Jacob Amis, 'The Jordanian Brotherhood in the Arab Spring', in *Current Trends in Islamist Ideology 14*, ed. Hillel Fradkin, Husain Haqqani, Eric Brown and Hassan Mneimeh (Washington, DC: Hudson Institute, 2013), 38–57. See also Ryan, *Jordan and the Arab Uprisings*, 19–42.

protests against the regime.[178] This did not change when, in 2013, the Muslim Brotherhood-led government in Egypt was overthrown by means of a military coup. Although the Jordanian branch of the organisation condemned the coup,[179] it explicitly stated that this event would have no effect on its own policies and that, as a result, it would not back down in Jordan.[180]

Because the organisation took a defiant approach, it became increasingly isolated in its positions, enabling the regime to direct its repressive measures to prevent a 'Jordanian Spring' more and more at the Brotherhood.[181] The organisation was not just coming under fire in Jordan, however. Besides the coup in Egypt and the ban on the Brotherhood there in 2013, Saudi Arabia and the United Arab Emirates also declared it to be a terrorist organisation for its role in the revolts across the Arab world. Given the close relations between the Gulf and Jordan and the latter's desire to keep events such as those that took place in Egypt at bay,[182] it was not surprising to hear talk of banning the Brotherhood in the kingdom, too. Although this threat was averted when dialogue between the regime and the Brotherhood was resumed

178 Agence France-Presse (AFP), 'Al-Urdunn: Taẓāhurāt li-"l-Ḥaraka al-Islāmiyya" Tuṭālibu bi-l-Iṣlāḥ', *Al-Ḥayāt* (http://alhayat.com/home/Print/504932?PrintPictures=0, accessed 22 April 2013), 19 April 2013; Taylor Luck, 'Muslim Brotherhood Returns to Streets with "Military Parade"', *The Jordan Times* (http://jordantimes.com/muslim-brotherhood-returns–to-streets-with-military-parade, accessed 22 April 2013), 20 April 2013; Taylor Luck, 'Muslim Brotherhood to Return to the Streets', *The Jordan Times* (http://jordantimes.com/muslim-brotherhood-to-return-to-the-streets, accessed 22 February 2013), 21 February 2013; Tāmir al-Ṣamādī, 'Al-Urdunn: ʿAwdat Taẓāhurāt "al-Ikhwān" wa-Ṣadamāt maʿa l-Shurṭa fī Maʿān wa-Irbid', *Al-Ḥayāt* (http://alhayat.com/home/Print/485942?PrintPictures=0, accessed 25 February 2013), 23 February 2013.

179 'Al-Murāqib al-ʿĀmm li-Ikhwān al-Urdunn Yastankiru Jarīmat al-Inqilāb al-Nakrāʾ fī Miṣr', *Al-Būṣala* (www.albosala.com/?id=111&artical=10901149&chng_tpl=print, accessed 5 July 2013), 4 July 2013; 'Shūrá Ikhwān al-Urdunn Yadīnu l-Inqilāb al-ʿAskarī fī Miṣr', *Al-Būṣala* (www.albosala.com/?id=111&artical=10901152&chng_tpl=print, accessed 5 July 2013), 4 July 2013; Bassām al-ʿUmūsh, 'Suqūṭ al-Dīmuqrāṭiyya bi-Isqāṭ Mursī', *Al-Būṣala* (www.albosala.com/?id=111&artical=10900633&chng_tpl=print, accessed 5 July 2013), 4 July 2013.

180 'Saʿīd: Lā Murājaʿa li-Ruʾyat Ikhwān al-Urdunn', *Al-Ghad* (www.allofjo.net/index.php?page=article&id=51652, accessed 13 December 2017), 22 July 2013; Mūsá Karāʿīn, 'Banī Irshīd: Al-Ḥukūma Lā Turīdu an Yakūna Ladaynā Ḥirāk Shaʿbī', *Al-Sabīl*, 8 July 2013, 3; Mūsá Karāʿīn, 'Manṣūr: Ḥamla Iʿlāmiyya li-Tashwīh al-Ḥaraka al-Islāmiyya', *Al-Sabīl*, 21 July 2013, 4; Mūsá Karāʿīn, 'Manṣūr: Man Yaḥlumu bi-Iḍʿāf al-Islāmiyyīn Wāhim', *Al-Sabīl*, 12 July 2013, 2.

181 Tāmir al-Ṣamādī, 'Al-Urdunn: Naḥwa Taḥālufāt Jadīda li-Muwājahat "al-Ikhwān"', *Al-Ḥayāt* (http://alhayat.com/home/print/461595?PrintPictures=0, accessed 13 December 2012), 13 December 2012.

182 Muḥammad al-Najjār, 'Al-Urdunn Yulawwiḥu bi-Ijrāʾāt Ḍidda l-Ikhwān', *Al-Jazīra* (www.aljazeera.net/home/print/f6451603-4dff-4ca1-9c10-122741d17432/d928b94a-013c-4ca8-ab7e-1083a548d6a6, accessed 15 August 2013), 29 July 2013.

and the king made clear he did not want to ban the organisation,[183] the situation remained volatile.

Rather than seeking integration into the political system at a time when it was vulnerable and – despite dialogue – still at odds with the regime, the IAF subsequently decided to boycott the elections of 2013, the first since the beginning of the Arab Spring. To the regime, these elections represented its continued commitment to democracy and reform and its ability to weather the storm that was the Arab Spring, although the first of these claims was questionable.[184] The IAF's boycott of the elections defied the regime's narrative and, indeed, analysts also pointed out that little had really changed.[185] The IAF itself adopted several amendments to its internal regulations later that year, but these seemed to have nothing to do with the regional or national circumstances.[186]

As such, it seemed that the Brotherhood was consistent and united in its policies towards the regime. Still, the organisation's increasingly confrontational stance after the beginning of the Arab Spring did not sit well with all of its members. While it was united in its demands for reform, particularly at first, its agreement on how to engage with the regime broke down as the Arab Spring increasingly turned out to be a disappointment. Partly out of unease with the defiant stance of the Brotherhood's leadership, but also building on existing disagreements (dealt with in the following chapters), some members of the organisation sought a broader, more inclusive approach to tackle the country's problems.[187] This resulted in 'The Jordanian Initiative for Building', better known as 'The ZamZam Initiative' because its founders had decided upon this in Hotel ZamZam in Amman in November 2012. Although ZamZam included

[183] Muḥammad al-Najjār, 'Rasāʾil Ījābiyya bayna l-Niẓām al-Urdunnī wa-l-Ikhwān', *Al-Jazīra* (https://eldorar.com/node/26199, accessed 14 December 2017), 17 September 2013; Tāmir al-Ṣamādī, 'Al-Urdunn: Jihāt Siyādiyya Taṭlubu Liqāʾ "al-Ikhwān"', *Al-Ḥayāt* (http://alhayat.com/home/Print/552851?PrintPictures=0, accessed 18 September 2013), 17 September 2013.

[184] Morten Valbjørn, 'The 2013 Parliamentary Elections in Jordan: Three Stories and Some General Lessons', *Mediterranean Politics* 18, no. 2 (2013): 311–17.

[185] Policy Analysis Unit ACRPS, *Political Reforms and Parliamentary Elections in Jordan: The Trials and Tribulations of Forming a New Government* (Arab Center for Research and Policy Studies: http://english.dohainstitute.org/release/d1297561-3df6-479a-a078-7f59d1b4688a# (accessed 20 March 2013), 6 March 2013); Nicholas Seeley, 'The Jordanian State Buys Itself Time', *Middle East Report Online* (www.merip.org/mero/mero021213, accessed 12 February 2013), 12 February 2013.

[186] '"Shūrá al-ʿAmal al-Islāmī" Yaqirru Taʿdīlāt ʿalá 11 Mādda wa-49 Bandan min Niẓāmihi l-Asāsī', *Al-Dustūr*, 17 November 2013, 8.

[187] For a detailed analysis of the Muslim Brotherhood's exclusive and inclusive tendencies during the 'Arab Spring', see Joas Wagemakers, 'Between Exclusivism and Inclusivism: The Jordanian Muslim Brotherhood's Divided Responses to the "Arab Spring"', *Middle East Law and Governance* 12, no. 1 (2020): 35–60.

many non-Islamist members and sought to solve the kingdom's problems in a broad-based – rather than Islamist – way, it was led by prominent IAF member Ruhayyil Gharayiba.[188]

While ZamZam did not strive for solutions that were against those proposed by the Muslim Brotherhood[189] and was explicitly meant as a broad initiative – not a political party – it was nevertheless perceived as an alternative to the Brotherhood.[190] This attitude was apparently also strongly represented within the upper echelons of the organisation, because the three main Brotherhood members involved with ZamZam – Ruhayyil Gharayiba, Nabil al-Kufahi and Jamil Duhaysat – were dismissed from the organisation in 2014.[191] Unsuccessful efforts were made to reconcile between the leadership and the three men by opponents of the dismissal and at the end of 2015, several hundreds of those who were unhappy about the treatment of the ZamZam members resigned.[192]

The resignation of several hundred members – including former General Controller of the Muslim Brotherhood, Salim al-Falahat, and former Secretary General of the IAF, Hamza Mansur – was only partly done out of frustration over the ZamZam members who had been dismissed. Apart from deeper ideological differences, which will be discussed in Chapters 4–6, there had also been internal elections in the IAF. These had resulted in the important position of head of the Consultation Council, previously held by the more moderate ʿAli Abu l-Sukkar, going to the more hawkish ʿAbd al-Muhsin al-ʿAzzam in

188 'Al-Duktūr Gharāyiba Yakshifu ʿan Maḍāmīn al-Liqāʾ fī Funduq ZamZam', *Shīḥān News* (www.shihannews.net/Print.aspx?ArticleNo=30102, accessed 29 November 2012), 27 November 2012.

189 Interview with Ruhayyil Gharayiba, Amman, 17 January 2013.

190 'Inqilāb fī l-Ikhwān ... Tafāṣīl Ijtimāʿ Funduq ZamZam', *Shīḥān News* (www.shihannews.net/Print.aspx?ArticleNo=30098, 29 November 2012), 27 November 2012.

191 'Taṣrīḥ Ṣafaḥī li-l-Maktab al-Iʿlāmī li-l-Ikhwān al-Muslimīn bi-Khuṣūṣ al-Ḥukm bi-Faṣl ʿAdad min Aʿḍāʾ al-Jamāʿa', *Al-Sabīl*, 22 April 2014, 3; Muʿādh al-Buṭūsh, 'Maṣādir Tuʾakkidu li-"*l-Ḥaqīqa al-Dawliyya*" Qarār "al-Ikhwān" bi-Faṣl al-Gharāyiba wa-l-Kūfaḥī wa-l-Duhaysāt', *Al-Ḥaqīqa al-Dawliyya* (http://factjo.com/pages/print.aspx?id=60749, accessed 21 April 2014), 20 April 2014; Taylor Luck, 'Muslim Brotherhood Expels Three Over ZamZam Initiative', *The Jordan Times* (www.jordantimes.com/news/local/muslim-brotherhood-expels-three-over-zamzam%E2%80%99-initiative, accessed 22 April 2014), 21 April 2014; Nasīm ʿUnayzāt, 'Faṣl Qiyādiyyī "ZamZam" al-Gharāyiba wa-l-Kūfaḥī wa-Duhaysāt min Jamāʿat al-Ikhwān', *Al-Dustūr*, 21 April 2014, 5.

192 Hadīl Ghabbūn, '300 ʿUḍw bi-'l-"Amal al-Islāmī" Yastaqīlūna', *Al-Ghad* (http://alghad.com/articles/912211, accessed 4 January 2016), 31 December 2015; Hadīl Ghabbūn, 'Istiqālat 400 ʿUḍw min "al-ʿAmal al-Islāmī" (al-Asmāʾ)', *Al-Ghad* (http://alghad.com/articles/912071, accessed 4 January 2016), 31 December 2015.

July 2014.[193] The following month, the hard-line Muhammad al-Zuyud was elected Secretary General of the IAF, rather than the more dovish Salim al-Falahat.[194] These elections thus confirmed a trend that had been discernible for years, namely, that 'hawks' gained more prominence at the expense of 'doves', to use the terminology widely applied in the Jordanian media.[195]

Underlying ideological differences, anger over the dismissal of the ZamZam members and frustration about the election results contributed to the decision of hundreds of Brotherhood members to resign in late 2015. These and other internal differences also had an even more devastating effect to the Muslim Brotherhood: since 2014, former General Controller ʿAbd al-Majid Dhunaybat had organised meetings for disaffected Brotherhood members who felt that the organisation was not being led properly, was too close-minded and was moving in the wrong direction. This ultimately resulted in the founding of a new Muslim Brotherhood (Jamʿiyyat Jamāʿat al-Ikhwān al-Muslimīn; the Society of the Muslim Brothers Association, hereafter: the New (Muslim) Brotherhood) in 2015.[196]

The defiant attitude as a result of the Arab Spring as well as the internal divisions within the Muslim Brotherhood made the organisation an easy target for regime repression. The latter was expressed in numerous ways since 2014, including arrests of Islamist activists,[197] the most prominent example of which was Zaki Bani Irshid, the then-Deputy General Controller of the Muslim Brotherhood. Bani Irshid was arrested in November 2014 for criticism he had expressed on Facebook about the United Arab Emirates' policy of designating the Muslim Brotherhood

193 Hadīl Ghabbūn, 'Al-ʿAzzām Raʾīsan li-Shūrá l-ʿAmal al-Islāmī wa-Taʾjīl Intikhāb al-Amīn al-ʿĀmm', *Al-Ghad* (www.alghad.com/articles/812452, accessed 21 November 2018), 5 July 2014.

194 Hadīl Ghabbūn, 'Al-Zuyūd Amīnan ʿĀmman li-"l-ʿAmal al-Islāmī" bi-l-Tazkiya', *Al-Ghad* (www.alghad.com/articles/819880, accessed 18 August 2014), 16 August 2014; Mūsá Karāʿīn, 'Bi-l-Tazkiya al-Zuyūd Amīnan ʿĀmman "li-l-ʿAmal al-Islāmī"', *Al-Sabīl*, 17 August 2014, 5.

195 The meaning of these terms and the fault-lines between them will be made clear later in this chapter.

196 Curtis R. Ryan, 'One Society of Muslim Brothers in Jordan or Two?', *Middle East Report Online* (http://merip.org/one-society-muslim-brothers-jordan-or-two, accessed 2 September 2015), 5 March 2015. The internal divisions in the Muslim Brotherhood, the influence of 'ZamZam' and the founding of the New Muslim Brotherhood are much more detailed than can be described here and would require a separate publication.

197 See, for instance, '"Al-ʿAmal al-Islāmī" wa-Niqābat al-Muhandisīn Yuṭālibān bi-Maʿlūmāt ʿan Tawqīf Thalātha Nāshiṭīn', *Al-Ghad* (http://alghad.com/articles/834667, accessed 6 November 2014), 5 November 2014; '"Al-ʿAmal al-Islāmī" Yuṭālibu bi-Kashf Makān Iʿtiqāl Maliṣa wa-Dawʿar wa-bnihi wa-l-Ifrāj ʿanhum', *Al-Sabīl*, 5 November 2014, 8.

a 'terrorist organisation'. This, according to the authorities, could hurt relations with 'an Arab brother state'.[198] In February 2015, the State Security Court found Bani Irshid guilty of this charge and sentenced him to eighteen months in prison,[199] although he was released earlier, in January 2016.[200] Some Islamists saw Bani Irshid's arrest as unprecedented[201] and IAF leader Muhammad al-Zuyud viewed these arrests as part of a broader policy to weaken the organisation.[202]

The repression against the Muslim Brotherhood really entered a new phase with the founding of the New Muslim Brotherhood. Dhunaybat, the leader of the latter, claimed he wanted to re-register his organisation because the leadership of the 'old' Brotherhood was illegitimate and because the organisation's position in the entire region was so precarious. As such, he wanted permission from the regime to 'continue' the (new) Brotherhood's work so as to be secure in its activities.[203] The original Muslim Brotherhood not only protested what it labelled a 'coup' against the organisation's leadership, which could effectively make them illegal, but also produced the documents proving that they had been given permission in 1946 and 1953 to be the Muslim Brotherhood in Jordan.[204] All of this was to no avail, however: the New Muslim Brotherhood was registered in March 2015, which also meant that no other group was allowed to use the name 'Muslim Brotherhood' without permission from the regime, thereby effectively rendering the original organisation unlicensed.[205]

198 Anas ʿAlī, '"Amn al-Dawla" Tuwaqqifu Zakī Banī Irshīd', *ʿAmmūn* (www.ammonnews.net/print.aspx?articleno=212480, accessed 21 November 2014), 20 November 2014.

199 'Bayān li-l-Ikhwān Yudīnu wa-Yastahjinu Ḥabs Banī Irshīd', *Al-Ghad* (http://alghad.com/articles/853399, accessed 16 February 2016), 15 February 2016.

200 Anas Ṣuwayliḥ, 'Al-Ifrāj ʿan Banī Irshīd', *Al-Dustūr*, 5 January 2016, 8.

201 ʿUmar al-ʿAyāṣira, 'Iʿtiqāl Banī Irshīd ... Marḥala Jadīda', *Al-Sabīl*, 23 November 2014, 2.

202 'Al-ʿAmal al-Islāmī: Hunāka Muḥāwalāt li-Iḍʿāf al-Ḥaraka al-Islāmiyya', *Al-Maqarr* (www.maqar.com/?id=70789, accessed 24 November 2014), 23 November 2014.

203 Mājid al-Amīr and Muḥammad al-Daʿma, 'Al-Murāqib al-ʿĀmm al-Sābiq li-"Ikhwān al-Urdunn": Qiyādat al-Ikhwān al-Muslimīn al-Ḥāliyya "Ghayr Sharʿiyya"', *Al-Sharq al-Awsaṭ* (http://aawsat.com/node/302751, accessed 3 March 2015), 2 March 2015.

204 Ḥātim al-Harsh, 'Al-Būṣala Tanshuru Wathāʾiq Tarkhīṣ al-Jamāʿa al-Rasmiyya ʿĀmmay 46/53', *Al-Būṣala* (http://albosa.la/TVRFeU1qazErdQ==, accessed 3 March 2015), 2 March 2015.

205 Hadīl Ghabbūn, 'Al-Dhunaybāt: Sanatawāṣalu maʿa Qawāʿid "al-Ikhwān"', *Al-Ghad* (http://alghad.com/articles/857546, accessed 10 March 2015), 10 March 2015. In May 2019, a court of cassation in Jordan ruled that the original Muslim Brotherhood has been illegal since 1953, because it failed to rectify its status in that year. See 'Court Deems Old Muslim Brotherhood Dissolved Since 1953', *The Jordan Times* (http://jordantimes.com/news/local/court-deems-old-muslim-brotherhood-dissolved-1953, accessed 13 June 2019), 13 June 2019.

Although the new situation of the Muslim Brotherhood did not take effect immediately, the New Brotherhood did want to take swift action against its namesake by demanding that the original organisation's headquarters be transferred to the new group,[206] for which they also got permission.[207] From that point on, the regime started closing Brotherhood (and, to a lesser extent, IAF) offices across the country, including the organisation's headquarters in Amman in 2016.[208] It also forced the pro-Brotherhood television channel al-Yarmuk to stop broadcasting from Amman,[209] sometimes prohibited the group from organising meals to break the fast during the month of Ramadan (*ifṭārs*)[210] and caused it to cancel its seventieth anniversary festival in 2015.[211]

The Muslim Brotherhood was obviously against the measures taken against it, but was not in a position to stop them. It did make three important changes in 2016, however. The first pertained to a long-held point of criticism often levelled against it, namely, that the Brotherhood was essentially a foreign organisation or at least not truly Jordanian. In early 2016, however, the Brotherhood formally cut ties with 'Cairo', thereby becoming an independent organisation.[212] The second decision was that, after the regime had decided to amend the electoral law back to the form it had in 1989[213] – a long-held demand by the Brotherhood – the

[206] Hadīl Ghabbūn, 'Al-Dhunaybāt: Sanaṭlubu Taslīm Maqarrāt "al-Ikhwān" Qarīban', *Al-Ghad* (http://alghad.com/articles/860938, accessed 27 March 2015), 27 March 2015.

[207] Hadīl Ghabbūn, 'Al-Dhunaybāt li-"*l-Ghad*": Man Yarfuḍu Naql al-Amlāk Lan Yabqá fī l-Jamāʿa', *Al-Ghad* (http://alghad.com/articles/873036, accessed 29 May 2015), 28 May 2015.

[208] Rabá Karāsina, 'Ighlāq al-Maqarr al-Tārīkhī li-"l-Ikhwān" fī Wasaṭ ʿAmmān', *Al-Būṣala* (http://albosa.la/TVRNMU5qVTMrdQ==, accessed 16 May 2016), 15 May 2016.

[209] 'Qanāt al-Yarmūk Tatawaqqaʿu Waqf Baththihā min ʿAmmān wa-Tattajihu li-l-ʿAmal min al-Khārij', *Al-Ghad* (www.alghad.com/articles/932817, accessed 18 April 2016), 18 April 2016.

[210] Rabá Karāsina, 'Iltifāf al-Kawādir Ḥawla l-Qiyāda al-Sharʿiyya Afshala l-Khaṭaṭ allatī Taḥāku Ḍidda l-Ikhwān', *Al-Būṣala* (http://albosa.la/TVRFNE56azQrdQ==, accessed 8 July 2015), 8 July 2015.

[211] '"Al-Ikhwān al-Muslimīn" Tuʿlinu ʿan Taʾjīl Iḥtifālihā', *Al-Sabīl*, 30 April 2015, 1; Nasīm ʿUnayzāt, '"Al-Ikhwān" Yuqarrirūna Taʾjīl al-Iḥtifāl bi-Dhikrá Taʾsīs al-Jamāʿa', *Al-Dustūr*, 30 April 2015, 1.

[212] Rabá Karāsina, 'Al-Khawālida: Taʿdīlāt al-Shūrá Akkadat ʿalá Istiqlāliyyat al-Jamāʿa', *Al-Būṣala* (http://albosa.la/TVRNd05qRTIrdQ==, accessed 15 February 2016), 13 February 2016; Khetam Malkawi, 'Muslim Brotherhood Ends Link with Egyptian Mother Group', *The Jordan Times* (www.jordantimes.com/news/local/muslim-brotherhood-ends-link-egyptian-mother-group, accessed 15 February 2016), 14 February 2016.

[213] Muṣʿab al-Ashqar, 'Al-Ḥukūma Taqirru Musawwadat Qānūn al-Intikhāb bi-l-ʿAwda li-89', *Al-Būṣala* (http://albosa.la/TVRJeE16WTUrdQ==, accessed 1 September 2015), 31 August 2015; Curtis R. Ryan, 'Deja vu for Jordanian Election Reforms', *The Washington Post* (www.washingtonpost.com/blogs/monkey-cage/wp/2015/09/02/deja-vu-for-jordanian-election-reforms/, accessed 3 September 2015), 2 September 2015.

IAF decided to end its boycott and participate in the elections of 2016,[214] eventually winning 10 seats (out of 130). Thirdly, and more importantly, the term limit of the Brotherhood's Executive Council was reached in 2016, which meant that Hammam Saʿid, the General Controller, as well as the other members of the Council had to leave. Given the fact that the Brotherhood was no longer licensed, however, they could not be replaced with newly and officially elected members, which resulted in a 'temporary' care-taker leadership,[215] which has remained the Brotherhood's leadership since then and, in a sense, marked the end of the organisation as it had existed for over seventy years.[216]

Divisions within the Muslim Brotherhood

The history of the Muslim Brotherhood in Jordan shows that the organisation, after having enjoyed strong ties with the regime, came under increasing pressure, particularly in the later years of King Husayn and even more so under King ʿAbdallah II. If we concentrate on the Brotherhood's behaviour in this period, we can see that the organisation elected fewer moderate people as it came under increasing pressure and was less willing to cooperate with the regime through parliamentary participation. This seems to bear out the inclusion-moderation thesis, which not only stresses that inclusion leads to moderation, but also that exclusion leads to radicalisation.

Yet there are several problems with this reasoning. Firstly, it does not account for some of the steps the Brotherhood took, such as the IAF's decision to participate in the elections in 2016. This happened at a time of unprecedented repression, but was a sign of moderation, which flies in the face of the inclusion-moderation thesis. Secondly, the Muslim

[214] Rabá Karāsina, '"Al-ʿAmal al-Islāmī" Yuqarriru l-Mushāraka fī l-Intikhābāt al-Niyābiyya', *Al-Būṣala* (http://albosa.la/TVRNM05ESTMrdQ==, accessed 13 June 2016), 11 June 2016; Khatem Malkawi, 'Islamists End Boycott, To Run for Elections in September', *The Jordan Times* (http://jordantimes.com/news/local/islamists-end-boycott-run-elections-september, accessed 13 June 2016), 11 June 2016.

[215] '"Al-Ikhwān" Tashkulu Lajna Muʾaqqata li-Idāratihā', *Al-Ghad* (http://alghad.com/articles/943962, accessed 13 June 2016), 11 June 2016; '"Al-Ikhwān al-Umm" Tashkulu Lajna Muʾaqqata li-Idārat al-Jamāʿa (Asmāʾ)', *Al-Būṣala* (http://albosa.la/TVRNM05ETTUrdQ==, accessed 13 June 2016), 11 June 2016.

[216] The New Muslim Brotherhood and ZamZam joined forces and set up their own political party, the National Congress Party (Ḥizb al-Muʾtamar al-Waṭanī), in June 2016. It won 5 seats (out of 130) in the parliamentary elections of that year. See Rabá Karāsina, '"Al-Tanmiya al-Siyāsiyya" Tatasallamu Ṭalaban Rasmiyyan li-Tarkhīṣ Ḥizb "ZamZam"', *Al-Būṣala* (http://albosa.la/TVRNNE16UXcrdQ==, accessed 30 June 2016), 28 June 2016.

Brotherhood has not just been influenced by what happens in Jordan, but also – and in different ways – by ideas from outside the kingdom, as the influence of the Arab Spring shows, and by what foreign Muslim scholars write. Inclusion or exclusion on a national level, in other words, is merely one of the factors influencing the group's moderation.

I argue that both points can be explained by analysing the Muslim Brotherhood's ideological divisions. The Brotherhood's behaviour was often strongly influenced by the Jordanian context, but what were the underlying ideological tendencies supporting it? The inclusion-moderation thesis also (or perhaps primarily) deals with ideological moderation, but we have not really looked at that yet. Moreover, it is clear from what we have seen in this chapter that the Muslim Brotherhood is actually a house divided and that its members have responded quite differently to the various challenges it has faced over the years. The conclusion that inclusion leads to moderation in this case does not pay full attention to these very real and important divisions. Although other scholars have certainly dealt with the Brotherhood's internal divisions in their work,[217] a full focus on them can shed new light on the inclusion-moderation thesis and how the different views by scholars on this thesis can be reconciled.

The different approaches towards Islamic tradition that we saw in Chapters 1 and 2 –*sharīʿa*-centred, *umma*-centred and balanced – can also be applied to the Jordanian Muslim Brotherhood's views on the state, political participation and societal rights and freedoms, as will happen in Chapters 4–6. Yet in order to do so, we must first look at where the fault-lines lie within the Muslim Brotherhood. As mentioned before, the Brotherhood is divided between 'hawks' and 'doves', terms that are used in Jordanian media, but also frequently appear in academic publications such as those mentioned above. These terms are often ill-defined, however, and frequently seem to refer to people's willingness to compromise or, for example, their attitude towards Sayyid Qutb.[218]

In order to give a more detailed picture of how the Muslim Brotherhood in Jordan is divided ideologically, I distinguish five dimensions of division within the organisation, of which the final two are most important in this book. The first of these refers to the identity of the Brotherhood: should it be a conservative missionary organisation focussing on *daʿwa* or an activist political one concentrating on policy matters? Some scholars have argued that *daʿwa* is the Muslim Brotherhood's

[217] Examples include Clark and Schwedler, 'Who Opened the Window?', 295–7; Schwedler, *Faith*, 163–4.
[218] Abu Rumman, *Muslim Brotherhood*, 34.

backbone that allows it to survive[219] and some important Jordanian members still focus primarily on missionary activities.[220] At the same time, however, parts of the organisation – especially the IAF, of course – are fully geared towards politics and, at most, seem to concentrate on *da'wa* only during a parliamentary boycott.[221]

The second and third dimensions of the Jordanian Muslim Brotherhood's dividedness are the organisation's character and openness. The former refers to whether the Brotherhood should focus first and foremost on the Palestinian question and support for Hamas or concentrate on internal Jordanian issues. While all Muslim Brothers are strong supporters of the Palestinians, they disagree on the priority their case should be given within the Jordanian Brotherhood.[222] The dimension of openness refers to whether the Brotherhood should operate in an exclusive way, striving to achieve its own Islamist interests, or work more inclusively by being open to other, non-Islamist groups and even joining coalitions with them.[223] Elements of this can be seen in the broad-based and inclusive ZamZam initiative and the Brotherhood's exclusive response to it.[224]

The most important fourth and fifth dimensions of dividedness (for this book) within the Muslim Brotherhood in Jordan are the group's Islamist ideology and its willingness to participate in an electoral process. The former refers to how the Brotherhood envisions the Jordanian state and society: as (part of) a caliphate or Islamic state and society or as entities that should be accepted and dealt with on their own terms. This dimension pertains to the Brotherhood's views on the state and societal rights and liberties and, as such, will be dealt with in Chapters 4 and 6. The organisation's willingness to participate, finally, is dealt with in Chapter 5 and divides those who prefer to boycott parliament and government from those who choose to participate in them.[225]

The first group mentioned with regard to each of these dimensions of dividedness can be labelled 'hawks' (roughly equal to 'radicals' in inclusion-moderation terms) while the second group may be referred to as 'doves' (or 'moderates'). The reality is, of course, that many Muslim

219 Itzchak Weismann, 'Framing a Modern Umma: The Muslim Brothers' Evolving Project of *Da'wa*', *Sociology of Islam* 3 (2015): 146–69.
220 See, for instance, Hammām Sa'īd, *Qawā'id al-Da'wa ilá llāh* (Amman: Dār al-Furqān li-l-Nashr wa-l-Tawzī', 2011).
221 Al-Budūr, *Al-Tajriba*, 131–2.
222 Brown, *Victory*, 103; Rosefsky Wickham, *Muslim Brotherhood*, 199.
223 Rosefsky Wickham, *Muslim Brotherhood*, 198–9; El-Said, *Pragmatism*, 8–9.
224 I have dealt extensively with this dimension of dividedness in the Jordanian Muslim Brotherhood in Wagemakers, 'Between Exclusivism and Inclusivism'.
225 Brown, *Victory*, 99, 102, 155; Moaddel, *Jordanian Exceptionalism*, 134–5.

Brothers are somewhere in between. Based on the dimensions given above, Part II will deal with the ideological divisions within the Muslim Brotherhood as pertaining to the subjects of the state, political participation and societal rights and liberties. This will not only show the limits of the terms 'hawks' and 'doves', but also that internal ideological divisions in terms of *sharīʿa*-centred, *umma*-centred and balanced approaches to Islamic tradition constitute an important factor in explaining the development of Islamist ideology in general, the Jordanian Muslim Brotherhood's behaviour in particular and how this relates to the inclusion-moderation thesis.

Part II

Divisions

4 Ideological Divisions on the State

The classical Sunni Islamic tradition was not homogeneous with regard to how the adjacent concepts of '*sharīʿa*', '*umma*' and '*sulṭa*' should be arranged in relation to the core concept of 'caliph'/'ruler' and neither was the early Muslim Brotherhood in Egypt, as we saw in Chapters 1 and 2. As such, the results of their conceptual decontestations differed with regard to the state. In classical times, the general tendency was towards a *sulṭa*-centred Islamic caliphate, while Rida argued for a spiritual caliphate and took an approach that balanced '*sharīʿa*' and '*umma*' with regard to the idea of an Islamic state. The latter was also advocated as an important goal by the early Muslim Brothers, although some of them took a balanced approach (al-Banna and al-Hudaybi), while others were clearly *sharīʿa*-centred (ʿAwda and Qutb).

Chapter 3 showed that the Jordanian Muslim Brotherhood is also quite divided. In order for us to find out to what extent Jordanian Muslim Brothers have *sharīʿa*-centred, *umma*-centred or balanced approaches to the state – the topic of this chapter – how this fits in with broader global Islamist discourse and how this relates to the 'inclusion-moderation' thesis, we must take a detailed look at the ideas the Jordanian Brotherhood has expressed on the state. This chapter therefore analyses the organisation's discourse on the caliphate, the Islamic state and how this is applied in the Jordanian context. As such, it shows the diversity of Islamist views on this matter and begins to give an idea of the Jordanian Muslim Brotherhood's divisions that partly account for why scholars have drawn such different conclusions with regard to the inclusion-moderation thesis.

The Caliphate

The Islamic caliphate, as we saw in Chapter 1, was the focal point of Islamic rule from the Middle Ages until the twentieth century and although it was contested or reinterpreted by modern scholars such as ʿAli ʿAbd al-Raziq and Muhammad Rashid Rida, it had functioned as the epitome of Islamic politics for centuries. So much so that thinkers associated with the Egyptian Muslim Brotherhood, even years after the Ottoman caliphate had been abolished, still talked about Islamic rule in terms of this system. Although not all early Brotherhood thinkers agreed on the use and meaning of the term 'caliph', as we saw in Chapter 2, they often did rely on classical ideas about the Islamic caliphate. This is hardly the case for members of the Jordanian Muslim Brotherhood, with one important exception.

Caliphate in Theory or in Practice?

Contemporary Islamic thinkers and scholars are often much further removed from the caliphate than early Muslim Brotherhood leaders like Hasan al-Banna, ʿAbd al-Qadir ʿAwda and Hasan al-Hudaybi were in their days, simply because much more time has passed since 1924. Scholars that have influenced the Jordanian Brotherhood, such as Yusuf al-Qaradawi and Hasan al-Turabi, appear not to see the caliphate as very important anymore. This does not mean that they have forgotten about the caliphate altogether or that they do not mourn its downfall; it simply implies that in their writings on Islamic rule in the twentieth and twenty-first centuries they tend to treat it merely as a historical phenomenon[1] or seem to view it as only indirectly and theoretically – rather than practically – relevant to today's discussions on Islamic politics.[2]

This same attitude is prevalent within the Jordanian Muslim Brotherhood. Talk of a caliphate is rare, even in publications in which one would expect this subject to be mentioned. In a two-volume study on political views by the prominent Jordanian Brother and former minister on behalf of the organisation Ishaq Farhan, for example, the caliphate

[1] See, for example, Muḥammad ʿImāra, *Al-Islām wa-l-Sulṭa al-Dīniyya* (Cairo: Dār al-Thaqāfa al-Jadīda, n.d.), 12–13; Yūsuf al-Qaraḍāwī, *Ummatunā bayna l-Qarnayn* (Cairo: Dār al-Shurūq, 2006 [2000]), 128–30.

[2] See, for instance, Hasan al-Turabi, 'The Islamic State', in *Princeton Readings in Islamist Thought: Texts and Contexts from al-Banna to Bin Laden*, ed. Roxanne L. Euben and Muhammad Qasim Zaman (Princeton, NJ, and Oxford: Princeton University Press, 2009), 213–23; Ḥasan al-Turābī, *Al-Siyāsa wa-l-Ḥukm: Al-Nuẓum al-Sulṭāniyya bayna l-Uṣūl wa-Sunan al-Wāqiʿ* (Beirut: Dār al-Sāqī, 2003). Yūsuf al-Qaraḍāwī, *Min Fiqh al-Dawla fī l-Islām: Makānatuhā ... Maʿālimuhā ... Ṭabīʿatuhā [wa-]Mawqifuhā min al-Dīmuqrāṭiyya wa-l-Taʿaddudiyya wa-l-Marʾa wa-Ghayr al-Muslimīn* (Cairo: Dār al-Shurūq, 2001 [1997]) is a special case, however, since the author does speak highly of the caliphate and clearly sees it as an ideal. Yet at the same time, he seems to use the tenets of the caliphate to come up with classical answers to modern questions, thereby showing that he may perhaps not want the caliphate back, but rather that people learn the lessons from how he believes this system was intended.

does not even come up.[3] The same applies to a reformist vision published as a booklet by the Jordanian Muslim Brotherhood and the IAF in 2005. Although the text of the booklet makes frequent use of Islamic concepts and texts, it does not dwell on the caliphate and, instead, expresses political views in the context of the Jordanian state.[4] Similarly, the IAF's regularly amended Basic Law statement published in 2018 remains silent on the caliphate and places the organisation's ambition to apply the *sharīʿa* squarely in the context of 'the resumption of the Islamic life of Jordanian society'.[5]

This lack of attention to the caliphate in Jordanian Brotherhood discourse cannot be because it does not have roots in classical Islamic political thought – because it does – or because the early Muslim Brothers in Egypt never mention it – because they do. Yet the latter also mostly moved away from the subject of the caliphate, even if they continued to use its terminology. Members of the Jordanian Brotherhood can therefore be said to have continued this growing realisation that the caliphate was not coming back. They appear to have done so for two reasons: firstly, given that the Jordanian Muslim Brotherhood does not – as mentioned before – have major scholars of its own, it seems likely that the organisation would follow global Islamist discourse as expressed by al-Qaradawi and others. Considering that such scholars seem to have moved beyond the caliphate (at least in practice), it is not surprising that Jordanian Brothers have done so, as well; secondly, because the Jordanian Muslim Brotherhood was accepted and licensed by the regime in 1946, the organisation had a strong interest in investing in its future in the Jordanian context, rather than in some potential future caliphate that might never materialise and might even jeopardise the safety and achievements they enjoyed in the Jordanian state.

Still, not all Muslim Brothers in Jordan agree on the rejection of the caliphate's practical relevance for the here and now. One Muslim scholar and long-time member of the Muslim Brotherhood, the aforementioned Muhammad Abu Faris (1938–2015), seems to view the theory of the caliphate as highly relevant in his description of modern-day Islamic politics. That he differs with global Islamist scholars like al-Qaradawi in

3 Isḥāq Aḥmad Farḥān, *Mawāqif wa-Ārāʾ Siyāsiyya fī Qaḍāyā Waṭaniyya wa-ʿArabiyya wa-Islāmiyya I* (Amman: Dār al-Furqān, 1999); Isḥāq Aḥmad Farḥān, *Mawāqif wa-Ārāʾ Siyāsiyya fī Qaḍāyā Waṭaniyya wa-ʿArabiyya wa-Islāmiyya II* (Amman: Dār al-Furqān, 2000).

4 Al-Ḥaraka al-Islāmiyya fī l-Urdunn, *Ruʾyat al-Ḥaraka al-Islāmiyya li-l-Iṣlāḥ fī l-Urdunn* (n. p.: 2005).

5 Ḥizb Jabhat al-ʿAmal al-Islāmī, *Al-Niẓām al-Asāsī* (n.p.: 2018), 4. I would like to thank Dīma Ṭahbūb, a Member of Parliament for the IAF, for providing me with a copy of this document.

this respect is perhaps not surprising, because when I interviewed him he indicated that al-Qaradawi was knowledgeable, but had not influenced him at all. He appears far more indebted to the classical Islamic tradition as seen through the prism of the early Egyptian Muslim Brothers' writings, as we will also see below.[6]

Abu Faris's basic premise with regard to politics in Islam is no different from that of other Muslim Brothers in Jordan (as will become clear later): he states that Islam 'encompasses rulings (*aḥkām*) that touch upon all areas of human life and that organise the relationship of man with his Lord, with himself, with his family and with other people'. These rulings, Abu Faris goes on, 'which must necessarily be applied in the reality of life, are in need of someone to execute their application'. They are, in other words, 'in need of a ruling power (*sulṭa ḥākima*)', a statement the author backs up with evidence from various sources of Islam.[7] Abu Faris thus sees the need for a ruler with *sulṭa* to apply the *sharīʿa*.[8]

Where Abu Faris differs from others in the Jordanian Muslim Brotherhood, however, is in his practical evaluation of the caliphate, or 'the greatest imamate (*al-imāma al-kubrá*)', which he labels 'the highest of general offices (*aʿlá l-wilāyāt al-ʿāmma*) in Islam'.[9] In a book dedicated to the political thought of Hasan al-Banna, Abu Faris ascribes such positive views on the caliphate to the Brotherhood's founder and cites precisely those quotations of al-Banna's views on the subject that were also given in Chapter 2.[10] He does the same with criticism of ʿAbd al-Raziq's book denying the religious obligation to set up a caliphate. While Abu Faris acknowledges that al-Banna did not mention ʿAbd al-Raziq's name in his own writings, he claims the former nevertheless refuted the latter to resist the development of 'this Western understanding of Islam, which the Orientalists and their like spread: the submissive Western imperialist Islam (*al-Islām al-istiʿmārī al-Gharbī al-dhalīl*)'.[11] Abu Faris shares al-Banna's views on this issue and spends over twenty pages defending the caliphate as a religious obligation against ʿAbd al-Raziq's claims.[12]

As much as Abu Faris agrees with al-Banna, he seems to reject the latter's (and possibly Rida's) tendency to accept multiple Muslim communities with different governments. While Rida suggested the transformation of the caliphate into an overarching spiritual authority

6 Interview with Muḥammad Abū Fāris, Amman, 21 January 2013.
7 Muḥammad ʿAbd al-Qādir Abū Fāris, *Al-Niẓām al-Siyāsī fī l-Islām* (Amman: Dār al-Furqān li-l-Nashr wa-l-Tawzīʿ, n.d.), 155–63. The quotations are from p. 155.
8 Ibid., 198.
9 Muḥammad ʿAbd al-Qādir Abū Fāris, *Al-Fiqh al-Siyāsī ʿinda l-Imām al-Shahīd Ḥasan al-Bannā* (Amman: Dār al-Bashīr li-l-Thaqāfa wa-l-ʿUlūm, 1999), 47.
10 Ibid., 47–8. 11 Ibid., 25–6. The quotation is on p. 25.
12 Abū Fāris, *Al-Niẓām*, 275–96.

and al-Banna even seemed to accept different nation states, Abu Faris appears to be having none of it. He weighs the evidence given by the majority of scholars who do not allow the presence of two imams at the same time[13] against that provided by the minority of *ʿulamāʾ* who do permit this[14] and, after his own analysis,[15] refutes the minority position[16] and concludes that 'it is not allowed to set up different governments and leaders of these governments. It is [also] not allowed to designate more than one imam at the same time'.[17]

One could argue that Abu Faris is merely stating Islamic political theory on the matter of the caliphate, rather than arguing for a practical implementation of this theory in Jordan. It is, indeed, true that Abu Faris's main book on the topic is a presentation of Islamic thought on this issue, not a call for action, let alone revolution. Still, the fact that the author also lists the exact criteria (and the scholarly discussions about some of them) for a Muslim ruler[18] suggests that he sees practical applicability in all of this. Moreover, even if Abu Faris's book was merely a theoretical exercise without any practical relevance, one could still say that the author apparently found the topic important enough to publish a book about it, rather than simply referring to one of the many classical works on the matter.

This impression is supported by Abu Faris's terminology. Rather than merely speaking of 'caliph', he also discusses the various terms for this position: *khalīfa*, *amīr al-muʾminīn* (leader of the believers) and *imām* (leader).[19] Moreover, Abu Faris uses the term '*raʾīs al-dawla al-Islāmiyya*' (the head of the Islamic state) throughout the book – though not consistently – to refer to the caliph, again suggesting that he sees a practical relevance for the doctrine of the caliphate in today's states. This is further confirmed when he suggests that these terms more or less mean the same thing and paraphrases ʿAwda's words on this matter, which were quoted in Chapter 2, stating: 'So caliphate (*al-khilāfa*), kingship (*al-mulk*) and imamate (*al-imāma*) are synonyms that point to the highest leadership (*al-riʾāsa al-ʿulyā*) of the [Islamic] state. They do not point to anything more than that.'[20]

Thus, with the exception of Abu Faris, for whom the caliphate is of great importance (including, apparently, in practice), the core concept of 'caliph' in Islamic political thought is not highly relevant for the Jordanian Muslim Brotherhood. What Abu Faris does have in common with other members of the organisation is his call for the application of the *sharīʿa*. Like them, as we will see below, he attempts to 'restore' the concept of '*sharīʿa*' to what he sees

[13] Ibid., 164–7. [14] Ibid., 167. [15] Ibid., 168–71. [16] Ibid., 171–4. [17] Ibid., 173.
[18] Ibid., 178–97. [19] Ibid., 174–8. [20] Ibid., 178.

as its rightful position as adjacent to the core concept of 'caliph' (or, more in line with the rest of the Brotherhood, 'ruler') in Islamic political thought. The lack of attention for 'caliph' in the Jordanian Brotherhood does not mean, however, that '*sharīʿa*' itself has become the new core concept. It is crucial that Islam is applied on a state level and in society and for that a ruler is needed. 'Ruler' thus remains central to the Brotherhood's ideology and must also be connected with '*sulṭa*', but it must simultaneously be closely tied with '*sharīʿa*'. The form in which the Brotherhood wants to place this system is not just a caliphate, but an Islamic state.

The Islamic State

A state, as we saw before, has many of the characteristics of an empire, but differs with regard to territory and borders. Given the similarities between them, it would be easy for Islamists to perpetuate classical ideas on the caliphate in the framework of a nation-state without changing much. This is, indeed, what Abu Faris seems to try in his work. He does not really appear to want the resurrection of the actual caliphate, but does seem to want to apply its exact elements to an Islamic state. Once the framework of the latter (rather than the caliphate) has been accepted as the norm, however, a broader range of possibilities of what this state should look like opens up, as this section shows.

Global Islamist Discourse on the Islamic State

Global Islamist thinkers and scholars whose names were mentioned to me by Jordanian Muslim Brothers as having influenced them seem to agree that Islam is inherently connected to politics. Rashid al-Ghannushi states that historical examples of Islamic political entities (such as the Prophet's government of Medina), the consensus of Muslim scholars on this issue and the necessity to have some sort of authority to apply and regulate Islam make clear that there is a firm link between Islam and politics.[21] Al-Ghannushi and others therefore criticise Muslim authors – especially ʿAbd al-Raziq – who deny this link, just as Abu Faris did. Yet unlike the latter, who was critical of the idea of denying the Islamic basis of the caliphate, al-Ghannushi seems to criticise ʿAbd al-Raziq for setting in motion a movement of

[21] Rāshid al-Ghannūshī, *Al-Ḥurriyyāt al-ʿĀmma fī l-Dawla al-Islāmiyya* (Beirut: Dār al-Mujtahid, 2011), 99–104.

secularist thinkers who tried to separate Islam from politics.[22] Al-Qaradawi, similarly, blames ʿAbd al-Raziq for stating that Islam is merely a spiritual religion with no connection to politics.[23]

To counter this view, al-Ghannushi shows that the scriptural evidence for Islamic rule makes clear that Muslims need to set up an Islamic state by citing many of the texts quoted in Chapters 1 and 2.[24] In fact, he claims that such a system derives its very legitimacy from its application of the *sharīʿa*,[25] which is simultaneously the justification for its presence.[26] Perhaps in an effort to distinguish the Islamic state from the oppressive regimes in the Arab world – or even from the '*sulṭa*-centred' approaches many classical scholars took – al-Ghannushi states that

> [t]he state in the Islamic conception (*al-taṣawwur al-Islāmī*) is not a weapon (*silāḥ*) in the hands of a class (*ṭabaqa*) to liquidate another class or oppositional group (*fiʾa muʿāraḍa*) – even though it is entitled to legitimate violence (jihad) to defend its domain against aggression – nor is it an instrument (*adāt*) to realise the glory of a people, race or sect (*majd shaʿb aw ʿirq aw ṭāʾifa*) at the expense of other peoples and races. On the contrary, it is an instrument for education (*li-l-tahdhīb*), upbringing (*al-tarbiya*), progress (*al-irtiqāʾ*) and the furnishing of abodes (*tawfīr munākhāt*) of freedom (*al-ḥurriyya*), justice (*al-ʿadl*) and purity (*al-taṭahhur*) [. . .].[27]

Al-Ghannushi thus not only stresses the necessity of an Islamic state, but also its deep – and, as he sees it, positive – involvement in people's lives.[28]

Similarly, al-Qaradawi, echoing al-Banna's words (cited in Chapter 2) about the need to give an Islamic state real meaning, states that

> the Islamic state (*dawlat al-Islām*) is 'an ideological, contractual state' (*dawla fikriyya ʿaqdiyya*), a state based on creed and methodology (*ʿaqīda wa-manhaj*), so it is not just 'a security apparatus' that protects the *umma* from internal attacks or outside invasion (*al-iʿtidāʾ al-dākhilī aw al-ghazw al-khārijī*). On the contrary, its duty (*waẓīfatahā*) is deeper and greater than that. Its duty is to educate the *umma* and to raise them on the teachings and principles (*taʿālīm wa-mabādiʾ*) of Islam.[29]

Al-Qaradawi goes on to claim that Muslims really need such a state to implement the *sharīʿa* and also argues that Islam is not apolitical but,

[22] Rāshid al-Ghannūshī, *Al-Dīmuqrāṭiyya wa-Ḥuqūq al-Insān fī l-Islām* (n.p.: Al-Dār al-ʿArabiyya li-l-ʿUlūm Nāshirūn/Markaz al-Jazīra li-l-Dirāsāt, n.d.), 10–11; al-Ghannūshī, *Al-Ḥurriyyāt*, 99.

[23] Yūsuf al-Qaraḍāwī, *Al-Siyāsa al-Sharʿiyya fī Ḍawʾ Nuṣūṣ al-Sharīʿa wa-Maqāṣidihā* (Cairo: Maktabat Wahba, 2008), 20–1.

[24] Al-Ghannūshī, *Al-Ḥurriyyāt*, 109–13. [25] Ibid., 113. [26] Ibid., 116. [27] Ibid., 252.

[28] See also Tamimi, *Rachid*, 93–9, for more on al-Ghannūshī's views on the Islamic state.

[29] Al-Qaraḍāwī, *Fiqh*, 19–20.

citing al-Banna, an all-encompassing system that includes the political sphere.[30]

Such an Islamic state obviously needs a leader if it is to serve its goal of implementing the *sharī'a*. According to al-Ghannushi, the leader of an Islamic state should have knowledge of Islam, be just, a sane adult and competent.[31] Interestingly, the requirement that the leader be Qurashi (i.e. a descendant of the Prophet Muhammad's Quraysh tribe), which is often mentioned as a condition of the caliphate[32] and which is dealt with extensively and supported by Abu Faris,[33] is treated as much less important by al-Ghannushi, who also raises several principled objections to it.[34] Moreover, al-Turabi emphasises that the ruler cannot simply do what he wants, but is subject to the norms of the *sharī'a* himself, as well:

> [A]n Islamic state is not an absolute or sovereign entity. It is subject to the higher norms of the shari'a that represent the will of God. Politically this rules out all forms of absolutism. Legally it paves the way for the development of constitutional law, a set of norms limiting state powers.[35]

The above makes clear that, unlike in classical Islam, no inordinate amount of weight is given to the adjacent concept of '*sulṭa*' in modern Islamic political thought as expressed by the contemporary scholars who influenced the Jordanian Brotherhood: the ruler must not be oppressive, he should apply the *sharī'a* and is also bound by Islamic law. Yet his position is also strongly linked to that of the *umma*. Citing the fourth caliph, 'Ali b. Abi Talib, al-Ghannushi states that 'the flock (*al-ra'iyya*) is not right (*laysa taṣluḥu*) except through the rightness of the rulers (*ṣalāḥ al-wulāt*) and the rulers are not right except through the uprightness of the flock (*istiqāmat al-ra'iyya*)', thereby underlining the extent to which ruler and *umma* need each other.[36]

In fact, al-Ghannushi states that it is the *umma*'s right to protect the religion 'through the world, that is: through politics'.[37] The relationship between the ruler and the ruled is dealt with in a more detailed way by al-Qaradawi, who states that 'the ruler (*al-ḥākim*) in Islam is the agent (*al-wakīl*) of the *umma*', echoing ideas that could also sometimes be found in classical Islamic political thought, as we saw in Chapter 1.[38] Al-Qaradawi goes further, however, and labels the ruler the *umma*'s 'employee' (*ajīr*), to whose services it is entitled, just like an employer is

[30] Ibid., 21–8. [31] Al-Ghannūshī, *Al-Ḥurriyyāt*, 178–80.
[32] See, for example, Lambton, *State*, 65. [33] Abū Fāris, *Al-Niẓām*, 193–7.
[34] Al-Ghannūshī, *Al-Ḥurriyyāt*, 180–1.
[35] Al-Turabi, 'Islamic State', 214; see also al-Turābī, *Al-Siyāsa*, 113.
[36] Al-Ghannūshī, *Al-Ḥurriyyāt*, 168–72. The quotation is on p. 168. [37] Ibid., 193.
[38] See also al-'Imāra, *Al-Islām*, 14.

to an employee's services.[39] Although the means through which the *umma* can participate in politics are dealt with in Chapter 5, it is interesting to see that to al-Qaradawi, who has influenced the Jordanian Brotherhood so much, the relationship between 'ruler' and '*umma*' – unlike what many scholars wrote in classical times – is devoid of any abuse of power (*sulṭa*).[40]

Yet the *umma* itself, at least in the writings of the early Egyptian Brotherhood thinker Sayyid Qutb, was also partly to blame for the absence of an Islamic state, since it lived in what he termed '*jāhiliyya*'. As we saw in Chapter 2, it was not entirely clear what Qutb meant by that and whether he believed Muslims in Egypt in his day were unbelievers or merely ignorant. Contemporary Muslim scholars who have influenced the Jordanian Brotherhood decontest such questions by essentially dismissing the value of '*jāhiliyya*' as a politically relevant peripheral concept. Al-Qaradawi, for instance, points out that modern-day Muslim societies are not like pre-Islamic Mecca. Unlike the latter, which was 'an unbelieving, pagan society (*mujtamaʿan wathaniyyan kāfiran*)', the majority of the *umma* is 'committed (*multazima*) to Islam'. Indeed, 'many of them pray, fast, pay alms and perform the pilgrimage'.[41] As such, al-Qaradawi states that Muslims who have been affected by a 'cultural invasion' should be treated as ignorant of Islam, but not as unbelievers.[42]

Muhammad Qutb (1919–2014), Sayyid's younger brother and a well-known interpreter of his sibling's writings, decontests the concept of '*jāhiliyya*' in a similar way. He describes the term as having either of two meanings: 'ignorance of the truth of the divinity of God and its features (*al-ulūhiyya wa-khaṣāʾiṣihā*)' or 'behaviour that is not determined (*ghayr al-munḍabiṭa*) by the divine norms (*bi-l-ḍawābiṭ al-rabbāniyya*), meaning, in other words: not following what God has revealed'.[43] Muhammad Qutb claims that the former meaning is the technical interpretation of the term '*jāhiliyya*' and the correct one.[44] The term '*ulūhiyya*' is often used to refer to the idea that only God may be worshipped and that, as a consequence, non-Islamic laws – equated here with false gods on the basis of Q. 9:31[45] – must be rejected and only Islamic laws may be followed,[46] a reasoning also

[39] Al-Qaraḍāwī, *Fiqh*, 35. [40] See also Rutherford, *Egypt*, 110–11.

[41] Yūsuf al-Qaraḍāwī, *Al-Ijtihād fī l-Sharīʿa al-Islāmiyya maʿa Naẓarāt Taḥlīliyya fī l-Ijtihād al-Muʿāṣir* (Cairo: Dār al-Qalam li-l-Nashr wa-l-Tawzīʿ, 2011), 260–1.

[42] Ibid., 262.

[43] Muḥammad Quṭb, *Ruʾya Islāmiyya li-Aḥwāl al-ʿĀlam al-Muʿāṣir* (Riyadh: Dār al-Waṭan li-l-Nashr, 1991), 15.

[44] Ibid., 17.

[45] This verse says, in part, 'They have taken their rabbis and their monks as lords (*arbāban*) apart from God.'

[46] See, for example, Joas Wagemakers, 'An Inquiry into Ignorance: A Jihādī-Salafī Debate on *Jahl* as an Obstacle to *Takfīr*', in *The Transmission and Dynamics of the Textual Sources of*

adopted by Sayyid Qutb himself.[47] Like al-Qaradawi, however, Muhammad Qutb de-radicalises this reasoning and deals with the concept of '*jāhiliyya*' virtually only with regard to the West[48] and its roots, which can supposedly be found mostly in Greek-Roman civilisation.[49]

The same de-radicalised decontestation takes place with regard to another peripheral concept strongly associated with Qutb (and Mawdudi): '*ḥākimiyya*'.[50] While both Mawdudi and Qutb treat it as indicating the absolute sovereignty of God as expressed in the full adoption of Islamic law, as we saw in Chapter 2, al-Qaradawi clearly makes the concept less controversial by claiming that it was not invented by both earlier scholars, but actually has roots in Islamic rule (*al-ḥukm al-sharʿī*) and is even hinted at in the Qurʾan, such as in various verses in Q. 6.[51] Moreover, al-Qaradawi claims that '*ḥākimiyya*' does not mean that all decisions are left to God and that people are precluded from legislating altogether.[52] It also does not mean, he states, that God appoints scholars or leaders who rule in his name. On the contrary, the *umma* is the source of 'the basis of political power (*sanad al-sulṭa al-siyāsiyya*). It is the one that chooses its rulers. It is the one that holds them accountable (*tuḥāsibuhum*) and that supervises them (*turāqibuhum*), even deposes them (*taʿziluhum*).'[53]

So the scholars influential to the Jordanian Brotherhood clearly make use of the classical tradition as well as early Egyptian Brothers' writings in their work on the Islamic state, but also build on them to give new meaning to those earlier writings. The latter is most evident from their attempt to propagate the idea of an Islamic state as a civil state (*dawla madaniyya*), which is clearly a step further than merely an Islamic state. The term 'civil state' is found in the writings of al-Ghannushi, for example, who presents this type of state as a golden mean between a secular state extolled by the people who build on ʿAbd al-Raziq's work, on the one hand, and a theocratic state as found in Shiite Iran nowadays, on the other.[54] Similarly, al-Qaradawi distinguishes the Islamic civil state from mediaeval Christian theocracy in the Roman Catholic Church as well as secularism.[55] Thus, al-Ghannushi writes, a civil state in Islam does not differ from modern democracies. The latter – as well as other states – 'are based on philosophical or moral foundations (*usus falsafiyya wa-qīmiyya*)

Islam: Essays in Honour of Harald Motzki, ed. Nicolet Boekhoff-van der Voort, Kees Versteegh and Joas Wagemakers (Leiden: Brill, 2011), 317, 320–2.

47 Quṭb, *Maʿālim*, 88–93. 48 Quṭb, *Ruʾya*, 18–21. 49 Ibid., 22–52.

50 For more on the usage of 'sovereignty' in Islamist thinking, see Andrew F. March, 'Genealogies of Sovereignty in Islamic Political Theology', *Social Research* 80, no. 1 (2013): 293–320.

51 Al-Qaraḍāwī, *Al-Siyāsa*, 18–19. 52 Al-Qaraḍāwī, *Fiqh*, 64. 53 Ibid., 62.

54 Al-Ghannūshī, *Al-Dīmuqrāṭiyya*, 11–13. 55 Al-Qaraḍāwī, *Fiqh*, 57–9.

that represent the greatest directions of their policies'. The same applies to an Islamic civil state, except for 'its divine moral authority (*marjaʿiyyatihā al-khulqiyya al-ʿulwiyya*), the authority of the *sharīʿa*'.[56]

The civil state with an Islamic authority thus seems to differ from the Islamic state propagated by the early Brotherhood leaders in the sense that the latter adopts the *rulings* of the *sharīʿa* as its entire legal system, deciding its every law, while the former merely treats the *sharīʿa* as a constitution: a broad set of *principles* that guide the legislative process. Individual laws, however, are decided upon by the people, not a group of religious scholars. This is also how the Egyptian Brotherhood seems to have adopted the idea of a civil state with an Islamic authority over the past decades and it has even made its way into the organisation's electoral manifestos.[57] Some have argued that this development brings the Brotherhood's ideology more in line with democracy and succeeds in integrating the latter with a state ruled by the *sharīʿa*.[58]

The fundamental contradiction between the supposed will of God – as expressed in the *sharīʿa* – and the will of the *umma*, which was discussed in Chapter 1, rears its head again here. If one assumes that Muslims will not choose anything that goes against the *sharīʿa*, as some early Islamist scholars – particularly Mawdudi – seemed to think (as we saw in Chapter 2), then this is not a problem. In reality, however, it is likely that Muslims will not always side with Islamic law in every instance. In such a case, which of the two prevails: the *sharīʿa* or the *umma*? The idea of a civil state seems to have solved this issue if the *sharīʿa* is reduced to a set of broad principles that everyone can agree on and that – crucially – can be changed by the *umma* if need be. Some scholars, however, question whether the civil state with an Islamic authority actually achieves this goal[59] or suggest that the *sharīʿa* may, in fact, still be quite intrusive in people's lives in such a state.[60]

Although they are not among the Muslim scholars mentioned to me as having influenced the Jordanian Brotherhood, some Islamist thinkers have tried to bring clarity to this issue by taking the idea of a civil state even further. The Egyptian Muhammad ʿImara (1931–2020), for example, similarly argues for a civil state[61] and also favourably compares this to a mediaeval Christian or modern-day Shiite theocracy.[62] Yet ʿImara,

[56] Al-Ghannūshī, *Al-Dīmuqrāṭiyya*, 14.
[57] Mohamed Fayez Farahat, 'Liberalizing the Muslim Brotherhood: Can It be Done?', *Arab Insight* 2, no. 6 (2009): 14–15.
[58] Harnisch and Mecham, 'Democratic Ideology'. [59] Rutherford, *Egypt*, 121–8.
[60] Moataz El Fegiery, *Tyranny of the Majority? Islamists' Ambivalence about Human Rights* (Madrid: Fride, 2012), 4–7; Tadros, *Muslim Brotherhood*, 47–57.
[61] ʿImāra, *Al-Islām*, 10. [62] Ibid., 22–8.

probably building on ʿAbd al-Raziq's work, argues in favour of such a state in the context of a separation of religion from politics[63] – which scholars like al-Ghannushi and al-Qaradawi are against – and, as such, also rejects the idea that the concept of '*ḥākimiyya*' has anything to do with governance,[64] again diverging from several early and contemporary Brotherhood scholars. Another thinker, the Saudi ʿAbdallah al-Maliki, does not go quite so far, but does address the likely clash between the *sharīʿa* and the will of the *umma* head on by explicitly privileging the latter over the former, because he believes that imposing the *sharīʿa* against the will of the people amounts to or will inevitably lead to tyranny.[65]

While the global Islamist scholars who have influenced the Jordanian Brotherhood do not take their views this far, they clearly go further than their predecessors in the organisation. Like them, they stress the adjacent concept of '*sharīʿa*', but decontest this differently by decoupling it from Qutb's peripheral concept of '*ḥākimiyya*'. As such, the *sharīʿa* becomes less a system of rulings that pervades everything than a collection of principles. (We will return to this matter in more detail in Chapter 6.) The same applies to the adjacent concept of '*umma*', which Brotherhood-inspiring global Islamist scholars decouple from Qutb's peripheral concept of '*jāhiliyya*'. As such, their decontestation of '*umma*' yields a community that can look to its ruler as its servant, rather than its master. This, in turn (and unlike al-Hudaybi), decontests the adjacent concept of '*sulṭa*' as necessary, but balanced with a more flexible conception of '*sharīʿa*' and an expanded mandate for '*umma*', resulting in an Islamic state that is civil in nature and in which its three adjacent concepts are ordered so that they tend towards being '*umma*-centred'.

The Jordanian Muslim Brotherhood on the Islamic State

Apart from actual calls for re-establishing the caliphate, as supported by groups such as the Islamic State and Hizb al-Tahrir, Islamist scholars thus present three different types of ruling systems: (1) a practical application of the caliphate's rules in the framework of a modern state, which Abu Faris seems to support; (2) an Islamic state characterised by the application of the *sharīʿa* (the option presented by some early Muslim Brothers in Egypt); and (3) a civil state that has the *sharīʿa* as its authority and gives the *umma* a certain amount of space to decide about individual laws, which the contemporary Islamist scholars mentioned above

[63] Ibid., 89–96. [64] Ibid., 36–88.
[65] ʿAbdallāh al-Mālikī, *Siyādat al-Umma qabla Taṭbīq al-Sharīʿa: Naḥwa Faḍāʾ Amthal li-Tajsīd Mabādiʾ al-Islām* (Beirut: Al-Shabaka al-ʿArabiyya li-l-Abḥāth wa-l-Nashr, 2012), especially 168–71.

support. The Jordanian Muslim Brotherhood's position in all of this has moved increasingly from an explicitly Islamic state to a civil state with an Islamic authority.

The Jordanian Brotherhood's general position on Islamic statehood (in a broad sense) is based on the idea of establishing justice (*ʿadl* or *ʿadāla*), which is considered an Islamic duty.[66] This means that people must be treated justly, 'irrespective of their languages (*lughātihim*), homelands (*awṭānihim*) or social circumstances (*aḥwālihim al-ijtimāʿiyya*)'.[67] This justice ensures, among other things, stability, flourishing societies and security and, as such, people are said to be just as dependent on justice as they are on rain.[68] This justice should also be the guiding light for rulers, as it allegedly was for rulers mentioned in the Qurʾan, like Dawud and Sulayman.[69] For this reason, rulers should take the general interests of the *umma* into account.[70] These interests and, indeed, justice in general are expressed most concretely in the form of the rule of Islam through the *sharīʿa*.[71]

The rule of Islam is thus of crucial importance to the Jordanian Muslim Brotherhood. As one scholar points out, the Muslim Brotherhood in Jordan 'operates in all its steps (*khaṭawātihim*), its hopes (*āmālihim*) and its actions (*aʿmālihim*) on [the basis of] the right guidance (*hudá*) of true Islam (*al-Islām al-ḥanīf*) as they have understood it'.[72] Another points out that the Jordanian Brotherhood strives for 'the application of the Islamic *sharīʿa* in all areas of political, educational, economic and social life' and 'preaching Islam to the people in the context of the sound understanding (*al-fahm al-ṣaḥīḥ*)'.[73] Although these statements are probably exaggerated, since the Muslim Brotherhood is often also led by pragmatic – rather than ideological – considerations, they do concur with the image the organisation wanted to convey at times.

That the importance of Islam should also be translated to the political sphere and government is clear from the Brotherhood's own general discourse. 'The Islam that the Muslim Brotherhood believes in', one scholar states, 'makes government into a pillar [of their ideology]'. As a result, the Brotherhood considers '[Islamic] rule (*al-ḥukm*) to be among the creeds and foundations (*ʿaqāʾid wa-uṣūl*), not among the issues of jurisprudence and branches (*fiqhiyyāt wa-furūʿ*)'.[74] It is therefore not surprising that when the organisation formulated its principles in 1954,

66 Abū Fāris, *Al-Niẓām*, 46–50. 67 Ibid., 51. 68 Ibid., 54–5.
69 Kāẓim ʿĀyish, 'Al-ʿAdl Asās al-Mulk', *Al-Sabīl*, 19 February 2013, 15.
70 Abū Fāris, *Al-Fiqh*, 45. 71 Abū Fāris, *Al-Niẓām*, 50–1.
72 Al-Budūr, *Al-Tajriba*, 23. 73 Gharāyiba, *Jamāʿat*, 33.
74 Al-Budūr, *Al-Tajriba*, 24. The terms '*uṣūl*' and '*furūʿ*' are also used in Islamic jurisprudence (*fiqh*), referring to the foundations of Islamic law and the applied results of these, respectively.

it stated that 'the Muslim Brotherhood rejects any system that is not founded on the basis of Islam (*asās al-Islām*)' and 'will not support any ruler (*ḥākim*) until he applies the *sharīʿa* of God on earth'.[75]

Such a statement may suggest that the Muslim Brotherhood did not support the ruling system in Jordan, whose king did not apply the *sharīʿa*, after all.[76] Moreover, the words 'on earth' suggest that the Jordanian Brotherhood may have had ambitions far beyond the borders of the kingdom and dreamed of a resurrected caliphate. Furthermore, we cannot simply dismiss the call for the application of Islamic law as something the Brotherhood may have wanted in the 1950s but has abandoned since then, as the organisation still values this greatly and sees it as an important demand.[77] In the 1990s, for example, during the government of Prime Minister Mudar Badran, in which the organisation took part, 'the Muslim Brotherhood had the basic demand of the application of the Islamic *sharīʿa* and this demand still stands'.[78]

As we saw in Chapter 3, however, the Brotherhood has shown itself to be quite pragmatic in the sense that it was willing to work with a regime that served its interests. This is also reflected in the way it calls for the application of the *sharīʿa*,[79] which is no longer presented by the organisation as the litmus test for the legitimacy of a state. The phrasing of the wish to apply the *sharīʿa*, in other words, has been adjusted throughout the years.[80] The most recent example of this is the IAF's Basic Law, published in 2018, which lists 'striving for the application of the Islamic *sharīʿa* in the different areas of life' as the first of its 'general goals'.[81] This reflects the importance the issue still holds for the IAF, but the statement's exact wording also shows that the organisation has toned down its rhetoric, no longer (explicitly) accepts or rejects a ruler on this basis and limits its ambitions in this regard to merely 'striving'. The question remains, however, in what governmental form the *sharīʿa* should ideally be applied.

Abu Faris, precisely because he seems to support the application of the caliphate's rules in the framework of a modern state, writes in some detail about what such a state should be like. He claims that a state is based on three pillars (the people (*al-shaʿb*), the territory (*al-iqlīm*) it occupies and the ruling power (*al-sulṭa al-ḥākima*))[82] and analyses how this came into

[75] Abū Fāris, *Ṣafaḥāt*, 11; al-ʿUbaydī, *Jamāʿat*, 150.
[76] Boulby, *Muslim Brotherhood*, 54.
[77] The Brotherhood's communiqués from the 1980s, for instance, regularly mention the application of the *sharīʿa* as an important goal. See Muḥammad al-Ḥasan, *Al-Ikhwān al-Muslimūn fī Suṭūr* (Amman: Dār al-Furqān li-l-Nashr wa-l-Tawzīʿ, 1990), 81, 87–91, 100, 169.
[78] Al-ʿUmūsh, *Maḥaṭṭāt*, 137.
[79] Boulby, *Muslim Brotherhood*, 54–5.
[80] Hamid, *Temptations*, 131–3.
[81] Ḥizb Jabhat al-ʿAmal al-Islāmī, *Al-Niẓām*, 4.
[82] Abū Fāris, *Al-Niẓām*, 131–2.

existence in the history of Islam.[83] In distinguishing an Islamic state from a non-Islamic one, Abu Faris paraphrases al-Banna's three principles, which we also saw in Chapter 2, claiming that an Islamic state is characterised by '(1) the responsibility of the ruler [as divided] between God and the people; (2) the unity of the Islamic *umma* on the basis of the Islamic creed; and (3) the respect for the will of the *umma* [. . .]'. He adds that 'if these principles are fulfilled in any state, then it is an Islamic state'.[84]

Again paraphrasing al-Banna, Abu Faris explains that an Islamic state should have an Islamic government, which is responsible for the actual application of the *sharīʿa*. In fact, he claims that 'Islam is not realised (*al-Islām lā yataḥaqqaqu*) the way God wants unless a government is set up that applies its rulings (*aḥkāmahu*) in all political, economic, legal, international and other matters of life'.[85] He cites the duties of an Islamic state that al-Banna listed, placing 'the execution of the Islamic law (*infādh al-qānūn al-Islāmī*)' at the top.[86] Although, as we saw above, Abu Faris is not representative of the entire Jordanian Brotherhood, his general ideas about an Islamic state as described here probably do represent a significant part of the organisation. Differences do not really start to appear until we focus on the Jordanian Brotherhood's views on the Islamic state in more detail.

Given the strong influence the early Egyptian Muslim Brotherhood thinkers have had on him, it is not surprising that – unlike al-Qaradawi and Muhammad Qutb – Abu Faris makes extensive use of Sayyid Qutb's peripheral concept of '*jāhiliyya*' and does not appear to tone down its implications. References to this concept can be found in multiple places in his publications, but most explicitly in a book he published on Islamic concepts (*mafāhīm Islāmiyya*). There he defines '*jāhiliyya*' as:

> any psychological position (*kull waḍʿ nafsī*) that rejects the right guidance through the direction of Islam (*ihtidāʾ bi-hady al-Islām*), rejects the appeal to God's *sharīʿa* (*al-taḥākum ilá sharʿ Allāh*); any organisational position (*kull waḍʿ tanẓīmī*) that rejects the sovereignty of God (*ḥākimiyyat Allāh*) for humanity and claims sovereignty for humanity apart from God and thus rejects the judgement by what God has sent down (*al-ḥukm bi-mā anzala llāh*); any position that presents itself (*yatamaththalu*) in deviance from the method of God (*inḥirāf min manhaj Allāh*); and any behaviour (*sulūk*) that contradicts a judgement of the Islamic *sharīʿa*.[87]

Unlike Muhammad Qutb, who would most likely have agreed with this definition but downplayed its political significance for the Muslim world,

[83] Ibid., 132–51. [84] Abū Fāris, *Al-Fiqh*, 51. [85] Ibid., 32. [86] Ibid., 33.
[87] Abū Fāris, *Mafāhīm Islāmiyya* (Amman: Dār al-Furqān li-l-Nashr wa-l-Tawzīʿ, 1994), 14.

Abu Faris states explicitly that this *jāhiliyya* is unbelief (*kufr*). Although he suggests that this should not be applied to individuals, he does seem to apply it to regimes, thereby underlining his rejection of 'un-Islamic' states.[88] This interpretation, though – again – not representative of the Jordanian Brotherhood as a whole, generally squares with the early views of the organisation about the application of the *sharīʿa* in the kingdom, as we saw above.[89]

Abu Faris further shows Qutb's influence on his work by making extensive use of the latter's peripheral concept of '*ḥākimiyya*'. Echoing the words of ʿAwda we saw in Chapter 2, Abu Faris writes that God has created the world and, as earth's owner, can do with it as he pleases. The system of laws God set up as part of creation must be followed by human beings. To refuse to do so would be to deny God his sovereignty over laws and, by extension, his ownership of creation.[90] Abu Faris therefore sees the application of Islamic laws as essential, precisely because it extends the *ḥākimiyya* of God to legislative issues, which was exactly what the prophets taught people, he claims.[91] Citing both ʿAwda and Qutb, Abu Faris writes that the Islamic *shahāda*, with its emphasis on *tawḥīd*, constitutes an affirmation of God's *ḥākimiyya* and a rejection of non-Islamic laws and means that anyone who does apply the latter – including regimes – is guilty of *kufr*.[92]

This radical interpretation of Qutb's work was at least partly rejected by other authors within the Jordanian Muslim Brotherhood. While many simply do not talk or write in terms of '*jāhiliyya*' or '*ḥākimiyya*',[93] one example of someone who does is the aforementioned Yusuf al-ʿAzm. The latter wrote a book about Qutb in which he is somewhat critical of him and – in line with al-Qaradawi – distinguishes between the concept of '*jāhiliyya*' and unbelief, particularly when applied to entire societies.[94] Another Jordanian Muslim Brother and major scholar of Qutb's work, Salah al-Khalidi, has similarly tried to reinterpret some of Qutb's

88 Ibid., 17. See also Muḥammad ʿAbd al-Qādir Abū Fāris, 'Yā Ḥukkām al-Muslimīn Urūnā Islāmakum al-Muʿtadil', *Al-Sabīl*, 3 September 2014, 9.

89 Interestingly, Ḥamīda Quṭb (1937–2012), Sayyid's younger sister, published an article in the Jordanian Muslim Brotherhood's weekly *Al-Kifāḥ al-Islāmī* in which she also used the term '*jāhiliyya*'. See Ḥamīda Quṭb, 'Dawr al-Ukht al-Muslima fī Nahḍat al-Islām al-Ḥadītha', *Al-Kifāḥ al-Islāmī*, 9 August 1954, 14.

90 Abū Fāris, *Al-Niẓām*, 17–21. 91 Ibid., 27. 92 Ibid., 28–34.

93 For an exception, see, for instance, Niḍāl al-Shiṭrāt, 'Siyādat al-Sharīʿa al-Islāmiyya Tuḥarriru l-Insān min Ḥukm al-Fard wa-l-Ghūghāʾiyya wa-l-Mizājiyya', *Al-Sabīl*, 17–23 March 1998, 14.

94 Yūsuf al-ʿAẓm, *Rāʾid al-Fikr al-Islāmī al-Muʿāṣir: Al-Shahīd Sayyid Quṭb, Ḥayātuhu wa-Madrasatuhu wa-Āthāruhu* (Beirut: Dār al-Qalam, 1980), 285–99. See also Gilles Kepel, *Muslim Extremism in Egypt: The Prophet and the Pharaoh*, trans. John Rothschild (Berkeley, CA, and Los Angeles: University of California Press, 2003 [1984]), 65–7.

more controversial positions in several books,[95] as has the previous leader of the Jordanian Brotherhood Hammam Sa'id, who views Qutb's use of '*jāhiliyya*' as referring to Muslims' shortcomings, rather than their supposed unbelief.[96] As such, most Jordanian Brothers either ignore Qutb's peripheral concepts altogether or dismiss them as politically irrelevant.

As a result, the type of state the Jordanian Muslim Brothers advocate ranges from the caliphate in the framework of a modern state (Abu Faris) to calls for an Islamic state. The idea of the latter, in which the *sharī'a* dominates, has traditionally been prevalent in Brotherhood discourse, with articles appearing in their periodicals advocating this system in the 1950s[97] and continuing to do so as late as the 1990s.[98] In fact, this position was also advocated more recently by the organisation's last real General Controller (i.e. before the regime allowed the founding of a new Muslim Brotherhood), Hammam Sa'id,[99] and is supported by other Brotherhood members like al-Khalidi, as well.[100]

From the 1990s on, however, new ideas of a civil state with an Islamic authority began to seep into the Jordanian Brotherhood's discourse, based on the writings of the contemporary global Islamist scholars discussed above.[101] Articles began appearing in the Jordanian Islamist press expressing a rejection of theocracy[102] or – with reference to

[95] See, for example, Ṣalāḥ 'Abd al-Fattāḥ al-Khālidī, introduction to *Ma'ālim fī l-Ṭarīq: Dirāsa wa-Taḥqīq*, ed. Ṣalāḥ 'Abd al-Fattāḥ al-Khālidī (Amman: Dār 'Ammār li-l-Nashr wa-l-Tawzī', 2009), 5–18.

[96] Interview with Hammām Sa'īd, Amman, 28 January 2013. As mentioned previously, the reception of Sayyid Quṭb's work among Jordanian Brothers is a major subject that deserves a separate publication and cannot be dealt with in detail here.

[97] See, for example, the articles by Muḥammad Asad (Leopold Weiss), 'Limādhā Nurīdu l-Dawla al-Islāmiyya?!', *Al-Kifāḥ al-Islāmī*, 29 March 1957, 9; Muḥammad Asad (Leopold Weiss), 'Limādhā Lā Nurīdu Dawla 'Almāniyya?', *Al-Kifāḥ al-Islāmī*, 5 April 1957, 4; Muḥammad Asad (Leopold Weiss), 'Limādhā Nurīdu l-Dawla al-Islāmiyya?!', *Al-Kifāḥ al-Islāmī*, 22 April 1957, 4.

[98] 'Al-Ḥukūma al-Muslima', *Al-Sabīl*, 17–23 October 1995, 3; Ibrāhīm Gharāyiba, 'Naḥwa Ru'ya Istrātījiyya li-l-'Amal al-Islāmī', *Al-Sabīl*, 2–9 November 1993, 15.

[99] Sayf al-Dīn Bākīr, 'Hammām Sa'id: Al-Umma 'alá Abwāb Qiyām Dawlat al-Islām', *Al-Sabīl*, 18 April 2013, 5.

[100] Interview with Ṣalāḥ al-Khālidī, Amman, 24 January 2013.

[101] For more on the Jordanian context in which discussions on a civil state came about, see Muḥammad Abū Rummān and Nifīn Bunduqjī, *Min al-Khilāfa al-Islamiyya ilá l-Dawla al-Madaniyya* (Amman: Friedrich Ebert Stiftung, 2018), 115–19.

[102] Īnās al-Khālidī, 'Mafhūm al-Sharī'a al-Islāmiyya fī l-Dustūr al-Urdunnī wa-l-Mīthāq al-Waṭanī', *Al-Sabīl*, 12–18 July 1994, 21. For a theoretically rich reflection on theocracy in the policy of the Jordanian Brotherhood, see Anne Sofie Roald, 'From Theocracy to Democracy? Towards Secularisation and Individualisation in the Policy of the Muslim Brotherhood in Jordan', *Journal of Arabic and Islamic Studies* 8, no. 7 (2008): 84–107.

al-Qaradawi – advocating an Islamic democracy in a civil state.[103] In line with contemporary global Islamist scholars and the Egyptian Muslim Brotherhood, this idea seems to have gained wide acceptance in the Jordanian organisation. The former Deputy General Controller Zaki Bani Irshid, for example, has expressed his support for a civil state with an Islamic authority on multiple occasions[104] and other prominent members of the organisation clearly agree.[105] This is not to say that there is consensus on this issue, however. There is still discussion on the civil state within the Jordanian Brotherhood,[106] but the trend seems dominant now,[107] especially among young members.[108]

The most prominent Muslim Brother in Jordan behind the idea of a civil state is Ruhayyil Gharayiba, who, together with Abu Faris, is also one of the few independent-minded and major Islamist scholars in the kingdom. Gharayiba claims that he has propagated this idea since 1995, when he presented the concept in his dissertation on the subject and also points out that the Egyptian and Syrian Muslim Brotherhoods have adopted similar positions.[109] Like global Islamist scholars before him, Gharayiba points out that there is no such thing as a clerical state in Islam as there was in the mediaeval Roman Catholic Church.[110] While he does not deny the importance of taking the time and period in which Muslims

103 Aḥmad Ḥamīḍ, 'Al-Dīmuqrāṭiyya al-Islāmiyya … Iʿādat al-Naẓar', *Al-Sabīl*, 26 April–5 May 1994, 15.

104 'Zakī Banī Irshīd: Nuʾakkidu l-Dawla al-Madaniyya bi-l-Urdunn', *Al-Būṣala* (http://albosa.la/TVRReU5EUXcrdQ==, accessed 7 September 2016), 6 September 2016; Hadīl Ghabbūn, 'Banī Irshīd: Naḥriṣu ʿalá Tajannub al-Ṣaddām maʿa l-ʿAlmāniyyīn', *Al-Ghad* (http://alghad.com/articles/1194122, accessed 18 October 2016), 18 October 2016; Rabá Karāsina, 'Banī Irshīd: Al-Sulṭa fī l-Dawla al-Islāmiyya Kamā Hiya fī l-Madaniyya', *Al-Būṣala* (http://albosa.la/TVRRM09UUTErdQ==, accessed 22 November 2016), 22 November 2016.

105 Interviews with Ruḥayyil Gharāyiba, Amman, 17 January 2013; ʿĀṭif al-Jawlānī, Amman, 14 June 2012; Ḥamza Manṣūr, Amman, 25 June 2012.

106 Hadīl Ghabbūn, 'Ijtimāʿ Qarīb li-Shūrá "al-ʿAmal al-Islāmī" wa-Tawajjuh li-Iʿādat Haykala Taṭwīriyya', *Al-Ghad* (http://alghad.com/articles/1179772, accessed 11 October 2016), 11 October 2016; Hadīl Ghabbūn, 'Al-ʿAzzām: Uṭrūḥāt "al-Dawla al-Madaniyya" Ijtihādāt Fardiyya', *Al-Ghad* (http://alghad.com/articles/1211612, accessed 26 October 2016), 26 October 2016; ʿAdnān ʿAlī Riḍā al-Naḥwī, 'Dawla Dīniyya am Madaniyya?', *Al-Sabīl*, 6 April 2011, 17. See also Abū Rummān and Bunduqjī, *Min al-Khilāfa*, 119–25.

107 Abū Fāris expressed his opposition to the concept of a civil state. Interview with Muḥammad Abū Fāris, Amman, 21 January 2013.

108 Abū Rummān and Bunduqjī, *Min al-Khilāfa*, 139–64.

109 Ruḥayyil Muḥammad Gharāyiba, 'Al-Islāmiyyūn wa-l-Dawla al-Madaniyya', *Al-Dustūr*, 11 November 2013, 20.

110 Ruḥayyil Muḥammad Gharāyiba, 'Lā Dawla Dīniyya fī l-Islām', *Al-Dustūr*, 1 November 2013, 16.

live into account,[111] he claims that a civil state is not just a solution to problems people have in the here and now, but also the 'original principle' (*mabda' aṣīl*) of statehood in Islam. This includes civil leadership, equal citizenship for all and 'the strengthening of the power of the people (*sulṭat al-sha'b*) in choosing the leader and holding him accountable (*ikhtiyār al-ḥākim wa-murāqabatihi*)', which he traces to early Islam.[112]

As we saw in Chapter 1, such elements can, indeed, be seen in early Islam, which – together with the early Muslim Brotherhood – remains an important source of inspiration for the organisation's members in Jordan today. Whereas Abu Faris clearly decontests both '*sharī'a*' and '*umma*' in line with 'Awda and Qutb, advocating an Islamic state on the basis of the rules of the caliphate, Gharayiba does so in a way that seems to view early Islamic rulers and early Brotherhood thinkers through the prism of contemporary Islamist scholars, resulting in a civil state with an Islamic authority. The next section deals with how all these ideas were put in practice in the Jordanian political context.

The Jordanian State

In dealing with how the various views espoused by the Jordanian Muslim Brotherhood about the state were applied in the kingdom, it is important to bear in mind what the *sharī'a* represents to the organisation and why its application is called for in the first place. While people in Western liberal democracies – perhaps having heard stories of beheadings and whippings supposedly based on Islamic law – may often think of the *sharī'a* as a source of oppression, this is not the case for the Jordanian Brotherhood. In line with classical scholars and the early Egyptian Brothers, they see the *sharī'a* not only as a guide for Muslim rulers, but also as a check on excessive power. As such, Jordanian Muslim Brothers do not see the *sharī'a* as a source of oppression, but as a source of divine liberation *from* oppression.

One may expect this attitude from the likes of Gharayiba, with his emphasis on citizens' right to choose their own ruler, but this is also found in Abu Faris's work, who dedicates one of his books to 'every *umma* that seeks to realise itself through its practice of its freedom

[111] Bassām Nāṣir, 'Dr. Irḥayyil [*sic*] Gharāyiba: Al-Dawla fī l-Fiqh al-Siyāsī al-Sunnī Laysat Ḥukūma Dīniyya bi-l-Mafhūm al-Gharbī wa-Innamā Dawla Madaniyya bi-Marja'iyya Islāmiyya', *Al-Sabīl*, 31 July 2009, 6.

[112] Ruḥayyil Muḥammad Gharāyiba, 'Madaniyyat al-Dawla fī l-Islām Mabda' Aṣīl', *Al-Dustūr*, 23 October 2016, 20. See also Nasīm 'Unayzāt, 'Al-Gharāyiba [*sic*]: "Al-Dawla" fī l-Islām "Madaniyya" Taqūmu 'alá Asās al-Muwāṭana wa-stī'āb Jamī' al-Afkār wa-l-Adyān', *Al-Dustūr*, 19 March 2013, 3.

(*mumārisatihā ḥurriyyatihā*) [. . .] and every official in Muslim countries who desires the respect of the will of the *umma* (*iḥtirām irādat al-umma*)'.[113] From the perspective of Abu Faris, who has spent much of his life living under oppressive rule and who has experienced first hand that even implicit support for certain positions can land you in prison in such a situation, the godly *sharīʿa* is precisely what frees people from man-made state repression and the whims of human dictators.

This section shows how such views on Islamic statehood have been translated into practice by the Jordanian Muslim Brotherhood, but also how they intersect with much less Islamically inspired ideas on the Jordanian regime and its king. This is where Islamist ideology takes a back seat and differences (and, perhaps, also tensions) between Jordanians of Palestinian descent and so-called East Jordanians come to light. As such, this section makes clear that it is not just ideological considerations shaped by the political context that decide the Jordanian Muslim Brothers' views on the kingdom and its regime, but also their national backgrounds.

Brotherhood Views of the Regime

Given the fact that the early Jordanian Brotherhood's stated point of view was not to accept regimes unless they applied the *sharīʿa*, at least some Brothers could be expected to be reluctant to accept the legitimacy of the regime in the Hashimite Kingdom. This was, indeed, the case. Abu Faris was among those sceptical of the regime. In one of his works, he states that 'the regimes that refuse the *sharīʿa* (*al-anẓima al-rāfiḍa li-sharʿ Allāh*) and are hostile to it and its supporters (*wa-l-muʿādiya lahu wa-li-awliyāʾihi*) are *jāhilī* regimes that one may not be loyal to'.[114] He also emphasises that this is a 'strategic difference' between the Brotherhood and regimes, 'not a tactical difference'.[115]

Abu Faris was perhaps the most prominent exponent of this point of view in the Jordanian Muslim Brotherhood, but not the only one. Bassam al-ʿUmush, a former member of the organisation who is strongly pro-regime, states that especially young Brothers 'talk about the king under the heading of the *ṭawāghīt* (idols)'.[116] The latter term, used by Qutb and others to refer to leaders who do not apply the *sharīʿa*, is a clear indication

[113] Muḥammad ʿAbd al-Qādir Abū Fāris, *Ḥukm al-Shūrá fī l-Islām wa-Natījatuhā* (Amman: Dār al-Furqān li-l-Nashr wa-l-Tawzīʿ, 1988), 7. This sentiment also strongly echoes the tone found in Quṭb's writings, as we saw in Chapter 2, but more generally in Quṭb, *Maʿālim*.

[114] Abū Fāris, *Ṣafaḥāt*, 14. [115] Ibid., 15. [116] Al-ʿUmūsh, *Maḥaṭṭāt*, 58.

of fundamental ideological disapproval.[117] One can imagine that such radical views on the Jordanian regime are not stated in public,[118] but al-ʿUmush names former General Controller Hammam Saʿid, long-time member ʿAli al-ʿUtum and Muhammad Abu Faris as exponents of a line of thinking that rejects the legitimacy of the Jordanian regime.[119]

Yet none of the people mentioned above actually advocates violence against the state or even the peaceful overthrow of the regime. In fact, as we saw in Chapter 3, the Muslim Brotherhood has been quite pragmatic in its dealings with the regime. Several (former) Brothers openly acknowledge that it was not so much their love for the regime that caused them to cooperate with it, but the interests they shared.[120] Even in the 1950s, the Brotherhood published its approval of the regime's policies if they agreed with them.[121] Abu Faris himself – in an implicit recognition of the regime – represented the IAF in parliament, although he later wrote that such things 'do not mean recognition of this regime (*lā yaʿnī l-iʿtirāf bi-hādhā l-niẓām*) and giving loyalty to it (*iʿṭāʾ al-walāʾ lahu*) if a regime does not apply Islam (*in kāna niẓāman lā yuṭabbiqu l-Islām*)'.[122] This means, in other words, that even the staunchest opponents of the Jordanian regime within the kingdom's Brotherhood are pragmatic in dealing with the state in practice.[123]

The same pragmatism is also displayed when we look at the justification of the Brotherhood's support for some of the major foreign policy decisions King Husayn took during his reign, which we saw in Chapter 3. Sometimes these decisions were simply in line with the Brotherhood's own, strongly anti-colonial or anti-Israel discourse. The Baghdad Pact of 1955, for example, was dismissed by Abu Faris as 'an imperialist pact'[124] and headlines in the Brotherhood weekly *Al-Kifah al-Islami* in the 1950s included: 'No imperialism, no communism and no regionalism (*lā istiʿmār wa-lā shuyūʿiyya wa-lā iqlīmiyya*). Instead [we want] a pious

117 See, for example, Quṭb, *Maʿālim*, 76.

118 This was also Abū Fāris's point of view. While he acknowledged and agreed with the literal and political interpretation of Q. 5:44, he was circumspect in whether or not this was applicable to the Jordanian king. The same applied to al-Khālidī. Interviews with Muḥammad Abū Fāris, Amman, 21 January 2013; Ṣalāḥ al-Khālidī, Amman, 24 January 2013.

119 Al-ʿUmūsh, *Maḥaṭṭāt*, 58–9.

120 Interviews with Ziyād Abū Ghanīma, Amman, 26 June 2012; Sālim al-Falāḥāt, Amman, 22 January 2013; ʿAwnī al-ʿUbaydī, Amman, 11 January 2014.

121 'Al-Shaʿb Yuʾayyidu l-Ḥusayn fī Nidāʾihi l-Tārīkhī', *Al-Kifāḥ al-Islāmī*, 8 February 1957, 2.

122 Abū Fāris, *Ṣafaḥāt*, 14.

123 Abū Fāris also confirmed this in my interview with him, as did al-Khālidī. Interviews with Muḥammad Abū Fāris, Amman, 21 January 2013; Ṣalāḥ al-Khālidī, Amman, 24 January 2013.

124 Abū Fāris, *Ṣafaḥāt*, 29.

Islamic creed (*ʿaqīda Islāmiyya ṣāliḥa*) from which a regime emanates (*yanbathiqu ʿanhā niẓām*) that makes humanity happy (*yusʿidu l-bashariyya*).'[125] The Eisenhower Doctrine was similarly dismissed by the Muslim Brotherhood as a blatant attempt to support Israel or as 'the new American imperialism' that 'would be fought with the same strength (*al-quwwa*), intensity (*al-shidda*) and struggle (*al-kifāḥ*) with which we fought the Baghdad Pact'.[126] In line with this anti-imperialist thinking, the organisation also supported the Arabisation of the Jordanian army, found it 'unacceptable' that the leader of their army was the British John Bagot Glubb and was happy when King Husayn dismissed him, 'ending the foreign leadership of the army'.[127]

At other times, the Muslim Brotherhood acted more out of its own interests than because of ideals it shared with the regime. This was the case, for example, with the Nasserist coup in the country in 1957. The Brotherhood was quite aware of the socialist and secular character of Nasser's regime in Egypt and also of the way the latter had cracked down on the Egyptian Muslim Brothers. As such, the organisation knew that its interests would not be served by a like-minded regime in Amman. It was therefore not only happy about the dismissal of the pro-Nasser Jordanian government of Prime Minister Sulayman al-Nabulsi in 1957,[128] but also applauded 'the failed plot' to overthrow the regime in Amman in the same year.[129] 'The leftists', al-ʿUmush states, 'declare their enmity towards Islam (*ʿadāʾahum li-l-Islām*); they see socialism as the solution (*al-ishtirākiyya hiya l-ḥall*), while the Brotherhood sees Islam as the solution.'[130] Abu Faris, for his part, describes Egypt under Nasser as 'the Egyptian idol regime (*niẓām al-ṭāghūt al-Miṣrī*)', apparently more willing to apply this label to Egypt than to his own state.[131] He also writes that 'the Muslim Brotherhood resisted (*taṣaddá*) this [Nasserist] movement in the army, outside of it and in the street, aiming at repelling the trouble for themselves (*ʿan anfusihim*), their possessions (*amwālihim*), their honour (*aʿrāḍihim*) and their blood (*dimāʾihim*)'. 'This is why', Abu Faris adds, 'the interest of the Muslim Brotherhood in repelling the trouble for themselves coincided with the interest of the regime in defending itself'.[132] Similarly, while members of the Brotherhood

[125] Al-ʿUmūsh, *Maḥaṭṭāt*, 106. Needless to say, this headline sounds much better in Arabic than in English.
[126] Abū Fāris, *Ṣafaḥāt*, 33. [127] Al-ʿUmūsh, *Maḥaṭṭāt*, 251. [128] Aruri, *Jordan*, 163.
[129] ʻʿAlá l-Muʾāmara al-Fāshila … wa-l-Baqiyya Taʾtī', *Al-Kifāḥ al-Islāmī*, 26 April 1957, 12.
[130] Al-ʿUmūsh, *Maḥaṭṭāt*, 50. [131] Abū Fāris, *Ṣafaḥāt*, 37. [132] Ibid., 39.

regretted the bloodshed between Muslims during Black September in 1970,[133] there was also understanding for the regime's actions.[134] The organisation's difficult decision to stay neutral (and thereby implicitly support the stronger side (the regime)) during this conflict was taken because the Brotherhood viewed the restoration of peace and quiet in Jordan as part of its interests.[135]

Yet it would be wrong to paint the entire Muslim Brotherhood in Jordan – as diverse as it is on the issue of the state – as guided primarily by pragmatism, suggesting mere business-like ties between the organisation and the regime. Apart from the antipathy towards leftists and Nasserism, some Brothers are also clearly more pro-regime than that. The most prominent exponent of this view is, perhaps, the aforementioned Bassam al-ʿUmush, a former Muslim Brother who left the organisation in 1997 because he disagreed with the Brotherhood's decision to boycott the elections in that year.[136] He was also one of the founders of the more pro-regime Islamic Centre Party.[137] While there are some differences in Islamist ideology between al-ʿUmush and others in the organisation,[138] the main reason he stands out seems not to be ideological, but national.

Like many others in the Brotherhood, al-ʿUmush has an East Jordanian, tribal background. As mentioned in Chapter 3, many of those who share this with him take pride in their Bedouin descent and view Jordanian society through this lens, often with accompanying scepticism towards the Palestinian inhabitants of the country. Because they tend to see the army, the tribes and especially the king as protectors of their heritage, such East Jordanians are frequently far more pro-regime than the kingdom's Palestinian inhabitants, who often have their own national – and highly politicised – sentiments with regard to a future Palestinian state.

Al-ʿUmush's views of the Jordanian regime are thus not naïve with regard to its Islamic credentials, but do represent a clearly East Jordanian attachment to especially the kings of Jordan that is not often found among Palestinian Jordanians. Al-ʿUmush describes the regime – despite its repression of the organisation sometimes – as highly supportive of the Brotherhood (and Hamas),[139] as the only one in the world that allows the organisation to function openly[140] and as having kings on whose order

133 Ibid., 49. 134 Al-ʿUmūsh, *Maḥaṭṭāt*, 74–86.
135 Interview with ʿAwnī ʿUbaydī, Amman, 11 January 2014.
136 Interview with Bassām al-ʿUmūsh, Amman, 30 January 2013. For more on al-ʿUmūsh's views on this boycott, see al-ʿUmūsh, *Maḥaṭṭāt*, 205–9.
137 Rosefsky Wickham, *Muslim Brotherhood*, 215. 138 Ibid., 215–16.
139 Al-ʿUmūsh, *Maḥaṭṭāt*, 24. 140 Ibid., 55.

the Brotherhood came into existence.[141] He also praises members of the royal family for taking a personal interest in the well-being of Brothers when they were ill.[142]

In al-ʿUmush's view, the relationship between the regime and the Brotherhood is based on a shared idea of stability and security in the country,[143] but also on the Islamic legitimacy of the Hashimite royal family.[144] These factors do play a role for the Muslim Brotherhood, but al-ʿUmush goes further by implicitly blaming the organisation itself for never having been allowed to form a government.[145] He also cites regime criticism of the Brotherhood for the latter's alleged disinterest in national occasions, such as Independence Day, and its supposed lack of patriotism.[146] Such calls for patriotism can also be found elsewhere in the Muslim Brotherhood,[147] but it is perhaps not an exaggeration that such open displays of love for Jordan and the king were more frequent in earlier times. In any case, al-ʿUmush laments the alleged lack of respect for the king among younger generations of Brothers. While older generations used terms like 'his majesty the king' for their monarch, he claims later Brothers merely refer to him as 'the head of the regime'.[148] Although he does not always say so openly, al-ʿUmush sometimes seems to blame Palestinian Jordanian members of the Brotherhood for this[149] and even believes that the number of members of parliament of Palestinian descent should be limited so as not to give the impression that Jordan is the homeland of the Palestinians in all but name.[150]

All of this shows that, quite apart from Islamist considerations, national backgrounds can sometimes influence the Brotherhood's views on the Jordanian state, as well.[151] It also reintroduces the adjacent concept of '*sulṭa*' in a new way. Previous generations of Islamists, as a response to a classical tradition of encroaching caliphal authority, had tried to decontest this concept as necessary but not overbearing in order to rescue '*sharīʿa*' and '*umma*' from falling into peripheral positions in the broader

141 Ibid., 164–5. 142 Ibid., 221–6. 143 Ibid., 26–7.

144 Ibid., 57. See also interview with ʿAwnī al-ʿUbaydī, Amman, 11 January 2014.

145 Al-ʿUmūsh, *Maḥaṭṭāt*, 270–1. 146 Ibid., 243.

147 Ruḥayyil Muḥammad al-Gharāyiba [*sic*], 'Bayna Haybat al-Dawla wa-Karāmat al-Muwāṭin', *Al-Dustūr*, 19 May 2015, 20.

148 Interview with Bassām al-ʿUmūsh, Amman, 30 January 2013.

149 Rosefsky Wickham, *Muslim Brotherhood*, 215.

150 Interview with Bassām al-ʿUmūsh, Amman, 30 January 2013. A more specific critique of the Brotherhood by al-ʿUmūsh can be found in his unpublished *Al-Ikhwān al-Muslimūn min al-Fikra al-Iṣlāḥiyya ilá l-Fikra al-Thawriyya*. I thank Bassām al-ʿUmūsh for providing me with a copy of this manuscript.

151 It must be said, however, that the Jordanian Muslim Brotherhood is one of the few political organisations in the country in which Jordanians of East Jordanian and Palestinian descent cooperate on an equal basis.

ideology. While other (and especially Palestinian) members of the Brotherhood in Jordan continued this line of thinking, al-ʿUmush decontests '*sulṭa*' in the Jordanian context as not just necessary, but also desirable for nationalist reasons.

Applied Ideological Views

Despite the differing views within the Muslim Brotherhood on the caliphate, an Islamic state and a civil state, as well as the added division of East Jordanian/Palestinian Jordanian sentiments, the organisation is united in its willingness to act within the framework of the Jordanian state, either out of pragmatism or patriotism (or both). The organisation does differ, however, with regard to how it applies its ideological views on the state in the Jordanian framework, with some striving to get their emphasis on the application of the *sharīʿa* translated into tangible reform measures, while others push their more people-oriented attitude to bring about change.

Those arguing in favour of an Islamic state claim, first and foremost, that reform of the Jordanian regime should be based on Islam, but – as mentioned – within the framework of the state. Abu Faris, using al-Banna as an example again, argues that in order to reach 'the end goal (*al-hadaf al-nihāʾī*)', which he states is 'the changing of the *jāhilī* circumstances (*al-awḍāʿ al-jāhiliyya*) and the resumption of Islamic life (*istiʾnāf al-ḥayāt al-Islāmiyya*)', the Muslim Brotherhood should work in 'gradual stages (*marāḥil mutadarrija*)'.[152] In practice, this means making people acquainted with the Muslim Brotherhood's views first, then choosing the right means to resume Islamic life and set up an Islamic state and, finally, practically executing the steps needed to realise this.[153] Among thinkers like Abu Faris, al-Khalidi and others, there is no doubt that this should result in a state where the *sharīʿa* permeates the entire system.[154] A like-minded Brother such as ʿAli al-ʿUtum therefore states that it should not be the people, but the *sharīʿa* that should be 'the owner of power and the ruler (*ṣāḥib al-sulṭa wa-l-sulṭān wa-l-ḥākim*) in all our affairs'.[155]

Although the end goal that Abu Faris and like-minded scholars such as al-Khalidi and others within the Muslim Brotherhood advocate is a far cry from what the state of Jordan represents today, they insist that they do not seek the overthrow of the regime.[156] Even during the 'Arab Spring', when

[152] Abū Fāris, *Al-Fiqh*, 37–8. [153] Ibid., 38.
[154] Ṣalāḥ al-Khālidī, 'Al-Nuwwāb wa-Ḥukm Allāh', *Al-Sabīl*, 25 January 2011, 17.
[155] ʿAlī al-ʿUtūm, 'Al-Islam wa-Naẓariyya: "Al-Umma Maṣdar al-Sulṭat"', *Al-Sabīl*, 13 March 2013, 15.
[156] Interviews with Muḥammad Abū Fāris, Amman, 21 January 2013; Ṣalāḥ al-Khālidī, Amman, 24 January 2013.

protesters across the Arab world were using the slogan 'the people want the downfall of the regime (*al-sha'b yurīdu isqāṭ al-niẓām*)', the Muslim Brotherhood in Jordan did not follow suit. This was perhaps the most vulnerable time for the Jordanian regime during King 'Abdallah II's reign, but – with only rare exceptions that did not represent the organisation as a whole[157] – the Muslim Brotherhood nevertheless virtually always confined itself to the slogan 'the people want the reform of the regime (*al-sha'b yurīdu iṣlāḥ al-niẓām*)'.[158]

These gradual and peaceful attempts to turn Jordan into an Islamic state were mostly made through the Brotherhood's and the IAF's participation in elections and parliament, which will be dealt with in Chapter 5, but also through the organisation's efforts to shape the aforementioned National Charter, which was ratified in 1991. Given that this was a new foundational document that was to give shape to the social contract between the king and the people for years to come, this was *the* moment to push for a greater role of the *sharī'a* in the Jordanian state's structure. The six Muslim Brothers and four independent Islamists (out of forty leading figures in total) who participated in the deliberations for the National Charter set out to make the *sharī'a* the *only* source (rather than merely *a* source) of legislation, thereby effectively securing that every new law must concur with Islamic law. In the end, a compromise solution (the *sharī'a* as the principle source of legislation) was accepted by the Brotherhood.[159] Still, as Moaddel has pointed out, this left a lot of uncertainty about how this was going to be applied and implemented and gave no guarantees of actual conformity with the *sharī'a*.[160]

A different direction was taken by those Brothers who advocated a civil state in the context of Jordan. As was made clear in a book published for the Brotherhood-affiliated Umma Centre for Studies and Research, which is led by Ruhayyil Gharayiba, such people also see Islam as a source of change and reform. The book presents reform (*iṣlāḥ*) as playing 'a central role (*dawran miḥwariyyan*)' in the Qur'an and as an

157 Bassām al-Badārīn, 'Hutāf "Isqāṭ al-Niẓām" Yashghalu l-Urdunn al-Rasmī wa-l-Sha'bī: Ri'āya Rasmiyya li-Riwāya Mutadaḥraja Tattahimu l-Ikhwān al-Muslimīn wa-Mu'ashshirāt Taḍlīl 'alá A'lá l-Mustawayāt', *Al-Quds al-'Arabī*, 27 November 2012, 6; Tāmir al-Ṣamādī '"Ikhwān" al-Urdunn Yarfa'ūna li-l-Marra al-Ūlá Shi'ār "Isqāṭ al-Niẓām"', *Al-Ḥayāt* (www.alhayat.com/Details/453556, accessed 28 November 2012), 17 November 2012.

158 Rabá Karāsina, '"Al-Ikhwān": Ikhtarnā Mā Ikhtārahu l-Sha'b min Shi'ār wa-Huwa "Iṣlāḥ al-Niẓām"', *Al-'Arab al-Yawm*, 20 November 2012, 7; Jākilīn Zāhir, 'Hammām Sa'īd: Lam Narfa' Shi'ār "Isqāṭ al-Niẓām" ... Bal Rafa'nā Iṣlāḥahu wa-Naṣr 'alayhi', *'Ammūn* (www.ammonnews.net/article/97317, accessed 12 December 2018), 16 September 2011.

159 Hamid, *Temptations*, 81; Moaddel, *Jordanian Exceptionalism*, 122.

160 Moaddel, *Jordanian Exceptionalism*, 122–4.

important part of 'the reformist messages of the prophets (*risālāt al-anbiyā' al-iṣlāḥiyya*)', including 'social reform, political reform and economic reform'.[161] It points to the many occurrences of derivatives of the word '*iṣlāḥ*' in the Qur'an and the Sunna, but also shows in what ways the message of Islam came to change and reform the existing mindsets, customs, beliefs and political and social practices of the people.[162]

Those advocating such Islam-inspired reform towards a civil state with an Islamic authority in Jordan do not deny the importance of the *sharīʿa*. The aforementioned former General Controller ʿAbd al-Majid Dhunaybat, for example, explicitly follows the Egyptian Brotherhood's lead in its reformist discourse on a civil state while acknowledging that there are 'definitive texts (*nuṣūṣ qāṭiʿa*) in matters of acts of worship and some [matters of] relations with others (*umūr al-ʿibādāt wa-baʿḍ al-muʿāmalāt*)' that cannot be overlooked. Like Rida and several early Egyptian Muslim Brothers before him, however, he argues that *ijtihād* may be applied. Echoing al-Banna's words we saw in Chapter 2, Dhunaybat advocates the use of *ijtihād* in areas 'in which there is no text from the Book, the Sunna or the consensus (*ijmāʿ*) of the *umma*'.[163]

Yet where al-Banna stops there, Dhunaybat adds that 'every period and place (*kull ʿaṣr wa-miṣr*) has its legislation and laws that agree with (*tatawā'amu maʿa*) its spirit and its recent developments (*rūḥihi wa-mustajaddātihi*) and serve man and respond to his needs'. Dhunaybat thus advocates the *sharīʿa*, but only as a general framework within which the people enjoy a lot of flexibility, not as a system whose exact rulings permeate all legislation. Interestingly, Dhunaybat even seems to like the idea of having the *sharīʿa* as 'the principle source (*al-maṣdar al-ra'īs*) of legislation', as it says in the Jordanian constitution. While the Muslim Brotherhood merely accepted this formula as a compromise in the negotiations for the National Charter in 1991, Dhunaybat seems to believe that this is what it should be.[164]

This broad – rather than detailed – role for the *sharīʿa* in this discourse is underlined further by stressing that it is the people or the *umma* who should be the source of power, as prominent Jordanian Brothers frequently do.[165] As an indication of how mainstream this

161 Adīb Fāyiz al-Ḍumūr, *Fiqh al-Iṣlāḥ wa-l-Taghyīr al-Siyāsī* (Amman: Dār al-Ma'mūn li-l-Nashr wa-l-Tawzīʿ, 2011), 41.

162 Ibid., 41–58.

163 ʿAbd al-Majīd Dhunaybāt, 'Ḥawla Barnāmij "al-Ikhwān" fī Miṣr', *Al-Ghad* (www.alghad.com/articles/546177, accessed 28 January 2013), 9 November 2007.

164 Ibid. See also Ibrāhīm Gharāyiba, *Al-Khiṭāb al-Islāmī wa-l-Taḥawwulāt al-Ḥaḍāriyya wa-l-Ijtimāʿiyya* (Amman: Dār Ward al-Urduniyya li-l-Nashr wa-l-Tawzīʿ, 2007), 34–5.

165 'Al-Falāḥāt: Lā Jaysh ladaynā fa-Jaysh al-Ḥirāk al-Shaʿbī Jayshunā', *Shīḥān News* (www.shihannews.net/Print.aspx?ArticleNo=28641, accessed 18 October 2012), 1 October 2012; 'Sālim al-Falāḥāt: Lan Nushārika fī l-Intikhābāt ... wa-Nuṣaʿʿidu

idea has become, the IAF's 2007 election manifesto mentions things like 'the *umma* is the source of powers', 'the strengthening of the Jordanian people with regard to choosing its government' and 'the will of the *umma*' under the heading 'Our electoral programme'.[166] Interestingly, references to the *sharī'a* do not occur until later in the manifesto, where they state that

> the vision and goals of the [Islamic Action Front] party (*ru'yat al-ḥizb wa-ahdāfahu*) stem from the intentions (*maqāṣid*)[167] of the Islamic *sharī'a*, namely, the preservation of the life of man (*ḥayāt al-insān*), his religion (*dīnihi*), his reason (*'aqlihi*), his freedom (*ḥurriyyatihi*), his possessions (*mālihi*) and his honour (*'irḍihi*).[168]

This view of the *sharī'a* as a system of general principles that leaves room for people's own legislation,[169] rather than detailed rulings that do not, is abetted by the idea of the ruler as an agent or employee of the people, which we saw earlier, and is also shared by proponents of a civil state in Jordan.[170]

Because of the breadth of this interpretation of the *sharī'a* and the important role played by the people, the civil state with an Islamic authority becomes a goal that far more people than just Islamists can unite around. As such, Brothers who support a civil state in Jordan advocate a broad reformist agenda vis-à-vis the state that is shared by a cross-section of society. Former General Controller Salim al-Falahat, for example, has stated that 'all popular movements (*jamī' al-ḥarakāt al-sha'biyya*) and party and national forces (*al-quwá al-waṭaniyya wa-l-ḥizbiyya*)' should be part of the efforts to reform the regime.[171] Similarly, then-IAF Secretary General Hamza Mansur called for 'the

Diḍḍa l-Niẓām Idhā Lam Yuṣliḥ', *Shīḥān News* (www.shihannews.net/Print.aspx?ArticleNo=29093, accessed 18 October 2012), 16 October 2012; Jamīl Abū Bakr, 'Ḥubb al-Waṭan ... wa-Raf' al-As'ār', *Al-Sabīl*, 7 November 2012, 1.

166 *Na'am ... Al-Islām Huwa l-Ḥall wa-ma'an ... li-Taḥqīq al-Ḥurriyya wa-l-'Adāla wa-l-Tanmiya wa-l-Iṣlāḥ wa-l-Waḥda ...: Al-Barnāmij al-Intikhābī li-Murashshaḥī Ḥizb Jabhat al-'Amal al-Islāmī li-Intikhābāt Majlis al-Nuwwāb al-Khāmis 'Ashara* (n.p.: 2011), 4–5.

167 This is a term from Islamic law that will be dealt with in more detail in Chapter 6.

168 *Na'am*, 6.

169 Gharāyiba further explains this by pointing to the multiple sources of Islam, which include not just the texts, but also the various means of arriving at different rulings, the interests of the people and the precedents of earlier Muslims. All of this adds up to a rather pluriform conception of the *sharī'a*. Interview with Ruḥayyil Gharāyiba, Amman, 16 June 2013.

170 Interviews with Jamīl Abū Bakr, Amman, 18 June 2012; 'Āṭif al-Jawlānī, Amman, 14 June 2012.

171 'Al-Falāḥāt: Lā Jaysh ladaynā fa-Jaysh al-Ḥirāk al-Sha'bī Jayshunā', *Shīḥān News* (www.shihannews.net/Print.aspx?ArticleNo=28641, accessed 18 October 2012), 1 October 2012.

founding of a broad Jordanian popular framework (*iṭār shaʿbī Urdunnī wāsiʿ*) that encompasses all who believe in reform'.[172] From such a broad perspective, it is not surprising that one author states that 'God's method of change (*manhaj Allāh al-taghyīrī*)' is a method that 'has brought together all reasonable views (*kull al-ārāʾ al-munṣifa*), Islamic and non-Islamic'.[173] Gharayiba points to Turkish President Recep Tayyip Erdogan as an example of what such a broad and not-explicitly Islamist coalition can bring about, arguing that in order to succeed, 'Islamic forces must work in the service of Islam through preparation, programmes and general service (*al-khidma al-ʿāmma*) to the people'.[174]

In practice, this reduced emphasis on the *sharīʿa* and strong focus on the *umma* results in demands that are only slightly less challenging to the government and even the regime of Jordan than the call for the application of the *sharīʿa*. Precisely because of their emphasis on the people, Brothers advocating a civil state call for measures against regime abuse, such as corruption and the strong influence of the security and intelligence services in Jordan, which probably enjoy widespread support.[175] More generally – and more controversially – the organisation has called for clear limits on the powers of the king.[176] In response to the question 'What do you mean by reform of the regime?', al-Falahat's first response was: 'We mean that the king has limited powers (*ṣalāḥiyyāt maḥdūda*) as opposed to broad powers (*ṣalāḥiyyāt wāsiʿa*) for the people.'[177]

From around 2007 onwards, such views have resulted in the concept of a constitutional monarchy (*malikiyya dustūriyya*), which is what many reform-minded Brothers have called for. Gharayiba, who claims to have introduced the idea in Jordan, states that it is particularly important to establish a true separation of powers and remove the king's influence from the legislative branch of government.[178] Probably because of the

172 'Manṣūr: Al-Iṣlāḥ al-Ḥaqīqī Yatamaththalu bi-Taʿdīlāt Dustūriyya wa-Tafʿīl al-Mawwād al-Ījābiyya', *Al-Sabīl*, 19 May 2011, 3.

173 Ruqayya al-Quḍāt, 'Al-Islām wa-l-Taghyīr al-Rāshid', *Al-Sabīl*, 3 October 2012, 14.

174 Ruḥayyil Gharāyiba, 'Fawz Ardughān wa-Mā Yanbaghī an Yuqāla', *Al-Dustūr*, 2 April 2014, 11, 16. The words cited are on p. 11.

175 'Al-Falāḥāt: Lā Jaysh ladaynā fa-Jaysh al-Ḥirāk al-Shaʿbī Jayshunā', *Shīḥān News* (www.shihannews.net/Print.aspx?ArticleNo=28641, accessed 18 October 2012), 1 October 2012; 'Sālim al-Falāḥāt: Lan Nushārika fī l-Intikhābāt ... wa-Nuṣaʿʿidu Diḍḍa l-Niẓām Idhā Lam Yuṣliḥ', *Shīḥān News* (www.shihannews.net/Print.aspx?ArticleNo=29093, 18 October 2012), 16 October 2012.

176 Muhannad Mubīḍīn, 'Maṭālib "al-Ikhwān" bi-Taʿdīl Mawwād fī l-Dustūr Tamassu Ṣalāḥiyyāt al-Malik ... Taʿkisu Ḥālat ʿadam Itmīnān Ladá l-Muwāṭinīn', *Al-Dustūr*, 15 October 2012.

177 'Sālim al-Falāḥāt: Lan Nushārika fī l-Intikhābāt ... wa-Nuṣaʿʿidu Diḍḍa l-Niẓām Idhā Lam Yuṣliḥ', *Shīḥān News* (www.shihannews.net/Print.aspx?ArticleNo=29093, 18 October 2012), 16 October 2012.

178 Interview with Ruḥayyil Gharāyiba, Amman, 17 January 2013.

challenge this concept therefore poses to the power of the king, several pro-monarchy East Jordanian Brothers felt this went too far and opposed the idea of a constitutional monarchy.[179] Some Brothers striving for an Islamic state also oppose it, however, not because it would limit the power of the king too much, but because it could imply a recognition of the monarchy.[180] The concept nevertheless seems to have gained support within the Jordanian Brotherhood[181] and even the king himself has stated that the country is a constitutional monarchy.[182] This immediately presents one of the problems that Jordanian Brothers advocating a civil state face: part of the reforms they call for have already been accepted in theory and are sometimes even in the constitution; they have just not been acted upon in practice by the king (yet).[183]

* * *

In conclusion, we can say that the Jordanian Brotherhood, like the early Egyptian branch of the organisation, has pushed back against too great an emphasis – in their view – on '*sulṭa*' as adjacent to the core ideological concept of 'ruler'. Interestingly, given the fact that Jordan is not a free country and, in effect, a relatively mildly repressive dictatorship, the idea of an overbearing '*sulṭa*' remains highly relevant for the Muslim Brotherhood, despite the absence of the caliphate, which was the reason classical Muslim scholars put so much emphasis on '*sulṭa*'. The Jordanian Brotherhood has countered this trend by emphasising Islamic rule through the application of the *sharīʿa*, thereby 'restoring' the latter from its peripheral position to one adjacent to the core concept of 'ruler'.

Yet the organisation cannot simply be labelled '*sharīʿa*-centred' in this respect, with the exception of Muhammad Abu Faris and like-minded others, who do privilege '*sharīʿa*' over other adjacent concepts. Several other Brothers are (or were) clearly in favour of an Islamic state that emphasises the *sharīʿa* and, like Mawdudi and others before them, seem to assume that this will more or less automatically dovetail with the will of the *umma*. Unlike this balanced approach, those arguing for a civil state tend more towards an *umma*-centred approach, emphasising the space for

179 Abū Rummān and Abū Haniyya, *Al-Ḥall*, 137–8.
180 Interview with Muḥammad Abū Rummān, Amman, 19 June 2012.
181 See, for example, ʿAbdallāh al-Shūbakī, 'Manṣūr: Al-Urdunniyyūn Irtaḍaw bi-l-Ḥukm al-Hāmishī Niyābiyyan Malakiyyan', *Al-Sabīl*, 29 June 2012, 8. Interview with Muḥammad Abū Rummān, Amman, 19 June 2012.
182 'Al-Malik: Al-Malakiyya fī l-Urdunn Malakiyya Dustūriyya … wa-Lā Amliku Sulṭa Muṭlaqa – 1', *Jirāsa* (www.gerasanews.com/article/60657, accessed 13 December 2012), 15 November 2011.
183 Interviews with Sālim al-Falāḥāt, Amman, 22 January 2013; Ruḥayyil Gharāyiba, Amman, 17 January 2013.

and the power of the people to decide the laws on the basis of a *sharīʿa* that has been 'constitutionalised' into a set of general principles, rather than detailed rulings. As such, they – in effect – privilege '*umma*' over '*sharīʿa*' as a concept adjacent to the core concept of 'ruler'. Dividing matters even more is the fact that some East Jordanian Brothers are quite positively inclined towards the king and, as such, are critical of reforms that challenge the monarchy too much. As such, their decontestation of '*sulṭa*' as a desirable necessity in Hashimite hands makes them balanced in a way we also saw in the case of al-Hudaybi in Chapter 2.

Thus, the Jordanian Muslim Brotherhood is quite divided on the question of the state, which begins to give us an idea of the complexity of drawing conclusions about the organisation with regard to the inclusion-moderation thesis. The analysis given above has shown that the Brotherhood is not homogeneous with regard to the political system in which it is supposed to participate and be included. Yet despite its divisions, the organisation is surprisingly united in its peaceful, non-revolutionary approach towards and its acceptance of the state, at least as a fait accompli. Whereas in Egypt and Syria the Brotherhood was sometimes involved in violence against the state in response to repression and radical groups sprang forth from within its ranks, this did not happen in Jordan. That is not to say that Jordan does not have radical Islamists, but these generally do not have backgrounds in the Brotherhood.[184]

The Brotherhood's moderation in this respect did not occur because radical ideas do not exist in classical Islamic political thought or the tradition of the Muslim Brotherhood itself – because they do. It has also become quite clear that at least some Jordanian Brothers have been influenced by radical early Egyptian Brotherhood thinkers like Sayyid Qutb, yet even they have not advocated armed revolution, let alone resorted to such means. It therefore seems likely that the Jordanian Brotherhood's united moderation towards the state – despite the organisation's ideological divisions and in line with Schwedler's conclusions – has come about as a result of the regime's policy of inclusion, thus supporting the inclusion-moderation thesis.

Still, the weight within the Jordanian Brotherhood seems to have shifted across ideological divisions from a *sharīʿa*-centred or balanced approach to an increasingly *umma*-centred approach since the 1990s and especially during the reign of King ʿAbdallah II. This further

[184] Beverley Milton-Edwards, 'Climate of Change in Jordan's Islamist Movement', in *Islamic Fundamentalism*, ed. Abdel Salam Sidahmed and Anoushiravan Ehteshami (Boulder, CO: Westview Press, 1996), 123–34; Joas Wagemakers, *A Quietist Jihadi: The Ideology and Influence of Abu Muhammad al-Maqdisi* (Cambridge: Cambridge University Press, 2012), 196–207.

moderation is surprising, since the Brotherhood was increasingly repressed in this period. This runs counter to the inclusion-moderation thesis, but is in line with Hamid's work. Two reasons can be given for this 'repression-moderation' explanation: firstly, by the time this repression began to take serious forms, the Brotherhood in Jordan had already experienced a long history of inclusion, thereby perhaps making it unlikely that the organisation would resort to unprecedented, radical and maybe even violent solutions in response to increased repression. This might have happened if the Brotherhood had been united in its views of the state and any alternative views would only have been found outside of the organisation's framework. Given the Brotherhood's ideological divisions, however, it was not only possible but even relatively easy for the group's members to gradually shift their views from one internal trend to another without leaving the organisation; secondly, the global Islamist discourse by which the Jordanian Brotherhood is strongly influenced has increasingly shifted towards ideological moderation.

These two reasons make it likely that the Jordanian Muslim Brotherhood would not respond with radical solutions to increasing repression but seek alternatives within its own existing moderate discourse, on the one hand, and follow the global Islamist trends in which moderate tendencies increasingly prevail, on the other. As such, we can say that the Brotherhood generally conformed to the inclusion-moderation thesis with regard to the state, but that within that framework regime repression caused the organisation to moderate even further as a result of the Brotherhood's ideological divisions and an increasingly moderate global Islamist discourse. The alternative to this process – radicalisation – would not only have meant an ideological break with global moderate Islamist discourse, but it would also have entailed an organisational break with the Jordanian Brotherhood itself. The Jordanian Muslim Brotherhood's divided views on the state within the context of the kingdom thus laid part of the foundation for its ideological moderation and helps explain how the organisation could moderate further under repression in the general context of moderation through inclusion. To be able to discern these divisions in a more detailed way and gain more insight into their complexity, we need to look at the Jordanian Muslim Brotherhood's views on political participation, to which we now turn.

5 Ideological Divisions on Political Participation

As Chapter 4 shows, both the exponents of an Islamic state ('hawks') and those who advocate a civil state in the form of a constitutional monarchy ('doves') demand reform of the regime. Although the former want an entirely new system in Jordan and the latter often point to already existing constitutional guarantees that they want to see realised in practice, they nevertheless both challenge the regime. In this sense, one could actually label both groups as 'hawks'. As such, the terms 'hawks' and 'doves', though useful as shorthand for broad trends within the Muslim Brotherhood in Jordan, are limited, conceal important differences and do not do justice to the ideological complexity of the organisation's views. This complexity is captured better through the use of the terms '*sharīʿa*-centred', '*umma*-centred' and 'balanced', especially if tendencies to stress '*sulṭa*' are also taken into account.

This becomes even clearer in this chapter, which deals with the Jordanian Muslim Brotherhood's views on political participation. It analyses the four different means of political participation distinguished in Chapters 1–2 (commanding right and forbidding wrong; consultation; oath of fealty; and obedience) that act as links between the core concept of 'ruler' and the adjacent concept of '*umma*' (and '*sharīʿa*'). It first deals with them from the point of view of global Islamist scholars who have influenced the Brotherhood in Jordan and then by analysing the divided ways in which the Jordanian organisation has used these itself. As such, it – again – shows the diversity of Islamist ideas on these issues and deepens our understanding of why the divisions within the Jordanian Brotherhood are so important with regard to the 'inclusion-moderation' thesis.

Commanding Right and Forbidding Wrong

The Qurʾanic duty of *al-amr bi-l-maʿrūf wa-l-nahy ʿan al-munkar* has taken multiple forms in classical Islam, as we saw in Chapter 1, with rulers increasingly interpreting and applying the concept in a way that suited their authority, rather than the *umma*'s ability to hold the caliph to account. The early leaders of the Muslim Brotherhood, however, while retaining the ineliminable feature of this concept – that right be commanded and wrong be forbidden – tried to reverse this situation by tying the *umma* to the quasi-contingent feature of commander/forbidder and the ruler to the person being commanded/forbidden again. Although al-Hudaybi took a mostly quietist position on this issue, al-Banna and especially ʿAwda embraced commanding right and forbidding wrong as a means to hold the ruler to account or even depose him. This way of thinking effectively reversed the classical development of this link between the core concept of 'ruler' and the adjacent concept of '*umma*', but did not provide it with concrete means to put it in practice. That was left to later generations of Islamist thinkers, including those in Jordan.

Global Islamist Discourse on Commanding Right and Forbidding Wrong

What is clear from the Qurʾanic verses and *ḥadīth*s underpinning the duty to command right and forbid wrong is that it has the potential to become a source of chaos and anarchy when used (or abused) by individual believers. Even if this duty may have been originally meant to act as a means for the *umma* (not the caliph) to assert itself in various ways, one can see why modern-day Muslim scholars have been cautious about it[1] and why authoritarian rulers have sometimes monopolised it for themselves, such as in Saudi Arabia.[2] Indeed, some contemporary radical Islamist groups have used the duty to command right and forbid wrong to justify violent acts against elements in society or the state.[3]

Among the global Islamist scholars that have influenced the Jordanian Brotherhood, relatively little attention is paid to commanding right and forbidding wrong, but those that do resort neither to the quietism of some non-Islamist scholars, nor to the radicalism of militant groups. Instead, they build on the activist interpretations espoused by early Muslim Brotherhood thinkers such as al-Banna. Perhaps the most specific of these is al-Ghannushi, who sees commanding right and forbidding

[1] Cook, *Commanding Right*, 522–8.

[2] Nabil Mouline, *Les clercs de l'islam: Autorité religieuse et pouvoir politique en Arabie Saoudite, XVIIIe-XXIe siècle* (Paris: Presses Universitaires de France, 2011), 259–97.

[3] Thomas Hegghammer and Stéphane Lacroix, 'Rejectionist Islamism in Saudi Arabia: The Story of Juhayman al-ʿUtaybi Revisited', *International Journal of Middle East Studies* 39, no. 1 (2007): 103–22; Roel Meijer, 'Commanding Right and Forbidding Wrong as a Principle of Social Action: The Case of the Egyptian al-Jamaʿa al-Islamiyya', in *Global Salafism: Islam's New Religious Movement*, ed. Roel Meijer (London: Hurst & Co., 2009), 189–220.

wrong as representing 'the task of supervision (*muhimmat al-raqāba*)', which – as the 'true owner of authority (*ṣāḥibat al-sulṭa al-ḥaqīqiyya*)' – the *umma* ought to take care of, either on an individual level or through the institutions of the state and society.[4] Like his ideological predecessors, al-Ghannushi points to the evidence in the sources to prove the necessity of commanding right and forbidding wrong and shows that even during the reign of the rightly guided caliphs, criticising the rulers and holding them to account was not unheard of.[5]

Al-Ghannushi goes further than other Brotherhood-affiliated thinkers, however. He states that the negligence of the *umma* in commanding right and forbidding wrong, particularly with regard to the wrongs of important people, is 'the direct reason (*al-sabab al-mubāshir*) for most of what has hit [the *umma*] in terms of catastrophes of despotism (*nakabāt al-istibdād*)'.[6] Given that the *umma* appoints a ruler 'to apply the *sharīʿa*, realise [the *umma*'s] interests and make justice prevail among [the members of the *umma*], so that security and prosperity (*al-amn wa-l-rakhāʾ*) prevail and dignity and freedom (*al-karāma wa-l-ḥurriyya*) are realised', it is 'the duty of the *umma* to remove him (*dafʿuhu*)' if he fails to do his job.[7] Interestingly, the duties whose neglect by the ruler can lead to deposing him include 'suspension of or aggression towards the *sharīʿa* of God, human rights and their freedom or neglect of their interests', according to al-Ghannushi.[8] This explicit mention of non-religious criteria suggests that even pious but dictatorial rulers could be subject to disposition through the commanding of right and forbidding of wrong.

In some of his writings, al-Ghannushi is adamant that 'forbidding wrong against the ruler and the resistance to his deviance and oppression (*inḥirāfihi wa-jawrihi*) are not the responsibility of one group from among the *umma*; on the contrary, they are the responsibility of all individuals and groups'. He ascribes scholars the job of pointing out what mistakes the rulers make, while imams in mosques can start campaigns against the wrongs in society and put pressure on the authorities, together turning the *umma* into 'a powerful front'.[9] The rest of the people can engage in activities such as marches, strikes and other peaceful means of resistance to tyranny.[10] If the *umma* holds its leaders to account in such a way, al-Ghannushi maintains, the ruler will have to respond.[11]

Al-Ghannushi thus maintains the connections between the quasi-contingent feature of the commander/forbidder and the *umma*, on the

[4] Al-Ghannūshī, *Al-Dīmuqrāṭiyya*, 21–2 (see also p. 37). The words quoted are on p. 21.
[5] Al-Ghannūshī, *Al-Ḥurriyyāt*, 201–3. [6] Ibid., 203. [7] Ibid. [8] Ibid.
[9] Ibid., 204.
[10] Al-Ghannūshī, *Al-Dīmuqrāṭiyya*, 22; al-Ghannūshī, *Al-Ḥurriyyāt*, 205–6.
[11] Al-Ghannūshī, *Al-Ḥurriyyāt*, 205.

one hand, and that of the person commanded/forbidden and the ruler, on the other, that Muslim Brothers like al-Banna and ʿAwda had established (or re-established) before. Unlike them, however, he makes the duty to command right and forbid wrong much more concrete by pointing to examples of what people can do to hold the rulers to account. As such, al-Ghannushi, through his more practical application of *al-amr bi-l-maʿrūf wa-l-nahy ʿan al-munkar*, decontests the position of the *umma* as firmly adjacent to the core concept of 'ruler' and does so in a more applied way than his ideological predecessors in the Muslim Brotherhood.

The Jordanian Muslim Brotherhood on Commanding Right and Forbidding Wrong

Although al-Ghannushi spoke in practical terms, he did not apply his ideas to a concrete context. Jordanian Muslim Brothers do seek to implement their views in the framework of a single state, which leads to even more practical ideas. The latter are part of a far more general desire for 'reform' on the part of the Muslim Brotherhood, which – as mentioned – is an important term for the organisation. It has played a prominent role in the organisation's ideology for years,[12] which has become even more explicit since the advent of the 'Arab Spring', not least in the Brotherhood's aforementioned slogan 'the people want the reform of the regime'. The Brotherhood's and IAF's leaders, ranging from the more accommodating Jamil Abu Bakr,[13] Salim al-Falahat[14] and Hamza Mansur[15] to the more confrontational Zaki Bani Irshid[16] and ʿAli al-ʿUtum,[17] are united in their calls for reform. In the Brotherhood's thinking, *al-amr bi-l-maʿrūf wa-l-nahy ʿan al-munkar* represents one of the primary means to achieve this.[18]

Although the belief in reform is widespread, the only member of the Jordanian Brotherhood who has written extensively about the role of commanding right and forbidding wrong in this respect is the aforementioned Muhammad Abu Faris. Like others before him, Abu Faris points

[12] See, for example, Al-Ḥaraka al-Islāmiyya fī l-Urdunn, *Ruʾyat*, 7–9.

[13] ʿAbdallāh al-Shūbakī, 'Al-Nāṭiq al-Iʿlāmī "li-l-Ikhwān": Taṭbīq Ruʾá l-Malik Hiya l-Ḥasm fī Jiddiyyat al-Iṣlāḥ', *Al-Sabīl*, 16 June 2011, 2; ʿAbdallāh al-Shūbakī, 'Al-Iṣlāḥ . . . Khuṭwatān li-l-Khalaf', *Al-Sabīl*, 3 April 2011, 1.

[14] Sālim al-Falāḥāt, 'Al-Iṣlāḥ aw al-Damār', *Al-Sabīl*, 16 June 2011, 12.

[15] 'Manṣūr', 3.

[16] Naṣr al-ʿUtūm, 'Banī Irshīd: Nadʿū ilá Ḥiwār Waṭanī Jādd Yuḥaqqiqu Iṣlāḥāt Ḥaqīqiyya', *Al-Sabīl*, 4 August 2013, 4.

[17] ʿAlī al-ʿUtūm, 'Al-Ikhwān al-Muslimūn fī Muqābalat Atlāntik maʿa l-Malik 1/2', *Al-Sabīl*, 3 April 2013, 15.

[18] Muḥammad Abū Fāris, 'Ilá l-Mushārikīn fī Masīrat "Inqādh al-Waṭan"', *Al-Sabīl*, 4 October 2012, 15.

to the evidence from the Qur'an and the Sunna that we saw in Chapter 1 to show the importance of this link between the core concept of 'ruler' and the adjacent concept of '*umma*'[19] and emphasises that it is a religious duty incumbent upon Muslims.[20] Interestingly and unlike many others, Abu Faris actually points out what 'right' and 'wrong' mean. Set against a background of belief in God, 'right' according to the *sharīʿa* is 'every belief (*iʿtiqād*), act (*ʿamal*), speech (*qawl*) or indication (*ishāra*) that the wise legislator (*al-shāriʿ al-ḥakīm*) has decided upon and has ordered in the form of a duty (*ʿalá wajh al-wujūb*) or an assignment (*al-nadb*)'.[21] 'Wrong' according to the *sharīʿa*, Abu Faris writes, is 'every belief, act or speech that the wise legislator rejects and forbids'.[22] He also points out that if the *umma* fails to command right and forbid wrong, God will punish this in various ways, such as by not answering the prayers of pious believers.[23]

Abu Faris's explanations are, in effect, still quite vague and beg the question who is responsible for commanding right and forbidding wrong, particularly if it is so important and its negligence will be punished. His use of the words 'wise legislator' may suggest that he sees the duty as the state's job and he does, indeed, appear to see a role for the state in this respect,[24] citing al-Banna's words that forbidding wrong by hand, such as closing off-licences, should be the prerogative of the government only.[25] This does not mean, however, that the state's application of this duty is always welcomed by Muslim Brothers. The Jordanian Brotherhood-affiliated Muslim scholar ʿAli al-Sawa, for example, criticises the way Saudi Arabia has wrongly applied the duty by employing uneducated people to enforce it, rather than exercising its power to command and forbid with knowledge and wisdom.[26]

This criticism of the state's handling of the duty to command right and forbid wrong hints at something both Abu Faris and al-Sawa see as very important, namely, that 'ordinary' Muslims should also be involved in its practice. Abu Faris discusses the question whether *al-amr bi-l-maʿrūf wa-l-nahy ʿan al-munkar* is an individual duty for every Muslim (*farḍ ʿalá l-ʿayn*) or a collective one that is fulfilled when a limited number of believers engages in it (*farḍ ʿalá l-kifāya*). Citing both classical as well as modern scholars such as Rida, Abu Faris states it is an individual duty for all Muslims, not just scholars. The latter, he claims, should lead and

19 Muḥammad ʿAbd al-Qādir Abū Fāris, *Al-Amr bi-l-Maʿrūf wa-l-Nahy ʿan al-Munkar* (Amman: Dār al-Furqān li-l-Nashr wa-l-Tawzīʿ, 1987), 15–18, 22–3.
20 Ibid., 30–40; Abū Fāris, *Mafāhīm*, 99–102.
21 Abū Fāris, *Al-Amr*, 18–19. The quotation is on p. 19. 22 Ibid., 20.
23 Ibid., 51–64. 24 Abū Fāris, 23–5. 25 Abū Fāris, *Al-Fiqh*, 41–2.
26 Interview with ʿAlī al-Ṣawā, Amman, 25 June 2012.

'carry the banner', but they 'have no weight if they are not surrounded by the believing masses (*al-jamāhīr al-mu'mina*) around them'.[27] Al-Sawa also sees *al-amr bi-l-ma'rūf wa-l-nahy 'an al-munkar* as a duty for all capable Muslims, although he stresses that they may only forbid wrong verbally – not by force – or by detesting it in their heart, echoing the important *ḥadīth* about this duty we saw in Chapter 1.[28]

The way the duty to command right and forbid wrong should be applied and towards whom is answered differently within the Jordanian Muslim Brotherhood. There appears to be widespread support for *da'wa* as a means to fulfil this duty: al-Sawa's words cited above seem to go in that direction; former General Controller of the Brotherhood 'Abd al-Majid Dhunaybat states in an interview that 'our relationship with the regime (*al-ḥukm*) in Jordan is based on the method of this *da'wa*, which is based on commanding right and forbidding wrong';[29] and the organisation's last elected General Controller, Hammam Sa'id, provides pointers on how to practise commanding right and forbidding wrong as *da'wa*, both verbally and in one's heart, in society.[30]

Abu Faris, too, sees a connection between *da'wa* and *al-amr bi-l-ma'rūf wa-l-nahy 'an al-munkar*,[31] but his tone is far more defiant than others' and – perhaps more importantly – he appears to see regimes – rather than societies – as the primary target of Islamic missionary activities. He states that 'Islam came to change *jāhilī* regimes, so how can those who call to God (*du'āt ilá llāh*) tie their work for the religion of God to permission from these regimes[?]'.[32] In this context, Abu Faris is not against *da'wa* in society, but does believe that its use is relatively limited 'when a preacher forbids people to drink wine, for example, in a society whose law permits wine and does not prosecute him who drinks it'.[33] As a result, Abu Faris believes commanding right and forbidding wrong should be directed first and foremost against regimes to bring about the application of Islamic law and points to examples of mediaeval as well as modern Muslim thinkers – including Sayyid Qutb – who expressed the duty to forbid wrong by standing up to the rulers.[34] In my interview with him, Abu Faris cited a famous *ḥadīth* stating that the best jihad is a word of truth to an oppressive ruler to underline his views on this point.[35]

[27] Abū Fāris, *Al-Amr*, 40–8. The quotation is on p. 48.
[28] Interview with 'Alī al-Ṣawā, Amman, 25 June 2012.
[29] 'Fī Ḥiwār Maftūḥ ma'a l-Murāqib al-'Āmm li-Jamā'at al-Ikhwān al-Muslimūn fī l-Urdunn', *Al-Qibla* 1, no. 3 (2002): 112.
[30] Sa'īd, *Qawā'id*, 148–55. [31] Abū Fāris, *Mafāhīm*, 99. [32] Ibid., 104.
[33] Abū Fāris, *Al-Amr*, 99. [34] Ibid., 73–83.
[35] Interview with Muḥammad Abū Fāris, Amman, 21 January 2013.

Some of this may sound confrontational, yet it continues a tradition that not only existed in classical Islam but is also espoused by modern-day thinkers such as al-Ghannushi. Moreover, it is important to bear in mind that none of this is intended to have violent implications. Like al-Sawa, Abu Faris explicitly rejects physical coercion and states that 'ordinary people (*ʿawwām al-nās*) do not have the right to use force (*wasīlat al-quwwa*) to reject wrong'.[36] Abu Faris – despite his desire to set up an Islamic state and his belief that Jordan does not deserve that label – states that repressive rulers should be advised and asked to leave. If they do not, they can be boycotted, which, he writes, is what is meant by the aforementioned *ḥadīth*'s admonition to forbid wrong with your heart.[37]

Yet Abu Faris does not limit *al-amr bi-l-maʿrūf wa-l-nahy ʿan al-munkar* to discreet verbal advice and quiet resistance in the heart, but explicitly expands on the former. He points out that one may also take action, which is the last phase in a gradual process of trying to change things when regimes deviate from the path of Islam.[38] Like al-Ghannushi, Abu Faris believes that this is not just the scholars' job, but should also include the people.[39] The natural result of this desire to forbid wrong by taking peaceful collective action against 'un-Islamic' regimes is, perhaps, protests in the streets such as those that took place in Jordan after the advent of the Arab Spring in 2011, as we saw in Chapter 3. In an opinion piece published in the Islamist *Al-Sabil* newspaper in October 2012, Abu Faris describes these as an expression of *al-amr bi-l-maʿrūf wa-l-nahy ʿan al-munkar* and urges demonstrators to be patient, to remain steadfast and not to respond to those who call for chaos.[40] He later explained to me that these demonstrations were meant to push back against injustice and – unsurprisingly, given how he sees the duty of commanding right and forbidding wrong – were not just allowed, but even compulsory.[41]

The Jordanian Muslim Brotherhood thus retains the quasi-contingent feature of the *umma* as the commander/forbidder with regard to the duty of *al-amr bi-l-maʿrūf wa-l-nahy ʿan al-munkar*. Where its members differ amongst themselves, however, is the quasi-contingent feature of the person commanded/forbidden. Whereas several Muslim Brothers in Jordan, though not averse to criticising the rulers, decontest this aspect of the duty as *daʿwa* in society, Abu Faris, while not against that, decontests it as directed primarily towards the rulers through both passive and active political action. As such, Abu Faris seems to have more in common with al-Ghannushi than with the Jordanian Brothers mentioned. Unlike

36 Abū Fāris, *Al-Amr*, 88. 37 Abū Fāris, *Al-Niẓām*, 273.
38 Abū Fāris, *Al-Fiqh*, 34–41. 39 Abū Fāris, *Al-Amr*, 100.
40 Abū Fāris, 'Ilá l-Mushārikīn', 15.
41 Interview with Muḥammad Abū Fāris, Amman, 21 January 2013.

al-Ghannushi, however, Abu Faris is quite *sharīʿa*-centred in his approach, decontesting *al-amr bi-l-maʿrūf wa-l-nahy ʿan al-munkar* as more closely linked with the adjacent concept of '*sharīʿa*' than with '*umma*', mostly seeing the latter as an instrument to achieve the former.

Despite these differences, the Jordanian Muslim Brothers mentioned have in common that all of them want to apply commanding right and forbidding wrong within the legal framework of the Jordanian state, so without resorting to revolution or violence. As such, even in times of a heightened sense of possible reform (during the Arab Spring), increased repression (under King ʿAbdallah II) and growing confrontationalism within the organisation's ranks (through the internal election of more 'hawkish' members), the Brotherhood did not advocate violence. This shows that even in such circumstances, the Muslim Brotherhood did not resort to means they had never used before, but remained within the 'moderate' framework that they had occupied for decades.

Consultation

The different links between the adjacent concepts of '*sharīʿa*' and '*umma*', on the one hand, and the core concept of 'ruler', on the other, are not entirely distinct. Since all connect the one with the other, it is not surprising that there is overlap between them. This also applies to *al-amr bi-l-maʿrūf wa-l-nahy ʿan al-munkar* and *shūrá*, the subject of this section. One author writing about the Muslim Brotherhood, for example, cites the reformist Muslim scholar Muhammad ʿAbduh as stating that the texts that establish the duty to command right and forbid wrong are 'the clearest and most explicit (*awḍaḥ wa-aṣraḥ*) Islamic legal source (*maṣdar sharʿī*) for the principle of consultation'.[42] Similarly, prominent Jordanian Muslim Brother Ishaq Farhan states that *shūrá* facilitates the representation of people, which in turn provides opportunities to command right and forbid wrong.[43]

Moreover, like *al-amr bi-l-maʿrūf wa-l-nahy ʿan al-munkar*, the scope of *shūrá* was limited in classical Islamic times. This was done through the policies of caliphs whose rule was perpetuated even if hardly any actual consultation had taken place and if the people deciding about succession – the *ahl al-ḥall wa-l-ʿaqd* – were limited in number and had little connection with the *umma* in general, as we saw in Chapter 1. As such, *shūrá*'s quasi-contingent feature of 'the people consulted' withered away, which

[42] Tawfīq Yūsuf al-Wāʿī, *Al-Fikr al-Siyāsī al-Muʿāṣir li-Tawajjuhāt al-Ikhwān al-Muslimīn* (Kuwait: Maktabat Ibn Kathīr, 2011), 57.

[43] Ishaq A. Farhan (Isḥāq Farḥān), *Islamic View Regarding Political Participation with Special Reference to the Jordanian Context* (Amman: Dār al-Furqān, 1998), 25.

favoured the ruler in mediaeval Islam. Chapters 1 and 2 showed that scholars like Rida and early Brotherhood thinkers like al-Banna, ʿAwda and Qutb tried to reverse this process by tying this feature more to the *umma* and by sometimes expanding the group of people who could be part of the *ahl al-ḥall wa-l-ʿaqd*. They simultaneously linked consultation with the *sharīʿa*, however, so that the actual room for the *umma* to decide about matters was strictly circumscribed. As such, the decontestations of *shūrá* we have seen so far are either *sharīʿa*-centred or balanced, but this changed in the hands of more recent global and Jordanian Islamists.

Global Islamist Discourse on Consultation

The concept of *shūrá* has been widely discussed by global Islamist thinkers, including those whom Jordanian Brothers say influenced them, and these debates have led to specific statements published by the Egyptian Muslim Brotherhood on this topic.[44] These various interpretations of consultation in modern Islam have, in turn, been the subject of academic publications, especially on the question of how *shūrá* – because of its ineliminable feature of mutual consultation with others – relates to democracy.[45] In their attempts to make sense of this question, global Islamist scholars clearly build on the classical Islamic tradition in which the concept of *shūrá* developed by pointing out the Qurʾanic verses in which (related forms of) the term appears and how this has been applied among early Islamic rulers.[46]

A central issue in the discussion on consultation and democracy among global Islamist scholars is where the ultimate authority lies in both systems.[47] Al-Turabi, for example, points out that with *shūrá*, Muslims place authority in the hands of God, while democracy is a system that relies on the people to have the final say, even if they do not take religion into account.[48] The latter, al-Turabi writes, is not allowed because

> [t]here is no room in Islam for popular rule cut off from the meanings of faith (*munqaṭiʿ ʿan maʿānī l-īmān*), because the Islamic religion is a religion based on the unity of God (*dīn tawḥīdī*) that encompasses life and completely grants it the

[44] Al-Wāʿī, *Al-Fikr*, 99–103.

[45] Jens Kutscher, 'Islamic Shura, Democracy, and Online Fatwas', *CyberOrient* 5, no. 2 (2011), www.cyberorient.net/article.do?articleId=7352 (accessed 23 May 2019); Uriya Shavit, 'Is *Shura* a Muslim Form of Democracy? Roots and Systemization of a Polemic', *Middle Eastern Studies* 46, no. 3 (2010): 349–74.

[46] Al-Ghannūshī, *Al-Ḥurriyyāt*, 119–20; al-Qaraḍāwī, *Al-Siyāsa*, 111–13; al-Wāʿī, *Al-Fikr*, 53–62.

[47] See, for example, al-Wāʿī, *Al-Fikr*, 64–6.

[48] Ḥasan al-Turābī, *Fī l-Fiqh al-Siyāsī* (Beirut: Al-Dār al-ʿArabiyya li-l-ʿUlūm Nāshirūn, 2010), 71.

meaning of worship and organises it through a total *sharīʿa*. There is no distinction between politics and religion or life generally and specifically.[49]

Al-Turabi goes on to state that democracy essentially does cut off politics from religion, thereby 'sharing the will of the people with its Creator'.[50] *Shūrá*, on the other hand, does not distinguish between politics and religion and therefore remains subservient to the responsibility Muslims have before God.[51]

Points of view such as al-Turabi's make one wonder where the line is between God's mandate and that of the people. What decisions, in other words, must be left to God and what questions may be decided by Muslims themselves through mutual consultation? An oft-heard answer to this question among Islamist scholars is that *shūrá* only applies to issues on which the Qurʾan and the Sunna (or, more specifically, the *sharīʿa*) are silent or unclear, meaning that there is only a limited number of questions that Muslims can legitimately decide for themselves in politics.[52] This again brings up the question that was posed in Chapter 1 to what extent the (presumably partly static) *sharīʿa* can be reconciled with an ever-changing *umma*. To several global Islamist scholars, this is clearly not a problem because they, like Mawdudi and others we have seen earlier, do not fear the will of the *umma* will clash with the *sharīʿa*. One of those is al-Qaradawi, who also claims that *shūrá* only applies to issues 'about which there is no text'[53] and who dismisses fears of a conflict between the *sharīʿa* and the *umma* by stating:

The rule of the people is not opposed to the rule of God. On the contrary, [it is opposed] to total authoritarianism (*ḥukm al-fard al-muṭlaq*). [In making this statement,] we assume that we are talking about the rule of a Muslim people in a Muslim country. Such [people] do not reject the rule of God, which is the rule of *shūrá* that rejects the rule of any obstinate tyrant (*kull jabbār ʿanīd*), the rule of pharaohs and of those who deem themselves gods (*mutaʾahhilīn*) on earth.[54]

Al-Turabi, similarly, denies that a contradiction between the *sharīʿa* and the *umma* is possible because an Islamic state is both 'a government of the shariʿa' and 'a popular government because the shariʿa represents the convictions of the people and, therefore, their direct will'.[55]

[49] Ḥasan al-Turābī, 'Al-Shūrá wa-l-Dīmuqrāṭiyya: Ishkālāt al-Muṣṭalaḥ wa-l-Mafhūm' (paper presented at the Maʿhad al-Dirāsāt al-Siyāsiyya wa-l-Istrātījiyya, Khartoum, Sudan, September 1984), 27. This paper was republished in al-Turābī, *Fī l-Fiqh*, 135–67.

[50] Al-Turābī, 'Al-Shūrá wa-l-Dīmuqrāṭiyya', 27. [51] Ibid., 31–2.

[52] Rutherford, *Egypt*, 118; Tadros, *Muslim Brotherhood*, 58.

[53] Al-Qaraḍāwī, *Al-Siyāsa*, 111. [54] Al-Qaraḍāwī, *Ummatunā*, 147.

[55] Al-Turabi, 'Islamic State', 216.

All of this suggests that in the eyes of global Islamist thinkers who have influenced the Jordanian Muslim Brotherhood, *shūrá* is basically democracy within the boundaries of the *sharīʿa*. Indeed, that is how some scholars see it, thereby echoing the views of several early Muslim Brothers we saw in Chapter 2. Like al-Banna and Mawdudi, scholars such as al-Qaradawi and al-Turabi take a balanced approach towards the adjacent concepts of '*sharīʿa*' and '*umma*' vis-à-vis the core concept of 'ruler'. Yet they also deepen the role of the *umma* within the framework of their balanced approach in various ways. One of these is to stress that the Qurʾanic order to engage in *shūrá* is clear textual proof of the role the *umma* should have in setting up an Islamic state in which the ruler, as we saw previously, is the agent or the representative of the community of Muslims.[56]

The belief that consultation is actually an order leads to other ways of building on earlier Brotherhood-related discourse on this matter, such as making the *shūrá*'s verdict binding.[57] As we saw in Chapter 2, al-Banna allowed the ruler to override the wishes of those he consulted and to pick the views he considered best. Al-Qaradawi – despite his admiration of the Brotherhood's founder – not only states that al-Banna's views do not accord with those of most classical and modern scholars, but also takes a different position himself, stating that the *ahl al-ḥall wa-l-ʿaqd*'s views are binding for the ruler and that if he consults people who disagree with him, the majority view should be taken into account.[58]

Another way in which global Islamist scholars differ from Rida and the early Muslim Brothers lies in the scope of who should be involved with *shūrá*. Whereas the earlier thinkers included only a select group of (religious) scholars or other prominent people, some Islamist thinkers include the entire *umma* in this.[59] Al-Turabi goes even further and not only states that all Muslims have inherited the caliphate as 'the people of consultation (*ahl al-shūrá*)',[60] but also claims that because of *shūrá*, participation in the running of public affairs through *ijtihād* and advice is incumbent upon every Muslim.[61] From this, it is perhaps only a small step to accepting modern-day parliaments as the contemporary forms of *shūrá*

[56] Al-Ghannūshī, *Al-Dīmuqrāṭiyya*, 16–17. For more on al-Ghannūshī's treatment of *shūrá* and how it fits in with his broader views on democracy, see March, 'Genealogies', 308–15; Shahin, *Political Ascent*, 220–5; Tamimi, *Rachid*, 79–91.

[57] Bruce K. Rutherford, 'What Do Egypt's Islamists Want? Moderate Islam and the Rise of Islamic Constitutionalism', *Middle East Journal* 60, no. 4 (2006): 713; Raghid El-Solh, 'Islamist Attitudes towards Democracy: A Review of the Ideas of al-Ghazālī, al-Turābī and ʿAmāra', *British Journal of Middle Eastern Studies* 20, no. 1 (1993): 59.

[58] Al-Qaraḍāwī, *Al-Siyāsa*, 114. [59] Rutherford, *Egypt*, 118.

[60] Al-Turābī, 'Al-Shūrá', 26. [61] Al-Turābī, *Fī l-Fiqh*, 96.

councils, with members of parliament acting as the *ahl al-ḥall wa-l-ʿaqd*, and encouraging everyone to participate, as al-Ghannushi does.[62]

Despite the deepening of the *umma*'s role, however, these approaches still remain balanced because they do not privilege either the adjacent concept of '*sharīʿa*' over '*umma*' or vice versa, allowing neither to recede to a peripheral position with regard to the core concept of 'ruler'. Yet al-Ghannushi, unlike several other global Islamist scholars, goes further. Whereas al-Qaradawi and al-Turabi view *shūrá* as an Islamically legitimate form of democracy, al-Ghannushi actually equates consultation with rule by the people, referring to 'the will of the *umma* that is expressed through free and organised expression by means of "*shūrá*" or, in modern terms (*bi-l-muṣṭalaḥ al-ḥadīth*), democracy'.[63]

Al-Ghannushi argues that '*shūrá* in Islam is the greatest source (*al-aṣl al-aʿẓam*) – after the text – on which the legitimacy of rule (*sharʿiyyat al-ḥukm*) is based'.[64] His ranking of consultation after the text (i.e. the Qurʾan and the Sunna) suggests a more *sharīʿa*-centred approach than I have suggested so far, but the question is what the scope of Islamic law's influence is and how much room it leaves for the *umma*. Citing the Egyptian intellectual ʿAbbas al-ʿAqqad (1889–1964), he states that there is no contradiction between 'the *umma* is the source of domination (*maṣdar al-siyāda*)' and 'the noble Qurʾan and the Prophetic Sunna are the source[s] of legislation (*maṣdar al-tashrīʿ*)'.[65] Unlike others, al-Ghannushi does not claim this because he believes Muslims will always choose the *sharīʿa*, but because – again citing al-ʿAqqad – 'the *umma* is the one that understands the Book and the Sunna, works with them and views them in its [own] circumstances to see when to apply [them] (*mawāḍiʿ al-taṭbīq*) and when to stop and amend [them]'.[66] Al-Ghannushi adds that 'the *sharīʿa* is not [a set of] frozen texts (*nuṣūṣ jāmida*)', suggesting that the *umma* ultimately decides how Islamic law should be viewed through the prism of *shūrá*.[67]

Seen in this light, it is not surprising that al-Ghannushi states that 'on the level of the system of ruling, all of its powers (*kull sulṭātihi*) are derived from the people (*min al-shaʿb*)'.[68] Al-Ghannushi can only reason this way because he views the *sharīʿa* as a flexible and – with regard to its influence in people's lives – limited collection of principles (rather than rules).

[62] Al-Ghannūshī, *Al-Ḥurriyyāt*, 127–33, 140. [63] Ibid., 13.
[64] Al-Ghannūshī, *Al-Dīmuqrāṭiyya*, 16. [65] Al-Ghannūshī, *Al-Ḥurriyyāt*, 135. [66] Ibid.
[67] Ibid.
[68] Al-Ghannūshī, *Al-Dīmuqrāṭiyya*, 16–17. Interestingly, al-Ghannūshī refers to 'the people' here, rather than to the *umma*, suggesting that he does not refer to the worldwide community of Muslims, but to a national community. This distinction is one to which we will return later in this chapter in the Jordanian context.

Indeed, he states that Muslims agree on the truth of certain 'definitive rulings as fixed through the text (*al-aḥkām al-qaṭʿiyya al-thābita bi-l-naṣṣ*), [but] they are very limited (*maḥdūda jiddan*) [in number]'.[69] Thus, by viewing the *sharīʿa* as largely subject to the *umma*'s interpretation and as flexible and limited in scope, al-Ghannushi creates more room for the *umma* to make its own decisions through *shūrá*.

As such, global Islamist scholars who have influenced the Jordanian Muslim Brotherhood have built on the classical heritage by 'restoring' one of *shūrá*'s quasi-contingent features ('the people consulted') and by continuing the early Muslim Brothers' trend of increasing the number of people who are included in this group of *ahl al-ḥall wa-l-ʿaqd*. In fact, scholars like al-Qaradawi and al-Turabi have expanded this group by tying it to the *umma* as a whole, while simultaneously continuing to limit its mandate through the boundaries of the *sharīʿa*. This shows their balanced approach of decontesting *shūrá* as a link with the core concept of 'ruler' that is equal in distance to the adjacent concepts of '*sharīʿa*' and '*umma*'. Al-Ghannushi, however, clearly privileges the latter over the former by decontesting *shūrá* as ultimately governed by the will of the *umma* within only a circumscribed number of broad, *sharīʿa*-based 'constitutionalised' limits. As such, al-Ghannushi tends towards an *umma*-centred approach. It is this increasingly 'moderate' global Islamist discourse that influenced the Jordanian Muslim Brotherhood most.

The Jordanian Muslim Brotherhood on Consultation

While the relative lack of prominent Jordanian Islamist scholars has contributed to the Brotherhood's greater susceptibility to global Islamist ones, the organisation's branch in the kingdom has obviously not simply copied and pasted whatever more famous thinkers from Egypt, Sudan and Tunisia have written. This is true in more than one way with regard to the topic of *shūrá*. On the one hand, the global Islamist scholars who have influenced the Jordanian Brotherhood deal with several dimensions of consultation, such as its all-encompassing (rather than just political) nature[70] and the role of the *umma*'s consensus in *shūrá*,[71] which hardly feature in the Jordanian Brotherhood's discourse.[72] On the other hand, despite (or perhaps because of) this narrower approach to *shūrá*, the organisation arguably also applies the meaning of consultation in greater

[69] Al-Ghannūshī, *Al-Ḥurriyyāt*, 127.
[70] Al-Turābī, *Fī l-Fiqh*, 100; al-Turābī, 'Al-Shūrá', 28–9.
[71] Al-Ghannūshī, *Al-Ḥurriyyāt*, 124–6, 133–6; al-Turābī, *Fī l-Fiqh*, 99–100.
[72] There are exceptions, of course, such as Abū Fāris, *Ḥukm*, 17.

detail than global Islamist scholars because of the practical Jordanian context it has to deal with, almost forcing it to somehow use the concept in a concrete way.

Shūrá, including its quasi-contingent feature of 'the people consulted', has long been quite important to the Jordanian Muslim Brotherhood in the context of its relationship with the Hashimite regime. Initially, the organisation's members seem to have viewed themselves as the ones who should give counsel to the king, so as to direct him towards a more Islamic policy.[73] In later works on the subject, Jordanian Brothers – like global Islamist scholars – point to the roots of *shūrá* in the Qur'an and the Sunna as well as the lives of early Muslims.[74] Abu Faris also states that consultation in Islam is limited by the boundaries of the *sharīʿa*, just as some global Islamist scholars have done.[75]

Similar to the non-Jordanian thinkers who have influenced the Brotherhood, the organisation's own members also deepen the role of the *umma*, even if they disagree on the scope of its mandate vis-à-vis the *sharīʿa*. This pertains, among other things, to the idea of *shūrá* as a duty incumbent upon the ruler, meaning that the latter has to consult others. Gharayiba, for example, indicates that there are classical and modern scholars who have weighed in on this subject and that those who believe consultation is a duty have the evidence on their side.[76] Abu Faris, in particular, pays considerable attention to juxtaposing the positions of the scholars (both classical and modern, including early Brothers) who believe the ruler is compelled to consult others[77] with the views of those who merely see this as recommended,[78] and squarely sides with the former.[79] He does the same with the question of whether the outcome of consultation is binding[80] or non-binding[81] to the ruler, again claiming that the former is correct.[82] Gharayiba agrees with this,[83] which means that both he and Abu Faris – like al-Qaradawi – differ with al-Banna on this point.

Despite the differences between Abu Faris and Gharayiba we saw earlier, both men thus decontest *shūrá* as compulsory for and binding to the ruler, thereby closely linking the quasi-contingent feature of 'the

[73] Boulby, *Muslim Brotherhood*, 54, 124.

[74] Abū Fāris, *Ḥukm*, 9–10; Abū Fāris, *Al-Niẓām*, 78–89; Ruḥayyil Gharāyiba, *Al-Ḥuqūq wa-l-Ḥurriyyāt al-Siyāsiyya fī l-Sharīʿa al-Islāmiyya* (Beirut: Al-Shabaka al-ʿArabiyya li-l-Abḥāth wa-l-Nashr, 2012), 255–7, 272–3.

[75] Muḥammad ʿAbd al-Qādir Abū Fāris, *Hādhā Huwa l-Ḥall* (Ṭanṭā: Dār al-Bashīr li-l-Thaqāfa wa-l-ʿUlūm, 1999), 63; Abū Fāris, *Ḥukm*, 11; Abū Fāris, *Al-Niẓām*, 100, 105–8.

[76] Gharāyiba, *Al-Ḥuqūq*, 257–61. [77] Abū Fāris, *Ḥukm*, 19–65. [78] Ibid., 67–81.

[79] Ibid., 83–5. [80] Ibid., 143–89. [81] Ibid., 89–141.

[82] Ibid., 191–3; Abū Fāris, *Al-Niẓām*, 88–9, 93–9. [83] Gharāyiba, *Al-Ḥuqūq*, 276–90.

people consulted' with the *umma*, which squares with the way they view *shūrá* in general, namely, as a means to limit the ruler's power and obtain freedom. As mentioned, such views should be seen in the context of Jordanian dictatorship in which – despite the absence of a caliphate – *sharīʿa* and *umma* still remain peripheral to the core concept of 'ruler'. As such, it is not surprising that Abu Faris, for example, believes that if the ruler does not accept *shūrá* as binding, 'it will lead to the despotism of the ruler (*istibdād al-ḥākim*) and his isolation (*infirādihi*) in deciding the fate of the *umma*'.[84] If he does accept consultation as binding, however, this 'preserves the personality of the Islamic *umma* (*shakhṣiyyat al-umma al-Islāmiyya*), its independence (*istiqlālihā*) and its distinction (*tamayyuzihā*)'[85] and leads to 'the widening of responsibility (*tawzīʿ li-l-masʾūliyya*), whether the result is positive or negative'.[86]

Such efforts to deepen the role of the *umma* are underlined by both men's attempts to tie *shūrá* to modern parliaments. This shows a flexibility in the interpretation of the idea of consultation that is shared by both *umma*-centred thinkers like Gharayiba and *sharīʿa*-centred ones like Abu Faris. The latter stated as far back as the 1980s that

> [n]o text is mentioned in the Book of God or in the Sunna of the Messenger of God [. . .] that shows us the manner of practising consultation (*kayfiyyat mumārasat al-shūrá*) and the commitment (*al-iltizām*) to this manner, just as no text is mentioned that compels the *umma* [to apply] a fixed number (*ʿadad muʿayyan*) [of candidates] for the *shūrá* council and the way to get to that number. In fact, this is one of the advantages of this eternal religion (*mumayyizāt hādhā l-dīn al-khālid*), which has not compelled the *umma* [to apply] a specific method (*uslūb muʿayyan*). It may be suitable at a time (*ṣāliḥan fī zaman*) and unsuitable for future times (*ghayr ṣāliḥ li-azmān mustaqbaliyya*).[87]

'The important thing from the Islamic point of view (*fī naẓar al-Islām*)', Abu Faris writes, 'is that the truth of consultation is carried out in society'.[88] He mentions several ways in which this can happen, including 'a council chosen through a direct election by the people', effectively equating consultation councils with parliaments.[89] Gharayiba does the latter more explicitly, simply stating that

> consultation councils (*majālis al-shūrá*) or legislative councils (*al-majālis al-tashrīʿiyya*) are invented names (*asmāʾ mustaḥdatha*) for what the jurisprudents

[84] Abū Fāris, *Ḥukm*, 83. [85] Ibid., 192. [86] Ibid., 194.
[87] Muḥammad Abū Fāris, 'Kayfiyyat al-Shūrá', *Al-Sabīl*, 26 October–2 November 1993, 23. This was originally published in Abū Fāris, *Al-Niẓām*, 108.
[88] Abū Fāris, 'Kayfiyyat', 23, Abū Fāris, *Al-Niẓām*, 109.
[89] Abū Fāris, 'Kayfiyyat', 23; Abū Fāris, *Al-Niẓām*, 111 (see also 237).

of the Muslims and their scholars (*fuqahāʾ al-Muslimīn wa-ʿulamāʾuhum*) used to call 'the people of loosening and binding' (*ahl al-ḥall wa-l-ʿaqd*).[90]

The term '*ahl al-ḥall wa-l-ʿaqd*' is specified even further by both men in their writings. Abu Faris states that

> [t]he people of consultation, they are the people in charge (*ūlū l-amr*), the ones who see (*aṣḥāb al-ruʾya*), those who are capable of producing an opinion (*yaqdurūna ʿalá ibdāʾ al-raʾy*) and solving problems (*ḥall al-mushkilāt*). [. . .] Those who know are more entitled to be consulted (*aḥaqq bi-l-mushāwara*) than those who do not know. [God] the exalted has said: 'Are they equal – those who know and those who know not?'[91]

The quotation above gives the impression that Abu Faris sees *shūrá*'s quasi-contingent feature of 'the people consulted' as a group of experts and this is, indeed, the case. He specifies his views on this by writing that 'the people of consultation are the people of loosening and binding', which include

> the ones who have an opinion, the thought leaders (*qādat al-fikr*), the masters of policy (*arbāb al-siyāsa*) and the commanders of armies (*umarāʾ al-juyūsh*). They are the ones who are specialised or experienced (*aṣḥāb al-ikhtiṣāṣ wa-l-khibra*) in any field of work (*fī kull fann min al-funūn*), such as agriculture (*al-zirāʿa*), trade (*al-tijāra*), industry (*al-ṣināʿa*), the economy (*al-iqtiṣād*) and matters of war (*shuʾūn al-ḥarb*).[92]

As such, Abu Faris does not include everyone in the *ahl al-ḥall wa-l-ʿaqd*, as some global Islamist scholars do, but stays closer to the ideas of some early Muslim Brothers by decontesting *shūrá* as a duty for the ruler whose result is binding, which can be achieved through parliaments and which preferably involves consulting experts.

Gharayiba does not fundamentally differ from Abu Faris with regard to who should be included among the *ahl al-ḥall wa-l-ʿaqd* in a consultation council. Although he initially points to broad and inclusive requirements such as justice, knowledge and wisdom as criteria for the people of loosening and binding,[93] he specifies this later to include a broad group of experts similar to the one Abu Faris mentions.[94] Gharayiba also makes clear that the *ahl al-ḥall wa-l-ʿaqd* should be elected by the entire *umma*, which they represent and whose affairs they must look after.[95] This is essential, Gharayiba states,

[90] Gharāyiba, *Al-Ḥuqūq*, 109.
[91] Abū Fāris, *Al-Niẓām*, 112. The quotation from the Qurʾān is from Q. 39:9.
[92] Ibid., 116. [93] Gharāyiba, *Al-Ḥuqūq*, 114. [94] Ibid., 271. [95] Ibid., 266.

because the entire *umma*, with all its individuals, can only realistically and rationally (*wāqiʿan wa-ʿaqlan*) manage these duties it is in charge of (*al-wājibāt al-munawwaṭa bihā*) through representation and delegation (*al-tamthīl wa-l-ināba*). That is why the *ahl al-ḥall wa-l-ʿaqd* are in charge of the task (*mahamma*) of representation and deputyship (*niyāba*) on behalf of the *umma*.[96]

The above suggests that Gharayiba decontests *shūrá* like Abu Faris and in some ways he does. Chapter 6 will show, however, that both men disagree on what groups in society should be included in or excluded from politics.

The final question with regard to *shūrá* we must answer now pertains to the concept's similarity to democracy. As we saw earlier, this is a matter that divided the global Islamist scholars who have influenced the Jordanian Muslim Brotherhood and we can see the same division within the organisation itself. The answer to this question is not just related to the decontestation of *shūrá* as such, which – as we saw directly above – is largely similar among Brothers as different as Abu Faris and Gharayiba, but also to the position one is willing to give to the *umma* in relation to both other adjacent concepts of '*sharīʿa*' and '*sulṭa*'. In other words, whether members of the Jordanian Brotherhood are *sharīʿa*-centred, *umma*-centred or balanced in their approach to the ruler makes a great difference in their willingness to equate *shūrá* with democracy.

In a study originally published in 1992, Chenivesse distinguishes three different attitudes towards the relationship between *shūrá* and democracy among the members of the Jordanian Muslim Brotherhood. One attitude rejects democracy and clearly holds on to *shūrá* as a superior alternative; a second accepts democracy, but prefers *shūrá* or sees the former as a stepping stone towards the latter; a third attitude, finally, embraces democracy and uses that term instead of or alongside *shūrá*.[97] Although the attitudes found among the Jordanian Muslim Brotherhood have shifted more towards the third group since the early 1990s, all three categories still exist and are therefore useful for our analysis here.[98]

The first category is represented most explicitly by Abu Faris. Although he clearly facilitates democracy through his deepening of the role of the *umma* in consultation, Abu Faris's pervasive *sharīʿa*-centredness prevents

96 Ibid.
97 Julien Chenivesse, 'Al-Ikhwān al-Muslimūn al-Urdunniyyūn wa-l-ʿAmaliyya al-Dīmuqrāṭiyya', in *Al-Ḥaraka al-Islāmiyya wa-l-Ḥuqūq wa-l-Ḥurriyyāt al-ʿĀmma*, ed. Ibrāhīm Gharāyiba (Amman: Markaz Dirāsāt al-Umma, 2002), 157–64. This study was originally published as 'Les freres musulmans Jordaniens face au processus de democratisation' by the Institut d'Etudes Politiques de Paris. Unfortunately, I have not been able to obtain the original French version of the article and have therefore relied on its Arabic translation.
98 For the purposes of clarity, the three categories are actually given in reverse order here compared with how Chenivesse presents them.

him from expanding the scope of the *umma*'s mandate vis-à-vis the adjacent concept of '*sharīʿa*'. As such, he adamantly rejects democracy. Like several global Islamist scholars who have influenced the Jordanian Brotherhood, Abu Faris distinguishes between the limits put on *shūrá* by the *sharīʿa*, on the one hand, and democracy, which he associates with personal freedoms he believes are contrary to Islamic law, on the other.[99] This is related to the fact that, according to Abu Faris, democracy is a secular system and one that is decided by human power, influence, sovereignty and laws.[100] When I confronted him with the belief of some Muslim Brothers that democracy could also be Islamic, he replied:

> There is no Islamic democracy. There is no Islamic democracy. Democracy . . . Its meaning is that domination is with the people (*al-siyāda li-l-nās*). No. The truth is that in Islam, no, domination is not with the people. Domination is with the *sharīʿa* and the laws of God.[101]

As such, Abu Faris does not view democracy as equal to *shūrá*, but sees its adoption in Muslim countries as 'the result of an intellectual raid (*ghazw fikrī*)' meant to defame various aspects of Islam.[102]

Although Abu Faris is perhaps the strongest ideological opponent of equating *shūrá* with democracy within the Jordanian Brotherhood, he is not the only one. Like-minded Jordanian Brother Salah al-Khalidi contends that *shūrá* is not only an alternative to democracy, but also a duty incumbent upon Muslims that was practised by the Prophet and his companions. Unlike in a democracy, in which – al-Khalidi states – 'nothing is sacred; everything can be voted on', in *shūrá* it is the *sharīʿa* that rules.[103] Another Brotherhood-affiliated scholar and author of several books on the organisation, ʿAwni al-ʿUbaydi, agrees with Abu Faris and similarly states that *shūrá* is superior to democracy, precisely because it acts within the boundaries of the *sharīʿa* and therefore cannot allow practices that are often seen as forbidden by Muslims, such as levying (usurious) interest (*ribā*).[104]

Brothers in the second group distinguished by Chenivesse are less adamant in their refusal to use the term 'democracy' and sometimes even partly accept the concept behind it, although they prefer *shūrá*. Hammam Saʿid, for example, accepts the *means* of democracy (choosing

99 Interview with Muḥammad Abū Fāris, Amman, 21 January 2013; Abū Fāris, *Hādhā*, 27–9.

100 Abū Fāris, *Hādhā*, 22–7. See also Abū Fāris, 'Al-Islām Huwa l-Ḥall. Hal al-Dīmuqrāṭiyya al-Ḥall?', *Al-Sabīl*, 14/20 September 1999, 17.

101 Interview with Muḥammad Abū Fāris, Amman, 21 January 2013.

102 Abū Fāris, *Hādhā*, 18.

103 Interview with Ṣalāḥ al-Khālidī, Amman, 24 January 2013.

104 Interview with ʿAwnī al-ʿUbaydī, Amman, 11 January 2014.

the ruler, general elections, etc.), but rejects its philosophical basis (popular sovereignty) because that may clash with Islam.[105] Similar ideas about democracy as partly (or even largely) acceptable have been expressed by other prominent members of the organisation like Ishaq Farhan.[106] Still others seem to agree with this, but appear to go further in their acceptance of democracy. Former General Controller ʿAbd al-Majid Dhunaybat, for example, states that 'democracy, in some of its methods (*asālībihā*), corresponds with (*tuwāzī*) *shūrá*. Democracy, as far as its mechanisms (*āliyātihā*) are concerned, we do not reject them (*lā nunkiruhā*)', suggesting he concurs with Saʿid. Yet he also appears to take his support for democracy further, viewing the means of democracy as 'the spirit and essence (*rūḥ wa-jawhar*) of *shūrá*' and 'the strengthening of the principle (*taʿzīz mabdaʾ*) of consultation'.[107]

The third category, finally, seems to have the upper hand in today's Jordanian Muslim Brotherhood.[108] This is perhaps not surprising. Once important members of the organisation even partly opened up to democracy, it gave them a chance to translate their popularity into representation and influence, which would be politically hard to give up for ideological reasons. The political process in Jordan thus facilitated the ideological direction that various members of the organisation (through their extensive discussions)[109] – as well as global Islamist scholars like al-Ghannushi – were going into anyway.[110] As a result, Jordanian Brothers increasingly unapologetically choose democracy and see this as a strategic – rather than merely a tactical – choice.[111]

The aforementioned Farhan, for example, while critical of what he labels 'the Western system of democracy', embraces democracy as 'the confirmation of our *shūrá* values (*taʾkīd qiyaminā l-shūriyya*)'.[112] He distinguishes five different components of democracy (parliament and elections; political parties and pluralism; freedom of expression and the press; commitment to the rule of law; and a just judiciary), all of which he supports.[113] Others point out that democracy provides greater detail to *shūrá*,[114] can be seen as its practical application[115] or is simply the same as

105 Interview with Hammām Saʿīd, Amman, 28 January 2013.
106 Farhan, *Islamic View*, 24–5.
107 'Fī Ḥiwār', 107–8. See also ʿAbd al-Majīd Dhunaybāt, 'Ḥawla Barnāmij "al-Ikhwān" fī Miṣr', *Al-Ghad* (www.alghad.com/articles/546177, accessed 28 January 2013), 9 November 2007.
108 Brown, *Victory*, 190–1. 109 Schwedler, *Faith*, 195–6.
110 Interview with ʿUrayb al-Rantāwī, Amman, 12 January 2013.
111 Robinson, 'Islamists', 378–9. 112 Farḥān, *Mawāqif I*, 15. 113 Ibid., 15–17.
114 Interview with Jamīl Abū Bakr, Amman, 18 June 2012.
115 Interview with Ḥamza Manṣūr, Amman, 25 June 2012.

consultation.[116] Given such views – as well as those that state that democracy is the best choice[117] – it is not surprising that recent policy documents published by the Brotherhood and/or the IAF use '*shūrá*' and 'democracy' more or less interchangeably[118] and that the regime is criticised for not being democratic enough.[119]

As mentioned, however, fully associating *shūrá*'s quasi-contingent feature of 'the people consulted' with the *umma*, even when provided with as much detail as some Jordanian Brothers have done, does not automatically amount to support for democracy, as Abu Faris shows. In fact, neither does equating '*shūrá*' and 'democracy' in and of itself translate into whole-hearted support for the latter since the recurring issue of the balance between the two adjacent concepts of '*sharīʿa*' and '*umma*' needs to be taken into account as well. If, as in Abu Faris and others' case, the former is a system of rulings that takes precedence over the latter, that is a *sharīʿa*-centred approach that can hardly be labelled 'democratic'. For that to happen, as we have discussed before, the *umma* must take precedence over the *sharīʿa*, which can happen by pushing the latter to a peripheral position vis-à-vis the core concept of 'ruler', or the *sharīʿa* itself should be made flexible and limited.

While the former option is, perhaps, a choice that an explicitly Islamist organisation is unlikely to make, the latter is not. As such, some Jordanian Brothers have abetted their embrace of democracy (through its equation with *shūrá*) by 'constitutionalising' the *sharīʿa* into a flexible set of guidelines with few fixed rules.[120] Several Jordanians affiliated with the Brotherhood indicate that the number of issues on which no consultation may take place is very limited, just like al-Ghannushi does, leaving more room for the *umma* to legislate.[121] This is also the area where Gharayiba differs starkly from Abu Faris. While they treated *shūrá*'s quasi-contingent feature of 'the people consulted' similarly, Gharayiba's *umma*-

[116] Interviews with ʿAlī Abū l-Sukkar, Amman, 27 June 2012; Zakī Banī Irshīd, Amman, 13 June 2012; Sālim al-Falāḥāt, Amman, 22 January 2013; Ruḥayyil Gharāyiba, Amman, 17 January 2013.

[117] Interviews with ʿĀṭif al-Jawlānī, Amman, 14 June 2012; Muḥammad al-Majālī, Amman, 17 June 2013.

[118] Al-Ḥaraka al-Islāmiyya fī l-Urdunn, *Ruʾyat*, 14, 16; Ḥizb Jabhat al-ʿAmal al-Islāmī, *Al-Niẓām*, 4–5.

[119] See, for example, Farḥān, *Mawāqif I*, 15–32; Farḥān, *Mawāqif II*, 11–12; Ḥamza Manṣūr, *Kalimāt wa-Mawāqif* (Amman: Dār al-Furqān li-l-Nashr wa-l-Tawzīʿ, 1998), 4, 92, 115; 'Al-Nāʾib Manṣūr: Al-Dīmuqrāṭiyya Tarājaʿat bi-Shidda baʿda l-Muʿāhada', *Al-Sabīl*, 16/22 January 1996, 3; 'Al-Dīmuqrāṭiyya al-Urdunniyya Tatarājaʿu Mundhu ʿĀmm 1993', *Al-Sabīl*, 12/18 April 2005, 4.

[120] Hamid, *Temptations*, 132–3.

[121] ʿAbd al-Jabbār Saʿīd, 'A-Shūrá am Dīmuqrāṭiyya?', *Al-Sabīl*, 21/27 December 1993, 18. Interview with Faraj Shalhūb, Amman, 21 June 2012.

centred approach causes him to divert greatly from Abu Faris's *sharī'a*-centred take on this matter. Gharayiba states:

> In reality, *shūrá* is an expression (*ta'bīr*) of the distinct space (*al-makāna al-bāriza*) that God [. . .] has given to the *umma* of the Muslims in the context of legislation (*al-tashrī'*) decided through the intentions of Islamic law (*maqāṣid al-sharī'a*) and its general principles (*wa-qawā'idihā l-'āmma*). [*Shūrá* is also an expression of] the broad mandates (*ṣalāḥiyyāt wāsi'a*) that God [. . .] has given to the *umma* with regard to adding to (*al-iḍāfa*) or renewing (*al-tajdīd*) [the *sharī'a*] within the greatest bases of Islamic law and its agreed upon fixed issues (*thawābitihā l-muttafaq 'alayhā*).[122]

Gharayiba, in other words, sees *shūrá* as providing the *umma* with a broad mandate to rule.

Elsewhere, Gharayiba distinguishes fixed issues in Islamic law (*thawābit*) from changeable ones (*mutaghayyirāt*) and states that the former are not only limited in number but also pertain to such basic creedal issues as the oneness of God (*waḥdāniyyat Allāh*) and the pillars of Islam. *Mutaghayyirāt*, however, represent the vast majority of Islamic legal issues, he claims, meaning that renewed *ijtihād* may be applied to them in every context and time, as long as they conform to the very broad 'spirit of the *sharī'a* and its general intentions'.[123] Thus, Gharayiba further supports his *umma*-centred approach to Islamist politics by decontesting *shūrá* as an Islamically inspired link between the adjacent concept of '*umma*' and the core concept of 'ruler' to create space for the people to rule democratically in a civil state with an Islamic authority.

Debating Political Participation

While Gharayiba is not representative of the Jordanian Muslim Brotherhood as a whole, the tendency over the past decades has clearly been towards a greater acceptance of democracy, as the analysis above makes clear. Moreover, the Brotherhood had already participated in the country's national elections several times when parliament was reinstated in 1989. This participation in the organisation's early decades had led to some debate within the Muslim Brotherhood in Jordan, but the majority view that supported political engagement prevailed, as it did in 1989.[124] There had also been a global debate on whether participation in parliaments was allowed, but among scholars sympathetic to and influential on

122 Gharāyiba, *Al-Ḥuqūq*, 282–3.
123 Ruḥayyil Gharāyiba, 'Mawāzīn Shar'iyya fī l-'Amal al-Siyāsī', *Al-Sabīl*, 19/26 October 1993, 15.
124 Schwedler, *Faith*, 155–9.

the Muslim Brotherhood this had overwhelmingly been accepted, partly because al-Banna had already participated in elections himself.[125]

Virtually all of this participation pertained to legislative – not executive – experience, however. Whereas a parliamentary presence allowed any party to remain steadfast in its views, participating in a government would mean making compromises and taking responsibility for them. Although engaging in the executive branch of politics had also been overwhelmingly approved of by global Islamist thinkers,[126] Jordanian Brotherhood-affiliated scholars nevertheless debated this issue when, apart from the continued parliamentary participation and the founding of a political party,[127] the option of joining the Jordanian government came up. This debate, organised as a forum in 1992, has received some attention from academics,[128] but needs to be dealt with here, not only to show the consolidation of a pro-participation attitude within the Muslim Brotherhood in Jordan, but also to add greater ideological and conceptual detail to the existing literature.

The participants in the forum included various scholars,[129] but the two most prominent among them were the aforementioned Muhammad Abu Faris, who opposed participation in government, and ʿUmar al-Ashqar (1940–2012), who argued in favour of governmental participation. The latter was a Salafi scholar of Palestinian descent who had spent much of his life in Kuwait but came to Jordan in the early 1990s.[130] Both Abu Faris and al-Ashqar had authored booklets in which they presented their points of view: *Participation in Government in Ignorant Regimes* (Abu Faris)[131]

125 Al-Ḍumūr, *Fiqh*, 263–303. Indeed, the only dissenters to this seem to be from among radical Islamist groups. For more on these and their views on democracy, see Joas Wagemakers, '"The *Kāfir* Religion of the West": *Takfīr* of Democracy and Democrats by Radical Islamists', in *Accusations of Unbelief in Islam: A Diachronic Perspective on* Takfīr, ed. Camilla Adang, Hassan Ansari, Maribel Fierro and Sabine Schmidtke (Leiden: Brill, 2016), 327–53.

126 Al-Ḍumūr, *Fiqh*, 307–77.

127 The founding of the IAF was mostly done for pragmatic reasons in the context of the regime's demands, as we saw in Chapter 3. The idea of a plurality of political parties had already been approved by Yūsuf al-Qaraḍāwī, however (Yūsuf al-Qaraḍāwī, 'Al-Taʿddudiyya al-Ḥizbiyya Ḍarūra Islāmiyya', *Al-Sabil*, 29 March–4 April 1994, 17), and, perhaps partly because of this, the founding of the IAF itself seems to have created relatively little stir. See Brown, *Victory*, 100; Hamid, 'Islamic Action Front', 545.

128 Al-Budūr, *Al-Tajriba*, 25–32; Gharyiba, *Jamāʿat*, 109–12; Hamid, *Temptations*, 161–2; Schwedler, *Faith*, 163–4.

129 Gharāyiba, *Jamāʿat*, 110–11.

130 Joas Wagemakers, 'Ashqar, ʿUmar Sulaymān', in *Encyclopaedia of Islam Three*, ed. Kate Fleet, Gudrun Krämer, Denis Matringe, John Nawas and Everett Rowson (Leiden: Brill, 2020), 2020-IV, 1–3.

131 Muḥammad ʿAbd al-Qādir Abū Fāris, *Al-Mushāraka fī l-Wizāra fī l-Anẓima al-Jāhiliyya* (Amman: Dār al-Furqān li-l-Nashr wa-l-Tawzīʿ, 1991).

and *The Ruling on Participation in Government and Parliaments* (al-Ashqar).[132]

Abu Faris's implicit starting point is that the regime in Jordan is a *jāhilī* one, which he defines as a regime that 'does not concede to God [. . .] through *ḥākimiyya*, thus applying a system of law other than the *sharīʿa* of God (*sharʿan ghayr sharʿ Allāh*) and refuses to consider Islam the only source (*al-maṣdar al-waḥīd*) of legislation'.[133] More specifically, he states that Islamic 'government' (*al-wizāra*, *al-ḥukūma*) or 'executive authority' (*al-sulṭa al-tanfīdhiyya*) is characterised by its Muslim members, its support for the duties (*farāʾiḍ*) of Islam and the execution of the religion's rulings and teachings (*aḥkām al-Islām wa-taʿālīmihi*), none of which he sees in *jāhilī* regimes.[134] Following the reasoning of ʿAwda and Qutb that we saw above, he believes that '*jāhilī*' applies to 'the regimes in the countries of the Arabs and the Muslims' and – citing several verses from the Qurʾan, including Q. 5:44 – states that this expels them from Islam.[135] He even cites ʿAwda's exact words quoted in Chapter 2 that a person guilty of such 'un-Islamic' rule 'is an unbeliever in whose heart there is not [even] an atom of Islam, even if he calls himself a Muslim'.[136]

Participation in a government guilty of 'un-Islamic' rule, Abu Faris claims, gives the impression that its legislation is legitimate. He states that this is not only a betrayal of the people who trust Islamists,[137] but also makes the latter share in the responsibility for such legislation.[138] That, in turn, gets them involved in the application of something other than the *sharīʿa*, which is forbidden.[139] Instead, Abu Faris writes

> Muslim are commanded by the *sharīʿa* not to believe in any idols (*yakfirū bi-kull ṭawāghīt*) on earth and to confront them (*yataṣaddū lahum*) and their infidel legislations (*li-sharāʾiʿihim al-kāfira*) through resistance (*bi-l-muqāwama*) and exposing their danger (*tibyān khuṭuratihā*) to the lives of people in [this] world and the hereafter (*fī l-dunyā wa-l-ākhira*).[140]

Although, as we saw above, Abu Faris does not advocate violence against the regime, he does tap into a long radical Islamist tradition – espoused by Qutb and others – of describing rulers who fail to apply Islamic law in full as objects of worship. While Abu Faris does not explicitly label those who follow such rulers as 'unbelievers' who serve other gods, al-Khalidi does suggest this by linking this matter to Q. 9:31[141] – like Qutb, as we saw in

132 ʿUmar Sulaymān al-Ashqar, *Ḥukm al-Mushāraka fī l-Wizāra wa-l-Majālis al-Niyābiyya* (Amman: Dār al-Nafāʾis li-l-Nashr wa-l-Tawzīʿ, 2009).
133 Abū Fāris, *Al-Mushāraka*, 17. 134 Ibid., 18. 135 Ibid., 17. 136 Ibid., 20.
137 Ibid., 20–1. 138 Ibid., 22. 139 Ibid., 37–9. 140 Ibid., 21.
141 Ṣalāh al-Khālidī, 'Wuʿūd al-Rasūl li-ʿAdī b. Ḥātim al-Ṭāʾī', *Al-Ribāṭ*, 4 November 1992, 7.

Chapter 4 – and, as such, seems to view the following of non-Islamic leaders as idolatrous worship.[142] To be sure, al-Khalidi does not apply *takfīr* to Jordanians who follow the regime's leaders or their laws and, in fact, he believes Qutb has been widely misunderstood on this point.[143] Yet it is also clear that this reasoning can lead to more drastic solutions – explicit *takfīr* of politicians and their supporters – than the ones Abu Faris and al-Khalidi espouse and among more radical Islamists it has, indeed, led to such outcomes.[144]

Yet Abu Faris does not just argue against governmental participation along religious lines. He also sees many supposedly un-Islamic regimes as autocratic and supportive of 'administrative and moral corruption (*al-fasād al-idārī wa-l-akhlāqī*)'[145] and believes they are responsible for pushing Islamist movements into concessions and creating divisions among them.[146] Citing the experience of both Qutb and al-Hudaybi in Egypt, Abu Faris also claims that the drawbacks of engaging with government outweigh the benefits.[147] Moreover, he believes that a small Islamist presence in a government will not help solve certain problems and that this failure will reflect badly on the Islamist movement as a whole.[148]

Governmental participation in *jāhilī* regimes is only allowed, Abu Faris claims, in exceptional cases, of which he names two. The first of these is the Qur'anic Yusuf, who served under a non-Muslim pharaoh in Egypt to provide food to save people from starvation. Abu Faris distinguishes this prophet from modern-day governments by pointing out that the former ruled at a time when the *sharīʿa* did not yet exist (and thus could not be applied), but that he nevertheless rejected ruling against revelation and refused idols. Moreover, Yusuf was only responsible for one task – feeding the people – and did not share in the responsibility of other aspects of government and was exceptionally suited for this job, in which he became the de facto ruler of the country.[149] The second example Abu Faris mentions is the Negus (al-Najāshī), the Christian ruler of Ethiopia whose rule some early Muslims are said to have lived under after having fled persecution in Mecca. Unlike today's regimes, Abu Faris writes, this ruler was just and provided the Muslims with freedom of worship, causing the Prophet to pray for him.[150] Such exceptions notwithstanding, Abu Faris maintains that the basic rule is that participation in government is not allowed.[151]

[142] Ṣalāh al-Khālidī, 'Arbāb ʿAṣriyyūn', *Al-Ribāṭ*, 11 November 1992, 7.
[143] Interview with Ṣalāḥ al-Khālidī, Amman, 24 January 2013.
[144] Wagemakers, 'Inquiry', 317, 320–2. [145] Abū Fāris, *Al-Mushāraka*, 24.
[146] Ibid., 25–7. See also 31–3. [147] Ibid., 28. [148] Ibid., 30. [149] Ibid., 39–48.
[150] Ibid., 48–53. [151] Ibid., 40.

Ironically, al-Ashqar, who argues in favour of governmental participation, agrees with Abu Faris's conclusion that participation in a government is not allowed if it does not rule on the basis of the *sharīʿa*. Citing the same texts as Abu Faris, al-Ashqar states that ruling according to something other than Islamic law is forbidden and *ḥākimiyya* should be with God, not the people.[152] He also claims that participation in 'un-Islamic' rule will cause Muslims to sin and differ with each other and – like al-Khalidi – cites Q. 9:31 to emphasise that following leaders who rule in contravention to the *sharīʿa* can be equated with worshipping other gods.[153] Like Abu Faris, al-Ashqar also mentions certain exceptions to the general rule that participation in 'un-Islamic' regimes is forbidden, namely, Yusuf, the Negus and *maṣlaḥa*.[154] The latter concept, as briefly referred to in Chapter 2, refers to the general interest and has been used by scholars to argue in favour of rulings that would otherwise be forbidden and this is precisely what al-Ashqar uses it for.

Yusuf, al-Ashqar states, lived in a society that 'without a doubt [. . .] was a *jāhilī* society that did not know Islam'.[155] Although al-Ashqar claims that Yusuf turned against the *jāhilī* nature of society through his behaviour and, as such, became one of the leaders of Egypt, second only to the pharaoh, he participated in a polytheist and unjust system in which he did not apply Islamic law and only made a specific contribution.[156] Al-Ashqar states that the fact that Yusuf nevertheless participated in this system must mean that it is allowed as an exception if one can serve the 'greatest general interest' (*maṣlaḥa kubrá*) or if one can ward off an 'imminent evil' (*sharr mustaṭīr*).[157] The author – frequently citing Qutb – rejects counter arguments such as that Yusuf was really in control of the entire regime.[158] Arguing that Yusuf, as a prophet, was sinless (*maʿṣūm*) and that his rule therefore must have accorded with the *ḥākimiyya* of God, al-Ashqar also dismisses the argument that Yusuf ruled at a time when the *sharīʿa* did not exist yet.[159] He concludes that, rather than a violation of God's sovereignty, Yusuf's participation was a sign of submission to Islam that allowed him to be used for a task that God had designated for him.[160]

Al-Ashqar thus differs with Abu Faris on the example of Yusuf, as he does on the Negus. According to al-Ashqar, the Negus converted to Islam and sums up a number of texts that seem to suggest that this was the case[161] and refutes those who claim that he remained a Christian.[162] The author also claims that the Negus may not have ruled according to Islam because 'externally, he fitted in with the situation (*innahu ẓāhir min al-ḥāl*)

152 Al-Ashqar, *Ḥukm*, 31. 153 Ibid., 32–3. 154 Ibid., 35. 155 Ibid., 36.
156 Ibid., 37–41. 157 Ibid., 41. 158 Ibid., 42–54. 159 Ibid., 54–60.
160 Ibid., 61–3. 161 Ibid., 69–75. 162 Ibid., 79–83.

that prevailed in his land (*allatī kānat sāʾida fī diyārihi*) and with the obstacles that obstructed his way (*al-ʿaqabāt allatī kānat taʿtariḍu ṭarīqahu*)'.[163] This suggests that the Negus could not rule on the basis of the *sharīʿa* because the (Christian) environment he was in did not allow him to. That, in turn, suggests that there are situations in which one cannot rule on the basis of the *sharīʿa*, but may still participate in ruling as such.

In this context, al-Ashqar distinguishes a fixed ruling (*ʿazīma*), which states that participation in 'un-Islamic' rule is not allowed, from a concession (*rukhṣa*), which entails an exception,[164] similar to what Gharayiba did with regard to Islamic law. Just as Yusuf and the Negus were exceptions, acting in the general interest of the Muslims can also be such an exception, al-Ashqar argues. So while participation in 'un-Islamic' government may be forbidden as a rule, it may also, in some cases, serve the *maṣlaḥa* of the *umma*.[165] While Abu Faris believes that the texts forbidding participation in 'un-Islamic' government overrule any interests that may be served by doing so anyway,[166] al-Ashqar mentions several examples of *maṣlaḥa* that justify it, such as doing away with the idea that Islamists cannot rule, increasing Islamist experience in governing and using the state to promote the religion.[167] Unsurprisingly, al-Ashqar, after going over a number of fatwas on this issue[168] as well as the arguments for and against participation,[169] eventually concludes that it is allowed to participate in governments not based on the *sharīʿa*.[170]

This discussion between the Brotherhood-affiliated scholars was also reflected in the Jordanian Islamist press in the years that followed the original forum.[171] As Schwedler has pointed out, al-Ashqar's views allowing participation in Jordanian governments were more representative of the Brotherhood's general views and, as such, prevailed over the increasingly marginalised views espoused by Abu Faris. Yet the latter remained within the organisation.[172] This way, just as *shūrá* (and, increasingly, democracy) had been decontested as an important link connecting the adjacent concept of '*umma*' with the core concept of 'ruler' through

163 Ibid., 75. 164 Ibid., 84–5. 165 Ibid., 103.

166 Muḥammad Abū Fāris, 'Ḥiwār maʿa l-Shaykh Yūsuf al-Qaraḍāwī ḥawla l-Mushāraka fī l-Wizāra fī l-Anẓima allatī Lā Tuṭabbiqu l-Islām', *Al-Sabīl*, 9/15 July 1996, 9; Muḥammad Abū Fāris, 'Ḥiwār maʿa l-Shaykh Yūsuf al-Qaraḍāwī ḥawla l-Mushāraka fī l-Wizāra fī l-Anẓima allatī Lā Tuṭabbiqu l-Islām', *Al-Sabīl*, 16/23 July 1996, 9. Abū Fāris expressed these views in a dialogue with al-Qaraḍāwī; however, not al-Ashqar.

167 Al-Ashqar, *Ḥukm*, 104–5. 168 Ibid., 106–12, 134–45. 169 Ibid., 113–33.

170 Ibid., 149.

171 See, for example, Ibrāhīm Gharāyiba, 'Al-Ikhwān al-Muslimīn wa-l-Mushāraka fī l-Wizāra', *Al-Sabīl*, 16/22 April 1996, 12; 'Al-Ashqar: Al-Mushāraka fī l-Majālis al-Niyābiyya Intikhāban wa-Tarshīḥan Ḥalāl Sharʿan', *Al-Sabīl*, 10/16 June 2003, 9.

172 Schwedler, *Faith*, 164.

parliament and a broad group of experts as the *ahl al-ḥall wa-l-ʿaqd*, the practical application of this had now also been decided upon. This meant that the Brotherhood's ideological path to political participation on all levels had been fully cleared.

The fact that the Brotherhood as an organisation had now decisively done away with religious obstacles to political participation did not mean that discussions on this subject ended completely[173] or that everyone agreed.[174] It did mean, however, that the question of participation was now debated in terms of the interests of the *umma* rather than the *sharīʿa*.[175] This became particularly clear in the elections of 1997, 2010 and 2013, which the Brotherhood-affiliated IAF boycotted. Rather than resorting to religious arguments against democracy or political participation, the IAF stated that foreign policy issues such as the normalisation with Israel (after the Wadi ʿAraba peace agreement in 1994) and the state's willingness to give in to the loan demands of the IMF were partly to blame for their decision to boycott the elections. Other factors included the regime's corruption, a press law the party disagreed with and, of course, the electoral law, as well as the accusation that the regime was retreating from the path of democratisation, did not enforce a proper separation of powers, did not give enough power and space to parliament and the opposition and limited people's freedoms.[176]

Although the IAF published its reasons for boycotting the 1997 elections in a statement on behalf of the entire party[177] and the decision had been adopted by the overwhelming majority (83.3 per cent) of the IAF's Shūrá Council's members,[178] there was internal opposition to it. This obviously did not come from Abu Faris, who – interestingly – did not rejoice that his anti-democratic views coincided with the IAF's decision to boycott the elections, but actually stuck to the party's line by mentioning

[173] See, for instance, Ṣalāḥ al-Khālidī, 'Hal al-Intikhābāt Wājib Sharʿan?!', *Al-Sabīl*, 23 October 2010, 9; 'Al-Duktūr ʿUmar al-Ashqar Yanfī Ṣudūr Ayy Fatwá ʿanhu Tuḥarrimu l-Mushāraka fī l-Intikhābāt al-Niyābiyya Tarshīḥan wa-Taṣwītan', *Al-Sabīl*, 3/9 June 2003, 1.

[174] See, for example, Ṣalāḥ al-Khālidī, 'Al-Nuwwāb wa-Ḥukm Allāh', *Al-Sabīl*, 25 January 2011, 17.

[175] 'Fī Ḥiwār', 108, 110. See also Schwedler, *Faith*, 166–7.

[176] Yūsuf al-ʿAẓm, *Bayādir wa-Ḥiṣād* (Amman: Dār al-Furqān li-l-Nashr wa-l-Tawzīʿ, 1998), 19–22; al-Budūr, *Al-Tajriba*, 126–7; Moaddel, *Jordanian Exceptionalism*, 135.

[177] 'Jabhat al-ʿAmal al-Islāmī Tuwaḍḍiḥu Asbāb Muqāṭaʿat al-Intikhābāt', *Al-Sabīl*, 29 July–4 August 1997, 1. For an English translation of the entire document, see Moaddel, *Jordanian Exceptionalism*, 191–8; Society of Muslim Brothers, 'Boycotting the 1997 Election in Jordan', in *Modernist and Fundamentalist Debates in Islam: A Reader*, ed. Mansoor Moaddel and Kamran Talattof (New York: Palgrave Macmillan, 2000), 301–7.

[178] 'Jabhat al-ʿAmal al-Islāmī Tuqarriru l-Muqāṭaʿa wa-bi-Aghlabiyya Sāḥiqa', *Al-Sabīl*, 29 July–4 August 1997, 17.

the same arguments given above.[179] Instead, the main – though not the only[180] – critic of this boycott was the aforementioned pro-regime Brother Bassam al-ʿUmush, who – as we saw in Chapter 3 – left the Brotherhood over the IAF's decision not to participate in 1997[181] and was among those disaffected Brothers who founded the Islamic Centre Party in 2001.[182] Although he later claimed in an interview that it was the ideological and organisational rigidity of the Brotherhood that made him quit the group,[183] this is not what he said at the time.

Given his slightly *sulṭa*-centred tendencies, it is not surprising that al-ʿUmush viewed the 1997 boycott as an affront to the king. Ignoring the measures the regime had taken against the IAF to limit its parliamentary presence (including the electoral law), al-ʿUmush questions why the party is so keen on winning many seats in parliament. If the party has no intention of dominating parliament with a majority anyway, 'what is the difference between their having twenty or fifteen representatives?'. Al-ʿUmush believes that the IAF should not push its luck with trying to win as many seats as possible because this may 'threaten the presence of parliament as a whole, where it is possible that the king uses his right to dissolve parliament'.[184]

As such, al-ʿUmush provides justification (or at least excuses) for the state's authoritarian approach in a way that, in a sense, resembles the *sulṭa*-centred classical Muslim scholars' attempts to incorporate the caliph's authority into their political philosophy. He also criticises the IAF's precise reasons for the boycott, however. Al-ʿUmush claims that the IAF has rarely been interested in legal reform before (so why complain about it now?), that this is not the time to protest peace with Israel, that amending laws one is unhappy about is done through parliament (not boycotts) and that the country's freedoms and its need for loans are hardly different from previous years.[185]

In 2010, the justification for the boycott of that year's elections was similarly framed in terms of the interests of the *umma*, not the application of the *sharīʿa*. As we saw in Chapter 3, the Brotherhood and the IAF elected several less accommodating members to important positions in the years prior to 2010, meaning that they were also less willing to overlook the regime's alleged transgressions now. Still, the decision to boycott the elections was not the work of a few hard-liners, but actually had widespread support within the party

[179] Abū Fāris, *Ṣafaḥāt*, 157–65. [180] Schwedler, *Faith*, 172.
[181] Maʾmūn ʿAyyāsh, 'Majlis Shūrá "al-Jabhat" Yarfuḍu Istiqālāt "6" min Aʿḍāʾ al-Maktab al-Tanfīdhī', *Al-Sabīl*, 16/22 September 1997, 4.
[182] Rosefsky Wickham, *Muslim Brotherhood*, 215. [183] Ibid., 215–16.
[184] Al-ʿUmūsh, *Maḥāṭṭāt*, 204. [185] Ibid., 206–8.

(70 per cent).[186] The main reason for the boycott was the Brotherhood's continued opposition to the electoral law, which kept recurring in publications about the issue.[187] Gharayiba describes the decision to boycott the elections as 'an attempt to stir the pot (*taḥrīk al-birka*), to get the societal dialogue going and to awaken the inattentive'.[188] Other prominent IAF members like Hamza Mansur[189] and Zaki Bani Irshid[190] point out that it was the political circumstances that caused them to boycott the elections, not their own supposed unwillingness to participate. As the head of the Brotherhood's Shūrá Council at the time, ʿAbd al-Latif ʿArabiyyat, points out:

> There is nothing new about the decision to boycott the parliamentary elections. The reasons for the boycott are known. If the reasons are taken away (*idhā uzīlat al-asbāb*) then it is possible to have another look at the decision. There is no going back on the decision to boycott as long as the reasons remain (*lā ʿawda ʿan qarār al-muqāṭaʿa mā lam tazāl al-asbāb*).[191]

Thus, for the IAF to return to participating in the elections, the regime needed to show that it was serious about political reform, especially of the electoral law.

This demand for political (rather than religious) reform was amplified by the Brotherhood and the IAF in the run-up to the elections of 2013, when – as we saw in Chapter 3 – Jordanian Islamists believed the time was right to push for real change in a region in which one regime seemed to be overthrown after another in the Arab Spring. This meant that the demand for a change in the electoral law was still expressed, but it was

186 Abū Rummān and Abū Haniyya, *Al-Ḥall*, 126–7; Rosefsky Wickham, *Muslim Brotherhood*, 208.

187 Fawzī ʿAlī al-Samhūrī, 'Al-Intikhābāt bayna l-Mushāraka wa-l-Muqāṭaʿa', *Al-Sabīl*, 24 July 2010, 11; Fawzī ʿAlī al-Samhūrī, 'Al-Muqāṭaʿa wa-l-Maṣlaḥa al-Waṭaniyya', *Al-Sabīl*, 25 September 2010, 11; Jamāl al-Shawāhīn, 'Muqāṭaʿat al-Intikhābāt am al-Ghuraf al-Mughlaqa', *Al-Sabīl*, 30 July 2010, 11; ʿAbdallāh al-Shūbakī, 'Abū Bakr: Al-Ḥaraka al-Islāmiyya Satadrusu Qānūn al-Intikhābāt li-Taḥdīd Mawqiʿihā min al-Mushāraka bi-l-Intikhābāt', *Al-Sabīl*, 8 June 2000, 4; 'Al-Murāqib al-ʿĀmm li-l-Ikhwān al-Muslimīn: Lā Qarār bi-l-Mushāraka fī l-Intikhābāt al-Muqbila . . . Wa-l-Ajwāʾ Ghayr Ījābiyya', *Al-Sabīl*, 5 March 2010, 3; 'Al-Ikhwān al-Muslimūn: Al-Intikhābāt al-Niyābiyya al-Muqbila Shakliyya', *Al-Sabīl*, 2 July 2010, 3.

188 Ruḥayyil Gharāyiba, 'Muqāṭaʿat al-Intikhābāt Laysat Qaṭīʿa maʿa l-Ḥāla al-Siyāsiyya', *Al-Sabīl*, 22 November 2010, 12.

189 Muḥammad al-Khawālida, 'Ḥamza Manṣūr: Muqāṭaʿat al-Intikhābāt Natīja Manṭiqiyya li-Insidād al-Ufuq al-Siyāsī', *Al-Sabīl*, 4 November 2011, 3.

190 Naṣr al-ʿUtūm, 'Banī Irshīd: Al-Muqāṭaʿa Laysat Qarāran Ḥizbiyyan Bal Ḥāla Siyāsiyya Mujtamaʿiyya Ṣanaʿathā Ḥālāt al-Ḥukūmāt al-Mutaraddiyya', *Al-Sabīl*, 28 October 2010, 5.

191 ʿAbdallāh al-Shūbakī, 'Al-Ḥaraka al-Islāmiyya Tatamassaku bi-Shurūt Muqāṭaʿat al-Intikhābāt al-Niyābiyya al-Muqbila', *Al-Sabīl*, 14 September 2010, 5.

accompanied by the broader call for constitutional reform. The latter included officially making the people the source of authority, limiting the powers of the king and broadening those of the people, establishing a true separation of powers, lessening the role of the military in people's lives, creating a constitutional court and having governments that reflect the balance of power in parliament.[192] Despite attempts by a new and relatively reformist prime minister, ʿAbdallah al-Nusur, to get the IAF to participate,[193] the party ultimately maintained its boycott and is said to have decided by a large internal majority to shun the elections of 2013.[194]

Whereas the situation prior to the elections in 2013 had been characterised by a certain amount of defiance on the part of the Brotherhood, things changed drastically in the run-up to the 2016 polls. As we saw in Chapter 3, the organisation's protests in the context of the Arab Spring had yielded little (if any) result, the regional repression of the Brotherhood also took on unprecedented forms in Jordan itself and three different groups (ZamZam, the New Muslim Brotherhood and hundreds of individual members) had split off from the organisation. Although it took some time, the Brotherhood and the IAF eventually did realise that times had changed, which was reflected in their discourse. For example, the IAF's Secretary General at the time, Muhammad al-Zuyud, significantly toned down the demands expressed in earlier years by stating that 'the party is prepared to participate in political life in the upcoming period, provided the one-vote electoral law is annulled'.[195]

Further realisation of the changing times could be seen in the decision the IAF took to form councils to study the question of participation in the 2016 elections,[196] rather than quickly dismissing this possibility, as it had done before. The IAF also indicated that, unlike in previous years, it was not striving for a boycott.[197] Elements within the Brotherhood, which by that time had already lost its official licence, even warned of 'the necessity

[192] 'Manṣūr: Lā Mushāraka fī l-Intikhābāt Dūna Iṣlāḥāt Ḥaqīqiyya Shāmila', *Al-Sabīl*, 4 October 2012, 1; 'Sālim al-Falāḥāt: Lan Nushārika fī l-Intikhābāt ... wa-Nuṣaʿʿidu Diḍḍa l-Niẓām Idhā Lam Yuṣliḥ', *Shīḥān News* (www.shihannews.net/Print.aspx?ArticleNo=29093, accessed 18 October 2012), 16 October 2012.

[193] Khaled Neimat, 'Islamists Reject New PM's Offer to Take Part in Polls', *The Jordan Times* (http://jordantimes.com/islamists-reject-new-pms-offer-to-take-part-in-polls, accessed 12 October 2012), 12 October 2012.

[194] Interview with ʿUrayb al-Rantāwī, Amman, 12 January 2013.

[195] 'Amīn ʿĀmm Ḥizb Jabhat al-ʿAmal al-Islāmī: Mustaʿiddūn li-l-Mushāraka fī l-Ḥayāt al-Siyāsiyya bi-Ḥāl Ilghāʾ al-Ṣawt al-Wāḥid', *Al-Ḥaqīqa al-Dawliyya* (http://factjo.com/pages/print.aspx?id=69627, accessed 25 September 2014), 25 September 2014.

[196] Hadīl Ghabbūn, '"Al-Ikhwān" Tushakkilu Lijānan Dākhiliyya li-Dirāsat al-Mushāraka bi-l-Intikhābiyyāt al-Niyābiyya', *Al-Ghad* (http://alghad.com/articles/930132, accessed 4 April 2016), 4 April 2016.

[197] '"Al-ʿAmal al-Islāmī": Muqāṭaʿat al-Intikhābāt Amr Lā Naṭmaḥu ilayhi', *Al-Dustūr*, 9 May 2016, 10.

of being conscious of the danger and the precariousness of the coming period (*ḍarūrat istishʿār al-marḥala al-qādima wa-diqqatihā*)'[198] and similar advice was given by Jordanian commentators.[199] Both the Brotherhood and the IAF thus seemed aware of the danger of continuing its 'radical' stance of refraining from parliamentary participation and the IAF's eventual decision to join the electoral process also reflected this, with al-Zuyud specifically mentioning the 'dangers and challenges' Jordan was going through[200] and the 'pressure' the party was under.[201] Unsurprisingly, the IAF was therefore not very enthusiastic about participating and openly stated that it saw this option as 'the lesser of two evils'[202] and chose this 'to make the highest national interest triumph'.[203]

The process of renewed electoral and parliamentary participation by the IAF was facilitated by the regime's decision to amend the electoral law to more or less the form it had in 1989. Given the fact that this change had been a key demand by the Muslim Brotherhood and the IAF and, indeed, larger parts of the opposition, this decision was widely hailed as a step in the right direction,[204] including by the Islamic Centre Party[205] and the New Muslim Brotherhood. The latter – in an apparent reference to the IAF – claimed that 'there is no excuse left for any party, group or opponent (*muʿāriḍ*) in Jordan not to participate in the elections [now]'.[206] Jordanians affiliated with the Brotherhood were more

198 'Shūrá l-Ikhwān al-Qānūniyya Yuqarriru l-Mushāraka bi-l-Intikhābāt al-Niyābiyya al-Muqbila', *Al-Ghad* (http://alghad.com/articles/929960, accessed 4 April 2016), 3 April 2016; '"Shūrá l-Ikhwān al-Qānūniyya" Yuqarriru l-Mushāraka bi-l-Intikhābāt al-Niyābiyya al-Muqbila', *Al-Dustūr*, 4 April 2016, 7.

199 Khetam Malkawi, '"Old" Brotherhood Advised to Partake in Next Polls as "Proof of Life"', *The Jordan Times* (http://jordantimes.com/news/local/old'-brotherhood-advised-partake-next-polls-proof-life', accessed 12 April 2016), 11 April 2016.

200 'Al-Zuyūd: Qarār al-Mushāraka Jāʾa bi-l-Tashāwur maʿa l-Quwá al-Waṭaniyya', *Al-Būṣala* (http://albosa.la/TVRNM05Ua3crdQ==, accessed 15 June 2016), 14 June 2016.

201 'Al-Zuyūd: Mushārakat al-Ḥizb fī l-Intikhābāt Inḥiyāzan li-l-Waṭan', *Al-Būṣala* (http://albosa.la/TVRNM05qSTQrdQ==, accessed 15 June 2016), 15 June 2016.

202 'Al-Zuyūd: Al-Mushāraka fī l-Intikhābāt Inḥiyāz li-l-Waṭan wa-Akhaff al-Ḍararayn', *Al-Ghad* (http://alghad.com/articles/953312, accessed 16 June 2016), 16 June 2016.

203 'Al-Zuyūd: Naḥnu Juzʾ min al-Waṭan Lā Nunākifu Aḥadan wa-Lā Nantaziʿu Dawr Ghayrinā', *Al-Dustūr*, 17 June 2016, 3.

204 Rabá Karāsina, 'Ḥizbiyyūn Yuraḥḥibūn bi-Mughādarat al-Ṣawt al-Wāḥid wa-Yantaqidūn Ilghāʾ al-Qāʾima al-Waṭaniyya', *Al-Būṣala* (http://albosa.la/TVRJeE1643o rdQ==, accessed 1 September 2015), 31 August 2015.

205 '"Al-Wasaṭ al-Islāmī": Qānūn al-Intikhāb Yuʿazzizu Dawr al-Nāʾib al-Siyāsī', *Al-Dustūr*, 9 September 2015, 11.

206 Nasīm ʿUnayzāt, '"Jamʿiyyat al-Ikhwān al-Muslimīn": Lā ʿUdhr li-ʿAdam al-Mushāraka fī l-Intikhābāt', *Al-Dustūr*, 2 September 2015, 5; 'Jamʿiyyat al-Ikhwān Turaḥḥibu bi-Qānūn al-Intikhāb wa-"Ghayr Murakhkhaṣa" Lam Tuʿlin Mawqifahā Baʿdu', *Al-Ghad* (http://alghad.com/articles/890637, accessed 2 September 2015), 1 September 2015.

cautious, with Gharayiba generally praising the law but also pointing out its flaws, for example.[207] Another Islamist commentator advised the IAF to 'take a positive position towards the [new electoral] law' and to present 'a different language than before, because today's demands and circumstances necessitate that'.[208]

Interestingly, in a way the IAF really began speaking a different language in the run-up to the 2016 election, namely, that of inclusion. To understand this, it is important to remember that particularly ZamZam, but also the New Brotherhood and, later, the group of hundreds of Brothers who left the organisation,[209] strove to set up less explicitly Islamist and more broad-based initiatives. Aware that Islamist groups were under fire in the region (and in Jordan) and conscious that broader parties would be more difficult to pigeonhole and suppress, the IAF tried to emulate the behaviour of groups like ZamZam by setting up the National Coalition for Reform (al-Taḥāluf al-Waṭanī li-l-Iṣlāḥ) through which it participated in the elections of 2016.[210] This coalition united the IAF 'with tribal and political forces' on the basis of 'a national political programme that will not include Islamist slogans (*shiʿārāt dīniyya*)'.[211]

The idea of a nationalist (and thus not Islamist) coalition was applied in practice through the inclusion of many people who were not members of the IAF,[212] a result of the party's express wish to diversify the membership of the alliance.[213] Bani Irshid stated that this coalition 'is not

207 Ruḥayyil Gharāyiba, 'Qānūn al-Intikhābāt', *Al-Dustūr*, 2 September 2015, 20.

208 ʿUmar ʿAyāṣira, 'Al-Niqāshāt wa-Qānūn al-Intikhāb', *Al-Sabīl*, 15 September 2015, 2.

209 Hadīl Ghabbūn, 'Al-Falāḥāt: Al-Yaʾs min Taṣwīb "al-Wāqiʿ al-Ikhwānī" Warāʾ Taʾsīs "al-Inqādh"', *Al-Ghad* (http://alghad.com/articles/1238022, accessed 8 November 2016), 8 November 2016.

210 Rabá Karāsina, '"Al-ʿAmal al-Islāmī" Yabdaʾu bi-ʿtimād Qawāʾim Murashshaḥa li-Khawḍ al-Intikhābāt', *Al-Būṣala* (http://albosa.la/TVRNNE9UWXgrdQ==, accessed 13 July 2016), 13 July 2016.

211 Hadīl Ghabbūn, '"Al-ʿAmal al-Islāmī" Yakhūḍu l-Intikhābāt bi-Qawāʾim Mukhtaliṭa', *Al-Ghad* (http://alghad.com/articles/1005422, accessed 15 July 2016), 14 July 2016.

212 Rabá Karāsina, '"Al-Būṣala" Tanshuru l-Qāʾima al-Awwaliyya li-Murashshaḥī "l-ʿAmal al-Islāmī"', *Al-Būṣala* (http://albosa.la/TVRNNU5qYzUrdQ==, accessed 25 July 2016), 25 July 2016; Khetam Malkawi, 'Islamists "Ready with Inclusive Tickets" as Polls Approach', *The Jordan Times* (http://jordantimes.com/news/local/islamists-ready-inclusive-tickets%E2%80%99-polls-approach, accessed 18 August 2016), 8 August 2016; '"Al-ʿAmal al-Islāmī" Yuʿlinu l-Qāʾima al-Awwaliyya li-Murashshaḥīhi li-l-Intikhābāt al-Niyābiyya', *Al-Dustūr*, 26 July 2016, 8; 'Islamists Ally with Other Forces, Including Christians, in Election Race', *The Jordan Times* (http://jordantimes.com/news/local/islamists-ally-other-forces-including-christians-election-race, accessed 18 August 2016), 17 August 2016.

213 Khetam Malkawi, 'Islamist Party Seeks to Diversify Membership – Spokesperson', *The Jordan Times* (http://jordantimes.com/news/local/islamist-party-seeks-diversify-membership-%E2%80%94-spokesperson, accessed 29 August 2016), 28 August 2016; '"Al-ʿAmal al-Islāmī" Yushakkilu Lajna li-Taqyīm Adāʾ al-Ḥizb wa-Iʿādat Haykalatihi', *Al-Būṣala* (http://albosa.la/TVRReE56WXkrdQ==, accessed

a tactical step; on the contrary, it represents a strategic project of the Islamic movement and the national Jordanian movement'.[214] Although it was left implicit, it is clear that through this discourse, 'the people' – long represented in the Brotherhood's discourse through the adjacent concept of '*umma*' – were now more and more associated with the citizens of Jordan, rather than the worldwide Muslim community. This was not just apparent through the lack of use of '*umma*', but also through the increasing efforts to show that the IAF was working 'in the service of Jordan'[215] or 'on the basis of the highest interests of the homeland'.[216]

As such, the decontestation of *shūrá* by the Brotherhood as a link between the adjacent concept of '*umma*' and the core concept of 'ruler' had come to its final destination in a national context. *Shūrá* was first decontested in a way that deepened the role of the *umma* and was ultimately often used as a synonym for democracy, the applicability of which was legitimised at all levels of politics. The role of the *umma* in this system was subsequently enlarged through a 'constitutionalised' interpretation of the *sharī'a* (thus making it more *umma*-centred) and finally specified as applying to Jordanian society, rather than the Muslim world as a whole. This 'Jordanised' decontestation of *shūrá* not only shows how far the Brotherhood has travelled in its ideological development, but – despite the IAF's modest results in the 2016 elections (10 seats out of 130) – also how 'moderate' it has become through its acceptance of broad-based participation.

Oath of Fealty and Obedience

As we saw in Chapters 1 and 2, the oath of fealty and obedience, the third and fourth links between the core concept of 'ruler' and the adjacent concept of '*umma*', were decontested in different ways. In classical Islam, *bay'a* was initially treated as a contractual relationship between the caliph and all Muslims, but one of the concept's quasi-contingent features – the ones pledging fealty – was later limited to a group of dignitaries. This resulted in an increasingly empty ritual of approval that is still practised by many dictatorial Arab regimes today, with little room for the people to get

29 August 2016), 28 August 2016; 'Lajna li-I'ādat Haykalat "al-'Amal al-Islāmī"', *Al-Dustūr*, 29 August 2016, 5.

214 Khalīl Qandīl, 'Banī Irshīd li-"l-Sabīl": Al-Taḥāluf al-Waṭanī li-l-Iṣlāḥ Mashrū' Istrātījī li-l-Ḥaraka al-Waṭaniyya al-Urdunniyya', *Al-Sabīl*, 10 September 2016, 3.

215 'Al-Khaṣāwina: Al-'Amal al-Islāmī Mutajadhdhira wa-Yatamaddada fī l-Mujtama'', *Al-Būṣala* (http://albosa.la/TVRNNE5EZ3krdQ==, accessed 1 July 2016), 1 July 2016.

216 'Al-Zuyūd Khilāl Ḥafl Takrīm li-l-Nuwwāb: Nas'á li-Da'm al-'Amal al-Mushtarak 'alá Qā'idat al-Maṣāliḥ al-'Ulyā li-l-Waṭan', *Al-Sabīl*, 1 October 2016, 2.

involved.[217] Rida, however, decontested *bayʿa* as a contract involving the *umma* again and tied its validity to the ruler's adherence to the *sharīʿa*. This trend was continued in slightly differing ways by early Muslim Brothers. In classical Islam, *ṭāʿa* similarly developed from obedience on the basis of the ruler's application of Islamic law to almost blind subservience, which Rida also tried to reverse again, in which he was followed by early Brothers in Egypt. How global Islamists as well as Jordanian Brothers decontested these concepts is dealt with in this section.

Global Islamist Discourse on the Oath of Fealty and Obedience

Given the fact that global Islamist thinkers who influenced the Jordanian Brotherhood have deepened the role of the *umma* in *shūrá*, it is perhaps not surprising that they also try to 'restore' the contractual nature of *bayʿa*, just like some early Muslim Brothers had done. Al-Turabi, for example, laments the development we saw in Chapter 1 of *bayʿa* from a 'serious, sincere contract (*ʿahdan ṣādiqan jāddan*)' into a stamp of approval for whatever ruler was in power.[218] Although several global Islamist scholars stress the contractual nature of the oath of fealty, some also point out that *bayʿa* is not the same as the concept of a social contract found in the work of Western philosophers like Jean-Jacques Rousseau. While the latter is used to establish a state, in Islam this is a command based on Qurʾanic texts. *Bayʿa* is therefore not used for this purpose, but rather to establish a contract between the ruler and the ruled, both al-Turabi and al-Ghannushi state.[219]

Interestingly, scholars like al-Ghannushi and al-Qaradawi differ with Rida and early Muslim Brothers by connecting *bayʿa* and *ṭāʿa* not only to the *sharīʿa*, but also to the will of the *umma* through *shūrá*. Both state that the oath of fealty does not just involve the ruler's application of the *sharīʿa*, but also his adherence to the will or the interests of the *umma*.[220] As such, al-Qaradawi writes, *bayʿa* can serve as a contractual means to make the ruler commit to the decisions of the *shūrá*.[221] Al-Ghannushi takes this even further by stating that the *umma* itself is the true vicegerent (*mustakhlaf*) of God's rule and through *bayʿa* merely delegates the job of actually applying this to a ruler.[222] In this system, which March refers to

[217] Elie Podeh, 'The *Bayʿa*: Modern Political Uses of Islamic Ritual in the Arab World', *Die Welt des Islams* 50, no. 1 (2010): 117–52.
[218] Al-Turābī, *Fī l-Fiqh*, 104.
[219] Al-Ghannūshī, *Al-Ḥurriyyāt*, 165–6; al-Turābī, 'Al-Shūrá', 13–14.
[220] Al-Ghannūshī, *Al-Ḥurriyyāt*, 192; Rutherford, 'What Do Egypt's Islamists Want?', 713.
[221] Al-Qaraḍāwī, *Al-Siyāsa*, 117. [222] Al-Ghannūshī, *Al-Ḥurriyyāt*, 167.

as 'the caliphate of man',[223] the ruler's breaking of the contract of *bayʿa* is not limited to violating the *sharīʿa*, but also includes going against the will of the *umma*. As such, the *umma*'s obedience to the ruler (and even the legitimacy of deposing him) is made partly conditional upon the ruler's willingness to listen to the people.[224]

By continuing the trend started by Rida and early Brothers of 'restoring' *bayʿa*'s quasi-contingent feature of 'the ones pledging fealty', global Islamist scholars who influenced the Brotherhood decontest the term as connected to both adjacent concepts of '*sharīʿa*' and '*umma*'. In the process, they essentially do the same with *ṭāʿa* by making it conditional upon adherence to the *sharīʿa* and listening to the *umma*. As such, they use *bayʿa* and *ṭāʿa* to put more emphasis on the *umma* vis-à-vis the core concept of 'ruler'. While this is tempered somewhat in al-Qaradawi's case by his generally balanced approach to Islamist ideology, al-Ghannushi only underlines his *umma*-centred approach this way.

The Jordanian Muslim Brotherhood on the Oath of Fealty and Obedience

Just as global Islamist scholars more or less extended their views on the other links between the core concept of 'ruler' and the adjacent concepts of '*sharīʿa*' and '*umma*' to *bayʿa* and *ṭāʿa*, so do Jordanian Muslim Brothers, although the latter do not write about the subjects much. The oath of fealty in the Jordanian Brotherhood is sometimes discussed within the confines of the organisation as a pledge of allegiance to the group's General Controller,[225] but also in the context of relations between the *umma* and the ruler. The main Jordanian scholars who deal with the subject are Abu Faris, who is quite aware of the concept's classical Islamic roots,[226] and Gharayiba, who also shows he realises that *bayʿa* can take the form of an ineffectual tradition,[227] which it took in mediaeval Islam, of course. The need for *bayʿa* as a means to decide relations with the ruler is clear[228] and so is the idea that it is not a one-sided concept but actually a contract involving both the ruler and the ruled.[229]

[223] March, 'Genealogies', 308–15, especially 310.
[224] Al-Ghannūshī, *Al-Ḥurriyyāt*, 189–91; Shahin, *Political Ascent*, 223.
[225] See, for instance, ʿAlī al-ʿUtūm, 'Al-Bayʿa fī Tanẓīm al-Ikhwān wa-Mutaṭallabātuhā 1/2', *Al-Sabīl*, 27 March 2013, 15; ʿAlī al-ʿUtūm, 'Al-Bayʿa fī Tanẓīm al-Ikhwān wa-Mutaṭallabātuhā 2/2', *Al-Sabīl*, 28 March 2013, 15.
[226] Abū Fāris, *Al-Niẓām*, 230, 299–303. [227] Gharāyiba, *Al-Ḥuqūq*, 185.
[228] Abū Fāris, *Al-Niẓām*, 245.
[229] Ibid., 309–10; Gharāyiba, *Al-Ḥuqūq*, 196; interviews with Sālim al-Falāḥāt, Amman, 22 January 2013; Ruḥayyil Gharāyiba, Amman, 17 January 2013.

Views within the Jordanian Brotherhood diverge, however, with regard to the type of contract *bay'a* represents. Several have stated that it equals that of a mandator (*muwakkil*) and an agent, with the *umma* representing the former and the ruler the latter.[230] Like global Islamist scholars who have influenced the Brotherhood in Jordan, Abu Faris deepens the role of the *umma* further by stating that 'the majority of the people should pledge fealty to the candidate for the leadership', thus not limiting *bay'a* to a select group of people.[231] Unlike al-Qaradawi and al-Ghannushi, however, Abu Faris does not set respecting the will of the *umma* as a condition for the ruler in a proper *bay'a* contract, but limits his requirements to 'that he rules on the basis of the Book of God and the Sunna of his messenger and that he establishes justice (*al-'adl*) among the people'.[232] We saw this rather vague term before in Chapter 1, where it was equated with rule according to the *sharī'a*, but Abu Faris leaves it undefined for now (but see below). Gharayiba sees it quite differently:

> The meaning of *bay'a* is a contract. [...] The people choose you and give you the legitimacy of this responsibility (*shar'iyyat hādhihi l-mas'ūliyya*), this position. That's why, in the end, this needs to translate into a person, the holder of the position (*ṣāḥib al-mawqi'*) [of ruler], but it is aimed at the expression of the collective will of the people (*maqṣūd irādat al-sha'b al-jam'iyya*). [...] There is no legitimacy, except through delegation of authority (*tafwīḍ*) by the people. *Bay'a* is an expression of the delegation of authority by the people.[233]

Like al-Qaradawi and especially al-Ghannushi, Gharayiba thus explicitly decontests *bay'a* as a contract connected to both adjacent concepts of '*sharī'a*' and '*umma*', thereby extending his *umma*-centred approach to Islamist ideology to the oath of fealty, just as Abu Faris does with his *sharī'a*-centred approach.

We can see the same division with regard to the term *ṭā'a*, which is also not discussed frequently by Jordanian Brothers. Abu Faris – with reference to Q. 4:59 on obedience to God, Muhammad and the rulers, which we saw above – states that in a truly Islamic state

> [e]very Muslim [...], in his capacity as a member of the community of Muslims (*jamā'at al-Muslimīn*), must listen to and obey (*yasma'a wa-yuṭī'a*) the rulers (*ūliyā' al-umūr*) in this Islamic state, such as the caliph, possessors of general duties (*aṣḥāb al-wilāyāt al-'āmma*) in the state like judges, regional rulers, military leaders, ministers and all who rule the Muslims.[234]

230 Abū Fāris, *Al-Niẓām*, 312; interview with Jamīl Abū Bakr, Amman, 18 June 2012.
231 Abū Fāris, *Al-Niẓām*, 245. 232 Ibid., 311.
233 Interview with Ruḥayyil Gharāyiba, Amman, 17 January 2013.
234 Abū Fāris, *Mafāhīm*, 110–11. The quotation is on p. 111.

Abu Faris thus advocates *ṭāʿa*, but only in the context of an Islamic state with a ruler who applies the *sharīʿa*. He confirms this by pointing out that *ṭāʿa* is only required if the ruler governs according to Islamic law, rules justly and does not order Muslims to sin.[235] With regard to *ṭāʿa*, Abu Faris does expand on what justice is in this context, stating that 'obedience to tyrannical rulers (*al-umarāʾ al-jāʾirīn*) is not obligatory, because tyranny is disobedience (*maʿṣiya*) and the tyrant is disobedient to God the Exalted', citing a *ḥadīth* in which the Prophet says that 'there is no obedience for him who does not obey God'.[236] This focus on just rule (rather than only the *sharīʿa*) does leave some room for the *umma* to withhold its *ṭāʿa* in cases where religion does not play a role. Abu Faris fills this space with the *umma*'s right to command right and forbid wrong, as we saw above.

Unlike Abu Faris's almost entirely *sharīʿa*-centred approach that does not really deviate from those of Rida, ʿAwda and other early Brothers in this respect, Gharayiba views things differently, although he agrees that Muslims may not obey orders to sin.[237] He writes that *ṭāʿa* is required when dealing with leaders who 'rule according to what God has sent down, rule with justice and produce confidence (*al-amānāt*) in the people',[238] thus adding an extra condition to those of Abu Faris that is so broad that it provides plenty of room for engagement by the *umma*. While Abu Faris creates some space for non-religious opposition, but only in response to oppressive rule, Gharayiba creates room for withholding obedience to a ruler who merely does not 'produce confidence', thus extending his *umma*-centred approach to *ṭāʿa* as well.

* * *

This chapter has shown a general tendency among both global Islamist scholars as well as Jordanian Muslim Brothers to move in the direction of an *umma*-centred approach by 'restoring' quasi-contingent features of the four links between the core concept of 'ruler' and the adjacent concept of '*umma*' in Islamic political thought. To be sure, some remained balanced in their approach to Islamist ideology and others even retained their *sharīʿa*-centredness. Yet even the latter at least deepened the role of the *umma* in some respects, underlining a trend towards greater emphasis on the *umma*'s role in political participation found among all thinkers dealt with in this chapter.

The more concrete application of commanding right and forbidding wrong, consultation, oath of fealty and obedience by global Islamist

[235] Abū Fāris, *Al-Niẓām*, 71–5. [236] Ibid., 72. [237] Gharāyiba, *Al-Ḥuqūq*, 348, 350.
[238] Ibid., 349.

scholars and especially the 'Jordanisation' of these terms in the context of the Hashimite Kingdom also show the often-intricate ideological differences between the players involved. As such, the suggestion that the terms 'hawks' and 'doves' to describe various Jordanian Brothers is not precise enough becomes even clearer than before. Abu Faris opposed political participation sometimes, for example, just as Bani Irshid did. While the former did so for religious reasons, however, the latter did so for pragmatic ones. Describing them both as 'hawks' therefore does not do justice to their respective ideological outlooks. Similarly, al-ʿUmush and Gharayiba are both often described as 'doves' for their willingness to participate. Yet the former does so because he is pro-regime, the latter out of pragmatism.

The labels '*sharīʿa*-centred', 'balanced' and '*umma*-centred' cover these divisions better than 'hawks' and 'doves' do, because they refer to the Brothers' deeper ideological motivations. Just as we saw in Chapter 4, and as Hamid argues, their views have generally grown more 'moderate' over the years in the sense that they have inclined towards a more democratic view of political participation. This moderation can be ascribed to the same two factors mentioned in Chapter 4: the organisation's long history of inclusion in Jordan and the 'moderate' global Islamist discourse that has influenced internal Brotherhood discussions throughout the years. As such, the regime's inclusion of the group has partly caused it to moderate. This complements Schwedler's argument, which states that not only inclusion but also internal ideological discussion is needed to facilitate moderation. While she limits this to intra-organisational debates, I argue that the international Islamist dimension of these discussions is also highly relevant.

These two factors have not solved divisions within the organisation, but they have united the group around a civil, non-violent and pragmatic course of action in which non-participation for Islamic reasons was no longer an option from the early 1990s onwards. It was this pragmatism that caused the organisation to 'radicalise' practically by boycotting several elections in times of greater repression, but simultaneously to continue to moderate ideologically as a result of continued (global) Islamist ideological development. The same reasons ultimately caused the IAF to participate in the 2016 elections again in an open and broad-based fashion, realising that in order to survive, no other option was available.

The organisation thus generally conformed to the inclusion-moderation thesis with regard to political participation, yet within that context, regime repression caused the group to moderate further. Apart from the organisation's history of inclusion and the 'moderate' global Islamist discourse affecting the group's internal debates, the divisions within the Brotherhood facilitated this process by allowing Brothers to shift position between confrontation (boycott) and accommodation (participation) within the group without having to leave it. Also, the split-offs from the organisation allowed the regime to exploit the divisions within the broader Islamist movement, essentially pick sides in its internal discussions and increase repression on the Brotherhood itself. Finally, these less explicitly Islamist split-offs showed the organisation that the way forward lay in broad-based participation, which the IAF adopted. As such, the Brotherhood's divisions on political participation and the flexibility it gave the organisation partly account for its ideological moderation and help explain how it could moderate further under repression in the general context of inclusion. Whether and how this attitude can be discerned in the Brotherhood's views on societal rights and freedoms is our final subject.

6 Ideological Unity on Societal Rights and Freedoms

One thing that has become quite clear over the past few chapters is that the Jordanian Muslim Brotherhood is highly divided over important issues, which has facilitated its moderation towards accepting the Jordanian state and democratic participation. This is not necessarily the case with regard to the Brotherhood's views on societal rights and freedoms, however. The Brotherhood and the IAF are, in fact, less widely divided between *sharīʿa*-centred, *umma*-centred and balanced approaches to Islamist ideology with regard to these issues. Partly as a consequence of this relative unity, the Brotherhood has not gone through the same process of moderation in this respect.

This chapter deals with the Jordanian Muslim Brotherhood's views on societal rights and freedoms. It starts with an analysis of whether and how Islamic law should be reformed according to global Islamist scholars who have influenced the Jordanian Brotherhood as well as the members of the organisation itself. It then moves on to analyse religious minority rights, women's rights and civil liberties from the perspective of both global Islamist scholars that Jordanian Brothers cite and the latter themselves. Although this chapter shows the Brotherhood's relative unity on the issues dealt with, this – conversely – nevertheless furthers our understanding of why the divisions within the organisation are so important with regard to the 'inclusion-moderation' thesis.

Reforming the *Sharīʿa*

The idea that the Jordanian Muslim Brotherhood's moderation in the areas of the state and political participation has not translated into more 'moderate' views on societal issues is not new. Rosefsky Wickham, for instance, writes: '[T]he IAF's commitment to democracy continues to be tempered by its opposition to individual freedom and equality when they are seen as conflicting with the Shariʿa and the fixed values of Jordanian society as they define them.'[1] As these words suggest, the topic of societal rights and freedoms is strongly connected to the subject of Islamic law and how this is interpreted. In order to appreciate the various points of view espoused by global as well as Jordanian Islamists presented below, it is therefore important to understand how these are rooted in a certain conception of the *sharīʿa*, which is why this topic is dealt with first.

Global Islamist Scholars on Reforming the Sharīʿa

Among the global Islamist scholars whom Jordanian Brothers say have influenced them, none has had a greater impact on their views of reforming Islamic law than Yusuf al-Qaradawi, which is why this section will focus on his writings. One could argue that the background to al-Qaradawi's reasoning on this topic is an idea that we saw before in the writings of al-Banna, namely, that Islam is a total system that encompasses everything. The *sharīʿa*, as such, should be applied to every aspect of life.[2] This does not mean, however, that al-Qaradawi believes Muslims should be trapped, as it were, within the confines of an unchanging *sharīʿa*. According to several global Islamist scholars, freedom is of paramount importance in Islam.[3] Yet al-Qaradawi believes that, to reform Islam and facilitate this freedom, other ideologies that have led to reform of religion in Western contexts, such as secularism, are unacceptable.[4] Thus, the *sharīʿa* must be reformed from within. How?

The starting point of al-Qaradawi's reformist view of the *sharīʿa* to provide as much freedom as possible is that all things are allowed (*ḥalāl*), unless an authoritative text says that it is forbidden (*ḥarām*). This idea is derived from several Qurʾanic verses (Q. 2:29: 'It is He who created for you all that is in the earth [...]' and similar verses like Q. 31:20 and Q. 45:13), but most explicitly from a *ḥadīth* that states: 'Whatever God has allowed in His book is allowed. Whatever He has forbidden is forbidden. Whatever He is silent about is kindness (*ʿafw*).'[5] To allow forbidden things or to forbid permitted ones, al-Qaradawi writes, is not only the sole prerogative of God and, as such, strictly prohibited to human beings,[6] but also leads to extremism, one way or the other.[7] In order to avoid this, Muslims should strive to occupy the centre (*wasaṭ*).[8]

[1] Rosefsky Wickham, *Muslim Brotherhood*, 209.
[2] Yūsuf al-Qaraḍāwī, *Madkhal li-Dirāsat al-Sharīʿa al-Islāmiyya* (Cairo: Maktabat Wahba, 2005), 233.
[3] Al-Ghannūshī, *Al-Dīmuqrāṭiyya*, 153–66, 172–5.
[4] Yūsuf al-Qaraḍāwī, *Wajhan li-Wajh . . . Al-Islām wa-l-ʿAlmāniyya* (Cairo: Dār al-Ṣaḥwa li-l-Nashr wa-l-Tawzīʿ, 1994), 73–4.
[5] Yūsuf al-Qaraḍāwī, *Al-Ḥalāl wa-l-Ḥarām fī l-Islām* (Cairo: Maktabat Wahba, 1999), 20–1.
[6] Ibid., 23–8. [7] Ibid., 19. [8] Ibid., 20.

The idea of clinging to some sort of middle position between two extremes is quite old in Islamic tradition and is also espoused by various other global Islamist scholars today.[9] Al-Qaradawi, however, is perhaps the primary exponent of a modern-day trend named after this idea: centrism (*wasaṭiyya*).[10] He describes this trend as the golden mean between various types of extremes,[11] but more specifically as the middle way between two approaches to the *sharīʿa*.[12] At the core of this centrism is the qualified appreciation of the aforementioned 'intentions of Islamic law' (*maqāṣid al-sharīʿa*),[13] the general principles underlying the *sharīʿa* in the context of which its individual rulings should be seen.[14] Al-Qaradawi neither literally wants to follow specific texts (*nuṣūs juzʾiyya*) of the *sharīʿa* that were decided upon at some point in history at the expense of the *maqāṣid*,[15] nor does he want to adhere only to the general intentions of Islamic law when that contradicts definitive texts.[16] Instead, his *wasaṭiyya* supposedly respects definitive texts from the Qurʾan and the Sunna, while adhering to the *sharīʿa*'s *maqāṣid* when such texts are absent. Al-Qaradawi believes this balanced approach represents 'the truth of Islam',[17] which also has consequences for the societal rights and freedoms dealt with in this chapter.[18]

Generally speaking, al-Qaradawi echoes the ideas we saw in Chapter 2 among early Brothers like al-Hudaybi that it is important in principle to stick to the specific texts with regard to *ʿibādāt*[19] and he cites several issues on which there are definitive texts that, as a result, must be adhered to instead of relying on the more general *maqāṣid*.[20] Resorting to these broad intentions of the *sharīʿa* is, however, the default choice with regard to *muʿāmalāt*.[21] This creates space for flexibility in interpreting the *sharīʿa*, a topic al-Qaradawi pays much attention to.[22] He focusses on various

9 Al-Ghannūshī, *Al-Dīmuqrāṭiyya*, 27–8, 79.

10 Bettina Gräf, 'The Concept of *Wasaṭiyya* in the Work of Yūsuf al-Qaraḍāwī', in *Global Mufti: The Phenomenon of Yusuf al-Qaradawi*, ed. Bettina Gräf and Jakob Skovgaard-Petersen (New York: Columbia University Press, 2009), 213–38. For more on the *wasaṭiyya*, see Baker, *Islam*, although Baker applies this term to a rather heterogeneous group whose methods are quite different. For more on this, see Ovamir Anjum, 'Dhimmi Citizens: Non-Muslims in the New Islamist Discourse', *ReOrient* 2, no. 1 (2016): 31–50.

11 Yūsuf al-Qaraḍāwī, *Kalimāt fī l-Wasaṭiyya al-Islāmiyya wa-Maʿālimihā* (Cairo: Dār al-Shurūq, 2011), 20–8.

12 Al-Qaraḍāwī, *Al-Ijtihād*, 233; al-Qaraḍāwī, *Al-Siyāsa*, 8–9.

13 Al-Qaraḍāwī, *Madkhal*, 55–79.

14 Felicitas Opwis, 'New Trends in Islamic Legal Theory: *Maqāṣid al-Sharīʿa* as a New Source of Law?', *Die Welt des Islams* 57 (2017): 7–32.

15 Al-Qaraḍāwī, *Al-Ijithād*, 230–1; al-Qaraḍāwī, *Al-Siyāsa*, 230–3.

16 Al-Qaraḍāwī, *Al-Ijtihād*, 231–3; al-Qaraḍāwī, *Al-Siyāsa*, 245–9.

17 Al-Qaraḍāwī, *Kalimāt*, 31–8. The quotation is on p. 31.

18 Ibid., 48–53.

19 Al-Qaraḍāwī, *Al-Siyāsa*, 272–3.

20 Ibid., 265–6.

21 Ibid., 273–4.

22 Yūsuf al-Qaraḍāwī, *ʿAwāmil al-Saʿa wa-l-Murūna fī l-Sharīʿa al-Islāmiyya* (Cairo: Maktaba Wahba, 2004); al-Qaraḍāwī, *Madkhal*, 147–230.

classical types of scholarly use of considered opinion (*ra'y*), such as juristic preference (*istiḥsān*),[23] to arrive at rulings on which no definitive texts exist and with regard to which mere analogical reasoning (*qiyās*) on the basis of other texts would yield unsatisfactory results.[24] Like al-Banna and other Brothers, including Jordanian ones we have seen in the context of their views on the state or political participation, al-Qaradawi also explicitly makes room for legal flexibility through *ijtihād*,[25] to whose exact criteria he dedicates much space in his work.[26]

Like Dhunaybat in the context of an Islamic state, as we saw in Chapter 4, al-Qaradawi also takes the changing times and circumstances into account,[27] stating that politics according to the *sharī'a* 'moves according to the movement of the *umma*'[28] and that 'we are in the fifteenth century *anno hegirae*, not in the tenth century or earlier'.[29] Al-Qaradawi sees such legal flexibility in the context of 'the jurisprudence of reality' (*fiqh al-wāqi'*), which entails that the *umma*'s changing interests can lead to different rulings based on *ijtihād*.[30] This also means that the *maṣlaḥa* of the *umma* may clash with the texts of the Qur'an and the Sunna.[31] Al-Qaradawi, for whom *maṣlaḥa* is a key concept,[32] even uses this to override definitive texts sometimes. He mentions, for example, that caliph 'Umar, despite a definitive verse in the Qur'an (Q. 5:38: 'And the thief, male and female: cut off the hands of both, as a recompense for what they have earned [. . .]'), did not punish this way during a famine. This punishment, al-Qaradawi states, was meant for actual thieves, not people who merely wanted to eat. In addition to the broader *umma*'s right to food, this meant that such punishment could not be applied. 'Umar therefore did not annul the general punishment, he writes, but temporarily suspended it in this particular situation.[33]

Al-Qaradawi thus adheres closely to definitive texts – mostly in the sphere of *'ibādāt*, but also in personal status issues, as we will see later on –

[23] Al-Qaraḍāwī, *'Awāmil*, 13–17; al-Qaraḍāwī, *Madkhal*, 155–8.

[24] See Wael B. Hallaq, *Sharī'a: Theory, Practice, Transformations* (Cambridge: Cambridge University Press, 2009), 50–1.

[25] Al-Qaraḍāwī, *Al-Ijtihād*, especially 6, 85–92, 123–66; al-Qaraḍāwī, *Madkhal*, 273–81. For more on al-Qaraḍāwī's views on *ijtihād*, see Mahmud El-Wereny, 'Reichweite und Instrumente islamrechtlicher Normenfindung in der Moderne: Yūsuf al-Qaraḍāwīs *iǧtihād*-Konzept', *Die Welt des Islams* 58 (2018): 65–100.

[26] Al-Qaraḍāwī, *Al-Ijtihād*, 17–73, 227–45. [27] Al-Qaraḍāwī, *Madkhal*, 235–48, 271–2.

[28] Al-Qaraḍāwī, *Al-Siyāsa*, 127. [29] Al-Qaraḍāwī, *Al-Ijtihād*, 239.

[30] Al-Qaraḍāwī, *Al-Siyāsa*, 287–8. [31] Ibid., 155–222.

[32] Armando Salvatore, 'Qaradawi's *Maslaha*: From Ideologue of the Islamic Awakening to Sponsor of Transnational Islam', in *Global Mufti: The Phenomenon of Yusuf al-Qaradawi*, ed. Bettina Gräf and Jakob Skovgaard-Petersen (New York: Columbia University Press, 2009), 239–50.

[33] Al-Qaraḍāwī, *Al-Siyāsa*, 202–7.

yet simultaneously takes the *maqāṣid al-sharīʿa* into account, clearly trying to balance between the rulings of Islamic law and the interests of the *umma*. The same conclusion can be drawn in Freeden's terms with respect to his decontestation of Islamist ideology and what, in this framework, a society in an Islamic state should look like: the ruler – the core concept – should emphasise both adjacent concepts of '*sharīʿa*' and '*umma*' in regulating society. As we will see later on with regard to the various societal rights and freedoms, al-Qaradawi is careful not to let either concept recede to a peripheral position.

The Jordanian Muslim Brotherhood on Reform of the Sharīʿa

Yusuf al-Qaradawi's views on reforming Islamic law appear to have been very influential on the members of the Jordanian Muslim Brotherhood, although not all have adopted them. Among those who have clearly not followed al-Qaradawi in his views on this issue is Muhammad Abu Faris. While he endorses the general idea of Islam as a broad and flexible religion, he does so in a very limited way by merely accepting the classical means of creating new rulings when no texts are available, such as *qiyās* and *istiḥsān*.[34] In what seems like a reference to scholars like al-Qaradawi, Abu Faris writes:

> There are those who claim that there is no escaping that we as Muslims adjust (*natakayyafu*) to the societies we live in, the governments that rule the Muslims by something other than Islam and the *jāhilī* regimes that are based on the disqualification of the *sharīʿa* of God (*istibʿād sharʿ Allāh*).[35]

Abu Faris rejects this view and states that Islam has come to change the various aspects of *jāhiliyya*, rather than be changed by them itself.[36] In his view, this entails that the *umma* should have little control over the contents of the *sharīʿa*, because people are likely to change their minds about what they think should be allowed or not, which he believes should be largely fixed.[37]

Abu Faris is not alone in such views within the Jordanian Brotherhood. Salah al-Khalidi, for example, told me:

> If you vote and the people want (usurious) interest (*ribā*) [to be levied], if 60 per cent want *ribā*, then yes, we will have *ribā*. [Yet] this is not acceptable in Islam. The duties and prohibitions (*al-wājibāt wa-l-muḥarramāt*) [of Islam] may not be subjected to a vote. [. . .] If Islam wants to apply what the people do not want to apply, Islam is above the law of democratic elections.[38]

[34] Abū Fāris, *Mafāhīm*, 59. [35] Ibid., 49. [36] Ibid., 51.
[37] Interview with Muḥammad Abū Fāris, Amman, 21 January 2013.
[38] Interview with Ṣalāḥ al-Khālidī, Amman, 24 January 2013.

Given such opposition to far-reaching reform of Islamic law, it is not surprising that al-Qaradawi's notion of *fiqh al-wāqiʿ* is rejected by Abu Faris. The latter sees this as a means of making prohibited concessions to society at the expense of the *sharīʿa*, which he describes as 'opposing a clear text (*naṣṣan ṣarīḥan*) in the Book of God based on the illusion of the jurisprudence of reality (*wahm fiqh al-wāqiʿ*)'.[39] Like al-Khalidi, Abu Faris mentions the example (among others) of *ribā*, which he believes is prohibited by a definitive text (Q. 2:275: 'God has permitted trafficking, and forbidden usury'), yet is nevertheless applied by banks in the Arab world as 'an economic necessity' to fit in with the international financial system and permitted 'in the name of *fiqh al-wāqiʿ*'.[40]

Instead, Abu Faris states that 'with us, there is only one jurisprudence, namely, *sharīʿa* jurisprudence (*al-fiqh al-sharʿī*)'.[41] Unlike *fiqh al-wāqiʿ*, this jurisprudence 'is taken from detailed evidence (*al-adilla al-tafṣīliyya*), meaning from Qurʾanic verses, prophetic *ḥadīth*s and matters of consensus (*masāʾil al-ijmāʿ*)'.[42] He blames proponents of *fiqh al-wāqiʿ* of 'trying their best to turn the texts from Qurʾanic verses and prophetic *ḥadīth*s upside down to give prevailing circumstances (*al-awḍāʿ al-qāʾima*) and false regulations (*al-taṣarrufāt al-bāṭila*) the attribute of legitimacy (*ṣifat al-sharʿiyya*), even if it is opposed to the *sharīʿa*'. Such evidence from the Qurʾan or the Sunna, Abu Faris writes, cannot be overridden, not even 'with the argument of *maṣlaḥa*'.[43]

Yet most prominent figures within the Muslim Brotherhood seem to disagree with Abu Faris and al-Khalidi in their views on the *sharīʿa* and, instead, are far more in line with al-Qaradawi's ideas. Salim al-Falahat and Hammam Saʿid, both former General Controllers of the Jordanian Brotherhood, told me that Islam is a broad religion that offers flexibility to its adherents.[44] Gharayiba is even against the term 'the application of the *sharīʿa*' because the latter is not a book whose rulings one can easily apply. Instead, he says:

> Islam has general principles. I believe mankind agrees on these principles. Islam wants honesty (*ṣidq*). It wants justice (*ʿadāla*). It wants tolerance (*musāmaḥa*). It wants agreement (*tawāfuq*). It wants good (*khayr*), fighting aggression (*muḥārabat al-ʿudwān*), fighting injustice (*ẓulm*), fighting corruption (*fasād*) and fighting evil (*al-ashrār wa-l-shurūr*). There is not a rational person in the world who does not agree [with these things].[45]

[39] Abū Fāris, *Mafāhīm*, 57. [40] Ibid., 56–7. [41] Ibid., 58. [42] Ibid., 59.
[43] Ibid., 56.
[44] Interviews with Sālim al-Falāḥāt, Amman, 22 January 2013; Hammām Saʿīd, Amman, 28 January 2013.
[45] Interview with Ruḥayyil Gharāyiba, Amman, 17 January 2013.

As with al-Qaradawi, however, this broad view of Islam does not mean that the religion only consists of general principles and has no specific rulings, as we will see later on. Indeed, the idea of holding on to a middle ground between two extremes can be found in the Jordanian Brotherhood's discourse, too.[46]

Not surprisingly, the *maqāṣid al-sharīʿa* are also stressed among Jordanian Brothers following al-Qaradawi's approach. Echoing Gharayiba's words cited above, the Muslim Brotherhood and the IAF state:

> Our complete political and ideological vision (*ruʾyatunā l-fikriyya wa-l-siyāsiyya al-kulliyya*) is based on the creed of the *umma* and the greatest intentions of the Islamic *sharīʿa* (*maqāṣid al-sharīʿa al-Islāmiyya al-kubrá*) in the protection of the soul (*ḥimāyat al-nafs*), the mind (*al-ʿaql*), the religion (*al-dīn*), the possessions (*al-māl*), the honour (*al-ʿirḍ*) and the establishment of justice (*iqāmat al-ʿadl*).[47]

The same document states that the *sharīʿa* encompasses both 'fixed texts and general intentions'.[48] Because some people do not understand these *maqāṣid al-sharīʿa*, Gharayiba states, 'they make [Islam] into a heavy burden (*ḥamlan thaqīlan*) and a shackle on the freedom of people (*qaydan ʿalá ḥurriyyat al-insān*)'.[49] Instead, the *sharīʿa* consists mostly of the aforementioned *mutaghayyirāt*, the elements of Islamic law that can be changed by the *umma* 'as long as they do not clash with the spirit of the *sharīʿa* and its general intentions (*rūḥ al-sharīʿa wa-maqāṣidihā l-ʿāmma*)'.[50] This can be done through various means,[51] including, most prominently, *ijtihād*.[52]

The room for the *umma*'s direct interpretation of the Qurʾan and the Sunna, independent of the schools of Islamic law, is seen by many prominent Jordanian Brothers as quite wide. Not only should the *sharīʿa*, whatever form it takes, be applied gradually,[53] but it should also be adjusted to the changing times and circumstances in which the *umma* lives. In his call for Islamic legal revisionism, Gharayiba states that Islam

46 Al-Ḍumūr, *Fiqh*, 61. 47 Al-Ḥaraka al-Islāmiyya fī l-Urdunn, *Ruʾyat*, 19.

48 Ibid., 19–20.

49 Ruḥayyil Muḥammad Gharāyiba, 'Al-Dīn Laysa Quyūdan wa-Aghlāqan', *Al-Dustūr*, 24 April 2015, 16.

50 Ruḥayyil Muḥammad Gharāyiba, 'Mawāzīn Sharʿiyya fī l-ʿAmal al-Siyāsī (1)', *Al-Sabīl*, 19–26 October 1993, 15.

51 Ruḥayyil Muḥammad Gharāyiba, 'Mawāzīn Sharʿiyya fī l-ʿAmal al-Siyāsī (2)', *Al-Sabīl*, 2–9 November 1993, 14.

52 'Fī Ḥiwār', 103–4; interviews with Ruḥayyil Gharāyiba, Amman, 17 January 2013; Hammām Saʿīd, Amman, 28 January 2013.

53 Bassām Nāṣir, 'Taṭbīq al-Sharīʿa bayna l-Ikhwān wa-l-Salafiyyīn', *Al-Sabīl*, 28 May 2013, 6.

> represents a broad cultural framework (*iṭāran ḥaḍāriyyan wāsiʿan*) for the entire *umma* in its different components and represents the collection of firmly established principles and norms (*majmūʿat al-mabādiʾ wa-l-qawāʿid wa-l-qiyam al-rāsikha*) that represent the rich ideological stock (*al-raṣīd al-fikrī al-ghanī*) and the measuring principle (*al-qāʿida al-miʿyāriyya*) for the derivation of laws and statutes (*ishtiqāq al-qawānīn wa-l-anẓima*) that take into account the temporal and local circumstance[s] of human gatherings (*al-ẓarf al-zamānī wa-l-makānī li-l-tajammuʿāt al-bashariyya*).[54]

While most other Jordanian Brothers will probably not go so far as to equate Islam with 'a broad cultural framework', as Gharayiba does, several others did tell me that the *sharīʿa* should constantly change with the place and time in which the *umma* finds itself[55] or that the reality in which Muslims live should be taken into consideration.[56] As a result, even some definitive texts can be overridden by *maṣlaḥa*, with Jamil Abu Bakr telling me exactly the same story about caliph ʿUmar suspending the punishment for thieves during a famine that al-Qaradawi used to make his point.[57]

One final area of reform of the *sharīʿa* in which some members of the Jordanian Brotherhood go further than al-Qaradawi, possibly because they are applying their views in an actual country, is that the implementation of Islamic law should be tied to its popular acceptance.[58] The idea that the *umma* needs to be generally supportive of the *sharīʿa* for it to be implemented can easily be tied to democracy: applying the *sharīʿa* (in whatever shape or form) without the consent of the people would be tyrannical and thus antithetical to the Brotherhood's increasingly democratic ideals. Yet this argument can also be turned around: if the majority of the people want to implement the *sharīʿa*, is applying it not the democratic thing to do? Multiple polls have, in fact, shown that the overwhelming majority of Jordanians prefer Islamic law to be implemented.[59] As such, conservative positions that some (or even

54 Ruḥayyil Gharāyiba, 'Al-Quwá al-Siyāsiyya wa-Ḍarūrat al-Murājaʿa', *Al-Būṣala* (www.albosala.com/?id=111&artical=10910515&chang_tpl=print, accessed 26 August 2013), 25 August 2013.

55 Interviews with Sālim al-Falāḥāt, Amman, 22 January 2013; Ruḥayyil Gharāyiba, Amman, 16 June 2013.

56 Interview with Hammām Saʿīd, Amman, 28 January 2013.

57 Interview with Jamīl Abū Bakr, Amman, 15 January 2013.

58 Interviews with Jamīl Abū Bakr, Amman, 15 January 2013; ʿAlī Abū l-Sukkar, Amman, 15 January 2013.

59 Hamid, *Temptations*, 57; ʿĀṭif al-Jawlānī, 'Al-Ghālibiyya al-Sāḥiqa min al-Urdunniyyīn Tuʿayyidu Taṭbīq al-Sharīʿa al-Islāmiyya', *Al-Sabīl*, 7–13 March 2000, 5; Pew Research Center, *The World's Muslims: Religion, Politics and Society* (www.pewforum.org/2013/04/30/the-worlds-muslims-religion-politics-society-overview/, accessed 24 June 2019), 30 April 2013.

many) in the organisation are unwilling to give up can easily be portrayed as mere reflections of society's views on such matters, as we will see below.

With regard to its views on Islamist thought and, more specifically, what role Islamic law should play in an Islamic state, the Muslim Brotherhood in Jordan is thus divided between *sharīʿa*-centred scholars such as Abu Faris and al-Khalidi, *umma*-centred ones like Gharayiba and a group of balanced Brothers in the middle. Whereas a more or less similar division led to highly diverse positions on political issues such as the state or parliamentary participation, this is far less the case with regard to societal rights and freedoms. The reason for this is the distinction between definitive texts whose meanings are fixed and the less explicit texts whose interpretations are not. All Brothers mentioned make this distinction, but draw the dividing line between the two categories elsewhere. Yet they nevertheless seem to agree that some of the societal issues dealt with below clearly fall in the former category.

Religious Minority Rights

As we saw in Chapter 1, the rights of religious minorities were interpreted differently from early Islam onwards, partly because the texts on the treatment of Jews and Christians were not always seen as very clear. As a result, views on how to deal with them varied between the strict application of the *sharīʿa*'s rules on *dhimma* and policies that seemed to be directed at taking these groups' interests into account. Rida tended more towards the latter, while early Muslim Brothers, particularly ʿAwda and Qutb, seem to have viewed Jews and Christians through the prism of the texts of the *sharīʿa* again and, as such, saw them as tolerated minorities on the basis of the concept of '*dhimma*'.

Over the past few decades, several studies have paid attention to Islamist views on religious minority rights,[60] including since the 'Arab Spring'.[61] Some publications deal with religious minority rights according to Islamists through the prism of the classical concept of '*dhimma*',[62] while others also treat this as an issue of non-Muslim citizenship in Muslim countries.[63] The concept of 'citizenship', often expressed in Arabic through the terms '*muwāṭana*' and '*jinsiyya*', has been the subject

[60] Scott, *Challenge*, 34–165; Wāʿī, *Al-Fikr*, 42–5.
[61] Maher Y. Abu-Munshar, 'In the Shadow of the "Arab Spring": The Fate of Non-Muslims under Islamist Rule', *Islam and Christian–Muslim Relations* 23, no. 4 (2012): 487–503; El Fegiery, *Tyranny*, 11–12.
[62] Scott, *Challenge*, 92–121.
[63] Ibid., 122–65; Jakob Skovgaard-Petersen, 'Brothers and Citizens: The Second Wave of Islamic Institutional Thinking and the Concept of Citizenship', in *The Crisis of Citizenship in the Arab World*, ed. Roel Meijer and Nils Butenschon (Leiden: Brill, 2017), 320–37.

of several book-length studies in the past few years[64] and it has also become increasingly popular among Islamist scholars, including the global and Jordanian ones dealt with below.

Global Islamist Scholars on Religious Minority Rights

One thing that global Islamist scholars who have influenced the Jordanian Brotherhood can agree on is that Jews and Christians should enjoy freedom of religion.[65] Q. 2:256, which we saw cited in Chapters 1 and 2 to indicate that there is no compulsion in religion, is quoted by global Islamist scholars, too. It is verses like these that lead the prominent Egyptian Islamist scholar Muhammad al-Ghazali (1917–1996) to state:

> Yes, believe if you want to. Or keep rejecting it and disbelieving it (*ibqaw alá inkārikum lahu wa-kufrikum bihi*) if you want to. Nobody will force you to be convinced of whatever you hate. The only means to faith that is pursued (*li-l-īmān al-manshūd*) is free knowledge (*al-ma'rifa al-ḥurra*), mere conviction (*al-iqtinā' al-mujarrad*) and humility (*al-khushū'*).[66]

The legitimacy of friendly relations with religious minorities is based, al-Qaradawi states, on a verse that al-Banna also cites in this respect (Q. 60:8), as we saw in Chapter 2, which justifies good ties with non-Muslims who did not attack or expel the early followers of the Prophet Muhammad. Al-Qaradawi believes that this verse and the one following it are about polytheists, meaning that Jews and Christians – as Muslims' fellow monotheists – should certainly be treated well.[67] More negative verses about Jews and Christians, al-Qaradawi writes, should be interpreted as directed at non-Muslims who were actively hostile to the early Islamic community, not at friendly Jewish neighbours or peaceful Christian acquaintances.[68] As such, al-Qaradawi portrays the history of Islam as one of tolerance towards Jews and Christians.[69]

Much of the debate about religious minority rights among global Islamist scholars who influenced the Jordanian Brotherhood is based on

[64] Nils A. Butenschon, Uri Davis and Manuel Hassassian, eds, *Citizenship and the State in the Middle East: Approaches and Applications* (Syracuse, NY: Syracuse University Press, 2000); Andrew F. March, *Islam and Liberal Citizenship: The Search for an Overlapping Consensus* (Oxford: Oxford University Press, 2009); Roel Meijer and Nils Butenschon, eds, *The Crisis of Citizenship in the Arab World* (Leiden: Brill, 2017).

[65] Al-Ghannūshī, *Al-Ḥurriyyāt*, 48; Muḥammad al-Ghazālī, *Hādhā Dīnunā* (Doha: Dār al-Thaqāfa, 1985), 59–62; Yūsuf al-Qaraḍāwī, *Ghayr al-Muslimīn fī l-Mujtama' al-Islāmī* (Cairo: Maktabat Wahba, 2005), 47–55; al-Turabi, 'Islamic State', 220.

[66] Al-Ghazālī, *Hādhā*, 59.

[67] Al-Qaraḍāwī, *Ghayr al-Muslimīn*, 6–7; al-Qaraḍāwī, *Al-Ḥalāl*, 290–1.

[68] Al-Qaraḍāwī, *Ghayr al-Muslimīn*, 72–5; al-Qaraḍāwī, *Al-Ḥalāl*, 293–6.

[69] Al-Qaraḍāwī, *Ghayr al-Muslimīn*, 56–60, 69–71.

the classical concept of *dhimma*.[70] Al-Qaradawi sees this concept as a contract of security through which non-Muslims can live under the protection of Islam and which entails certain rights and duties.[71] These rights include protection,[72] freedom of religion,[73] the freedom to work[74] and the freedom to be in governmental positions,[75] except for certain jobs that are meant to be taken by Muslims, such as the caliphate, top positions in the army and judges presiding over cases involving only Muslims. The caliphate, al-Qaradawi states, is the succession of the Prophet, which cannot be done by a non-Muslim. Similarly, leading an army in Islam means waging jihad, which is reserved for Muslims, and judging Muslims' cases is done on the basis of the *sharīʿa*, justifying the exclusion of people who do not follow this legal system themselves.[76]

The duties of non-Muslims under the system of *dhimma* basically involve only two things: the first is that they adhere to and live within the boundaries of the Islamic laws and norms of the land;[77] the second is that they pay the *jizya*. While the former is perhaps not very controversial, the latter clearly is because it can easily be portrayed as a form of discrimination against non-Muslims, as we saw in Chapter 1. That same chapter also mentions a different interpretation, however, and since the exact reason behind the *jizya* is not clear, global Islamist scholars who have influenced the Jordanian Brotherhood resort to the latter. Al-Ghannushi and al-Qaradawi state that jihad is only waged by Muslims and, as such, non-Muslims should contribute to military affairs financially, making the *jizya* – in al-Qaradawi's words – merely 'a financial substitute for "military service (*al-khidma al-ʿaskariyya*)"',[78] which can be discarded if non-Muslims join in the actual military defence of Muslim lands.[79]

This transition from *jizya* as a means of humiliating non-Muslims to something akin to military service that can be ignored in countries with conscription for all takes the different interpretations of *dhimma* a step further than what happened in classical Islam. It also takes it more in the direction of the modern term 'citizenship', which implies equal rights and duties for all in modern nation-states, regardless of people's religion.[80] In

70 See, for example, Warren and Gilmore, 'One Nation', 228–9, 231–5.
71 Al-Qaraḍāwī, *Ghayr al-Muslimīn*, 7–8. 72 Ibid., 9–18.
73 Rāshid al-Ghannūshī, *Ḥuqūq al-Muwāṭana: Ḥuqūq Ghayr al-Muslim fī l-Mujtamaʿ al-Islāmī* (Herndon, VA: Al-Maʿhad al-ʿĀlamī li-l-Fikr al-Islāmī, 1993 [1989]), 65–8; al-Qaraḍāwī, *Ghayr al-Muslimīn*, 18–22.
74 Al-Qaraḍāwī, *Ghayr al-Muslimīn*, 22–3. 75 Ibid., 23. 76 Ibid., 23–4.
77 Ibid., 34. 78 Ibid., 36–7. The quotation is on p. 37.
79 Al-Ghannūshī, *Ḥuqūq*, 99–102; al-Qaraḍāwī, *Ghayr al-Muslimīn*, 39; al-Qaraḍāwī, *Ummatunā*, 205.
80 Warren and Gilmore, 'Rethinking Neo-Salafism', 3–6.

fact, although he defends the concept of *dhimma*, as we saw above, al-Qaradawi acknowledges that this term may cause non-Muslims to fear discrimination and therefore advocates dropping it altogether in favour of 'citizenship'.[81] Contentwise, however, the latter is clearly based on the interpretation of *dhimma* given above, just as it is inspired by the aforementioned early Muslim community of Medina and especially its 'constitution', with its equal treatment of Jews and Muslims.[82] Al-Turabi even states that

> [t]he constitutional history of the Muslims (*tārīkh al-Muslimīn al-dustūrī*) really began through the *hijra* [to Medina in 622] with the founding of the Sunni state in Medina. That state was the first of its time founded on the basis of a written constitution (*dustūr maktūb*). This document was a treaty of citizenship (*'ahdan li-l-muwāṭana*) between the different people of Medina.[83]

As such, the global Islamist scholars dealt with here have no objection to using the term 'citizenship' as the modern version of *dhimma*.[84]

Still, as far-reaching as the global Islamist scholarly discourse on religious minority rights is, some differences between Muslims and non-Muslims remain. The first of these pertains to non-Muslim proselatisation, which al-Qaradawi does not believe should be allowed,[85] although other global Islamist scholars are more tolerant of this.[86] A second, important difference concerns the political rights of non-Muslims in an Islamic state and society. The global Islamist scholars who have influenced the Jordanian Brotherhood agree that non-Muslims have the right to be members of parliament[87] because there are no texts forbidding it[88] and they also believe non-Muslims may hold positions in government.[89] They exclude them from the presidency of an Islamic state, however,

[81] Warren and Gilmore, 'One Nation', 229.

[82] Al-Ghannūshī, *Al-Dīmuqrāṭiyya*, 46, 63–4, 117, 182–8; al-Ghannūshī, *Ḥuqūq*, 48–50.

[83] Al-Turābī, *Fī l-Fiqh*, 170.

[84] Al-Ghannūshī, *Al-Ḥuqūq*, 7; al-Ghannūshī, *Al-Ḥurriyyāt*, 47; al-Qaraḍāwī, *Ummatunā*, 203.

[85] Warren and Gilmore, 'One Nation', 233.

[86] Rāshid al-Ghannūshī, 'Al-Aḥzāb Ghayr al-Islāmiyya fī l-Dawla al-Islāmiyya', *Al-Sabīl*, 1–7 March 1994, 17; al-Ghannūshī, *Al-Ḥurriyyāt*, 49; al-Turabi, 'Islamic State', 222.

[87] Rāshid al-Ghannūshī, 'Al-Aḥzāb Ghayr al-Islāmiyya fī l-Dawla al-Islāmiyya', *Al-Sabīl*, 1–7 March 1994, 17; al-Ghannūshī, *Al-Ḥurriyyāt*, 142–4; Rutherford, *Egypt*, 116; Rutherford, 'What Do Egypt's Islamists Want?', 718–19. The latter two sources indicate that al-Qaraḍāwī believes parliament should retain a Muslim majority to preserve its Islamic character, however.

[88] Al-Ghannūshī, *Al-Ḥurriyyāt*, 142; al-Qaraḍāwī, *Min Fiqh*, 194.

[89] Al-Ghannūshī, *Ḥuqūq*, 78–9; Rutherford, *Egypt*, 116; Rutherford, 'What Do Egypt's Islamists Want?', 718.

claiming that this job requires protecting Islam and must therefore be left to a Muslim.[90]

This means that, as reformist as some of these global Islamist scholars are, there are clear lines that even they will not cross. While the 'constitutionalisation' of the *sharīʿa* in the works of al-Ghannushi meant that he could embrace democracy and deepen his *umma*-centred approach to Islamist ideology by decontesting '*umma*' as adjacent to the core concept of 'ruler', this is not the case with regard to his views on religious minority rights. As Tamimi points out, al-Ghannushi attempts to explain why it is obvious that an Islamic state has a Muslim ruler and tries to minimise the differences in citizenship rights between Muslims and non-Muslims.[91] Yet in the end, both al-Ghannushi and other global Islamist scholars give too much weight to the adjacent concept of '*sharīʿa*' at the expense of '*umma*' to end these differences altogether, meaning that their approach to Islamist ideology with regard to religious minority rights is essentially a balanced one.

The Jordanian Muslim Brotherhood on Religious Minority Rights

Just like their global Islamist scholarly sources of influence, Jordanian Brothers agree on the importance of freedom of religion. According to Gharayiba, 'all jurisprudents and scholars (*kull al-fuqahāʾ wa-l-ʿulamāʾ*) and all Muslim thinkers (*jamīʿ al-mufakkirīn al-Muslimīn*) agree that religious freedom (*al-ḥurriyya al-dīniyya*) is a settled principle (*aṣl maqṭūʿ bihi*) in Islam'.[92] This does, indeed, seem to be widely shared among the members of the Jordanian Muslim Brotherhood, with one of them pointing to the friendly ties Hasan al-Banna had with some Coptic Christians in Egypt,[93] while others stress the importance of Q. 2:256 and the freedom of conscience that they believe is implied in this verse.[94] Gharayiba states that while Muslims are commanded to do *daʿwa* to non-Muslims to bring them to Islam, they may not be forced or coerced into this religion and should be reasoned with in a friendly manner, citing Q. 2:256 and other verses to prove his point. Muslims, he makes clear, should also take

[90] Rāshid al-Ghannūshī, 'Al-Aḥzāb Ghayr al-Islāmiyya fī l-Dawla al-Islāmiyya', *Al-Sabīl*, 1–7 March 1994, 17; al-Ghannūshī, *Ḥuqūq*, 79; Rutherford, *Egypt*, 116; Rutherford, 'What Do Egypt's Islamists Want?', 718–19.

[91] Tamimi, *Rachid*, 77–8.

[92] Ruḥayyil Muḥammad Gharāyiba, 'Ḥurriyyat al-Iʿtiqād wa-l-Qaḍāyā al-Shāʾika', *Al-Dustūr*, 16 February 2016, 20.

[93] Interview with Ziyād Abū Ghanīma, Amman, 26 June 2012.

[94] Interviews with Jamīl Abū Bakr, Amman, 18 June 2012; Zakī Banī Irshīd, Amman, 13 June 2012; Sālim al-Falāḥāt, Amman, 22 January 2013; Faraj Shalhūb, Amman, 21 June 2012.

care not to defame non-Muslims' religions and the latter have the right to worship as they wish, except in places where Muslims gather.[95]

According to Gharayiba, the freedom non-Muslims enjoy in an Islamic society brings with it certain rights that are shared by Muslims, such as social and economic rights, like the right to possess property, as well as general freedoms such as freedom of expression.[96] As he told me in one of my conversations with him, in his view

> [a]ll of them, in rights and duties, are equal. [. . .] There is no difference between a Muslim and a non-Muslim in the political community, in their citizenship (*jinsiyya*) of the state, at all. There is no difference in any rights or duties. The only distinction is in religious questions and personal circumstances (*al-aḥwāl al-shakhṣiyya*) [like marriage, divorce, etc., which they can do] as they want according to the beliefs they adhere to. It is not permitted to impose another religion on them. That alone is the distinction.[97]

Just like al-Qaradawi does, Abu Faris legitimises such friendly relations with non-Muslims based on their behaviour, stating – with reference to Q. 60:8 – that non-Muslims who are peaceful and do not help the enemies of the believers must be treated well and should be protected, but that the same may not happen with those who do turn against Muslims.[98] Both Gharayiba and Abu Faris point out that this explains why Islam has historically been so tolerant towards Jews and Christians.[99]

As with global Islamist scholars who have influenced Jordanian Brothers, the latter themselves also partly use the concept of '*dhimma*' to support their views. Jamil Abu Bakr uses the protection inherent to *dhimma* to claim that it is 'the responsibility of the majority (*mas'ūliyyat al-aghlabiyya*) to protect the minority (*ḥimāyat al-aqalliyya*) and not at the expense of their rights'.[100] Gharayiba also describes *dhimma* as a contract that serves to protect non-Muslims,[101] is rooted in the life of the Prophet Muhammad and his companions[102] and gives Jews and Christians the right to settle in the lands of Islam and provides them with religious freedom, the inviolability of their lives and possessions and protection.[103] Moreover, Gharayiba sees a deeper meaning to *dhimma*

[95] Ruḥayyil Gharāyiba, *Al-Jinsiyya fī l-Sharī'a al-Islāmiyya* (Beirut: Al-Shabaka al-'Arabiyya li-l-Abḥāth wa-l-Nashr, 2011), 120–2.

[96] Ibid., 122–4. [97] Interview with Ruḥayyil Gharāyiba, Amman, 16 June 2013.

[98] Abū Fāris, *Al-Fiqh*, 65–6; interview with Muḥammad Abū Fāris, Amman, 21 January 2013.

[99] Abū Fāris, *Al-Fiqh*, 66; Ruḥayyil Muḥammad Gharāyiba, 'Maḥaṭṭāt Tārīkhiyya fī l-'Alāqa al-Islāmiyya al-Masīḥiyya', *Al-Dustūr*, 19 May 2014, 20, 13.

[100] Interview with Jamīl Abū Bakr, Amman, 18 June 2012.

[101] Gharāyiba, *Al-Jinsiyya*, 51. [102] Ibid., 52–5.

[103] Gharāyiba, *Al-Ḥuqūq*, 65–9; Gharāyiba, *Al-Jinsiyya*, 58–60, 62–4.

as a kind of *da'wa* for Islam by showing the religion's kindness to non-Muslims. Probably in response to the practices of the militant group the Islamic State (IS), which applied the *dhimma* by force in parts of Iraq and Syria at the time, Gharayiba states that the concept

> has become a way of blood (*ṭarīqan li-l-dam*), dismay (*al-ru'b*), hatred (*al-bughḍ*), expulsion (*al-tashrīd*), cutting off heads (*qaṭ' al-ru'ūs*), the weakening of the state (*iḍ'āf al-dawla*), the division of society (*taqsīm al-mujtama'*), the crumbling of the national fabric (*taftīt al-nasīj al-waṭanī*), the defamation of the religion (*tashwīh al-dīn*) [. . .].[104]

Instead, he argues, it should be 'among the most successful ways that lead to the conversion to Islam'.[105] Given this context, it is not surprising that Gharayiba and others argue that the *jizya* is not a means to denigrate non-Muslims, but a payment in lieu of military service on behalf of Islam that enables them to have a stake in society and that is annulled if Jews and Christians join the army.[106]

Yet like the global Islamist scholars discussed above, members of the Jordanian Brotherhood have increasingly discussed religious minority rights in terms of citizenship, not *dhimma*, using the latter as a source of authentically Islamic inspiration rather than as a functional concept for today's society.[107] Interestingly, Gharayiba sees *dhimma* as one of the two ways of obtaining citizenship in the lands of Islam (the other being conversion) and thus integrates the classical concept in the modern one.[108] Gharayiba describes citizenship in numerous ways, but it can be defined as the contractual relationship between individuals (both Muslim and non-Muslim) with the state that entails rights and duties.[109] Apart from *dhimma* as a source of inspiration for citizenship, the 'constitution of Medina' is also frequently mentioned as an example for today's societies.[110] Because of

104 Ruḥayyil Muḥammad Gharāyiba, 'Bayna Fiqh al-Kulliyyāt wa-Fiqh al-Juz'iyyāt', *Al-Dustūr*, 26 August 2014, 16.

105 Gharāyiba, *Al-Jinsiyya*, 64.

106 Ibid., 61–2, 132–5; Ruḥayyil Muḥammad Gharāyiba, 'Qiṣṣat al-Jizya', *Al-Būṣala* (www.albosala.com/?id=111&artical=10807624&chng_tpl=print, accessed 29 April 2013), 28 April 2013; interviews with Jamīl Abū Bakr, Amman, 18 June 2012; 'Abd al-Laṭīf 'Arabiyyāt, Amman, 20 June 2012.

107 Abū Rummān and Bunduqjī, *Min al-Khilāfa*, 186; Gharāyiba, *Jamā'at*, 101. The term 'citizens' has, in fact, been used for decades by the Jordanian Brotherhood to indicate both Muslim and non-Muslim Jordanians. See, for example, 'Ayyuhā l-Muwāṭinūn ... Muslimūn wa-Masīḥiyyūn ... Kūnū 'alá Ḥadhar', *Al-Kifāḥ al-Islāmī*, 26 August 1954, 7.

108 Gharāyiba, *Al-Jinsiyya*, 41–2.

109 Gharāyiba, *Al-Ḥuqūq*, 53–63; Gharāyiba, *Al-Jinsiyya*, 14–30.

110 Gharāyiba, *Al-Ḥuqūq*, 57–60; Gharāyiba, *Al-Jinsiyya*, 37–40; Ruḥayyil Muḥammad Gharāyiba, 'Ḥurriyyat al-I'tiqād wa-l-Qaḍāyā al-Shā'ika', *Al-Dustūr*, 16 February 2016, 20; Ruḥayyil Muḥammad Gharāyiba, 'Qiṣṣat al-Jizya', *Al-Būṣala* (www.albosala.com/?id=111&artical=10807624&chng_tpl=print, accessed 29 April

these roots, as well as the global Islamist discourse on this matter, the term 'citizenship' is used among a wide variety of Jordanian Brothers in their discourse on religious minority rights now.[111]

There are differences between the various Jordanian Brothers on this topic, but they are smaller than what we saw in the previous two chapters. Abu Faris believes non-Muslims should not play a role in *shūrá* councils because this did not happen in early Islam either and because it would be strange to have a non-Muslim decide about the application of the *sharīʿa*.[112] Gharayiba, however, believes that non-Muslims can play a role in parliament with regard to worldly affairs[113] and can vote on who the ruler should be,[114] referring to Jordanian Christians as 'partners on earth and [in] the homeland (*shurakāʾ fī l-arḍ wa-l-waṭan*), partners in power and responsibility (*al-sulṭa wa-l-masʾūliyya*), partners in money and wealth (*al-māl wa-l-tharwa*) and partners in damage and profit (*al-ghurm wa-l-ghunm*)'.[115]

With regard to non-Muslims in government, Abu Faris – echoing al-Banna – makes this conditional on necessity and believes they should be kept out of leadership positions.[116]

Dhunaybat states that non-Muslims can become prime minister, but does not discuss the position of head of state, possibly because 'king' is not even theoretically a position that ordinary citizens may ever obtain in Jordan.[117] Gharayiba, despite his major differences with Abu Faris, more or less agrees with the latter, perhaps guided by conservative views on this matter in Jordanian society or the belief that, unlike the famine in caliph ʿUmar's ruling, Christian rights to become heads of state do not justify overriding Qurʾanic texts. In any case, he states that positions like those of

2013), 28 April 2013; interviews with Jamīl Abū Bakr, Amman, 18 June 2012; ʿAbd al-Laṭīf ʿArabiyyāt, Amman, 20 June 2012; ʿAlī al-Ṣawā, Amman, 25 June 2012.

111 Mohammad Ghazal, '"Islamists Should Show Good Faith by Committing to Openness"', *The Jordan Times* (http://jordantimes.com/islamists-should-show-good-faith-by-committing-to-openness, accessed 18 November 2013), 17 November 2013; interviews with Jamīl Abū Bakr, Amman, 18 June 2012; ʿAbd al-Laṭīf ʿArabiyyāt, Amman, 20 June 2012; Muḥammad Abū Fāris, Amman, 21 January 2013; Zakī Banī Irshīd, Amman, 13 June 2012; Ibrāhīm Gharāyiba, Amman, 25 June 2013; ʿĀṭif al-Jawlānī, Amman, 14 June 2012; ʿAlī al-Ṣawā, Amman, 25 June 2012; Faraj Shalhūb, Amman, 21 June 2012.

112 Abū Fāris, *Al-Niẓām*, 118–19.

113 Gharāyiba, *Al-Ḥuqūq*, 143–4; Gharāyiba, *Al-Jinsiyya*, 117–19.

114 Gharāyiba, *Al-Ḥuqūq*, 207–8.

115 Ruḥayyil Muḥammad Gharāyiba, 'Al-Masīḥiyyūn wa-l-Muwāṭana', *ʿAmmūn* (www.ammonnews.net/print.aspx?articleno=170325, accessed 21 October 2013), 21 October 2013.

116 Abū Fāris, *Al-Fiqh*, 66–7.

117 ʿAbd al-Majīd Dhunaybāt, 'Ḥawla Barnāmij "al-Ikhwān" fī Miṣr', *Al-Ghad* (www.alghad.com/articles/546177, accessed 28 January 2013), 9 November 2007.

ruler and leader of the army should not be held by non-Muslims. The reason for this is that they are Islamic tasks inextricably tied to Islam through texts such as the aforementioned Q. 4:59 as well as Q. 4:83 ('[. . .] if they had referred it to the Messenger and those in authority among them [. . .]'), which he believes refer to Muslim leaders only. This is confirmed, Gharayiba believes, by Q. 4:141 ('[. . .] God will not grant the unbelievers any way over the believers.').[118]

Because of such supposedly definitive texts, ideologically diverse men like Abu Faris and Gharayiba basically agree on the idea that some political positions should be off-limits to non-Muslims. Ironically, Gharayiba's views on reform of Islamic law enables him to 'constitutionalise' the *sharīʿa* by reducing it to broad guidelines and limiting its fixed texts to religious issues, as we saw before, but the supposedly religious basis of the political positions to which these texts are tied are simultaneously precisely what keeps him from allowing non-Muslims to fill them. In other words, while Gharayiba's specific decontestation of '*sharīʿa*' ensures his *umma*-centred approach with regard to the state and political participation, it also means that he takes a more text-based approach in some aspects of religious minority rights. As such, while Abu Faris remains *sharīʿa*-centred through his privileging of the adjacent concept of '*sharīʿa*' over '*umma*', many other Jordanian Brothers – including Gharayiba – are better described as balanced in their approach to religious minority rights in Islamist ideology.

Women's Rights

From the point of view of the *sharīʿa*, what mostly seemed to differentiate women from non-Muslim minorities was that the former – unlike the latter – were more or less assumed to agree with Islamic law, as we saw in Chapter 1. Rida seems to have made more of an effort than classical scholars to take the wishes of the *umma*'s female half into account by providing flexibility in the context of the *sharīʿa*, but ultimately stuck to the texts on this issue, which are relatively explicit and, as such, often seen as definitive. Chapter 2 showed that the early Muslim Brothers, particularly al-Sibaʿi, tended towards a *sharīʿa*-centred approach again, limiting women's opportunities to work, keeping *ikhtilāṭ* to a minimum and preferably keeping them out of politics altogether, instead focussing on women's roles as wives and mothers. Global Islamist scholars who have influenced the Jordanian Brotherhood and members of the organisation

[118] Gharāyiba, *Al-Jinsiyya*, 106–13.

itself have developed beyond these ideas somewhat, but – again – not drastically.

Global Islamist Scholars on Women's Rights

Just like other topics discussed above, ideological developments on women's rights have been widely debated in Brotherhood circles.[119] One issue that features prominently in these debates is equality between men and women. Interestingly, various scholars portray men and women as equal human beings[120] and, for instance, apply the command to cast down your eyes and guard your private parts found in Q. 24:30, 31, as we saw in Chapter 1, to both men and women,[121] but in the end they clearly acknowledge more rights for men than for women. The difference in inheritance between men and women, referred to in Q. 4:11, 176 and discussed in Chapter 1, is explained by al-Ghazali and al-Qaradawi, for example, as compensation for the dower (*mahr*) a man has to pay to his wife at the start of their marriage.[122] Similarly, al-Turabi – who is (rightly) credited with calling attention to and widening women's rights in his writings[123] – states that 'men have no power over women, except in the context of marriage (*fī iṭār al-zawjiyya*)'.[124] As such, these scholars, rather than trying to reinterpret texts on the basis of the *umma*'s changed circumstances, explain why holding on to them is the right thing to do.

The same continuation of earlier ideas on the basis of what the scholars consider to be definitive texts can be seen with regard to the issue of gender-mixing. Al-Ghazali explicitly forbids *ikhtilāṭ* in any situation in which love or flirtation is involved.[125] Al-Ghannushi mentions that gender-mixing is quite common and often allowed in Islam, but only in situations in which 'the virtue of the gaze (*ʿiffat al-naẓar*) and the purity

[119] El Fegiery, *Tyranny*, 9–10; Barbara Freyer Stowasser, 'Yūsuf al-Qaraḍāwī on Women', in *Global Mufti: The Phenomenon of Yusuf al-Qaradawi*, ed. Bettina Gräf and Jakob Skovgaard-Petersen (New York: Columbia University Press, 2009), 181–211; al-Wāʿī, *Al-Fikr*, 184–201.

[120] Al-Ghannūshī, *Al-Dīmuqrāṭiyya*, 160; Muḥammad al-Ghazālī, *Mushkilāt fī Ṭarīq al-Ḥayāt al-Islāmiyya* (Cairo: Nahḍat Miṣr li-l-Ṭabāʿa wa-l-Nashr wa-l-Tawzīʿ, 2003), 50; Yūsuf al-Qaraḍāwī, *Markaz al-Marʾa fī l-Ḥayāt al-Islāmiyya* (Amman: Dār al-Furqān li-l-Nashr wa-l-Tawzīʿ, 1996), 9–16; Muḥammad Quṭb, *Qaḍiyyat al-Tanwīr fī l-ʿĀlam al-Islāmī* (Cairo: Dār al-Shurūq, 2002 [1999]), 57; Ḥasan al-Turābī, *Al-Marʾa bayna l-Uṣūl wa-l-Taqālīd* (Khartoum: Markaz Dirāsāt al-Marʾa, 2000), 8.

[121] Al-Ghazālī, *Hādhā Dīnunā*, 153–4; al-Qaraḍāwī, *Al-Ḥalāl*, 138–9; al-Turābī, *Al-Marʾa*, 16.

[122] Al-Ghazālī, *Hādhā Dīnunā*, 51–2; al-Qaraḍāwī, *Markaz*, 23–7.

[123] Abdelwahid, *Rise*, 141–8; El-Affendi, *Turabi's Revolution*, 173–5.

[124] Al-Turābī, *Al-Marʾa*, 11. See also Stowasser, 'Yūsuf', 203.

[125] Al-Ghazālī, *Hādhā Dīnunā*, 154–5.

of heart (*ṭahārat al-qalb*)' can be maintained.[126] Al-Qaradawi essentially agrees, writing that *ikhtilāṭ* is not forbidden in Islam if it serves a legitimate purpose,[127] although he is careful to point out that the type of 'total gender-mixing (*al-ikhtilāṭ al-muṭlaq*)' seen in the West has led to a decline in norms as well as a rise in the number of deadly diseases and children born out of wedlock.[128] With regard to Qur'anic verses like Q. 33:33, which calls on women to remain in their houses (as we saw in Chapter 1), al-Ghannushi does not take an obvious stand,[129] but al-Turabi states that Q. 33:53 – about the need for separation between men and women, as mentioned in Chapter 1 – only applies to the Prophet's wives, not women in general.[130]

The issues of gender-mixing and leaving one's house are obviously related to all kinds of activities, including having a job. Global Islamist scholars who influenced the Jordanian Brotherhood sometimes justify excluding women from certain professions because it is a question of honour for a man to provide for his family (rather than letting his wife do that)[131] or because some professions allegedly do not square with women's nature or competence.[132] Yet the topic of women's professional work is simultaneously a good illustration of al-Qaradawi's reformist position that if there is no text forbidding something, it is allowed. As al-Ghannushi points out:

> This question [of women working], which started as a consequence of the Muslims' contact with European civilisation, is a problem that was not mentioned in the *fiqh* books of old (*kutub al-fiqh qadīman*). So the jurisprudents did not ask themselves[:] Does a woman have the right to participate in the economic production process (*ḥarakat al-intāj al-iqtiṣādī*) or not? Despite the fact that Islam confirms the responsibility of the man to provide for his family (*al-infāq ʿalá baytihi*) to free the woman to raise her children (*li-tufarrigha l-marʾa li-tarbiyat abnāʾihā*), no special limits have been placed on her that prevent her from engaging in economic activity.[133]

Al-Ghannushi therefore asks, 'by means of what *sharīʿa* text is a woman prevented from doing noble work?'[134] Given the apparent absence of such a text, it is not surprising that al-Ghannushi comes out in favour of women working outside the house, provided they do not neglect their

126 Al-Ghannūshī, *Al-Marʾa*, 81–2 (the words quoted are on p. 82); Muhammad Mahmoud, 'Women and Islamism: The Case of Rashid al-Ghannushi of Tunisia', in *Islamic Fundamentalism*, ed. Abdel Salam Sidahmed and Anoushiravan Ehteshami (Boulder, CO: Westview Press, 1996), 258–9.
127 Al-Qaraḍāwī, *Markaz*, 41–56. 128 Ibid., 59–66. The words quoted are on p. 59.
129 Al-Ghannūshī, *Al-Marʾa*, 83–4; Mahmoud, 'Women', 259.
130 Al-Turābī, *Al-Marʾa*, 13–14. 131 Quṭb, *Qaḍiyyat*, 60.
132 Al-Qaraḍāwī, *Markaz*, 16–23. 133 Al-Ghannūshī, *Al-Marʾa*, 74. 134 Ibid., 75.

roles as wives and mothers.[135] Al-Qaradawi agrees with this, allowing women to work in principle as long as their husbands and families come first[136] and the job itself is Islamically legitimate, allows them to work around other women and enables them to maintain their decency (*adab*).[137]

Similar requirements are given with regard to a job in politics for women, meaning that global Islamist scholars allow women – within limits – to run for and hold public office.[138] Al-Qaradawi, for instance, claims that the order for women to stay in their houses (Q. 33:33) was directed at the Prophet's wives. Moreover, the necessity of getting religious women – rather than secular ones – involved in politics is an additional reason for them to leave their homes to engage in political activities.[139] More controversial in this regard is the issue of women in leadership positions, which global Islamist scholars base on several texts, the most prominent of which are Q. 4:34, about men being the managers of women's affairs (cited in Chapter 1), and a specific *ḥadīth*: 'A people (*qawm*) ruled by (*wallaw amrahum*) a woman will not be successful (*lan yufliḥa*).'[140]

Such authoritative texts cannot simply be ignored, of course, apparently meaning that somehow men must have leadership roles over women. Al-Ghannushi cites Mawdudi as someone who excludes women from politics altogether on the basis of these texts, but makes clear he disagrees with him by explicitly allowing women to occupy a whole range of leadership positions in politics,[141] although he has certain conditions: while he believes that Q. 4:34 refers to husbands' management of the affairs of their wives – not men's management of women's affairs in general, thus concurring with al-Turabi's statement mentioned above – he also believes that men should remain a majority in parliament and that the *ḥadīth* mentioned means women cannot be caliphs or heads of state.[142] Al-Qaradawi agrees and similarly excludes

[135] Ibid., 75–7.
[136] Al-Qaraḍāwī, *Markaz*, 159–61, 163–4; al-Qaraḍāwī, *Ummatunā*, 175–6.
[137] Al-Qaraḍāwī, *Markaz*, 161–3.
[138] Al-Ghannūshī, *Al-Mar'a*, 120; al-Qaraḍāwī, *Markaz*, 31–2; Rutherford, 'What Do Egypt's Islamists Want?', 717–18.
[139] Stowasser, 'Yūsuf', 204.
[140] *Ṣaḥīḥ al-Bukhārī*, book 59 ('Kitāb al-Maghāzī'), *bāb* 'Kitāb al-Nabī Ṣallá llāh ʿalayhi wa-Sallam ilá Kisrá wa-Qayṣar', no. 709.
[141] Al-Ghannūshī, *Al-Ḥurriyyāt*, 144–50; al-Ghannūshī, *Al-Mar'a*, 111–29.
[142] Al-Ghannūshī, *Al-Mar'a*, 119. Al-Ghannūshī's choice of words ('the general leadership over the *umma* (*al-wilāya al-ʿāmma ʿalá l-umma*), meaning being the head of state (*ayy ri'āsat al-dawla*)') suggests he equates the one with the other, while they are obviously two different things in our day and age. This makes it rather unclear what he means exactly.

women from the caliphate or from being heads of state,[143] partly because he believes women generally do not have the energy for such a job.[144]

A similar process to what we saw with regard to religious minority rights can thus also be discerned here: while global Islamist scholars are willing to decontest the concept of '*umma*' – in this case Muslim women – as being more adjacent to the core concept of 'ruler' than the early Brothers allowed for, their means of reforming Islamic law can only take them so far because of what they see as definitive texts that may not be overruled. As such, they cannot be said to take a *sharīʿa*-centred approach to Islamist thought with regard to women's rights, like al-Sibaʿi and his contemporaries did, but their emphasis on the rules of the *sharīʿa* at the expense of women's rights is not *umma*-centred either. Instead, they take a balanced approach to this part of Islamist thought.

The Jordanian Muslim Brotherhood on Women's Rights

To the Brotherhood in Jordan, the issue of women's rights presents just as much of a dilemma between a sort of text-based conservatism, on the one hand, and the need to change along with society, on the other, as it does for global Islamist scholars. In fact, given that the Jordanian Brotherhood is focussed on one society in particular and is, in a sense, accountable to the members of that society, one could argue that the organisation is even more caught up in this dilemma.[145] The Brotherhood's conservatism with regard to women's rights is not merely informed by religious texts, however, but sometimes also by anti-Western ideas, expressed to reject the 'decadent' culture of the West affecting their own,[146] or what may be more culturally inspired ideas on the proper roles of men and women in the family and in society. While these are often framed as Islamic, they are presented as obvious truths, rather than convictions supported by texts.[147]

[143] Al-Qaraḍāwī, *Min Fiqh*, 165. Just like al-Ghannūshī, al-Qaraḍāwī uses words ('the general leadership over the entire *umma* (*al-wilāya al-ʿāmma ʿalá l-umma kullihā*), meaning being the head of state (*ayy riʾāsat al-dawla*)') that suggest an equation between the caliphate and the head of state. This leaves unclear where al-Qaraḍāwī stands on women as heads of state.

[144] Al-Qaraḍāwī, *Markaz*, 32.

[145] For more on this, see Clark, 'Conditions', 548–55; Lisa Taraki, 'Islam Is the Solution: Jordanian Islamists and the Dilemma of the "Modern Woman"', *British Journal of Sociology* 46, no. 4 (1995): 643–61; Lisa Taraki, 'Jordanian Islamists and the Agenda for Women: Between Discourse and Practice', *Middle Eastern Studies* 32, no. 1 (1996): 140–58.

[146] Moaddel, *Jordanian Exceptionalism*, 139–40; *Naʿam*, 12; ʿAlī al-ʿUtūm, 'Al-Marʾa bayna l-Islām wa-Aʿdāʾihi', *Al-Sabīl*, 27 May 2010, 15.

[147] See, for instance, 'Al-Marʾa al-Urdunniyya', *Al-Kifāḥ al-Islāmī*, 8 February 1957, 5; Suʿād ʿAbd al-Fattāḥ Kutūʿa, 'Ḥuqūq al-Marʾa wa-Wājibātuhā fī l-Islām', *Al-Kifāḥ al-Islāmī*, 15 March 1957, 5; Al-Zahrāʾ ʿAbd al-Majīd, 'Al-Marʾa wa-l-Bināʾ al-Ijtimāʿī', *Al-Ribāṭ*,

Within this context, however, the Jordanian Brotherhood also focusses on the textual issues we saw above. Just like global Islamist scholars who influenced them, Jordanian Brothers regularly point to the idea that men and women are equal in their eyes in terms of humanity and dignity.[148] Abu Faris claims that with regard to inheritance, Islam has improved women's rights in comparison with pre-Islamic times, when women did not receive any inheritance.[149] Gharayiba agrees, in a way, by blaming the deviation from Islam for injustice towards women:

> There is no escaping that we acknowledge the presence of clear injustice to the woman that sometimes comes wrapped in religion (*mughallaf bi-l-dīn*). There is an inheritance of social behaviour, impressions and tendencies (*mawrūth min al-sulūkāt wa-l-inṭibāʿāt wa-l-ittijāhāt al-ijtimāʿiyya*) that contradicts the essence of Islam, its spirit and its general intentions (*jawhar al-Islām wa-rūḥahu wa-maqāṣidahu l-ʿāmm*).[150]

Gharayiba made this statement in a context in which IS was widely criticised for raping women and selling them as slaves at markets, perhaps explaining why he also states that 'the woman is an independent being (*kāʾin mustaqill*) through protection and responsibility in [this] world and the hereafter, not a creature that follows the man'.[151]

Gharayiba may, however, also have referred to some of the beliefs held by members of the Brotherhood and the IAF themselves, who have also been criticised for their record on women's rights. Perhaps the most important example of this is the IAF's opposition to outlawing honour killings. Jordanian law has long had provisions allowing the murderers of adulterous women to escape punishment if they committed their crime to restore their family honour. Although women's rights activists have campaigned against this practice for years, supported by King ʿAbdallah II's aunt Princess Basma, the law remained in place partly because of the IAF, which did not condone the murder of adulterers as such, but firmly opposed adultery on the basis of the *sharīʿa*,[152] causing it to vote against

10 February 1993, 14; Muʾmina Maʿālī, 'Mushārakat al-Zawj wa-l-Abnāʾ fī Aʿmāl al-Manzil Ḥāla Ghāʾiba ʿan Mujtamaʿātinā!', *Al-Sabīl*, 4 May 2010, 9. Īmān al-Quḍāt, 'Dawr al-Marʾa al-Muslima ... wa-Kalām Ākhar ...', *Al-Ribāṭ*, 16 September 1992, 14.

148 Farhan, *Islamic View*, 38; Al-Ḥarakat al-Islāmiyya fī l-Urdunn, *Ruʾyat*, 48–50.

149 Muḥammad ʿAbd al-Qādir Abū Fāris, *Mubtadiʿāt wa-ʿĀdāt wa-Ḥukm al-Sharʿ fīhā* (Amman: Dār ʿAmmār, 2000), 44.

150 Ruḥayyil Muḥammad Gharāyiba, 'Inṣāf al-Marʾa wa-Ḥimāyat al-Usra', *Al-Dustūr*, 10 June 2015, 16.

151 Ibid.

152 'Jabhat al-ʿAmal al-Islāmī: Ḥadhf al-Mādda (340) Yaʿnī Qatl al-Ghayra al-Sharīfa ʿalá l-Aʿrāḍ', *Al-Sabīl*, 15/21 February 2000, 5; Ṭāriq Dīlwānī, 'Al-Ikhtilāṭ fī l-Masābiḥ wa-Ilghāʾ al-Mādda (340) ʿAjl min Muṭālabat al-Nuwwāb bi-Taṭbīq al-Sharīʿa al-Islāmiyya', *Al-Sabīl*, 29 February–6 March 2000, 4.

the law's amendment several times.[153] For similar reasons, and sometimes in cooperation with conservative tribal members of parliament, the IAF has also opposed easing divorce regulations for women, raising the minimum age of marriage for girls or allowing courts to inform wives of their husbands' polygamy.[154]

With regard to *ikhtilāṭ*, the Jordanian Brotherhood has a similarly conservative record. Abu Faris is generally against it and portrays it as a moral danger,[155] while Farhan warns that it may lead to forbidden deeds.[156] Indeed, the Brotherhood issued explicit calls for gender segregation in schools in the late 1980s and early 1990s[157] and has also tried to implement such policies itself at ministries when some of its members were ministers in the early 1990s.[158] One author writing in *Al-Sabil* around the same time states that *ikhtilāṭ* is only allowed when the situation necessitates it, such as during a war.[159] Based on several *ḥadīth*s, Abu Faris similarly rejects the idea of women travelling alone, so without their husbands or a guardian, including if the purpose of the trip is useful, such as to seek education or to go on a pilgrimage.[160] Yet there are also members of the Brotherhood who have different ideas about this issue. Gharayiba, for instance, believes that Q. 33:33 only commands the Prophet's wives – not modern-day women – to stay in their houses[161] and sees no religious objections to women obtaining a visa without their husbands' permission.[162]

Although Brotherhood opinion – like Jordanian public opinion in general[163] – is mixed on the matter of *ikhtilāṭ* and women travelling without their husbands' permission, the issue is important enough for them to take a strong stand on. This became very clear when Prime Minister ʿAbdallah al-Nusur addressed the International Coordinating Committee of National Institutions for the Promotion and Protection of

[153] The law was eventually changed in 2017, although not enough according to human rights campaigners. See 'Jordan: Parliament Passes Human Rights Reform', *Human Rights Watch* (www.hrw.org/news/2017/10/04/jordan-parliament-passes-human-rights-reforms, accessed 28 July 2019), 4 October 2017.

[154] Clark, 'Conditions', 549–50; Rosefsky Wickham, *Muslim Brotherhood*, 211–13. With regard to divorce, Rosefsky Wickham notes, however, that the IAF's objections were mostly procedural, rather than ideological.

[155] Abū Fāris, *Al-Fiqh*, 59–62. [156] Farhan, *Islamic View*, 40.

[157] Manṣūr, *Kalimāt*, 76–7; El-Said, *Pragmatism*, 30. [158] El-Said, *Pragmatism*, 31.

[159] Usāma al-Ḥamd, 'Al-Muslima bayna l-ʿAmal al-ʿĀmm wa-l-Ikhtilāṭ', *Al-Sabīl*, 31 May–6 June 1994, 15.

[160] Abū Fāris, *Mubtadiʿāt*, 53–4. [161] Gharāyiba, *Al-Ḥuqūq*, 119.

[162] Rabá l-Farakh, 'Ḥaqq al-Marʾa fī l-Ḥuṣūl ʿalá Jawāz Safar Dūna Sharṭ', *Al-Sabīl*, 26 December–2 January 1996, 5.

[163] Jalnār Fahīm, 'Al-Ikhtilāṭ Athnāʾ al-Dirāsa ... Hal Yakūnu l-Miṣyada?', *Al-Sabīl*, 1/7 June 1999, 18.

Human Rights in early November 2012. During his address, al-Nusur stated that Jordan had accepted the 1979 Convention for the Elimination of All Forms of Discrimination against Women (CEDAW)[164] with some reservations (including with regard to women's right to travel without their husbands' or guardians' consent), but that these would be resolved soon. Although Jordan had signed CEDAW as far back as 1992, it was ratified with these reservations in 2007, but the government decided to lift them in 2009, to protests from the Brotherhood and others, who claimed the right of women to travel without consent clashed with the *sharīʿa*.[165]

After al-Nusur had made his remarks, IAF Secretary General Hamza Mansur demanded an apology from the prime minister, stating that the articles on which the government had previously expressed its reservations 'clash with the principles of our religion and our pure Jordanian norms (*qiyaminā l-Urdunniyya al-aṣīla*) and threaten the well-being of the Jordanian family (*salāmat al-usra al-Urdunniyya*) and societal security (*al-amn al-mujtamaʿī*)'.[166] Mansur was not alone, however. Religious scholars affiliated with the Brotherhood[167] – but also those who were not[168] – condemned CEDAW for the same reasons, as did unaffiliated experts.[169] Female members of the organisation were perhaps the most outspoken in their opposition, demanding that al-Nusur retract his remarks[170] or viewing CEDAW in the context of 'the presence of the spirit of the conspiracy (*rūḥ al-muʾāmara*) and the evil of the scheming intention (*sūʾ al-qaṣd al-mubayyit*) against the woman in general and the Muslim woman in particular'.[171] Prominent Member of Parliament for the IAF Dima Tahbub warns against adopting Western customs like CEDAW and

164 See www.un.org/womenwatch/daw/cedaw/ (accessed 28 June 2019).

165 '"Al-Ikhwān al-Muslimūn": Al-Ḥukūma Tastahtiru bi-l-Sharʿ al-Ḥanīf', *Al-Sabīl*, 13 August 2009, 2; Rana Husseini, 'Islamists Urge Ensour to Retract Statement on CEDAW Reservations', *The Jordan Times* (http://vista.sahafi.jo/art.php?id=04d1fb2c79a3634f43ddf9b47bec406068026d3d, accessed 28 June 2019), 11 November 2012; Petra, '"Al-Iftāʾ": Kull Mā Khālafa l-Sharīʿa fī Muʿāhadat "Sīdāw" Ḥarām wa-Lā Yajūzu l-ʿAmal bihi Ka-Ḥuriyyat al-Zawja fī an Taskuna wa-Tusāfira Kamā Tashāʾu', *Al-Sabīl*, 3 August 2009, 6.

166 'Manṣūr Yastahjinu Taṣrīḥāt Ḥawla "Sīdāw" wa-Yuṭālibu l-Nusūr bi-l-Iʿtidhār', *Shīḥān News*, 10 November 2012; interview with Jamīl Abū Bakr, Amman, 15 January 2013.

167 Mūsá Karāʿīn, 'Lajnat ʿUlamāʾ al-Ḥaraka al-Islāmiyya: Taṣrīḥāt al-Nusūr Ḥawla Sīdāw Tatanāqaḍu wa-Aḥkām al-Sharīʿa wa-l-Qānūn', *Al-Sabīl*, 14 November 2012, 2.

168 Muḥammad al-Zuyūd, '"ʿUlamāʾ al-Urdunn" Tuṭālibu l-Nuwwāb bi-ʿAdam Rafʿ al-Taḥaffuẓāt ʿan Māddatayn fī "Sīdāw"', *Al-Raʾy*, 11 December 2013.

169 'Khubarāʾ: Ittifāqiyyat "Sīdāw" Tataʿāraḍu maʿa Siyādat al-Dustūr', *Al-Sabīl*, 6 December 2012, 2.

170 Rana Husseini, 'IAF Women Members Protest Against CEDAW', *The Jordan Times* (http://vista.sahafi.jo/art.php?id=1ba5f261c6fcc98e7c3baba060faf0af8cbfb6ce, accessed 28 June 2019), 13 November 2012.

171 Ruqayya al-Quḍāt, '"Sīdāw" wa-l-Majāl al-Ākhar', *Al-Sabīl*, 23 November 2012, 5.

calls for relying on the *sharī'a* as the solution to women's problems, instead.[172]

Interestingly, and as Hamid has also pointed out,[173] because of the fairly wide support for such socially conservative points of view among the Jordanian population in general, the Brotherhood's positions are actually quite in line with those of society at large. As such, they can easily be portrayed as reflections of the popular will, which – in turn – can be presented as proof of the organisation's embrace of democracy. Indeed, as Rosefsky Wickham writes, 'the very responsiveness of the IAF's leaders to the views of its base has impeded progressive reform in the group's agenda'.[174] Echoing this, prominent members of the Jordanian Brotherhood told me that global agreements such as CEDAW do not take into account the specifics of individual countries and that, as such, certain aspects about universal women's rights are not acceptable in their particular society, which they believe should be respected.[175]

Given such norms about women both in- and outside the Brotherhood, it is not surprising that when the issue of women having jobs outside the house comes up, similar reservations apply. Abu Faris explicitly states that Islam gives women the right to work, but also that this right is limited by conditions, including that paid work is not an alternative to a woman's role as a mother, that she needs the job (i.e. not just because she wants to work) and that the job 'fits her femininity and her dignity (*unūthatihā wa-karāmatihā*)' and does not contradict the *sharī'a*.[176] Although some point to examples from Islamic history – such as Khadija, a business woman and the Prophet's first wife – to show that women should be allowed to work,[177] others comment on this issue in a way that shows scepticism towards women working[178] or explicitly mentions conditions such as those named by Abu Faris.[179] Even a light-hearted article offering advice for women working ('do not drink too much coffee and tea', 'do not worry

172 Dīma Ṭāriq Ṭahbūb, 'Abā Zuhayr Hal Tarḍá "Sīdāw" li-Zawjatika wa-bnatika wa-Ḥafīdatika?', *Al-Sabīl*, 8 November 2012, 15; Dīma Ṭāriq Ṭahbūb, 'Al-Nisā' ... ilá l-Khalaf Darra', *Al-Sabīl*, 11 December 2012, 15.

173 Hamid, *Temptations*, 80. 174 Rosefsky Wickham, *Muslim Brotherhood*, 218.

175 Interviews with Jamīl Abū Bakr, Amman, 15 January 2013; 'Alī Abū l-Sukkar, Amman, 15 January 2013.

176 Abū Fāris, *Mubtadi'āt*, 41.

177 Yāsir Abū Hilāla, 'Al-Usra wa-'Amal al-Mar'a ... Kalām Ākhar', *Al-Sabīl*, 16/22 August 1994, 7.

178 'Abd al-Salām Abū Riyāsh, 'Al-Mar'a al-'Āmila ... Wājibāt – 'Awā'iq – Ṭumūḥāt', *Al-Ribāṭ*, 11 November 1992, 13; Nānsī Dalkī, 'Radd 'alá Maqāl al-Mar'a al-Muslima wa-l-'Amal al-'Āmm', *Al-Sabīl*, 31 May–6 June 1994, 15.

179 Mundhir Zaytūn, ''Amal al-Mar'a fī Ḍaw' al-Sharī'a (1)', *Al-Sabīl*, 25 January 2011, 17; Mundhir Zaytūn, ''Amal al-Mar'a fī Ḍaw' al-Sharī'a (2)', *Al-Sabīl*, 26 January 2011, 11.

about tomorrow', etc.) is written in the context of women taking care of their children on top of their job.[180]

While all Brothers seem to agree that women are allowed to work, albeit subject to certain conditions, they do not agree on whether a woman should be allowed to work in politics. Abu Faris believes that a woman – like a man – should command right and forbid wrong,[181] but he also states that the Prophet never chose women to be among the *ahl al-ḥall wa-l-ʿaqd* and neither did he involve women in consultation and decision-making.[182] Citing aforementioned texts such as Q. 4:34 and the *ḥadīth* about a people being ruled by a woman not being successful, Abu Faris writes that a *shūrá* council may not include women[183] and further justifies such ideas by stating that

> a man is more competent than a woman (*al-rajul akfaʾ min al-marʾa*) intellectually (*ʿaqlan*) and with regard to capabilities (*qudran*), even in things that are particular to her (*khuṣūṣiyyātihā*) and her prerogative (*ikhtiṣāṣihā*), like cooking (*al-ṭuhá*), making her clothes (*ṣanʿ libāsihā*), sewing them (*khiyāṭahu*) and repairing them (*taṣḥīḥahu*). Because it is known that the greatest chefs in the world (*aʿẓam ṭuhāt al-ʿālam*) are men, just like the greatest fashion designers for women (*aʿẓam muṣammimī l-izyāʾ li-l-nisāʾ*) are men.[184]

This opposition to women in politics was not just a theoretical issue, which became quite clear in 2001 when, during a conference of the IAF, a representative of the women's section of the party was supposed to give a speech and several Brothers opposed to this walked out. First and foremost among them was Abu Faris,[185] although he did eventually come to respect Hayat al-Musaymi, a female representative on behalf of the IAF after the 2003 elections, for her dedication and seriousness.[186]

Although Abu Faris's views on women in politics are not entirely out of tune with those in Jordanian society in general,[187] they seem to be a minority view within the Brotherhood itself. Thinkers like Gharayiba do allow a woman to work in politics,[188] as do Ishaq Farhan – explicitly invoking al-Banna's example[189] – and others who point to women's participation in 'political' acts in early Islam, such as the *hijra* to

[180] '24 Naṣīḥa li-l-Marʾa al-ʿĀmila', *Al-Sabīl*, 2/8 April 2002, 11.
[181] Abū Fāris, *Al-Fiqh*, 59. [182] Ibid., 65. [183] Abū Fāris, *Al-Niẓām*, 120–1.
[184] Abū Fāris, *Al-Fiqh*, 64. [185] Abū Haniyya, *Al-Marʾa*, 65.
[186] Rosefsky Wickham, *Muslim Brotherhood*, 218.
[187] 'Natāʾij al-Istiṭlāʿ Kamā Yuwaḍḍiḥuhā l-Jadwal al-Tālī', *Al-Sabīl*, 10/16 June 1997, 4. This survey showed 50 per cent in favour of women entering parliament (48 per cent against).
[188] Gharāyiba, *Al-Ḥuqūq*, 115, 205–7.
[189] 'Tarshīḥ al-Masīra al-Shūriyya al-Dīmuqrāṭiyya wa-l-Taṣaddī li-l-Taṭbīʿ maʿa l-ʿAdū al-Ṣihyūnī min Awluwiyyāt al-Ḥaraka al-Islāmiyya', *Al-Sabīl*, 15/21 February 1994, 14.

Medina and the oath of fealty to the Prophet.[190] While the organisation as a whole indicates that a woman is first and foremost a wife and a mother, it also states that there is no text in the *sharīʿa* that prevents women from participating in politics, meaning that it is allowed,[191] which is also reflected in its official documents.[192] Women's participation in politics is also seen as a form of commanding right and forbidding wrong.[193]

The proof of the pudding is in the eating, of course, and the question is to what extent women have been able to make the leap from theoretically being allowed to engage in political action to actually representing the IAF in parliament.[194] Throughout the years, a number of women have served on the IAF's Shūrá Council,[195] starting with Nawal al-Faʿuri in 1993,[196] rising to a total of nine women fifteen years later.[197] Past and present members of parliament on behalf of the IAF include the aforementioned Hayat al-Musaymi and Dima Tahbub. Yet the number of women active in the IAF is still very small compared to the number of men in the party. This is partly the result of the female members' own view that they need to balance parliamentary work with their responsibilities at home,[198] but also of a lack of effort on behalf of the party leadership. Although as far back as 1992, the then-Secretary General of the IAF, Ishaq Farhan, expressed the hope that women would find their way into the party,[199] several members of the Brotherhood have called for more action on this point,[200] with al-Musaymi stating in 1997:

> The Islamic movement has developed amazingly (*taṭawwuran hāʾilan*) in some areas, but it has not developed on the subject of the woman, just as I do not consider [that] the matter of delay (*amr al-taʾkhīr*) on the subject of the woman has come as the result of external factors or some internal factors. The idea [of women being less important] is found among the people in the nature of upbringing (*ṭabīʿat al-tarbiya*), that the woman is a secondary thing (*shayʾ thānawī*).[201]

While it is obviously true that political participation means more than being on the electoral list of a party, as Arwa l-Kilani, the then-head of the

190 ʿAbd al-Jabbār Saʿīd, 'Mushārakat al-Marʾa fī Majlis al-Nuwwāb Taʾṣīl Sharʿī', *Al-Sabīl*, 10/16 June 2003, 7.
191 Abū Haniyya, *Al-Marʾa*, 63. 192 Al-Ḥaraka al-Islāmiyya fī l-Urdunn, *Ruʾyat*, 51.
193 Farhan, *Islamic View*, 41–2; Gharāyiba, *Jamāʿat*, 104.
194 For an in-depth treatment of this question, see Clark and Schwedler, 'Who Opened the Window?'.
195 Abū Haniyya, *Al-Marʾa*, 66. 196 El-Said, *Pragmatism*, 30.
197 Rosefsky Wickham, *Muslim Brotherhood*, 215–16. 198 Ibid., 216.
199 'Al-Marʾa wa-Jabhat al-ʿAmal al-Islāmī', *Al-Ribāṭ*, 27 October 1992, 13.
200 Ibrāhīm Gharāyiba, 'Al-Ḥaraka al-Islāmiyya wa-l-Dīmuqrāṭiyya', *Al-Sabīl*, 7/12 June 1994, 7; Marwá Jābir, 'Al-Marʾa fī Jabhat al-ʿAmal al-Islāmī … Wāqiʿ wa-Ṭumūḥ', *Al-Sabīl*, 31 May–6 June 1994, 15.
201 Rabá l-Farakh and Jullanār Fahīm, 'Dawr al-Marʾa al-Muslima … Al-Wāqiʿ wa-l-Ṭumūḥ', *Al-Sabīl*, 8/14 April 1997, 4.

Women's Section of the IAF, pointed out in 1999,[202] the issue of more prominent and even leadership positions for women in the party remains a topic of discussion.[203]

Part of this discussion in the Jordanian Brotherhood about women and political leadership is religious in nature, which is also how global Islamist scholars who have influenced the organisation deal with it. Based on the *ḥadīth* about female leadership mentioned before, Abu Faris excludes women from all leadership positions in politics (as well as other areas of life).[204] The IAF as a whole, however, has long advocated the position that women are allowed to have many roles of political leadership,[205] a topic that Gharayiba has extensively discussed in his work, eventually reaching the same conclusion.[206] Prominent members of the Brotherhood have even stated that a woman – subject to the conditions about her role as a wife and mother – is allowed to become prime minister.[207] While in Jordan this is the highest office attainable for ordinary Jordanians,[208] the hypothetical question of a woman being the caliph or head of state has also been asked. Just like with the idea of having a non-Muslim as president or king, this is basically unacceptable to members of the Jordanian Brotherhood,[209] including Gharayiba.[210]

As with the Brotherhood's position on non-Muslims, the organisation is thus fairly united on the issue of women's rights. While *sharīʿa*-centred scholars such as Abu Faris clearly deviate from the mainstream within the Brotherhood, the rest are quite homogeneous in decontesting the adjacent concept of '*sharīʿa*' as dominant in the social sphere and privileging it over '*umma*'. In politics, most seem to agree that only the position of head of state is off-limits to women, even if this is merely a theoretical notion in the Jordanian context, making their approach to this aspect of Islamist thought a balanced one. Despite his slightly greater willingness to be *umma*-centred with regard to women than with non-Muslims, it is

202 Arwá l-Kīlānī, 'Limādhā Ghābat al-Marʾa ʿan al-Intikhābāt al-Baladiyya fī Qawāʾim Jabhat al-ʿAmal al-Islāmī', *Al-Sabīl*, 20/26 July 1999, 14.
203 Rabá Karāsina, 'Shūrá "l-ʿAmal al-Islāmī" Yabḥathu Taʿdīlāt Niẓām al-Ḥizb Nihāyat al-Shahr', *Al-Būṣala* (http://albosa.la/TVRJd056VXcrdQ==, accessed 21 August 2015), 20 August 2015.
204 Abū Haniyya, *Al-Marʾa*, 62.
205 Clark and Schwedler, 'Who Opened the Window?', 301.
206 Gharāyiba, *Al-Ḥuqūq*, 115–31.
207 ʿAbd al-Majīd Dhunaybāt, 'Ḥawla Barnāmij "al-Ikhwān" fī Miṣr', *Al-Ghad* (www.alghad.com/articles/546177, accessed 28 January 2013), 9 November 2007; interview with Jamīl Abū Bakr, Amman, 15 January 2013. See also interview with ʿUrayb al-Rantāwī, Amman, 12 January 2013.
208 Abū Rumman and Abū Haniyya, *Al-Ḥall*, 96.
209 Clark and Schwedler, 'Who Opened the Window?', 301; Gharāyiba, *Jamāʿat*, 104; interview with Jamīl Abū Bakr, Amman, 15 January 2013.
210 Abū Haniyya, *Al-Marʾa*, 62; Gharāyiba, *Al-Ḥuqūq*, 131.

nevertheless interesting that Gharayiba, though limiting the application of definitive texts about men's power over women to their smallest possible practical relevance (the position of head of state), still feels there are textual lines he will not cross.

Civil Liberties

The topics of freedom of speech and the freedom to leave Islam were, as we saw in Chapter 1, dealt with quite differently in classical Islam. While all believed insulting God and the Prophet was wrong, views were divided over what punishment this deserved. Some scholars believed it should be death, while others claimed that this was only appropriate if the defamation of Islam had been accompanied by sowing chaos among believers or showing hostility to the Muslim polity. The latter explanation was also supported by Qur'anic verses and early Islamic examples on privacy and the belief that privately committed sins should not be punished. The same reasoning was given with regard to apostasy, with some scholars viewing *ridda* as worthy of death in and of itself, while others believed this only applied when apostasy was accompanied by hostility to the *umma* or treason. The early Muslim Brothers, unlike on other subjects, did not comment much on these topics beyond condemnations of 'Western' freedoms and stating that expression should be limited by the boundaries of the *sharīʿa*. Global Islamist scholars and Jordanian Brothers have made more extensive use of classical Islam in this respect, however, as we will see in this section.

Global Islamists on Civil Liberties

The issue of freedom of speech is sometimes dealt with by global Islamist scholars who have influenced the Jordanian Brotherhood in the context of freedom in general, particularly in connection with the West. Al-Qaradawi is sceptical of Western influence[211] and criticises Western countries for viewing freedom as sacred, but being less strict about it with regard to the dictatorial rulers of many Arab and Muslim countries.[212] Apart from this perceived hypocrisy on the part of Western countries, he also criticises specific societal freedoms found in Western countries, such as the right to commit adultery and gay marriage, which he believes are clearly at odds with the *sharīʿa*.[213]

This does not mean, however, that global Islamist scholars do not believe in freedom. Al-Turabi, for example, believes that Islam represents

[211] Al-Qaraḍāwī, *Ummatunā*, 77–95. [212] Ibid., 23–4. [213] Ibid., 26.

true freedom because it liberates people from human obstacles and sets them on the path to worship God. Other forms of freedom exist, al-Turabi admits, but they are not complete, like Islam, which has freed mankind from the *jāhiliyya* and remains a guiding light for continued freedom.[214] Al-Ghannushi concurs, viewing God as the source of freedom, which means it is not just a right, but also a duty to be free.[215] In line with this thinking, al-Qaradawi states with regard to freedom of speech that

> [t]he time has come for us to welcome freedom of the word (*ḥurriyyat al-kalima*), even if it is in opposition to our direction or our politics (*wa-law kānat mu'āraḍatan li-ttijjāhinā aw siyāsatinā*). We will not benefit – on the contrary, we will suffer greatly (*nataḍarraru kathīran*) – if we silence the tongues (*akhrasnā l-alsina*) and break the pens (*kasarnā l-aqlām*). Because God has created the tongues to speak and the pens to write and to express.[216]

This seemingly strong commitment to freedom of speech is qualified, however, by certain conditions. Al-Ghazali, for instance, writes that freedom of thinking should not be confused with 'freedom of desire' (*ḥurriyyat al-shahwa*), which should be limited.[217] One of these limits is that Muslim sensibilities should be respected, meaning that people are not allowed to insult Islam, the Prophet or the Qur'an.[218]

Given the things that people should take into account with regard to free speech, it is not surprising that al-Qaradawi also views apostasy, which he sees as part of a greater plan by Christians to fight Islam, as a threat to Muslim societies.[219] Just like in classical Islam, al-Qaradawi cites the *ḥadīth*s we saw in Chapter 1 to justify his conclusion that apostates should be executed.[220] Yet al-Qaradawi's generally balanced approach to Islamist ideology, as well as his emphasis on the societal impact of freedom of speech, leads him to follow the second way of dealing with apostasy we saw in Chapter 1, namely, that a *murtadd* 'is not merely an unbeliever in Islam; he, in fact, has waged war on [Islam] and its *umma*', either by hand or verbally. If such a person persists in this behaviour, al-Qaradawi states, he should be killed.[221] This punishment,

214 Al-Turābī, *Fī l-Fiqh*, 59–71. 215 Al-Ghannūshī, *Al-Ḥurriyyāt*, 35–43.
216 Yūsuf al-Qaraḍāwī, 'Ḥawla Ḥaqq al-Muslimīn fī Ḥurriyyat al-Kalima', *Al-Sabīl*, 5 January 2010, 1.
217 Al-Ghazālī, *Hadhā Dīnunā*, 42–3.
218 Al-Qaraḍāwī, *Ghayr al-Muslimīn*, 45. Other limits less connected with freedom of speech include not being allowed to drink wine or eat pork publicly or sell those items to Muslims or eat in public during Ramadan. See ibid., 46.
219 Al-Qaraḍāwī, *Jarīmat al-Ridda . . . wa-'Uqūbat al-Murtadd fī Ḍaw' al-Qur'ān wa-l-Sunna* (Amman: Dār al-Furqān li-l-Nashr wa-l-Tawzī', 1996), 44–6.
220 Ibid., 46–52. 221 Ibid., 53–4.

in other words, is not because of an apostate's change of heart about religion, which will only be punished in the hereafter,[222] but because of his open and public change of loyalty from Islam to something else. This is so detrimental to the Islamic nature of Muslim societies, al-Qaradawi states, that not punishing it would cause society to 'perhaps develop into bloody conflict and even civil war'.[223]

Although al-Qaradawi is careful to point out that the practice of *takfīr* is one that should be handled with extreme caution, should only be dealt with by scholars and political authorities and should include giving the culprit a chance to repent,[224] his views are obviously a far cry from total freedom to leave Islam. Indeed, famous 'apostates' such as the author Salman Rushdi are described by al-Qaradawi as deserving of the death penalty.[225] Yet al-Qaradawi does not simply apply *sharīʿa* texts to lax Muslims or those who convert to Christianity, for example, but significantly narrows the group to whom this punishment can be applied by contextualising the relevant *ḥadīth*s and, as such, tying apostasy to the public disavowal of Islam and even linking it to sowing chaos in society. His balanced approach to this aspect of Islamist ideology is not just very old, as we saw in Chapter 1, but this decontestation of the role of both adjacent concepts of '*sharīʿa*' and '*umma*' is also shared by earlier reformers,[226] as well as other global Islamist scholars who have influenced the Jordanian Muslim Brotherhood.[227]

The Jordanian Muslim Brotherhood on Civil Liberties

In contrast to their ideas on the state and political participation, ʿUrayb al-Rantawi, a Jordanian expert on Islamist movements, calls the Jordanian Brotherhood's views on civil liberties 'a grey zone' because they have not been reformed equally clearly.[228] Like al-Ghannushi, Gharayiba states that freedom stems from the *sharīʿa* and, like al-Turabi, claims that applying the God-given rights that Islam provides is a form of worship.[229] Indeed, the importance of various types of freedom is regularly stressed in official documents

[222] Ibid., 54–5. [223] Ibid., 56–7. [224] Ibid., 58–63. [225] Ibid., 60.
[226] Peters and De Vries, 'Apostasy', 17.
[227] Al-Ghannūshī, *Al-Ḥurriyyāt*, 50–2; al-Ghannūshī, *Al-Dīmuqrāṭiyya*, 165; al-Ghazālī, *Hādhā Dīnunā*, 202–3; Tamimi, *Rachid*, 78.
[228] Interview with ʿUrayb al-Rantāwī, Amman, 12 January 2013.
[229] Gharāyiba, *Al-Ḥuqūq*, 361–2.

produced by the Jordanian Muslim Brotherhood or the IAF,[230] sometimes with reference to textual sources such as Q. 2:256 as proof of their validity.[231]

Gharayiba also traces freedom of speech to Islam and sees it as 'an original right of the *sharīʿa*', using the same Q. 2:256 to underline his statement.[232] Abu Faris also defines freedom of speech in the context of Islam by stating that it means

> that a human being in Islamic society and in the Islamic state – whether Muslim or non-Muslim, man or woman – is free in his thinking and expressing his opinion (*tafkīrihi wa-ibdāʾ raʾyihi*), whether the opinions he expresses concur with [those of] others or differ from them. Perhaps it is criticism (*naqdan*) of the views of others who disagree (*li-ārāʾ al-mukhālifīn*) or opposition to them (*muʿāraḍa lahum*) in their verbal and practical behaviour (*taṣarrufātihim al-qawliyya wa-l-ʿamaliyya*).[233]

Moreover, the Brotherhood and the IAF often mention it as an important freedom[234] and both organisations regularly call for the release of political prisoners[235] and freedom of the press.[236] The latter is taken so seriously by the IAF that it condemned a raid by the security forces on the offices of

230 '"Al-ʿAmal al-Islāmī": Al-Ḥurriyyāt al-ʿĀmma Waṣalat li-Ḥāla Mutaraddiyya', *Al-Būṣala* (http://albosa.la/TVRFek1qUXkrdQ==, accessed 19 March 2015), 18 March 2015; '"Al-ʿAmal al-Islāmī" Yastahjinu Taraddī Ḥālat al-Ḥurriyyāt al-ʿĀmma fī l-Urdunn', *Al-Sabīl*, 19 March 2015, 8; *Al-Taqrīr al-Idārī li-Kutlat Nuwwāb Ḥizb Jabhat al-ʿAmal al-Islāmī fī Majlis al-Nuwwāb al-Urdunnī al-Rābiʿ ʿAshara 2003–2007* (n.p.: n.d.), 23–4; Al-Ḥaraka al-Islāmiyya fī l-Urdunn, *Ruʾyat*, 30–4.

231 Aḥmad Nawfal, 'Falsafat al-Ḥurriyya fī Hādhā l-Dīn', *Al-Sabīl*, 25 December 2009, 11; ʿUmar Zurayqāt, 'Ḥuqūq al-Insān bayna l-Qurʾān wa-l-Iʿlān wa-l-Dustūr', *Al-Sabīl*, 5/11 July 1994, 20.

232 Gharāyiba, *Al-Ḥuqūq*, 293–4.

233 Bassām Nāṣir, 'Ḥurriyyat al-Raʾy fī l-Islām Hal Hiya Maftūḥa bi-Lā Suqūf?', *Al-Sabīl*, 5 June 2009, 6.

234 '"Al-ʿAmal al-Islāmī": Al-Dhahāb ilá l-Intikhābāt al-Niyābiyya fī Ghiyāb al-Tawāfuq al-Waṭanī "Khaṭaʾ Fādiḥ"', *Al-Dustūr*, 6 December 2012, 5; '"Al-ʿAmal al-Islāmī": Muḍī fī l-Intikhābāt al-Muqbila Istinsākh li-l-Majlis al-Sābiq', *Al-Sabīl*, 6 December 2012, 3; 'Al-Falāḥāt: Lā Jaysh Ladaynā fa-Jaysh al-Ḥirāk al-Shaʿbī Jayshunā', *Shīḥān News* (www.shihannews.net/Print.aspx?ArticleNo=28641, accessed 18 October 2012), 1 October 2012; Fawzī ʿAlī al-Samhūrī, 'Ḥurriyyat al-Taʿbīr wa-l-Tajammuʿ bayna l-Nuṣūṣ wa-l-Maḥākim', *Al-Sabīl*, 24 September 2013, 12.

235 Hadīl Ghabbūn, '"Al-ʿAmal al-Islāmī" Yujaddidu l-Muṭālaba bi-Ilghāʾ "Amn al-Dawla" wa-Qānūn Manʿ al-Irhāb', *Al-Ghad* (http://alghad.com/articles/871394, accessed 20 May 2015), 20 May 2015; Ḥamdān al-Ḥāj, '"Ḥurriyyāt al-ʿAmal al-Islāmī" Tadʿū li-l-Ifrāj ʿan Muʿtaqalī l-Raʾy wa-Ilghāʾ Qānūn Manʿ al-Irhāb', *Al-Dustūr*, 20 May 2015, 9; Khalīl Qandīl, 'Ḥurriyyāt al-ʿAmal al-Islāmī: Intikāsa Kabīra fī Wāqiʿ al-Ḥurriyyāt', *Al-Būṣala* (http://albosa.la/TVRFMk5UY3grdQ==, accessed 20 May 2015), 19 May 2015.

236 *Naʿam*, 6–7; '... wa-Yadʿū l-Ḥukūma ilá Murājaʿat Siyāsatihā Izāʾ al-Ḥurriyyāt al-ʿĀmma wa-l-Ṣaḥafiyya', *Al-Sabīl*, 5 May 2014, 3; Gharāyiba, *Al-Ḥuqūq*, 319–22.

the Jordanian newspaper *Al-Ra'y*,[237] which is often quite critical of the Muslim Brotherhood. As Gharayiba points out, however, freedom of speech serves the general interest – rather than the organisation's own narrow interests – because it is a means towards progress, a tool to reform the rule of the country and a means to resist injustice and tyranny.[238]

Although, like al-Qaradawi's views cited earlier, these words sound like ringing endorsements of freedom of speech, they are actually limited to speech directed at the political powers that be, rather than at religion or religious people, for example. While Gharayiba, unlike al-Qaradawi, explicitly states that freedom need not be a recipe for chaos and conflict,[239] he and others nevertheless come up with a number of preferred or prescribed limits to what may be freely expressed. Abu Faris claims that freedom of speech cannot be absolute, 'especially with regard to that which is related to the texts of the Qur'anic revelation and the pure Prophetic Sunna' and cannot include calls for unbelief or 'moral depravity (*al-ifsād al-akhlāqī*)'.[240] Others concur, stating that freedom of speech should be civil and respectful and should not lead to 'chaos and division [. . .] or the spread of atheism (*al-ilḥād*), desires (*al-ahwā'*) and heretical religious innovations (*al-bida'*) among Muslims'.[241] Gharayiba similarly believes that speech in Islam should be well intended, believed by the speaker to be true, expressed with knowledge, friendliness and balance through legitimate means.[242]

The Muslim Brotherhood in Jordan does not just believe such conditions to freedom of speech are sensible, but has officially rejected views that substantially clash with theirs. In 1990, for example, the organisation condemned the participation of what it described as 'atheist' political parties, which it did not consider part of the nation.[243] More recently, the Brotherhood has called for people who spread a pamphlet that supposedly insulted Islam to be prosecuted[244] and once stated that '[i]t is unacceptable [. . .] to exploit the right to freedom of expression to pour [one's] outrage over religious people and the Islamists'.[245] Indeed, former

237 '"Al-'Amal al-Islāmī": Yudīnu qtiḥām al-Ajhiza al-Amniyya li-"l-Ra'y"', *Al-Būṣala* (www.albosala.com/?id=111&artical=10987953&chng_tpl=print, accessed 13 November 2013), 13 November 2013.

238 Gharāyiba, *Al-Ḥuqūq*, 301–7.

239 Ruḥayyil Muḥammad Gharāyiba, 'Al-Ḥurriyya Laysat Khurūjan 'alá l-Qiyam', *Al-Dustūr*, 3 June 2015, 20.

240 Bassām Nāṣir, 'Ḥurriyyat al-Ra'y fī l-Islām Hal Hiya Maftūḥa bi-Lā Suqūf?', *Al-Sabīl*, 5 June 2009, 6.

241 Karīm Kashākish, 'Ḥurriyyat al-Ra'y wa-l-Fikr fī l-Islām', *Al-Sabīl*, 20/26 July 1999, 5.

242 Gharāyiba, *Al-Ḥuqūq*, 323–30.

243 Hamid, *Temptations*, 186.

244 'Al-Ikhwān al-Muslimūn: Manshūr al-Siyāḥa Iftirā' 'alá l-Nabī', *Al-Sabīl*, 18 November 2009, 3.

245 Press statement by Islamists published on 3 November 1989, cited in Dieterich, 'Weakness', 138.

Jordanian Muslim Brother Ibrahim Gharayiba – and brother of Ruhayyil – claims he left the organisation because of an article he wrote that the Brotherhood did not like. This was a sign, Gharayiba writes, of the organisation's belief that 'it applies a truth that has been revealed from heaven, which is why any difference [of opinion] with them is a difference [of opinion] with God'.[246]

Gharayiba's words may be an exaggeration, but it is interesting to see that even in one of the areas in which the Brotherhood has staunchly defended freedom of speech – the press – it believes there should be limits. This was made quite clear after twelve members of the editorial board of the French satirical magazine *Charlie Hebdo*, which had published cartoons on Islam and the Prophet Muhammad, were killed in a terrorist attack on 7 January 2015. Although the IAF condemned the attack,[247] its condemnation quickly turned into a more general rejection of 'extremism in all its forms' and the magazine's 'insulting of the Messenger of God (*al-isāʾa li-rasūl Allāh*)'[248] and ended with the IAF demanding an official apology from the French government.[249] As with other issues we have seen in this chapter, these sentiments appeared entirely in step with the feelings of other Jordanians: Muslim scholars unaffiliated with the Brotherhood,[250] the Royal Court,[251] 'ZamZam'[252] and demonstrators in Amman[253] all condemned the magazine's defamation of the Prophet. The Ministry of Religious Endowments even suggested Friday sermons condemn both the attack and 'the chaos of freedom of expression'.[254]

[246] Markaz Ḥimāyat wa-Ḥurriyyat al-Ṣaḥafiyyīn, *Qamʿ*, 246–7. The words quoted are on p. 246.

[247] '"Al-ʿAmal al-Islāmī" Yastankiru l-Hujūm ʿalá Ṣaḥīfat "Shārlī" bi-Faransā', *Al-Sabīl*, 11 January 2015, 1.

[248] 'Al-Ikhwān al-Muslimīn Tudīnu Kull Ashkāl al-Taṭarruf', *Al-Ghad* (http://alghad.com/articles/847634, accessed 15 January 2015), 15 January 2015. See also '"Al-Ikhwān al-Muslimīn": Narfuḍu l-Isāʾa li-l-Anbiyāʾ Kāffatan wa-Nudīnu l-Mumārasāt allatī Tughadhdhī Mashāʿir al-Karāhiyya wa-Tusīʾu li-l-Adyān', *Al-Sabīl*, 16 January 2015, 3; Ḥamdān al-Ḥaj, '"Al-Ikhwān al-Muslimīn" Tudīnu l-Isāʾa li-l-Nabī l-Karīm wa-l-Lujūʾ ilá l-Taṭarruf wa-l-ʿUnf', *Al-Dustūr*, 16 January 2015, 3.

[249] '"Al-ʿAmal al-Islāmī" Yuṭālibu Faransā bi-ʿtidhār li-l-Muslimīn', *Al-Sabīl*, 27 January 2015, 4.

[250] Ḥamdān al-Ḥāj, 'Rābiṭat ʿUlamāʾ al-Urdunn: Al-Isāʾa li-l-Rasūl Mukhaṭṭaṭ Khabīth li-Ithārat al-Karāhiyya wa-l-Ṣirāʿ bayna l-Umam', *Al-Dustūr*, 16 January 2015, 3.

[251] Ḥātim al-ʿAbbādī, 'Al-Dīwān al-Malikī Yudīnu Isāʾat "Tshārlī Ībdū" li-l-Rasūl al-Karīm', *Al-Raʾy*, 16 January 2015, 1.

[252] '"ZamZam": Khayr Radd ʿalá Ahl al-Isāʾa Yakūnu bi-Ḥusn al-Tamaththul li-Manẓūmat al-Islām al-Qīmiyya', *Al-Ghad* (http://alghad.com/articles/848036, accessed 19 January 2015), 18 January 2015.

[253] 'Masīrat al-Ḥusaynī: "Illā Rasūl Allāh"', *Al-Maqarr* (www.maqar.com/?id=74740, accessed 16 January 2015), 16 January 2015.

[254] 'Iqtirāḥ "Shārlī Ībdū" Mādda li-Khuṭbat al-Jumʿa', *Al-Maqarr* (www.maqar.com/?id=74726, accessed 16 January 2015), 16 January 2015. When a Christian Jordanian named Nāhiḍ Ḥatar was murdered in Amman in September 2016 for publishing

The Brotherhood's views on the related issue of apostasy are similar, but less clear. Gharayiba has formulated the most detailed ideas on this matter, listing the verses and *ḥadīth*s about the topic we saw in Chapter 1[255] and reaching a conclusion similar to that of the global Islamist scholars dealt with above (some of whom, including al-Ghannushi, he mentions):[256] execution should only be applied to someone guilty of 'parting with the community (*mufāraqat al-jamāʿa*), meaning rebellion against (*al-khurūj ʿalá*) the regime of the state'.[257] It is, as such, the political consequences of apostasy, not the mere change of religion, that makes it such a problem. Gharayiba agrees with al-Qaradawi that *ridda* can cause chaos in society and also believes that because people enter Islam voluntarily as if it were a contract, they should not be allowed to leave easily. As such, he sees this as a matter outside the parameters of freedom of speech and as a 'dangerous crime'.[258]

Many people seem to share Gharayiba's point of view on apostasy in the sense that they see *ridda* as more than a change of religion. What must be added for apostasy to become punishable by death, however, is not always clear and does not always amount to revolt against the regime, thereby lowering the bar for execution. Abu Faris, for example, does link punishment for apostates to parting with the community of Muslims, although it is unclear if he sees this as a revolt, like Gharayiba does.[259] Jamil Abu Bakr appears to see openly switching back and forth between religions as so detrimental to society that it merits punishment, although only after exhausting every other option.[260] Likewise, for ʿAli Abu l-Sukkar, it is the open and public display of one's apostasy that is the

a cartoon that some viewed as mocking God, the Brotherhood and the IAF both condemned the murder without paying much attention to the cartoon's content. The difference with *Charlie Hebdo*'s cartoons may have been that unlike that magazine, Ḥatar was on trial in Jordan, meaning that legal action had already been taken against him. See '"Al-ʿAmal al-Islāmī" Yudīnu Ḥādithat Ightiyāl Ḥatar', *Al-Ghad* (http://alghad.com/articles/1148482, accessed 26 September 2016), 25 September 2016; '"Al-Ikhwān al-Umm": Maqtal al-Kātib Ḥatar Jarīma Bashiʿa wa-Mudāna', *Al-Būṣala* (http://albosa.la/TVRRek5ERXcrdQ==, accessed 26 September, 2016), 25 September 2016; Rana Husseini, 'Suspect in Hattar's Murder Identified', *The Jordan Times* (www.jordantimes.com/news/local/suspect-hattar%E2%80%99s-murder-identified, accessed 3 July 2019), 25 September 2016.

255 Gharāyiba, *Al-Ḥuqūq*, 313; Gharāyiba, *Al-Jinsiyya*, 173.

256 Gharāyiba, *Al-Ḥuqūq*, 315.

257 Ibid., 314. See also Ruḥayyil Muḥammad Gharāyiba, 'Ḥurriyyat al-Iʿtiqād wa-l-Qaḍāyā al-Shāʾika', *Al-Dustūr*, 16 February 2016, 20; interviews with Ruḥayyil Gharāyiba, Amman, 17 January 2013; Faraj Shalhūb, Amman, 15 January 2013.

258 Gharāyiba, *Al-Ḥudūd*, 315–17. The words quoted are on p. 317.

259 Abū Fāris, *Mafāhīm*, 113–14; interview with Muḥammad Abū Fāris, Amman, 21 January 2013.

260 Interview with Jamīl Abū Bakr, Amman, 15 January 2013. See also al-Qaraḍāwī, *Jarīmat*, 55.

problem, not the change of religion itself.[261] Some dissenting voices believe in the first approach to apostasy distinguished in Chapter 1 – a mere change of religion is worthy of the death penalty in an Islamic state – and publish in the Jordanian Islamist *Al-Sabil* newspaper sometimes,[262] but these do not seem to play a prominent (or even any) role in the Brotherhood.

Still, that the public display of a change of religion should meet with such suspicion out of fear it might destabilise society is striking. Several Brothers, as with other societal rights and freedoms dealt with in this chapter, explained such aspects as specific to Muslim countries,[263] sometimes comparing it with criminalising Holocaust denial in certain European states: while illiberal, it is nevertheless accepted because of some countries' specific histories.[264] Moreover, despite their slight differences in point of view, all those I asked about this agreed that, in accordance with the Qurʾanic verses on privacy mentioned in Chapter 1, people should be judged on their outward and public behaviour, not on sins they commit in the private sphere.[265] Spying in people's houses to find out what they are doing is therefore out of the question. In order to stress this, Jamil Abu Bakr even recounted to me the story we saw in Chapter 1 about caliph ʿUmar, who discovered a man sinning in his own house but did not punish him for it.[266] This explanation also squares with that of the state's General Fatwa Department, which claims that those who outwardly profess Islam should be treated as Muslims, without questioning their inner faith.[267]

Jordanian Muslim Brothers, like the global Islamist scholars who have influenced them so much, are thus more united on civil liberties than they are on the questions of the state and political participation and even on the topic of rights for religious minorities and women. Unlike on any of these issues, nobody clearly privileges the adjacent concept of '*sharīʿa*' over '*umma*', but – and this is unique about the Brotherhood's views on civil liberties – nobody looks at this issue entirely through the prism of the

261 Interview with ʿAlī Abū l-Sukkar, Amman, 15 January 2013.
262 Bassām Nāṣir, 'Ḥukm al-Ridda wa-Qatl al-Murtadd bayna Ruʾyatayn Fiqhiyyatayn Mukhtalifatayn', *Al-Sabīl*, 18 April 2009, 7.
263 Interviews with Jamīl Abū Bakr, Amman, 15 January 2013; Sālim al-Falāḥāt, Amman, 22 January 2013.
264 Interview with ʿAlī Abū l-Sukkar, Amman, 15 January 2013.
265 Interviews with Muḥammad Abū Fāris, Amman, 21 January 2013; Ruḥayyil Gharāyiba, Amman, 17 January 2013; Ṣalāḥ al-Khālidī, Amman, 24 January 2013.
266 Interview with Jamīl Abū Bakr, Amman, 15 January 2013.
267 'Al-Iftāʾ: Al-Qatl bi-Ḥujjat al-Ridda Mukhālif li-Taʿālīm al-Islām', *Al-Ghad* (http://alghad.com/articles/857625, accessed 11 March 2015), 10 March 2015; '"Al-Iftāʾ": Qatl Dāʿish li-l-Muslimīn bi-Ḥujjat al-Ridda wa-l-Kufr Mukhālif li-Taʿālīm al-Islām', *Al-Dustūr*, 3 March 2015, 14.

umma's interests either. Instead, all – including Abu Faris and Gharayiba – deal with civil liberties by decontesting '*sharī'a*' as partly fixed but also as partly modified by the interests of the *umma*, leading to a balanced approach to Islamist thought in which an Islamic state is a regime that uses its three adjacent concepts equally: '*sulṭa*' is applied to work on behalf of and with input from '*umma*', which is both facilitated and limited by '*sharī'a*'.

* * *

The Jordanian Muslim Brotherhood has displayed a wide array of views on a range of topics, but this is far less on display with regard to societal rights and freedoms, in which a few outliers such as Abu Faris are mostly – though not even always – *sharī'a*-centred, while the rest all take a balanced approach to this aspect of Islamist ideology. Such approaches have a long history, sometimes going all the way back to classical Islam, eventually reaching the Jordanian Brotherhood through the first Brothers from Egypt and Syria. Given that, in the Introduction, we defined 'moderation' in this respect as greater freedom on a societal level, we can conclude that this has only partly happened and certainly to a far lesser extent than what we saw with regard to the topics of the state and political participation.

Apart from the long-existing balanced approach to Islamic political thought and the global Islamist reformist discourse that has also remained balanced and has influenced the Jordanian Brotherhood as such, there are three reasons for the lack of substantial moderation in the area of societal rights and freedoms. The first is that, unlike the topics dealt with in Chapters 4 and 5, the authoritative religious texts underpinning Islamist thought on societal rights and freedoms are relatively often definitive in nature, making them harder to reinterpret than others, with even reformist scholars proving unwilling to go against the apparently obvious meaning of the texts.

The second reason for the lack of substantial moderation in the Jordanian Muslim Brotherhood on the issue of societal rights and freedoms lies in the context of Jordan. The latter is a generally conservative country whose inhabitants are often religious and – opinion polls show – would mostly like to see the *sharī'a* applied, whatever that means to them. The Brotherhood originates from this climate and, as such, reflects its values. This, in turn, entails that the organisation is likely to have views similar to those in broader society, on the one hand, but also that it wants to give voice to such views for democratic reasons, on the other. In such a context, if reform on especially women's rights and civil liberties are not supported by the people, they are unlikely to be espoused by the Brotherhood.

Thirdly and finally – and most importantly in this study – the lack of moderation with respect to societal rights and freedoms can be explained by the Brotherhood's ideological unity (and lack of substantial discussion) on this topic, underlining Schwedler's work on the importance of ideological debates with regard to moderation. Unlike with regard to the state and political participation, on which the Brotherhood was strongly divided, the organisation has been mostly united in its views on religious minority rights, women's rights and civil liberties. This means not only that the notion of 'hawks' and 'doves' becomes even more blurred than we have already seen, but also that the organisation lacks an ideological vanguard pushing for new ideas. As such, it does not have the ideological flexibility that would have come with that and would have facilitated a shift in views, like it did with regard to the state and political participation. The Brotherhood's lack of divisions on societal rights and freedoms thus facilitated its dearth of substantial moderation in this respect. Taking into consideration the presence of the pervasive factors influencing the organisation – Islamic tradition, global Islamist discourse, authoritative religious texts, a conservative society and greater ideological homogeneity – this is unlikely to change anytime soon.

Conclusion

The Brotherhood-affiliated driver of the slow car mentioned in the Introduction most likely wanted to portray his organisation as law abiding. Although I think he was rather disingenuous about the state of his vehicle, I do believe this book has shown that he was right about the willingness of the Muslim Brotherhood in Jordan to play by the rules. This conclusion summarises my findings on this law-abiding organisation, focussing on the development of Islamic political thought, the Jordanian Brotherhood's historical and ideological trajectories and its place in the debate on the 'inclusion-moderation' thesis. Finally, it answers the question of how and why the Jordanian Brotherhood has moderated its views and positions on the topics of the state, political participation and societal rights and freedoms in the period 1946–2016 and what the wider implications of this are.

The Development of Islamic Political Thought

The development of Islamic political thought was analysed in this book with the aid of Michael Freeden's ideas on ideology, treating the latter as flexible and dynamic and consisting of core, adjacent and peripheral concepts. The former are central to an ideology while adjacent ones revolve around them and give more concrete meaning to them. Peripheral concepts flavour the core and adjacent ones without being vital to an ideology themselves. In this study, I describe 'caliph' or, later, 'ruler' as the core concept of Islamist thought since this is the basis on which other concepts build and around which everything revolves. '*Sharīʿa*', '*umma*' and '*sulṭa*' all figure as adjacent concepts to 'caliph'/'ruler', giving meaning to it, but sometimes falling to a peripheral position. Scholars who decontest one of these concepts as the most important one are labelled '*sharīʿa*-', '*umma*-' or '*sulṭa*-centred', while I call those who do not privilege any of these over the others 'balanced'.

Another piece of analysis inspired by Freeden's work was used on a conceptual – rather than an ideological – level. I have argued that the two most important adjacent concepts analysed in this study – '*sharīʿa*' and '*umma*' – have four different links with the core concept of 'caliph'/ 'ruler': commanding right and forbidding wrong, consultation, the oath of fealty and obedience. Each of these four links has an ineliminable feature that the concept cannot do without (respectively: that right be commanded and wrong be forbidden, that consultation take place, that fealty be pledged and that someone be obeyed), and quasi-contingent features that refer to the subject and object of these duties, which are highly important, but can be ascribed to different actors.

The Caliphate/State

Because the Sunni view of an Islamic state had 'caliph', as the ruling authority, as its core concept, '*sulṭa*' was naturally adjacent to it, vesting a lot of power in the hands of the ruler. Although the adjacent concept of '*sharīʿa*' was supposed to act as a check on caliphs, there was little that could be done when they abused their power and held on to it irrespective of religious legitimacy. As a result, '*sharīʿa*' drifted to a peripheral position vis-à-vis 'caliph' in classical Islam, with Muslim scholars increasingly taking a *sulṭa*-centred approach to Islamic political thought to justify this development. The nineteenth- and twentieth-century reformist scholar Muhammad Rashid Rida lamented the decline of the caliphate, but did accept it, arguing instead for a renewed, spiritual caliphate that acted as a sort of commonwealth encompassing the new nation-states in the Middle East. He thereby paved the way for changing the meaning of the core concept of 'caliph' as a specific form of ruling authority to the more general 'ruler'.

The trend of moving away from the caliph and towards an Islamic state governed by a pious ruler was continued by early Muslim Brothers in Egypt, although they did look at such a system through the prism of the caliphate's rules. Like Rida, early leaders of the Muslim Brotherhood like Hasan al-Banna, ʿAbd al-Qadir ʿAwda, Sayyid Qutb and Hasan al-Hudaybi decontested the adjacent concept of '*sharīʿa*' as a necessary condition for proper Islamic rule, re-emphasising it as a check on the ruler's power. In their quest to push back against the *sulṭa*-centred approach that had developed over the centuries, ʿAwda and Qutb tended towards a *sharīʿa*-centred approach. Qutb did so most explicitly by coupling the peripheral concept of '*ḥākimiyya*' to '*sharīʿa*', resulting in an all-encompassing emphasis on Islamic law, while simultaneously pairing '*umma*' with the peripheral concept of '*jāhiliyya*', which entailed that the Muslim community was not so much in charge, but should be led instead. Al-Banna and al-Hudaybi, however, were more balanced, with the latter's attempts to counter Qutb's radicalism making him emphasise the adjacent concept of '*sulṭa*' again.

The global Islamist scholars who have influenced the Jordanian Brotherhood were even further removed from the caliphate and dealt with it even less as a practical matter of direct relevance today than their early Brotherhood predecessors. Moreover, while, like them, they emphasised the adjacent concept of '*sharīʿa*', they decontested it differently by untying it from the Qutbian peripheral concept of '*ḥākimiyya*'. This way, the *sharīʿa* could become a set of principles rather than a collection of rulings that permeates everything. This also applies to the adjacent concept of '*umma*', which global Islamist scholars detached from Qutb's peripheral concept of '*jāhiliyya*'. As a result, the way they decontested '*umma*' created a religious community with a ruler acting not as its master, but as its servant. Such decontestations acknowledged the adjacent concept of '*sulṭa*' as necessary, but balanced it with a 'constitutionalised' view of '*sharīʿa*' and a broader mandate for '*umma*'. This resulted in a civil Islamic state in which the order of the adjacent concepts tended towards being '*umma*-centred'.

Political Participation

Just like classical scholars effectively justified turning '*sharīʿa*' into a peripheral concept vis-à-vis the core concept of 'caliph', so they did with '*umma*' by legitimising the marginalisation of people's participation in politics and the limitation of their ability to hold their ruler to account, thus effectively taking a *sulṭa*-centred approach. This was done by explaining quasi-contingent features of the various links between 'caliph' and '*umma*' (and '*sharīʿa*') in a way that benefitted the ruler. Concretely, rulers took it upon themselves to command right and forbid wrong (rather than letting the *umma* do this), limited the number of people who needed to be consulted or to pledge fealty to legitimise the caliphate and wanted the *umma* to obey them even if their rule did not accord with the *sharīʿa*. Since the scholars were more or less forced to deal with this, such *sulṭa*-centred decontestations of the *umma*'s role in the caliphate became part of Islamic political thought. Rida, however, recoupled the quasi-contingent features of consultation and the oath of fealty with broader sections of '*umma*' (within the confines of '*sharīʿa*') and conditioned obedience on the ruler's reliance on '*sharīʿa*' again. Thus, by saving both '*umma*' and '*sharīʿa*' from their peripheral positions and decontesting them as fully adjacent to the core concept of 'ruler', Rida took a balanced approach towards Islamic political thought.

Early Muslim Brothers also decontested '*umma*' differently than classical scholars did. Despite differences among them, al-Banna, ʿAwda and al-Hudaybi all reconnected *al-amr bi-l-maʿrūf wa-l-nahy ʿan al-munkar*'s quasi-contingent feature of 'those who command/forbid' with '*umma*' again, providing ordinary Muslims with the means of holding the rulers to account. The same applies to *shūrá*, which early Brothers decontested as being slightly more tied to '*umma*' than in classical times, but mostly as connected to the adjacent concept of '*sharīʿa*'. With regard to *bayʿa*, the same development can be seen, but al-Hudaybi again emphasised the adjacent concept of '*sulṭa*' a bit more than others, which is also the case with *ṭāʿa*: while other early Brothers tied obedience to the adjacent concept of '*sharīʿa*', al-Hudaybi also appeared to see obeying the ruler in power as a good thing in and of itself. As such, the early Brothers differed amongst themselves with regard to political participation, with ʿAwda and Qutb clearly taking *sharīʿa*-centred approaches, while al-Banna and al-Hudaybi balanced the different adjacent concepts.

With regard to *al-amr bi-l-maʿrūf wa-l-nahy ʿan al-munkar*, the Tunisian global Islamist scholar Rashid al-Ghannushi continued the trend set by early Muslim Brothers of associating the quasi-contingent feature of 'those who command/forbid' with the adjacent concept of '*umma*'. He went further than they, however, by explicitly treating it as a means to depose a ruler, even for non-religious reasons, and allowing the entire *umma* to get involved in this duty. Al-Ghannushi did the same with *shūrá*. While Yusuf al-Qaradawi and Hasan al-Turabi, like the early Brothers, tied one of the concept's quasi-contingent features ('the people consulted') to the adjacent concept of '*umma*' and also increased the number of people involved in consultation, they continued to circumscribe the *shūrá*'s mandate by limiting it to things not dealt with in the *sharīʿa*. This balanced approach contrasted with al-Ghannushi's *umma*-centred approach, which privileged '*umma*' over '*sharīʿa*' by limiting the latter to a small number of 'constitutionalised' principles. The global Islamist scholars also, finally, continued the work of Rida and the early Brothers in their attempts to 'restore' the quasi-contingent feature of 'the ones pledging fealty' to *bayʿa*, thereby getting the *umma* involved in a contractual relationship with the ruler again. They essentially did the same with *ṭāʿa*, making it not only conditional on the ruler's adherence to the *sharīʿa*, but also to his willingness to take the *umma*'s views into account, which particularly the *umma*-centred al-Ghannushi stressed.

Societal Rights and Freedoms

Classical Islamic views on non-Muslims were rather divided between a more *sharīʿa*-centred stance that concentrated on humbling Jews and Christians and something resembling a rudimentary *umma*-centred approach that sought to look at Islamic law through the prism of tolerance of others, as expressed in the 'constitution of Medina' and verses like Q. 2:256. Issues such as the *dhimma* and the payment of the *jizya* were interpreted along the same lines. This was different, however, for women's rights, on which there were quite a few relatively clear texts that seemed to suggest that women were equal to men in some respects, but clearly different in others, such as inheritance, marriage and the freedom to travel unsupervised. Given that Muslim women – because they are Muslims – were presumed to agree with Islamic rules governing their behaviour, this could be described as a balanced approach to applying the appropriate rules to believing women. Civil liberties, finally, proved to be a struggle among classical scholars between the adjacent concepts of '*sharīʿa*' and '*umma*'. Some believed that blasphemy and apostasy were punishable by death in and of themselves because there were texts suggesting that, while others believed this only applied if people expressed them by causing civil strife or treason. Several centuries later, Rida basically followed the second, more balanced approach towards religious minorities and also strove to take women's rights into account, although he did not ultimately question the validity of certain classical interpretations.

With regard to societal rights and freedoms, al-Banna balanced the requirements of the *sharīʿa* as he saw them with the interests of Coptic Christians in Egypt, whereas the *sharīʿa*-centred approach of ʿAwda and Qutb – while emphasising equality and freedom of religion – clearly denied non-Muslims certain rights, particularly in the political sphere. This emphasis on the adjacent concept of '*sharīʿa*' could be seen even more clearly in early Brothers' views on women's rights: issues such as gender-mixing, professional work, the freedom of movement and politics were all limited on the basis of Islamic law, particularly by the Syrian Muslim Brother Mustafa al-Sibaʿi. Civil liberties were equally submitted to the rulings of Islamic law, giving less room to '*umma*' than some classical scholars and confirming the *sharīʿa*-centred approach of the early Brothers.

Global Islamist scholars who influenced the Jordanian Brotherhood clearly moved beyond early Brothers' views by taking the changing times and circumstances into account when interpreting the *sharīʿa* in what is referred to as *fiqh al-wāqiʿ*. Guided by a method that allows all things not explicitly forbidden in the sources and that relies on the general intentions of the *sharīʿa*, they used tools like *ijtihād* to serve the interests of the *umma* and provide it with more freedom. In this spirit, they clearly sided with the more tolerant view of religious minority rights developed in classical Islam, acknowledging the legitimacy of freedom of religion, friendly ties with non-hostile non-Muslims and rights for Jews and Christians on the basis of *dhimma* (or, increasingly, citizenship). The *jizya*, in their view, was a substitute for military service that could be lifted if they joined the army. They did exclude non-Muslims from certain top positions in the political, legal and military spheres, however. Global Islamist scholars also kept these positions from being occupied by women, whom they saw as equal to men as human beings, but not in their duties in the family, in society and in politics. While they were more open to *ikhtilāṭ* and women working outside the home than early Brothers, they nevertheless preferred to restrict this somewhat and believed women should focus on their families, which should be headed by their husbands. On civil liberties, finally, the global Islamist scholars who have influenced the Jordanian Brotherhood argued strongly in favour of freedom of speech, but on the condition that Islam not be insulted. They viewed apostates similarly to the more tolerant view expressed in classical Islam, namely, that these should only be killed if they accompanied their unbelief with a public disavowal of the religion and civil strife. On all these issues, global Islamist scholars' decontestations showed more flexibility than those of some early Brothers, yet it was also clear that there were some definitive texts these scholars definitely wanted to uphold, making their approach a balanced one.

The Jordanian Muslim Brotherhood's Historical and Ideological Trajectories

The Muslim Brotherhood in Jordan, a local branch of the broad and activist original group founded by Hasan al-Banna in Egypt in 1928, was founded in 1945 and was officially recognised by the Jordanian regime in 1946. Working as a religious and charitable organisation, it became increasingly politicised from the 1950s onwards, but mostly with a focus on the Palestinian question and Western influence. As such, it differed with the regime sometimes, but – through a combination of pro-Hashimite tendencies, shared anti-Nasserist sentiments and a realisation that the stability of Jordan ought to be preserved – it repeatedly sided with the regime in times of trouble. Its activities in this period (1946–1989) were mostly confined to social and charitable work, although some of its members were also involved in fighting Israel and the organisation as a whole participated in parliament.

The late 1980s saw an upsurge in protests against the regime because of its economic policies, causing King Husayn to start what looked like a process of liberal and democratic reform. This expressed itself most clearly in parliamentary elections in 1989, during which the Brotherhood did quite well. Shortly thereafter, the organisation was even briefly part of the government before founding the Islamic Action Front as its separate political party in 1992. Unhappy about the success the Brotherhood enjoyed in 1989, the regime took several measures – most prominently by changing the electoral law – through which it limited the IAF's influence, resulting in a worse outcome for the party in the 1993 elections. Because of this, as well as dissatisfaction about reform in the country and especially the Israeli–Jordanian Wadi ʿAraba peace agreement in 1994, the IAF boycotted the elections in 1997.

In 1999, King Husayn died and was succeeded by his son ʿAbdallah II. The latter was less familiar with and less sympathetic towards the Brotherhood and was more inclined to view Islamism through the lens of security, rather than politics or religion. As a result, the new king became increasingly repressive of the Brotherhood, which continued to participate in elections in 2003 and 2007. Internally, however, the Brotherhood had changed. Not only had a more moderate group split off from the main organisation in the form of the Islamic Centre Party, which was founded in 2001, but the remaining group also elected increasingly confrontational leaders. It was therefore not surprising that the Brotherhood decided to boycott the elections in 2010, an attitude that was strengthened by the 'Arab Spring', which made the organisation believe this was the opportune moment to push for more reform and also boycott the elections in 2013. Not everyone agreed, however, and through a series of dismissals, resignations and split-offs, several new organisations came into existence, including the broad-based ZamZam initiative in 2012 and an entirely new Muslim Brotherhood in 2015. These divisions not only weakened the Brotherhood, but also made it more susceptible to regime pressure, which was increased to such an extent that the original Brotherhood was essentially outlawed, while the New Brotherhood was given a licence. Forced to dance to the regime's tune, the Brotherhood cut ties with other branches of the organisation and the IAF participated in the 2016 elections again.

The Jordanian Muslim Brotherhood on the State

In the context of the changing circumstances that the Kingdom of Jordan offered the Brotherhood, it – like the global Islamist scholars it was influenced by – did not put much emphasis on the caliphate as a practical and directly relevant system, with the exception of Muhammad Abu Faris, who appears to have wanted it applied in Jordan. In this context, he emphasised the application of the *sharīʿa* and explicitly tied this to Qutb's (and Mawdudi's) peripheral concept of '*ḥākimiyya*', just as he did with their peripheral concept of '*jāhiliyya*' with regard to the adjacent concept of '*umma*'. As such, he advocated a *sharīʿa*-centred, caliphate-oriented Islamic state. Other Muslim Brothers had also long pushed for the application of the *sharīʿa*, but only in the context of an Islamic state and without (or only with depoliticised) references to Qutb's peripheral concepts of '*jāhiliyya*' and '*ḥākimiyya*'. Their *sharīʿa*-centred approach gradually made way, however, for the more *umma*-centred idea of a civil state with an Islamic authority, likely inspired by global Islamist scholars who influenced the organisation and advocated most by Jordanian Brother Ruhayyil Gharayiba.

Even the Brothers who rejected the Jordanian regime as '*jāhilī*' or 'un-Islamic', however, were pragmatic in dealing with it in practice and certainly did not advocate its (violent) overthrow. The entire Jordanian Brotherhood supported the regime for ideological or pragmatic reasons, with some East Jordanian members – most prominently Bassam al-ʿUmush – also adding nationalist, pro-Hashimite motives to these, thus – in a sense – re-emphasising '*sulṭa*' as adjacent to the core concept of 'ruler'. With regard to the scope of the *sharīʿa*'s application, some *sharīʿa*-centred Brothers like Abu Faris wanted it applied in every sphere of life, while other, balanced Brothers accepted making it merely the principle source of law. The increasing number of *umma*-centred Brothers calling for a civil state, meanwhile, decontested the *sharīʿa*'s role in politics as that of a flexible set of principles, like the global Islamist scholars by whom they had been influenced, providing them with a 'constitutionalised' form of Islamic law that left more room for the *umma* and the idea of a constitutional monarchy in Jordan.

The Jordanian Muslim Brotherhood on Political Participation

The Brotherhood in Jordan decontested the duty of *al-amr bi-l-maʿrūf wa-l-nahy ʿan al-munkar* in the context of reform and continued the trend set by early Brothers and global Islamist scholars of associating the quasi-contingent feature of 'those who command/forbid' with the *umma*. Some of them explicitly stated, however, that the execution of the duty by hand should be the prerogative of the state, not individual Muslims, who should limit themselves to commanding and forbidding with the tongue or in their hearts. One of the means to do so was *daʿwa*, directed either at society or the state. In the case of the latter, collective action such as protests – joined not just by scholars, but also by the masses – is one form of commanding right and forbidding wrong that Abu Faris – like al-Ghannushi – explicitly endorsed. Unlike al-Ghannushi, however, he did so from a *sharīʿa*-centred point of view in which he saw the *umma* as a means to achieve the implementation of Islamic law.

The application of *shūrá* by Jordanian Brothers to a large extent also followed the previous views expressed by early members of the Egyptian organisation and global Islamist scholars, but was more practically applied in the Hashimite Kingdom. Scholars ranging from Abu Faris to Gharayiba believed that *shūrá* was a duty upon the ruler, that it could be applied through a parliament and that the group of people involved should be broader than classical scholars believed. Jordanian Brothers differed on the extent to which *shūrá* could be associated with democracy, however. *Sharīʿa*-centred scholars like Abu Faris believed that God's sovereignty made the former superior to the latter, while balanced Brothers partially accepted democracy. A larger group of *umma*-centred members decontested *shūrá* as a synonym of democracy, limiting the *sharīʿa* to 'constitutionalised' principles and a small number of definitive texts (mostly on religious issues) that cannot be changed.

The theoretical process of accepting democracy did not mean that the Brotherhood also wanted to participate in government, which necessarily required concessions to one's beliefs. To decide on whether this was allowed or not, a debate between several Jordanian scholars was organised in 1992. Abu Faris was the most prominent opponent of governmental participation on the basis of the *sharīʿa*, while ʿUmar al-Ashqar argued in favour of this by pointing to the interests of the *umma*. The latter position was adopted by the organisation, thereby clearing the way for the Brotherhood's political participation on all levels. From then on, the decision to participate in or boycott parliamentary elections was based on interests, not religious rulings. It was also on the basis of nationalist – not religious – reasons that al-ʿUmush, with his slightly *sulṭa*-centred tendencies, objected to parliamentary boycotts – which enjoyed broad support within the IAF – and left the party. In 2016, however, several groups had left the Brotherhood, which had come under unprecedented pressure from the regime. In this climate, in which the regime also changed the country's electoral law back to a form that was acceptable to the IAF, the latter decided to stop its boycott and participate in the elections again with a broad-based manifesto and a 'Jordanised' national discourse, rather than a strictly Islamist one.

With regard to *bayʿa* and *ṭāʿa*, Jordanian Brothers came to quite different conclusions: while Abu Faris, in a further confirmation of his *sharīʿa*-centredness, did connect *bayʿa* to the adjacent concept of '*sharīʿa*', he made no effort to increase the influence of '*umma*' over it, unlike global Islamist scholars before him. He did the same with *ṭāʿa*, making it conditional on the ruler's adherence to the *sharīʿa*, although he left some room for the *umma* to oppose tyranny as well. Gharayiba, however, explicitly decontested *bayʿa* as a contract tied to both '*sharīʿa*' and '*umma*' and created more room for the latter to withhold its obedience to the ruler, not just in cases of tyranny, thereby underlining his own *umma*-centred approach to Islamist ideology.

The Jordanian Muslim Brotherhood on Societal Rights and Freedoms

For all their dividedness on the state and political participation, the Jordanian Muslim Brothers were quite united on societal rights and freedoms. This is strongly related to their views on the *sharīʿa*. While some, such as Abu Faris, saw Islamic law as having only limited flexibility and opposed global Islamists' ideas on *fiqh al-wāqiʿ*, others did take Jordanian society's views into account, while still others, such as Gharayiba, viewed Islam as a 'broad cultural framework' that offers wide leeway for Muslims' interests through means such as *ijtihād*. In a sense, this reflected the Jordanian Brotherhood's increasingly democratic views, but – conversely – it also allowed Jordan's conservative society to keep the organisation from greater ideological moderation with regard to societal rights and freedoms.

In this context, Jordanian Brothers generally thought like the global Islamist scholars that they have been influenced by, supporting freedom of religion and good relations with friendly non-Muslims and viewing the concept of '*dhimma*' as providing Jews and Christians with general equality to Muslims. Like them, they also saw the *jizya* as a substitute for military service that has become superfluous through full citizenship. Despite this flexibility, the definitive texts about religious issues that were often marginalised when discussing the state or political participation now came into play with regard to positions that were seen as inextricably tied to Islam, such as the head of state or the leader of the army. As a result, all prominent Jordanian Brothers excluded non-Muslims from such positions, uniting almost all of them around a balanced approach to Islamist ideology.

A similar process took place with regard to women's rights. Jordanian Brothers claimed women are equal to men as human beings, just as global Islamist scholars stated, but were restrictive in practice, particularly with regard to the matter of honour killings as a result of adultery, in which they ultimately believed it was more important to oppose extra-marital sex than to defend women's rights. The same restrictive attitude could be seen in their views on *ikhtilāṭ*, although they did allow work outside the home, provided women take care of their families first. With regard to women in politics, some – like Abu Faris – wanted to keep this exclusively male, while others were more open to the idea, although they also excluded women from the position of head of state. With the exception of men like Abu Faris, the Brotherhood thus took a balanced approach on this issue.

Civil liberties, finally, were treated in a similar way by Jordanian Brothers. Like global Islamist scholars that have influenced them, they favoured free speech, but mostly directed this at political rulers, not at religious sensibilities, which they condemned. Apostasy, too, was a matter rejected by Jordanian Brothers, but was seen as worthy of the death penalty in an Islamic state only if accompanied by a public disavowal of Islam and the civil strife that this entailed, although they differed on what this meant. Both positions reflected popular sentiment in Jordanian society and were partly legitimised as such, too. They also represented a balanced approach to Islamist ideology in this respect, privileging neither '*sharīʿa*' nor '*umma*' over the other.

The Inclusion-Moderation Thesis

What does all of this mean for the Jordanian Muslim Brotherhood's position in the inclusion-moderation thesis? In the Introduction, I defined moderation as a tendency towards a peaceful and non-revolutionary attitude to the state, an inclination towards a democratic view of political participation and a move towards greater freedom on a societal level. The reason the Jordanian Brotherhood has moderated with regard to its ideology and its behaviour throughout the seventy-year history dealt with in this book is not so much related to rewards the regime has given the group (in the form of greater liberalisation, for instance), but to three other factors: Islamic political thought, the organisation's long history of political inclusion in Jordan and the Brotherhood's ideological divisions.

Firstly, the Jordanian Muslim Brotherhood sees itself as part of and clearly builds on a long and highly diverse tradition of Islamic political thought, stretching back all the way to early Islam, through modern reformist scholars such as Rida and members of the early Muslim Brotherhood in Egypt and Syria. This tradition was perpetuated by global Islamist scholars that have – by Jordanian Brothers' own admission – had a profound effect on their thinking, which can also be discerned in much of their own ideas, partly irrespective of the organisation's position in

Jordan. This has resulted in moderation with regard to the state and political participation, based on flexible interpretations of a malleable tradition. At the same time, it has not led to much moderation (though not radicalisation either) with regard to societal rights and freedoms because the Brotherhood often based its views on these issues on (stricter interpretations of) definitive texts, which also have a long pedigree in Islamic thought. The fact that such views were widely shared in a Jordanian society that the Brotherhood was not only rooted in but also wanted to represent was not conducive to more moderate interpretations either.

Secondly, echoing Schwedler's work, the Brotherhood in Jordan has enjoyed inclusion in the country's political system for decades, which has tied its fate to the Hashimite Kingdom and its stability, providing a strong incentive to moderate its views, which it did. The past few decades, however, have witnessed more repression of the organisation, which – conversely – has led to greater radicalisation of the Brotherhood's behaviour in the form of electoral boycotts and the election of less accommodating members to the group's decision-making bodies. All of this confirms the inclusion-moderation thesis, bearing out the conclusions of those who apply this thesis to the Jordanian Brotherhood.

Yet – in line with Hamid's conclusions – the period of repression of the Brotherhood has not caused it to radicalise ideologically, but has witnessed their becoming more moderate, suggesting that it is not inclusion, but repression that causes them to moderate. This is correct, but only in the context of the organisation's earlier moderation as a result of global Islamist discourse and its political inclusion. In other words, the Brotherhood had already shed much of its 'radical' ideology – its rejection of democracy, for example – by the time regime repression started because it had been thoroughly moderated by the ideas of certain global Islamist scholars and its decades-long inclusion. This meant that an interest-based radicalisation of its behaviour was possible by boycotting the elections, but truly ideological radicalisation was no longer an option since the group had progressed too thoroughly and too organically to return to more radical views.

Thirdly, there are the Brotherhood's ideological divisions. The Jordanian Brotherhood is highly divided, yet it is also clear that some parts of the organisation, particularly members such as Muhammad Abu Faris and Salah al-Khalidi, have not moderated at all. Moreover, the terms 'hawks' and 'doves', used to label the Brotherhood's confrontational and accommodating members, respectively, appear to be less useful when analysed in detail because they do not take the Brothers' motivations into account. Those who want to boycott elections, for example, can be lumped together, even though their motivations may be rooted in either ideological anti-democratic views or the pragmatic belief that it is useless to participate. Similarly, those advocating participation may do so for pragmatic reasons, but also for nationalist ones, while 'hawks' and 'doves' actually hold quite similar views with regard to societal rights and freedoms. A division of Brotherhood members in balanced, *sharī'a-* or *umma*-centred ones does take their motivations into account and also clarifies how divergent approaches can reach similar conclusions with regard to societal rights and freedoms based on their views of Islamic law.

Most importantly, ideological divisions on the state among Jordanian Brothers created flexibility within the organisation, enabling it to debate and shift to more moderate positions when needed without having to leave the Brotherhood altogether. The same applied with regard to political participation, but here internal ideological divisions and the split-offs that this eventually led to also made the organisation as a whole vulnerable to regime pressure. The fact that the IAF decided to moderate under this pressure by participating in the elections of 2016 – rather than to radicalise – was not only the result of a long tradition of ideological moderation, but also of the realisation that the party only needed to shift back to behaviour it had displayed many times before – parliamentary participation – to save its skin. By contrast, the ideological unity within the Brotherhood on societal rights and freedoms deprived the organisation of flexibility in this regard, contributing to its lack of moderation on this issue. The reason for the Jordanian Muslim Brotherhood's ideological and behavioural moderation in the period 1946–2016 therefore lies in the tradition of Islamic political thought on which it builds and of which it is also part, the long period of political inclusion it enjoyed in Jordan and the ideological divisions within its own ranks.

The Muslim Brotherhood in Jordan: Between Cats and Conspiracies

Once, during my fieldwork in Jordan, I interviewed a Brotherhood-affiliated scholar in Amman who kept reminding me during our conversation that his organisation is peaceful and that Islam, similarly, does not condone terrorism or mindless violence, much like the Brother who drove me home in his slow but noisy car. When this scholar, one of his students and I walked outside after the interview, I saw two stray cats fighting fiercely with each other. When I pointed this out to my host and his student, the former quipped: 'There is no connection between this behaviour and Islam whatsoever!' We all laughed at his joke, but there was a seriousness to his remark that did not escape my attention. Indeed, the tendency to ascribe inherently violent traits to Islam or to accuse the Brotherhood of forming a global conspiracy is very much alive, as is the habit among some Muslims to deny the link between Islam and certain phenomena they do not like.

The idea that the Jordanian Muslim Brotherhood is (part of) a conspiracy was always problematic, but its 70-year-old history, the 90-year-old history of the Egyptian organisation on which it builds and the 1,400-year-old Islamic political tradition of which it is part makes it downright absurd to believe that the group has kept up its plots across national borders for so long. Moreover, the Brotherhood's deep ideological divisions, expressed in diverse views as well as several acrimonious splits-offs, make the chances of the organisation's being part of a sinister global plot even less likely. Indeed, if the members of the Jordanian Brotherhood *are* secretly conspiring to control the world, it must be said that they are evidently quite bad at it.

At the same time, the Jordanian Muslim Brotherhood is not exactly like the fighting cats outside the scholar's home either, with no connection to Islam whatsoever. While there are several reasons for the 'fighting' within the organisation, the fact that its members have widely diverging interpretations of Islam is certainly one of them. As the Freedenesque analysis in this book has shown, these interpretations are structurally related to each other and cohere through the use of similar concepts, but differ in how they are decontested in the broader ideological framework and combined with other concepts, just like with liberalism or other ideologies. As such, this study of the Jordanian Muslim Brotherhood not only shows the development of Islamic political thought, the historical and ideological trajectories of the organisation and its position in the inclusion-moderation debate, but also what a rich, diverse and dynamic tradition Islamism and, even more so, Islam really is.

Glossary

Note: several of the terms mentioned here have multiple meanings. I have chosen to focus only on those meanings used in this study. Less important terms or those used only once in the book are not listed here, but explained where they occur in the text.

ʿadāla – see *ʿadl.*

ʿadl – justice. The establishment of justice has long been seen as a primary task of the caliph (*khalīfa*, q.v.) or ruler (*ḥākim*, q.v.) in Islamic political thought.

aḥkām (sing. *ḥukm*) – rulings, specifically the rulings of the *sharīʿa* (q.v.). See also *maqāṣid.*

ahl al-dhimma – the people of protection, a term mostly used to refer to Jews and Christians who, as a protected religious minority, could live among Muslims under certain conditions, including the payment of a poll tax (*jizya*, q.v.). See also *dhimma.*

ahl al-ḥall wa-l-ʿaqd – 'the people of loosening and binding', a group of religious scholars (*ʿulamāʾ*, q.v.) or other dignitaries who pledged an oath of fealty (*bayʿa*, q.v.) to the caliph (*khalīfa*, q.v.) on behalf of the *umma* (q. v.) or chose the ruler (*ḥākim*, q.v.).

ahl al-kitāb – the people of the Book, a term mostly used to refer to Jews and Christians.

al-amr bi-l-maʿrūf wa-l-nahy ʿan al-munkar – commanding right and forbidding wrong. This Qurʾanic duty takes many forms and is sometimes used as a tool to hold the ruler (*ḥākim*, q.v.) to account. In this study, *al-amr bi-l-maʿrūf wa-l-nahy ʿan al-munkar* also functions as one of four links between the adjacent concept of '*umma*' (q.v.) (and '*sharīʿa*', q.v.) and the core Islamist ideological concept of 'caliph'/'ruler' (*khalīfa*, q.v.). See also *bayʿa, shūrá* and *ṭāʿa.*

ʿaqīda – creed.

bayʿa – oath of fealty. This pledge of allegiance to a ruler (*ḥākim*, q.v.) takes different forms and is sometimes used to indicate the contractual nature between the ruler and the ruled. In this study, *bay'a* also functions as one of four links between the adjacent concept of '*umma*' (q.v.) (and '*sharī'a*', q.v.) and the core Islamist ideological concept of 'caliph'/'ruler' (*khalīfa*, q.v.). See also *al-amr bi-l-ma'rūf wa-l-nahy 'an al-munkar*, *shūrá* and *ṭā'a*.

da'wa – the call to Islam, missionary work. This is historically an important activity engaged in by the Muslim Brotherhood in Jordan.

dawla – state. The term is also used to refer to an empire.

dhimma – protection. This term was used to refer to the protective system that mostly Jews and Christians lived under when they were settled amongst Muslims. It entailed, among other things, paying the poll tax (*jizya*, q.v.) and has been used by global Islamist scholars (*'ulamā'*, q.v.) who have influenced the Jordanian Muslim Brotherhood as well as members of the latter itself to grant citizenship (*jinsiyya*, q.v., *muwāṭana*, q.v.) to religious minorities. See also *ahl al-dhimma*.

*dhimmī*s – see *ahl al-dhimma*.

farḍ 'alá l-kifāya – collective duty, meaning that only a limited number of Muslims need to act upon it, as opposed to an individual duty (*farḍ 'alá l-'ayn*), which needs to be performed by all Muslims.

fawḍá – chaos, civil strife. Muslim scholars (*'ulamā'*, q.v.) have long seen this as something that should be punished and avoided as much as possible, although it does not carry the same religious connotation as *fitna* (q.v.).

fiqh – jurisprudence, the study of the *sharī'a* (q.v.). See also *fiqh al-wāqi'*.

fiqh al-wāqi' – the jurisprudence of reality. This represents the practice among Muslim scholars (*'ulamā'*, q.v.) to take the changing circumstances into account when ruling on matters of the *sharī'a* (q.v.). See also *fiqh*.

fitna – chaos, civil strife. Muslim scholars (*'ulamā'*, q.v.) have long seen this as something that should be punished and avoided as much as possible. See also *fawḍá*.

fuqahā' – Muslim scholars of Islamic jurisprudence. See also *'ulamā'*.

ḥadīth (pl. *aḥādīth*, but given as *ḥadīth*s in this study) – a story consisting of a chain of transmitters (*isnād*) and some content (*matn*) containing information about or from the first generations of Muslims, particularly the Prophet Muhammad. *Ḥadīth*s have played a major role in the formation of Islamic law (*sharī'a*, q.v.).

ḥākim – ruler. See also *imām*, *khalīfa*.

ḥākimiyya – sovereignty. In the work of Mawdudi, Qutb and others, this term refers to the sovereignty of God in all things, especially legislation.

hijra – emigration. Most often used to refer to the emigration of the Prophet Muhammad and the early community of Muslims (*umma*, q.v.) from Mecca to Medina in 622.

ḥukm – rule. See also *aḥkām*.

ʿibādāt – acts of worship. According to some scholars (*ʿulamāʾ*, q.v.), these are not subject to changing interpretations but guided by definitive texts. See also *muʿāmalāt*.

ijmāʿ – consensus, specifically the consensus among Muslim scholars (*ʿulamāʾ*, q.v.) on Islamic legal issues.

ijtihād – independent reasoning on the basis of the scriptural sources of Islam without necessarily remaining within the limits of one Islamic legal school of thought (*madhhab*). It is an important tool for the reform (*iṣlāḥ*, q.v.) of the *sharīʿa* (q.v.).

ikhtilāṭ – gender-mixing. The Muslim Brotherhood often takes a dim view of this, although they mostly do not believe it is altogether forbidden.

imām – leader. This term is often used to refer to the caliph (*khalīfa*, q.v.). See also *ḥākim*, *imāma*.

imāma – imamate, leadership. This term is often used to refer to the caliph (*khalīfa*, q.v.), when it is sometimes labelled 'the greatest imamate' (*al-imāma al-kubrá* or *al-imāma al-ʿuẓmá*). See also *khilāfa*, *mulk*.

īmān – faith. See also *kufr*, *murtadd*, *ridda*, *takfīr*.

iṣlāḥ – reform. This term carries a very positive connotation among Islamists, who see Islam itself as a religion of reform.

istiḥsān – juristic preference. This tool can be used as a source of the *sharīʿa* (q.v.) when no definitive texts exist and analogical reasoning (*qiyās*, q.v.) does not yield a satisfactory result.

jāhiliyya – the pre-Islamic period of supposed ignorance. More specifically, the term used by Qutb and others to describe the state of Muslim societies today.

jinsiyya – citizenship. See also *muwāṭana*.

jizya – poll tax paid mostly by Jews and Christian in classical Islam. Global Islamist scholars (*ʿulamāʾ*, q.v.) who have influenced the Jordanian Muslim Brotherhood and members of the latter itself have argued that this was not a discriminatory tax, but a financial compensation for the fact that Jews and Christians did not participate in fighting a jihad for the Muslim empire (*dawla*, q.v.). See also *ahl al-dhimma*, *dhimma*.

khalīfa (pl. *khulafāʾ*) – caliph. The position of caliph was the successor to the Prophet Muhammad and the (theoretical) ruler (*ḥākim*, q.v.) of the Muslim community (*umma*, q.v.) throughout much of Islamic history. In this study, 'caliph'/'ruler' (*khalīfa*, q.v.) also functions as the core concept of Islamist political thought. See also *ḥākim*, *imām*.

khilāfa – caliphate. A system of Muslim rule (*ḥukm*, q.v.) led by a caliph (*khalīfa*, q.v.). See also *imāma*, *mulk*.

kufr – unbelief. See also *īmān*, *murtadd*, *ridda*, *takfīr*.

maqāṣid – intentions, specifically the underlying intentions of the *sharīʿa* (q.v.). See also *aḥkām*.

maṣlaḥa – general interest. In the *sharīʿa* (q.v.), this term is used to avoid certain rulings (*aḥkām*, q.v.) to serve the interests of the *umma* (q.v.).

muʿāmalāt – relations with others. According to some scholars (*ʿulamāʾ*, q.v.), these are subject to changing interpretations. See also *ʿibādāt*.

mulk – kingship. See also *imāma*, *khilāfa*.

murtadd – apostate. Many Muslim scholars (*ʿulamāʾ*, q.v.) believe such a person should be punished by execution for his or her apostasy (*ridda*, q. v.), but they differ on whether the term refers to someone who has merely left Islam or has done so in combination with causing chaos and civil strife (*fawḍá*, q.v., *fitna*, q.v.). See also *īmān*, *kufr*, *takfīr*.

muwāṭana – citizenship. See also *jinsiyya*.

nāʾib – representative. According to some scholars (*ʿulamāʾ*, q.v.), both in classical and modern times, the ruler (*ḥākim*, q.v.) should be a representative of the *umma* (q.v.), working on its behalf rather than the other way round. See also *wakīl*.

qiyās – analogical reasoning. This is often used as a source of the *sharīʿa* (q.v.).

raʾy – (considered) opinion. This can be used as a source of the *sharīʿa* (q.v.).

ribā – (usurious) interest.

ridda – apostasy. Many Muslim scholars (*ʿulamāʾ*, q.v.) believe this should be punished by executing the apostate (*murtadd*, q.v.), but they differ on whether the term refers to merely leaving Islam or doing so in combination with causing chaos and civil strife (*fawḍá*, q.v., *fitna*, q.v.). See also *īmān*, *kufr*, *takfīr*.

shahāda – the Islamic confession of faith that there is only one god and that Muhammad is the messenger of God. See also *tawḥīd, ulūhiyya.*

sharīʿa – Islamic law. The term refers to the path Muslims should follow, which is supposedly embodied by the numerous writings on Islamic legal issues. Global Islamist scholars (*ʿulamāʾ*, q.v.) have made extensive efforts to reform (*iṣlāḥ*, q.v.) the *sharīʿa*, which has influenced many members of the Jordanian Muslim Brotherhood. In this study, '*sharīʿa*' also functions as a concept adjacent to the core Islamist ideological concept of 'caliph'/'ruler' (*khalīfa*, q.v., *ḥākim*, q.v.).

shūrá – consultation. According to Islamists, this Qurʾan-based term refers to the consultation between a ruler (*ḥākim*, q.v.) and the ruled and, according to many, acts as a form of or even a synonym for democracy. In this study, *shūrá* also functions as one of four links between the adjacent concept of '*umma*' (q.v.) (and '*sharīʿa*', q.v.) and the core Islamist ideological concept of 'caliph'/'ruler' (*khalīfa*, q.v.). See also *al-amr bi-l-maʿrūf wa-l-nahy ʿan al-munkar, bayʿa* and *ṭāʿa.*

sulṭa – power. In this study, *sulṭa* also functions as a concept adjacent to the core Islamist ideological concept of 'caliph'/'ruler' (*khalīfa*, q.v., *ḥākim*, q.v.).

ṭāʿa – obedience. This Qurʾan-based duty refers to the obedience that must be shown to the ruler (*ḥākim*, q.v.). In this study, *ṭāʿa* also functions as one of four links between the adjacent concept of '*umma*' (q.v.) (and '*sharīʿa*', q.v.) and the core Islamist ideological concept of 'caliph'/'ruler' (*khalīfa*, q.v.). See also *al-amr bi-l-maʿrūf wa-l-nahy ʿan al-munkar, bayʿa* and *shūrá.*

takfīr – excommunication, the expulsion of Muslims from the community of believers (*umma*, q.v.). Muslim Brothers use this sometimes, but are generally quite careful in applying it to others. See also *īmān, kufr, murtadd, ridda.*

ṭawāghīt (sing. *ṭāghūt*) – idols. The term is sometimes used to label rulers (*ḥākim*, q.v.) who do not rule by the *sharīʿa* (q.v.).

tawḥīd – the unity of God. See also *shahāda, ulūhiyya.*

ʿulamāʾ – Muslim scholars. See also *fuqahāʾ.*

ulūhiyya – divinity, which refers to the idea that only God may be worshipped. See also *shahāda, tawḥīd.*

umma – the worldwide community of Muslims. Among some global Islamist scholars (*ʿulamāʾ*, q.v.) who have influenced the Jordanian Muslim Brotherhood, as well as among some members of the organisation itself, the term is sometimes also used to refer to their national community of citizens. In this study, *umma* also functions as a concept adjacent to the core Islamist ideological concept of 'caliph'/'ruler' (*khalīfa*, q.v., *ḥākim*, q.v.).

wakīl – agent. According to some scholars (*ʿulamāʾ*, q.v.), both in classical and modern times, the ruler (*ḥākim*, q.v.) should be an agent of the *umma* (q.v.), serving it rather than acting as its master. See also *nāʾib*.

wasaṭiyya – centrism. In the context of Islamism, it is often used to indicate the alleged golden mean in Islamic jurisprudence (*fiqh*, q.v.) of relying on definitive texts in some matters and using the intentions (*maqāṣid*, q.v.) of the *sharīʿa* (q.v.) in others.

Bibliography

Below is a non-exhaustive list of sources. For reasons of space, the numerous references to newspapers and *ḥadīth* collections have been omitted.

Interviews

The list of interviews given below only shows those semi-structured interviews with the people who allowed me to use their names.

Jamīl Abū Bakr, Amman, 18 June 2012, 15 January 2013
Muḥammad Abū Fāris, Amman, 21 January 2013
Ziyād Abū Ghanīma, Amman, 26 June 2012
Ḥusayn Abū Rummān, Amman, 16 June 2012
Muḥammad Abū Rummān, Amman, 19 June 2012
ʿAlī Abū l-Sukkar, Amman, 27 June 2012, 15 January 2013
ʿAbd al-Laṭīf ʿArabiyyāt, Amman, 20 December 2012
Zakī Banī Irshīd, Amman, 13 June 2012
Jamīl Duhaysāt, Amman, 18 June 2014
Sālim al-Falāḥāt, Amman, 22 January 2013
Ibrāhīm Gharāyiba, Amman, 25 June 2012
Ruḥayyil Gharāyiba, Amman, 17 January 2013, 16 June 2013, 15 June 2014
Shadi Hamid, Amman, 11 August 2008
ʿĀṭif al-Jawlānī, Amman, 14 June 2012
Ṣalāḥ al-Khālidī, Amman, 24 January 2013
Nabīl al-Kūfaḥī, Amman, 29 January 2014
Muḥammad al-Majālī, Amman, 17 June 2013
Ḥamza Manṣūr, Amman, 25 June 2012
ʿUrayb al-Rantāwī, Amman, 12 August 2008, 12 January 2013
Hammām Saʿīd, Amman, 28 January 2013
ʿAlī al-Ṣawā, Amman, 25 January 2012
Faraj Shalhūb, Amman, 21 June 2012, 15 January 2013
Sulaymān al-Shiyāb, Amman, 15 June 2012
ʿAwnī al-ʿUbaydī, Amman, 11 January 2014
Bassām al-ʿUmūsh, Amman, 30 January 2013

Media

Agence France-Presse
ʿAmmūn
Al-ʿArab al-Yawm
Al-Būṣala
Al-Dustūr
Al-Ghad
Al-Ḥaqīqa al-Dawliyya
Al-Ḥayāt
Al-Jazīra
Jirāsa
The Jordan Times
Al-Kifāḥ al-Islāmī
Al-Maqarr
Petra
Al-Quds al-ʿArabī
Al-Raʾy
Al-Ribāṭ
Al-Sabīl
Al-Sharq al-Awsaṭ
Shīḥān News
The Washington Post

Works Cited

Primary Sources (Arabic, English)

ʿAbd al-Rāziq, ʿAli. *Al-Islām wa-Uṣūl al-Ḥukm*. Beirut/Cairo: Dār al-Kitāb al-Lubnānī/Dār al-Kitāb al-Miṣrī, 2012 [1925].
Abū Fāris, Muḥammad ʿAbd al-Qādir. *Al-Amr bi-l-Maʿrūf wa-l-Nahy ʿan al-Munkar*. Amman: Dār al-Furqān li-l-Nashr wa-l-Tawzīʿ, 1987.
Al-Fiqh al-Siyāsī ʿinda l-Imām al-Shahīd Ḥasan al-Bannā. Amman: Dār al-Bashīr li-l-Thaqāfa wa-l-ʿUlūm, 1999.
Hādhā Huwa l-Ḥall. Ṭanṭā: Dār al-Bashīr li-l-Thaqāfa wa-l-ʿUlūm, 1999.
Ḥukm al-Shūrá fī l-Islām wa-Natījatuhā. Amman: Dār al-Furqān li-l-Nashr wa-l-Tawzīʿ, 1988.
Mafāhīm Islāmiyya. Amman: Dār al-Furqān li-l-Nashr wa-l-Tawzīʿ, 1994.
Mubtadiʿāt wa-ʿĀdāt wa-Ḥukm al-Sharʿ fīhā. Amman: Dār ʿAmmār, 2000.
Al-Mushāraka fī l-Wizāra fī l-Anẓima al-Jāhiliyya. Amman: Dār al-Furqān li-l-Nashr wa-l-Tawzīʿ, 1991.
Al-Niẓām al-Siyāsī fī l-Islām. Amman: Dār al-Furqān li-l-Nashr wa-l-Tawzīʿ, n.d.
Ṣafaḥāt min al-Tārīkh al-Siyāsī li-l-Ikhwān al-Muslimīn fī l-Urdunn. Amman: Dār al-Furqān, 2000.
Abū Ghanīma, Ziyād. *Al-Ḥaraka al-Islāmiyya wa-Qaḍiyyat Filasṭīn*. Amman: Dār al-Furqān li-l-Nashr wa-l-Tawzīʿ, 1989.

Al-Amāna al-ʿĀmma li-Ḥizb Jabhat al-ʿAmal al-Islāmī. Amman: Al-Muʾtamar al-ʿĀmm li-Ḥizb Jabhat al-ʿAmal al-Islāmī, 2002.

al-Ashqar, ʿUmar Sulaymān. *Ḥukm al-Mushāraka fī l-Wizāra wa-l-Majālis al-Niyābiyya*. Amman: Dār al-Nafāʾis li-l-Nashr wa-l-Tawzīʿ, 2009.

ʿAwda, ʿAbd al-Qādir. *Al-Islām wa-Awḍāʿunā al-Qānūniyya*. N.p.: 1967 [1951].

Al-Islām wa-Awḍāʿunā al-Siyāsiyya. N.p.: n.d.

Al-Māl wa-l-Ḥukm fī l-Islām. Dammam and Riyadh: Al-Dār al-Saʿūdiyya li-l-Nashr wa-l-Tawzīʿ, 1984 [1951].

al-ʿAẓm, Yūsuf. *Bayādir wa-Ḥiṣād*. Amman: Dār al-Furqān li-l-Nashr wa-l-Tawzīʿ, 1998.

Rāʾid al-Fikr al-Islāmī al-Muʿāṣir: Al-Shahīd Sayyid Quṭb, Ḥayātuhu wa-Madrasatuhu wa-Āthāruhu. Beirut: Dār al-Qalam, 1980.

al-Bannā, Ḥasan. *Majmūʿat Rasāʾil al-Imām al-Shahīd Ḥasan al-Bannā*. N.p.: Dār al-Tawzīʿ wa-l-Nashr al-Islāmiyya, 1992.

Farhan, Ishaq (Isḥāq A. Farḥān). *Islamic View Regarding Political Participation with Special Reference to the Jordanian Context*. Amman: Dār al-Furqān, 1998.

Mawāqif wa-Ārāʾ Siyāsiyya fī Qaḍāyā Waṭaniyya wa-ʿArabiyya wa-Islāmiyya I. Amman: Dār al-Furqān, 1999.

Mawāqif wa-Ārāʾ Siyāsiyya fī Qaḍāyā Waṭaniyya wa-ʿArabiyya wa-Islāmiyya II. Amman: Dār al-Furqān, 2000.

'Fī Ḥiwār Maftūḥ maʿa l-Murāqib al-ʿĀmm li-Jamāʿat al-Ikhwān al-Muslimūn fī l-Urdunn'. *Al-Qibla* 1, no. 3 (2002): 94–114.

al-Ghannūshī, Rāshid. *Al-Dīmuqrāṭiyya wa-Ḥuqūq al-Insān fī l-Islām*. N.p.: Al-Dār al-ʿArabiyya li-l-ʿUlūm Nāshirūn/Markaz al-Jazīra li-l-Dirāsāt, n.d.

Ḥuqūq al-Muwāṭana: Ḥuqūq Ghayr al-Muslim fī l-Mujtamaʿ al-Islāmī. Herndon, VA: Al-Maʿhad al-ʿĀlamī li-l-Fikr al-Islāmī, 1993 [1989].

Al-Ḥurriyyāt al-ʿĀmma fī l-Dawla al-Islāmiyya. Beirut: Dār al-Mujtahid, 2011.

Gharāyiba, Ruḥayyil. *Al-Ḥuqūq wa-l-Ḥurriyyāt al-Siyāsiyya fī l-Sharīʿa al-Islāmiyya*. Beirut: Al-Shabaka al-ʿArabiyya li-l-Abḥāth wa-l-Nashr, 2012.

Al-Jinsiyya fī l-Sharīʿa al-Islāmiyya. Beirut: Al-Shabaka al-ʿArabiyya li-l-Abḥāth wa-l-Nashr, 2011.

al-Ghazālī, Muḥammad. *Hādhā Dīnunā*. Doha: Dār al-Thaqāfa, 1985.

Mushkilāt fī Ṭarīq al-Ḥayāt al-Islāmiyya. Cairo: Nahḍat Miṣr li-l-Ṭabāʿa wa-l-Nashr wa-l-Tawzīʿ, 2003.

Al-Ḥaraka al-Islāmiyya fī l-Urdunn. *Ruʾyat al-Ḥaraka al-Islāmiyya li-l-Iṣlāḥ fī l-Urdunn*. N.p.: 2005.

al-Ḥasan, Muḥammad. *Al-Ikhwān al-Muslimūn fī Suṭūr*. Amman: Dār al-Furqān li-l-Nashr wa-l-Tawzīʿ, 1990.

Ḥizb Jabhat al-ʿAmal al-Islāmī. *Al-Niẓām al-Asāsī*. N.p.: 2018.

al-Huḍaybī, Ḥasan. *Duʿāt Lā Quḍāt*. Cairo: Dār al-Tawzīʿ wa-l-Nashr al-Islāmiyya, 1977.

ʿImāra, Muḥammad. *Al-Islām wa-l-Sulṭa al-Dīniyya*. Cairo: Dār al-Thaqāfa al-Jadīda, n.d.

al-Khālidī, Ṣalāḥ ʿAbd al-Fattāḥ. Introduction to *Maʿālim fī l-Ṭarīq: Dirāsa wa-Taḥqīq*, edited by Ṣalāḥ ʿAbd al-Fattāḥ al-Khālidī, 5–18. Amman: Dār ʿAmmār li-l-Nashr wa-l-Tawzīʿ, 2009.

al-Mālikī, ʿAbdallāh. *Siyādat al-Umma qabla Taṭbīq al-Sharīʿa: Naḥwa Faḍāʾ Amthal li-Tajsīd Mabādiʾ al-Islām*. Beirut: Al-Shabaka al-ʿArabiyya li-l-Abḥāth wa-l-Nashr, 2012.
Manṣūr, Ḥamza. *Kalimāt wa-Mawāqif*. Amman: Dār al-Furqān li-l-Nashr wa-l-Tawzīʿ, 1998.
Naʿam ... Al-Islām Huwa l-Ḥall wa-maʿan ... li-Taḥqīq al-Ḥurriyya wa-l-ʿAdāla wa-l-Tanmiya wa-l-Iṣlāḥ wa-l-Waḥda ...: Al-Barnāmij al-Intikhābī li-Murashshaḥī Ḥizb Jabhat al-ʿAmal al-Islāmī li-Intikhābāt Majlis al-Nuwwāb al-Khāmis ʿAshara. N.p.: 2011.
al-Qaraḍāwī, Yūsuf. *ʿAwāmil al-Saʿa wa-l-Murūna fī l-Sharīʿa al-Islāmiyya*. Cairo: Maktaba Wahba, 2004.
Ghayr al-Muslimīn fī l-Mujtamaʿ al-Islāmī. Cairo: Maktabat Wahba, 2005.
Al-Ḥalāl wa-l-Ḥarām fī l-Islām. Cairo: Maktabat Wahba, 1999.
Al-Ijtihād fī l-Sharīʿa al-Islāmiyya maʿa Naẓarāt Taḥlīliyya fī l-Ijtihād al-Muʿāṣir. Cairo: Dār al-Qalam li-l-Nashr wa-l-Tawzīʿ, 2011.
Jarīmat al-Ridda ... wa-ʿUqūbat al-Murtadd fī Ḍawʾ al-Qurʾān wa-l-Sunna. Amman: Dār al-Furqān li-l-Nashr wa-l-Tawzīʿ, 1996.
Kalimāt fī l-Wasaṭiyya al-Islāmiyya wa-Maʿālimihā. Cairo: Dār al-Shurūq, 2011.
Madkhal li-Dirāsat al-Sharīʿa al-Islāmiyya. Cairo: Maktabat Wahba, 2005.
Markaz al-Marʾa fī l-Ḥayāt al-Islāmiyya. Amman: Dār al-Furqān li-l-Nashr wa-l-Tawzīʿ, 1996.
Min Fiqh al-Dawla fī l-Islām: Makānatuhā ... Maʿālimuhā ... Ṭabīʿatuhā [wa-] Mawqifuhā min al-Dīmuqrāṭiyya wa-l-Taʿaddudiyya wa-l-Marʾa wa-Ghayr al-Muslimīn. Cairo: Dār al-Shurūq, 2001 [1997].
Al-Siyāsa al-Sharʿiyya fī Ḍawʾ Nuṣūṣ al-Sharīʿa wa-Maqāṣidihā. Cairo: Maktabat Wahba, 2008.
Ummatunā bayna l-Qarnayn. Cairo: Dār al-Shurūq, 2006 [2000].
Wajhan li-Wajh ... Al-Islām wa-l-ʿAlmāniyya. Cairo: Dār al-Ṣaḥwa li-l-Nashr wa-l-Tawzīʿ, 1994.
Quṭb, Muḥammad. *Qaḍiyyat al-Tanwīr fī l-ʿĀlam al-Islāmī*. Cairo: Dār al-Shurūq, 2002 [1999].
Ruʾya Islāmiyya li-Aḥwāl al-ʿĀlam al-Muʿāṣir. Riyadh: Dār al-Waṭan li-l-Nashr, 1991.
Quṭb, Sayyid. *Al-ʿAdāla al-Ijtimāʿiyya fī l-Islām*. 27th ed. Cairo: Dār al-Shurūq, 2009.
Maʿālim fī l-Ṭarīq. 6th ed. Beirut and Cairo: Dār al-Shurūq, 1979.
Maʿālim fī l-Ṭarīq: Dirāsa wa-Taḥqīq. Edited by Ṣalāḥ ʿAbd al-Fattāḥ al-Khālidī. Amman: Dār ʿAmmār, 2009.
Riḍā, Muḥammad Rashīd. *Ḥuqūq al-Nisāʾ fī l-Islām wa-Ḥaẓẓuhunna min al-Iṣlāḥ al-Muḥammadī al-ʿĀmm*. Beirut and Damascus: Al-Maktab al-Islāmī, 1984.
Al-Khilāfa aw al-Imāma al-ʿUẓmá. N.p.: Maṭbaʿat al-Manār bi-Miṣr, n.d.
Saʿīd, Hammām. *Qawāʿid al-Daʿwa ilá llāh*. Amman: Dār al-Furqān li-l-Nashr wa-l-Tawzīʿ, 2011.
al-Sibāʿī, Muṣṭafá. *Al-Marʾa bayna l-Fiqh wa-l-Qānūn*. 7th ed. Beirut: Dār al-Warrāq, 1999.

Society of Muslim Brothers. 'Boycotting the 1997 Election in Jordan'. In *Modernist and Fundamentalist Debates in Islam: A Reader*, edited by Mansoor Moaddel and Kamran Talattof, 301–7. New York: Palgrave Macmillan, 2000.

Al-Taqrīr al-Idārī li-Kutlat Nuwwāb Ḥizb Jabhat al-ʿAmal al-Islāmī fī Majlis al-Nuwwāb al-Urdunnī al-Rābiʿ ʿAshara 2003–2007. N.p.: n.d.

al-Turābī, Ḥasan. *Fī l-Fiqh al-Siyāsī*. Beirut: Al-Dār al-ʿArabiyya li-l-ʿUlūm Nāshirūn, 2010.

'The Islamic State'. In *Princeton Readings in Islamist Thought: Texts and Contexts from al-Banna to Bin Laden*, edited by Roxanne L. Euben and Muhammad Qasim Zaman, 213–23. Princeton, NJ, and Oxford: Princeton University Press, 2009.

Al-Marʾa bayna l-Uṣūl wa-l-Taqālīd. Khartoum: Markaz Dirāsāt al-Marʾa, 2000.

Al-Siyāsa wa-l-Ḥukm: Al-Nuẓum al-Sulṭāniyya bayna l-Uṣūl wa-Sunan al-Wāqiʿ. Beirut: Dār al-Sāqī, 2003.

'Al-Shūrá wa-l-Dīmuqrāṭiyya: Ishkālāt al-Muṣṭalaḥ wa-l-Mafhūm'. Paper presented at the Maʿhad al-Dirāsāt al-Siyāsiyya wa-l-Istrātījiyya, Khartoum, Sudan, September 1984.

al-ʿUbaydī, ʿAwnī Jadwaʿ. *Jamāʿat al-Ikhwān al-Muslimīn fī l-Urdunn wa-Filasṭīn, 1945–1970: Ṣafaḥāt Tārkhiyya*. Amman: 1991.

Ṣafaḥāt min Ḥayāt al-Ḥāj ʿAbd al-Laṭīf Abū Qūra, Muʾassis Jamāʿat al-Ikhwān al-Muslimīn fī l-Urdunn. Amman: Markaz Dirāsāt wa-Abḥāth al-ʿAmal al-Islāmī, 1992.

al-ʿUmūsh, Bassām ʿAlī. *Al-Ikhwān al-Muslimūn min al-Fikra al-Iṣlāḥiyya ilá l-Fikra al-Thawriyya* (unpublished manuscript).

Maḥaṭṭāt fī Tārīkh Jamāʿat al-Ikhwān al-Muslimīn fī l-Urdunn. Amman: Al-Akādīmiyyūn li-l-Nashr wa-l-Tawzīʿ, 2008.

Secondary Sources (Arabic, Dutch, English, French, German)

Abdelwahid, Mustafa A. *The Rise of the Islamic Movement in Sudan (1945–1989)*. New York: Edwin Mellen Press, 2008.

Abed-Kotob, Sana. 'The Accommodationists Speak: Goals and Strategies of the Muslim Brotherhood of Egypt'. *International Journal of Middle East Studies* 27, no. 3 (1995): 321–39.

Abou El Fadl, Khaled. *Rebellion & Violence in Islamic Law*. Cambridge: Cambridge University Press, 2001.

Abu-Amr, Ziad. *Islamic Fundamentalism in the West Bank and Gaza: Muslim Brotherhood and Islamic Jihad*. Bloomington and Indianapolis, IN: Indiana University Press, 1994.

Abū Haniyya, Ḥasan. *Al-Marʾa wa-l-Siyāsa min Manẓūr al-Ḥarakāt al-Islāmiyya fī l-Urdunn*. Amman: Friedrich Ebert Stiftung, 2008.

Abu Jaber, Kamel S. and Schirin H. Fathi. 'The 1989 Jordanian Parliamentary Elections'. *Orient: Deutsche Zeitschrift für den modernen Orient* 31, no. 1 (1990): 67–86.

Abu-Munshar, Maher Y. 'In the Shadow of the "Arab Spring": The Fate of Non-Muslims under Islamist Rule'. *Islam and Christian–Muslim Relations* 23, no. 4 (2012): 487–503.
Abu-Odeh, Adnan. *Jordanians, Palestinians & the Hashemite Kingdom in the Middle East Peace Process*. Washington, DC: United States Institute of Peace, 1999.
Abu Rumman, Mohammad Suliman (Muḥammad Abū Rummān). *The Muslim Brotherhood in the 2007 Jordanian Parliamentary Elections: A Passing 'Political Setback' or Diminished Popularity?* Amman: Friedrich Ebert Stiftung, 2007.
Abū Rummān, Muḥammad and Ḥasan Abū Haniyya. *Al-Ḥall al-Islāmī fī l-Urdunn: Al-Islāmiyyūn wa-l-Dawla wa-Rihānāt al-Dīmuqrāṭiyya wa-l-Amn*. Amman: Friedrich Ebert Stiftung, 2012.
Abū Rummān, Muḥammad and Nifīn Bunduqjī. *Min al-Khilāfa al-Islamiyya ilá l-Dawla al-Madaniyya*. Amman: Friedrich Ebert Stiftung, 2018.
Adams, Charles J. 'The Ideology of Mawlana Mawdudi'. In *South Asian Politics and Religion*, edited by Donald Eugene Smith, 371–97. Princeton, NJ: Princeton University Press, 1966.
'Mawdudi and the Islamic State'. In *Voices of Resurgent Islam*, edited by John L. Esposito, 99–133. Oxford: Oxford University Press, 1983.
El-Affendi, Abdelwahab. *Turabi's Revolution: Islam and Power in Sudan*. London: Grey Seal Books, 1991.
Afsaruddin, Asma. 'Loyalty and Obedience to the Ruler: Religious Obligation or a Practical Necessity?' *The Muslim World* 106 (2016): 361–73.
'Theologizing about Democracy: A Critical Appraisal of Mawdudi's Thought'. In *Islam, the State, and Political Authority: Medieval Issues and Modern Concerns*, edited by Asma Afsaruddin, 131–54. New York: Palgrave Macmillan, 2011.
Alon, Yoav. *The Making of Jordan: Tribes, Colonialism and the Modern State*. London and New York: I.B. Tauris, 2007.
The Shaykh of Shaykhs: Mithqal al-Fayiz and Tribal Leadership in Modern Jordan. Stanford, CA: Stanford University Press, 2016.
Amawi, Abla M. 'The 1993 Elections in Jordan'. *Arab Studies Quarterly* 16, no. 3 (1994): 15–27.
Amis, Jacob. 'The Jordanian Brotherhood in the Arab Spring'. In *Current Trends in Islamist Ideology 14*, edited by Hillel Fradkin, Husain Haqqani, Eric Brown and Hassan Mneimeh, 38–57. Washington, DC: Hudson Institute, 2013.
al-Anani, Khalil. 'Egypt's Muslim Brotherhood: From Opposition to Power and Back Again. A Study in the Dynamics of their Rise and Fall'. In *The Prospects of Political Islam in a Troubled Region: Islamists and Post-Arab Spring Challenges*, edited by Mohammed Abu Rumman, 75–87. Amman: Friedrich Ebert Stiftung, 2018.
Inside the Muslim Brotherhood: Religion, Identity, and Politics. Oxford: Oxford University Press, 2016.
'Rethinking the Repression-Dissent Nexus: Assessing Egypt's Muslim Brotherhood's Response to Repression since the Coup of 2013'. *Democratization* 26, no. 8 (2019): 1329–41.
'Understanding Repression-Adaptation Nexus in Islamist Movements'. In *Adaptation Strategies of Islamist Movements*. POMEPS Studies 26, 4–7.

Washington, DC: Project on Middle East Political Science (POMEPS), 2017.

'Upended Path: The Rise and Fall of Egypt's Muslim Brotherhood'. *Middle East Journal* 69, no. 4 (2015): 527–43.

Anjum, Ovamir. 'Dhimmi Citizens: Non-Muslims in the New Islamist Discourse'. *ReOrient* 2, no. 1 (2016): 31–50.

Politics, Law, and Community in Islamic Thought: The Taymiyyan Moment. Cambridge: Cambridge University Press, 2012.

Antonius, George. *The Arab Awakening.* New York: Capricorn Books, 1965 [1946].

Arberry, A. J. *The Koran Interpreted.* New York: Touchstone, 1955.

Arigita, Elena and Rafael Ortega. 'From Syria to Spain: The Rise and Decline of the Muslim Brothers'. In *The Muslim Brotherhood in Europe*, edited by Roel Meijer and Edwin Bakker, 189–208. London: Hurst & Co., 2012.

Arjomand, Saïd Amir. 'The Constitution of Medina: A Sociolegal Interpretation of Muhammad's Acts of Foundation of the *Umma*'. *International Journal of Middle East Studies* 41, no. 4 (2009): 555–75.

Aruri, Naseer H. *Jordan: A Study in Political Development (1921–1965)*. The Hague: Martinus Nijhoff, 1972.

Atzori, Daniel. *Islamism and Globalisation in Jordan: The Muslim Brotherhood's Quest for Hegemony*. London and New York: Routledge, 2015.

Auda, Gehad. 'The "Normalization" of the Islamic Movement in Egypt from the 1970s to the early 1990s'. In *Accounting for Fundamentalisms: The Dynamic Character of Movements*, edited by Martin E. Marty and R. Scott Appleby, 374–412. Chicago, IL, and London: University of Chicago Press, 1994.

Aveni, Adrian F. 'Organizational Linkages and Resource Mobilization: The Significance of Linkage Strength and Breadth'. *Sociological Quarterly* 19, no. 2 (1978): 185–202.

Al-Awadi, Hesham. *In Pursuit of Legitimacy: The Muslim Brothers and Mubarak, 1982–2000.* London and New York: I.B. Tauris, 2004.

El-Awaisi, Abd Al-Fattah Muhammad. *The Muslim Brothers and the Palestine Question, 1928–1947.* London and New York: I.B. Tauris, 1998.

El-Azhary Sonbol, Amira. 'Egypt'. In *The Politics of Islamic Revivalism: Diversity and Unity*, edited by Shireen Hunter, 23–38. Bloomington and Indianapolis, IN: Indiana University Press, 1988.

Baker, Raymond William. 'Invidious Comparisons: Realism, Postmodern Globalism and Centrist Islamic Movements in Egypt'. In *Political Islam: Revolution, Radicalism or Reform?*, edited by John L. Esposito, 115–33. Boulder, CO: Lynne Rienner Publishers, 1997.

Islam without Fear: Egypt and the New Islamists. Cambridge, MA, and London: Harvard University Press, 2003.

Bakker, Edwin. 'The Public Image of the Muslim Brotherhood in the Netherlands'. In *The Muslim Brotherhood in Europe*, edited by Roel Meijer and Edwin Bakker, 169–88. London: Hurst & Co., 2012.

Batatu, Hanna. 'Syria's Muslim Brethren'. In *State and Ideology in the Middle East and Pakistan*, edited by Fred Halliday and Hamza Alavi, 112–32. London: Macmillan, 1988.

Bayat, Asef. *Making Islam Democratic: Social Movements and the Post-Islamist Turn*. Stanford, CA: Stanford University Press, 2007.

Bayat, Asef, ed. *Post-Islamism: The Changing Faces of Political Islam*. Oxford: Oxford University Press, 2013.

Baylocq, Cédric. 'The Autonomisation of the Muslim Brotherhood in Europe: *Da'wa*, *Mixité* and Non-Muslims'. In *The Muslim Brotherhood in Europe*, edited by Roel Meijer and Edwin Bakker, 149–68. London: Hurst & Co., 2012.

Baylouny, Anne Marie. 'Militarizing Welfare: Neo-liberalism and Jordanian Policy'. *Middle East Journal* 62, no. 2 (2008): 104–23.

Becker, Petra. 'Die syrische Muslimbruderschaft bleibt ein wichtiger Akteur'. *SWP-Aktuell* 52 (2013): 1–8.

Belén Soage, Ana. 'Ḥasan al-Bannā and Sayyid Quṭb: Continuity or Rupture?' *The Muslim World* 99 (2009): 294–311.

'Yusuf al-Qaradawi: The Muslim Brothers' Favorite Ideological Guide'. In *The Muslim Brotherhood: The Organization and Policies of a Global Islamist Movement*, edited by Barry Rubin, 19–37. New York: Palgrave Macmillan, 2010.

Belén Soage, Ana and Jorge Fuentelsaz Franganillo. 'The Muslim Brothers in Egypt'. In *The Muslim Brotherhood: The Organization and Policies of a Global Islamist Movement*, edited by Barry Rubin, 39–56. New York: Palgrave Macmillan, 2010.

Binder, Leonard. *Islamic Liberalism: A Critique of Development Ideologies*. Chicago, IL, and London: University of Chicago Press, 1988.

Black, Antony. *The History of Islamic Political Thought: From the Prophet to the Present*. New York: Routledge, 2001.

Bondokji, Neven. 'The Prospects of Islamic Movements and Parties in Jordan'. In *The Prospects of Political Islam in a Troubled Region: Islamists and Post-Arab Spring Challenges*, edited by Mohammed Abu Rumman, 159–69. Amman: Friedrich Ebert Stiftung, 2018.

Bosworth, C. E., Manuela Marin and A. Ayalon. 'Shūrā'. In *Encyclopaedia of Islam: New Edition*, vol. 9, edited by C. E. Bosworth, 504–6. Leiden: E.J. Brill, 1997.

Boulby, Marion. *The Muslim Brotherhood and the Kings of Jordan, 1945–1993*. Atlanta, GA: Scholars Press, 1999.

Bouzenita, Anke Iman. 'Early Contributions to the Theory of Islamic Governance: 'Abd al-Raḥmān al-Awzā'ī'. *Journal of Islamic Studies* 23, no. 2 (2012): 137–64.

Bowen, Innes. 'The Muslim Brotherhood in Britain'. In *The Muslim Brotherhood in Europe*, edited by Roel Meijer and Edwin Bakker, 111–26. London: Hurst & Co., 2012.

Brand, Laurie A. 'The Effects of the Peace Process on Political Liberalization in Jordan'. *Journal of Palestine Studies* 28, no. 2 (1999): 52–67.

'Palestinians and Jordanians: A Crisis of Identity'. *Journal of Palestine Studies* 24, no. 4 (1995): 46–61.

Brooke, Steven. 'The Muslim Brotherhood in Europe and the Middle East: The Evolution of a Relationship'. In *The Muslim Brotherhood in Europe*, edited by Roel Meijer and Edwin Bakker, 27–49. London: Hurst & Co., 2012.

Brown, Jonathan A. C. 'The Issue of Apostasy in Islam'. Yaqeen Institute, https://yaqeeninstitute.org/en/jonathan-brown/apostasy/ (accessed 8 July 2017), 5 July 2017.

Misquoting Muhammad: The Challenge and Choices of Interpreting the Prophet's Legacy. London: Oneworld, 2014.

Brown, Nathan J. *Jordan and Its Islamic Movement: The Limits of Inclusion?* Carnegie Papers no. 74. Washington, DC: Carnegie Endowment for International Peace, 2006.

When Victory Is Not an Option: Islamist Movements in Arab Politics. Ithaca, NY, and London: Cornell University Press, 2012.

Brynen, Rex. 'Economic Crisis and Post-rentier Democratization in the Arab World: The Case of Jordan'. *Canadian Journal of Political Science/Revue canadienne de science politique* 25, no. 1 (1992): 69–97.

al-Budūr, Bakr Muḥammad. *Al-Tajriba al-Niyābiyya li-l-Ḥaraka al-Islāmiyya fī l-Urdunn, 1989–2007*. Amman: Dār al-Ma'mūn li-l-Nashr wa-l-Tawzī', 2011.

Buehler, Matt. 'The Threat to "Un-moderate": Moroccan Islamists and the Arab Spring'. *Middle East Law and Governance* 5 (2013): 213–57.

Burgat, François. *Face to Face with Political Islam*. London and New York: I.B. Tauris, 2005 [1996].

Burgat, François and William Dowell. *The Islamic Movement in North Africa*. Austin, TX: University of Texas Press, 1993.

Burr, J. Millard and Robert O. Collins. *Sudan in Turmoil: Hasan al-Turabi and the Islamist State*. Princeton, NJ: Markus Wiener Publishers, 2010.

Butenschon, Nils A., Uri Davis and Manuel Hassassian, eds. *Citizenship and the State in the Middle East: Approaches and Applications*. Syracuse, NY: Syracuse University Press, 2000.

Calvert, John. *Sayyid Qutb and the Origins of Radical Islamism*. London: Hurst & Co., 2010.

Caridi, Paola. *Hamas: From Resistance to Government*. Translated by Andrea Teti. New York: Seven Stories Press, 2012 [2009].

Carré, Olivier and Michel Seurat. *Les frères musulmans (1928–1982)*. Paris: L'Harmattan, 1983.

Cavatorta, Francesco and Fabio Merone. 'Moderation Through Exclusion? The Journey of the Tunisian *Ennahda* from Fundamentalist to Conservative Party'. *Democratization* 20, no. 5 (2013): 857–75.

Charillon, Frédéric and Alain Mouftard. 'Jordanie: Les élections du 8 novembre 1993 et le processus de paix'. *Monde arabe/Maghreb-Machrek*, no. 144 (1994): 40–54.

Chehab, Zaki. *Inside Hamas: The Untold Story of the Militant Islamic Movement*. New York: Nation Books, 2007.

Chenivesse, Julien. 'Al-Ikhwān al-Muslimūn al-Urdunniyyūn wa-l-'Amaliyya al-Dīmuqrāṭiyya'. In *Al-Ḥaraka al-Islāmiyya wa-l-Ḥuqūq wa-l-Ḥurriyyāt al-'Āmma*, edited by Ibrāhīm Gharāyiba, 155–77. Amman: Markaz Dirāsāt al-Umma, 2002.

Clark, Janine A. 'The Conditions of Islamist Moderation: Unpacking Cross-ideological Cooperation in Jordan'. *International Journal of Middle East Studies* 38, no. 4 (2006): 539–60.

Islam, Charity, and Activism: Middle-Class Networks and Social Welfare in Egypt, Jordan, and Yemen. Bloomington and Indianapolis, IN: Indiana University Press, 2004.

'Patronage, Prestige, and Power: The Islamic Center Charity Society's Political Role within the Muslim Brotherhood'. In *Islamist Politics in the Middle East: Movements and Change*, edited by Samer S. Shehata, 68–87. London and New York: Routledge, 2012.

Clark, Janine A. and Jillian Schwedler. 'Who Opened the Window? Women's Activism in Islamist Parties'. *Comparative Politics* 35, no. 3 (2003): 93–312.

Cohen, Mark R. *Under Crescent & Cross: The Jews in the Middle Ages*. Princeton, NJ: Princeton University Press, 2008 [1994].

Conduit, Dara. *The Muslim Brotherhood in Syria*. Cambridge: Cambridge University Press, 2019.

'The Syrian Muslim Brotherhood and the Spectacle of Hama'. *Middle East Journal* 70, no. 2 (2016): 211–26.

Cook, Michael. *Ancient Religions: Modern Politics: The Islamic Case in Comparative Perspective*. Princeton, NJ, and Oxford: Princeton University Press, 2014.

Commanding Right and Forbidding Wrong in Islamic Thought. Cambridge: Cambridge University Press, 2001.

Crone, Patricia. *God's Rule – Government and Islam: Six Centuries of Medieval Islamic Political Thought*. New York: Columbia University Press, 2004.

Crone, Patricia and Martin Hinds. *God's Caliph: Religious Authority in the First Centuries of Islam*. Cambridge: Cambridge University Press, 2003 [1986].

Dalacoura, Katerina. *Islamist Terrorism and Democracy in the Middle East*. Cambridge: Cambridge University Press, 2011.

Dann, Uriel. *King Hussein and the Challenge of Arab Radicalism: Jordan, 1955–1967*. Oxford: Oxford University Press, 1989.

Della Porta, Donatella and Mario Dani. *Social Movements: An Introduction*. Malden, MA: Blackwell Publishing, 2006 [1999].

Dieterich, Renate. 'The Weakness of the Ruled Is the Strength of the Ruler: The Role of the Opposition in Contemporary Jordan'. In *Jordan in Transition: 1990–2000*, edited by George Joffé, 127–48. London: Hurst & Co., 2002.

Dijk, Teun A. van. *Ideology: A Multidisciplinary Approach*. London: Sage Publications, 1998.

al-Ḍumūr, Adīb Fāyiz. *Fiqh al-Iṣlāḥ wa-l-Taghyīr al-Siyāsī*. Amman: Dār al-Ma'mūn li-l-Nashr wa-l-Tawzī', 2011.

Ebstein, Michael. *In the Shadows of the Koran: Said* [*sic*] *Qutb's Views on Jews and Christians as Reflected in his Koran Commentary*. Research Monographs on the Muslim World 2, no. 4. Washington, DC: Hudson Institute, 2009.

Elshobaki, Amr. 'The Muslim Brotherhood – Between Evangelizing and Politics: The Challenges of Incorporating the Brotherhood into the Political Process'. In *Islamist Politics in the Middle East: Movements and Change*, edited by Samer S. Shehata, 107–19. London and New York: Routledge, 2012.

Enayat, Hamid. *Modern Islamic Political Thought*. Austin, TX: University of Texas Press, 1982.

Escobar Stemmann, Juan José. 'The Crossroads of Muslim Brothers in Jordan'. In *The Muslim Brotherhood: The Organization and Policies of a Global Islamist*

Movement, edited by Barry Rubin, 57–71. New York: Palgrave Macmillan, 2010.

Farahat, Cynthia. 'The Muslim Brotherhood, Fountain of Islamist Violence'. *Middle East Quarterly* 24, no. 2 (2017).

Farahat, Mohamed Fayez. 'Liberalizing the Muslim Brotherhood: Can It be Done?' *Arab Insight* 2, no. 6 (2009): 11–23.

Farschid, Olaf. 'Hizbiya: Die Neuorientierung der Muslimbruderschaft Ägyptens in den Jahren 1984 bis 1989'. *Orient* 30, no. 1 (1989): 53–74.

Fathi, Schirin. *Jordan: An Invented Nation? Tribe-State Dynamics and the Formation of National Identity*. Hamburg: Deutsches Orient-Institut, 1994.

El Fegiery, Moataz. *Tyranny of the Majority? Islamists' Ambivalence about Human Rights*. Madrid: Fride, 2012.

Forstner, Martin. 'Auf dem legalen Weg zur Macht? Zur Politischen Entwicklung der Muslimbruderschaft Ägyptens'. *Orient* 29, no. 3 (1988): 386–422.

Frampton, Martyn. *The Muslim Brotherhood and the West: A History of Enmity and Engagement*. Cambridge, MA, and London: Belknap/Harvard University Press, 2018.

Freeden, Michael. *Ideologies and Political Theory: A Conceptual Approach*. Oxford: Oxford University Press, 1996.

Ideology: A Very Short Introduction. Oxford: Oxford University Press, 2003.

Liberal Languages: Ideological Imaginations and Twentieth-Century Progressive Thought. Princeton, NJ, and Oxford: Princeton University Press, 2005.

Freeden, Michael, ed. *Reassessing Political Ideologies: The Durability of Dissent*. London and New York: Routledge, 2001.

Freer, Courtney. *The Changing Islamist Landscape of the Gulf Arab States*. Washington, DC: The Arab Gulf States Institute in Washington, 2016.

'Exclusion-Moderation in the Gulf Context: Tracing the Development of Pragmatic Islamism in Kuwait'. *Middle Eastern Studies* 54, no. 1 (2018): 1–21.

Rentier Islamism: The Influence of the Muslim Brotherhood in Gulf Monarchies. Oxford: Oxford University Press, 2018.

Freij, Hanna Y. and Leonard C. Robinson. 'Liberalization, the Islamists, and the Stability of the Arab State: Jordan as a Case Study'. *The Muslim World* 86, no. 1 (1996): 1–32.

Friedmann, Yohanan. *Tolerance and Coercion in Islam: Interfaith Relations in the Muslim Tradition*. Cambridge: Cambridge University Press, 2003.

Gaffney, Frank. *The Muslim Brotherhood in the Obama Administration*. Sherman Oaks, CA: The David Horowitz Freedom Center, 2012.

Gerring, John. 'Ideology: A Definitional Analysis'. *Political Research Quarterly* 50, no. 4 (1997): 957–94.

Gharāyiba, Ibrāhīm. *Jamāʿat al-Ikhwān al-Muslimīn fī l-Urdunn, 1946–1996*. Amman: Markaz al-Urdunn al-Jadīd li-l-Dirāsāt and Dār Sindbād li-l-Nashr, 1997.

Al-Khiṭāb al-Islāmī wa-l-Taḥawwulāt al-Ḥaḍāriyya wa-l-Ijtimāʿiyya. Amman: Dār Ward al-Urduniyya li-l-Nashr wa-l-Tawzīʿ, 2007.

El-Ghobashy, Mona. 'The Metamorphosis of the Egyptian Muslim Brothers'. *International Journal of Middle East Studies* 37 (2005): 373–95.

Goffman, Erving. *Frame Analysis: An Essay on the Organization of Experience*. New York: Harper & Row, 1974.

Gräf, Bettina. 'The Concept of *Wasaṭiyya* in the Work of Yūsuf al-Qaraḍāwī'. In *Global Mufti: The Phenomenon of Yusuf al-Qaradawi*, edited by Bettina Gräf and Jakob Skovgaard-Petersen, 213–38. New York: Columbia University Press, 2009.

Gräf, Bettina and Jakob Skovgaard-Petersen, eds. *Global Mufti: The Phenomenon of Yusuf al-Qaradawi*. New York: Columbia University Press, 2009.

Gubser, Peter. *Politics and Change in Al-Karak, Jordan*. Oxford: Oxford University Press, 1973.

Gunning, Jeroen. *Hamas in Politics: Democracy, Religion, Violence*. London: Hurst & Co., 2007.

Habib, Randa. *Hussein and Abdullah: Inside the Jordanian Royal Family*. Translated by Miranda Tell. London: Saqi, 2010.

Hallaq, Wael B. *The Impossible State: Islam, Politics, and Modernity's Moral Predicament*. New York: Columbia University Press, 2013.

Sharī'a: Theory, Practice, Transformations. Cambridge: Cambridge University Press, 2009.

Hamid, Shadi. 'Arab Islamist Parties: Losing on Purpose?' *Journal of Democracy* 22, no. 1 (2011): 68–80.

'The Islamic Action Front in Jordan'. In *The Oxford Handbook of Islam and Politics*, edited John L. Esposito and Emad el-Din Shahin, 544–57. Oxford: Oxford University Press, 2013.

Islamic Exceptionalism: How the Struggle over Islam Is Reshaping the World. New York: St. Martin's Press, 2016.

'New Democrats? The Political Evolution of Jordan's Islamists'. Paper presented at the CSIC Sixth Annual Conference 'Democracy and Development: Challenges for the Islamic World', Washington, DC, United States of America, 22–23 April 2005.

Temptations of Power: Islamists & Illiberal Democracy in a New Middle East. Oxford: Oxford University Press, 2014.

al-Hanashi, Abdul Latif. 'Tunisia: The Impact of Democratic Transition on the Ennahda Party'. In *The Prospects of Political Islam in a Troubled Region: Islamists and Post-Arab Spring Challenges*, edited by Mohammed Abu Rumman, 53–65. Amman: Friedrich Ebert Stiftung, 2018.

Hansen, Stig Jarle and Mohamed Husein Gaas. 'The Ideological Arena of the Wider Muslim Brotherhood'. In *The Muslim Brotherhood Movement in the Arab Winter*, edited by Stig Jarle Hansen, Mohamed Husein Gaas and Ida Bary, 7–19. Cambridge, MA: Harvard Kenney School Belfer Center for Science and International Affairs, 2017.

Hansen, Stig Jarle, Mohamed Husein Gaas and Ida Bary, eds. *The Muslim Brotherhood Movement in the Arab Winter*. Cambridge, MA: Harvard Kenney School Belfer Center for Science and International Affairs, 2017.

Harmsen, Egbert. *Islam, Civil Society and Social Work: Muslim Voluntary Welfare Associations in Jordan between Patronage and Empowerment*. Amsterdam: Amsterdam University Press, 2008.

Harnisch, Chris and Quinn Mecham. 'Democratic Ideology in Islamist Opposition? The Muslim Brotherhood's "Civil State"'. *Middle Eastern Studies* 45, no. 2 (2009): 189–205.

Hegghammer, Thomas. ''Abdallāh 'Azzām and Palestine'. *Die Welt des Islams* 53, nos. 3–4 (2013): 353–87.

Hegghammer, Thomas and Stéphane Lacroix. 'Rejectionist Islamism in Saudi Arabia: The Story of Juhayman al-'Utaybi Revisited'. *International Journal of Middle East Studies* 39, no. 1 (2007): 103–22.

Heywood, Andrew. *Politics*. New York: Palgrave, 2002 [1997].

Hinnebusch, Raymond A. 'Syria'. In *The Politics of Islamic Revivalism: Diversity and Unity*, edited by Shireen T. Hunter, 39–56. Bloomington and Indianapolis, IN: Indiana University Press, 1988.

Holtmann, Philipp. 'After the Fall: The Muslim Brotherhood's Post Coup Strategy'. *Perspectives on Terrorism* 7, no. 5 (2013): 198–204.

El Houdaiby, Ibrahim. *From Prison to Palace: The Muslim Brotherhood's Challenges and Responses in Post-Revolution Egypt*. N.p.: Fride/Hivos, 2015.

Hourani, Albert. *Arabic Thought in the Liberal Age, 1798–1939*. Cambridge: Cambridge University Press, 1983 [1962].

Hroub, Khaled. 'Die Aktuelle Politik von Hamas: Überleben ohne Strategie'. *Inamo* 8, no. 32 (2002): 15–17.

Hamas: A Beginner's Guide. London and Ann Arbor, MI: Pluto Press, 2006.

Hamas: Political Thought and Practice. Washington, DC: Institute for Palestine Studies, 2000.

'A "New Hamas" through Its New Documents'. *Journal of Palestine Studies* 35, no. 4 (2006): 6–27.

Husaini, Ishak Musa. *The Moslem Brethren: The Greatest of Modern Islamic Movements*. Westpoint, CT: Hyperion Press, 1986 [1956].

International Crisis Group (ICG). *Dealing with Hamas*. Middle East Report no. 21. Amman and Brussels: ICG, 2004.

Enter Hamas: The Challenge of Political Integration. Middle East Report no. 49. Amman and Brussels: ICG, 2006.

Jordan's 9/11: Dealing with Jihadi Islamism. Middle East Report no. 47. Amman and Brussels: ICG, 2005.

Iskander Monier, Elizabeth and Annette Ranko. 'The Fall of the Muslim Brotherhood: Implications for Egypt'. *Middle East Policy* 20, no. 4 (2013): 111–23.

Jawad, Nazek. 'Democracy in Modern Islamic Thought'. *British Journal of Middle Eastern Studies* 40, no. 3 (2013): 327–39.

Jenkins, J. Craig. 'Resource Mobilization Theory and the Study of Social Movements'. *Annual Review of Sociology* 9 (1983): 527–53.

Jensen, Michael Irving. *The Political Ideology of Hamas: A Grassroots Perspective*. Translated by Sally Laird. London and New York: I.B. Tauris, 2010 [2009].

'Jordan: Parliament Passes Human Rights Reform'. *Human Rights Watch*, www.hrw.org/news/2017/10/04/jordan-parliament-passes-human-rights-reforms (accessed 28 July 2019), 4 October 2017.

Jung, Dietrich and Marie Juul Petersen. '"We Think That This Job Pleases Allah": Islamic Charity, Social Order, and the Construction of Modern Muslim Selfhoods in Jordan'. *International Journal of Middle East Studies* 46 (2014): 285–306.

Al Kadi, Alia. 'Between Foreign Policy and the *Umma*: The Muslim Brotherhood in Egypt and Jordan'. *The Muslim World* 109 (2019): 240–60.

al-Kanbouri, Idriss. 'Morocco's Islamists: Action Outside Religion'. In *The Prospects of Political Islam in a Troubled Region: Islamists and Post-Arab Spring Challenges*, edited by Mohammed Abu Rumman, 67–74. Amman: Friedrich Ebert Stiftung, 2018.

Kandil, Hazem. *Inside the Brotherhood*. Cambridge: Polity Press, 2015.

Katz, Kimberley. *Jordanian Jerusalem: Holy Places and National Spaces*. Gainesville, FL: University of Florida Press, 2005.

Keddie, Nikki R. *Sayyid Jamal Ad-Din 'Al-Afghani': A Political Biography*. Berkeley and Los Angeles, CA, and London: University of California Press, 1972.

Kedourie, Elie. *Afghani and ʿAbduh: An Essay on Religious Unbelief and Political Activism in Modern Islam*. London: Frank Cass & Co., 1997 [1966].

Kepel, Gilles. *Muslim Extremism in Egypt: The Prophet and the Pharaoh*. Translated by John Rothschild. Berkeley, CA, and Los Angeles: University of California Press, 2003 [1984].

Khan, Siraj. 'Blasphemy against the Prophet'. In *Muhammad in History, Thought and Culture: An Encyclopedia of the Prophet*, edited by Coeli Fitzpatrick and Adam H. Walker, 59–68. Santa Barbara, CA: ABC-CLIO, 2014.

Khatab, Sayyed. *The Political Thought of Sayyid Qutb: The Theory of Jahiliyyah*. London and New York: Routledge, 2006.

The Power of Sovereignty: The Political and Ideological Philosophy of Sayyid Qutb. London and New York: Routledge, 2006.

Al-Khazendar, Sami. *Jordan and the Palestine Question: The Role of Islamic and Left Forces in Foreign Policy-Making*. Reading, UK: Ithaca Press, 1997.

Khosrokhavar, Farhad. 'The Muslim Brotherhood in France'. In *The Muslim Brotherhood: The Organization and Policies of a Global Islamist Movement*, edited by Barry Rubin, 137–47. New York: Palgrave Macmillan, 2010.

King Abdullah II of Jordan. *Our Last Best Chance: The Pursuit of Peace in a Time of Peril*. London: Viking, 2011.

Kister, M. J. 'Notes on an Account of the Shura Appointed by ʿUmar b. al-Khattab'. *Journal of Semitic Studies* 9 (1964): 320–6.

Klandermans, Bert and Suzanne Staggenborg, eds. *Methods of Social Movement Research*. Minneapolis, MN: University of Minnesota Press, 2002.

Klein, Menachem. 'Hamas in Power'. *Middle East Journal* 61, no. 3 (2007): 442–59.

Kutscher, Jens. 'Islamic Shura, Democracy, and Online Fatwas'. *CyberOrient* 5, no. 2 (2011). www.cyberorient.net/article.do?articleId=7352 (accessed 23 May 2019).

Lahoud, Nelly. *Political Thought in Islam: A Study in Intellectual Boundaries*. London and New York: Routledge, 2005.

Lambton, Ann K. S. *State and Government in Medieval Islam – An Introduction to the Study of Islamic Political Theory: The Jurists*. New York: Routledge, 1991 [1981].

Landau-Tasseron, Ella. *Leadership and Allegiance in the Society of the Muslim Brothers*. Washington, DC: Center on Islam, Democracy, and the Future of the Muslim World at the Hudson Institute, 2010.

The Religious Foundations of Political Allegiance: A Study of Bayʿa in Pre-modern Islam. Research Monographs on the Muslim World 2, no. 4. Washington, DC: Hudson Institute, 2010.

Lappen, Alyssa A. 'The Muslim Brotherhood in North America'. In *The Muslim Brotherhood: The Organization and Policies of a Global Islamist Movement*, edited by Barry Rubin, 161–79. New York: Palgrave Macmillan, 2010.

Laraña, Enrique, Hank Johnston and Joseph R. Gusfield, eds. *New Social Movements: From Ideology to Identity*. Philadelphia, PA: Temple University Press, 1994.

Lauzière, Henri. *The Making of Salafism: Islamic Reform in the Twentieth Century*. New York: Columbia University Press, 2016.

Lea-Henry, Jed. 'The Life and Death of Abdullah Azzam'. *Middle East Policy* 25, no. 1 (2018): 64–79.

Lefèvre, Raphaël. *Ashes of Hama: The Muslim Brotherhood in Syria*. Oxford: Oxford University Press, 2013.

Legrain, Jean-François. 'Hamas as a Ruling Party'. In *Islamist Politics in the Middle East: Movements and Change*, edited by Samer S. Shehata, 183–204. London and New York: Routledge, 2012.

Levitt, Matthew. *Hamas: Politics, Charity, and Terrorism in the Service of Jihad*. New Haven, CT, and London: Yale University Press, 2006.

Levy-Rubin, Milka. *Non-Muslims in the Early Islamic Empire: From Surrender to Coexistence*. Cambridge: Cambridge University Press, 2011.

Lewis, Bernard. *The Jews of Islam*. Princeton, NJ: Princeton University Press, 2014 [1984].

Lia, Brynjar. 'Autobiography or Fiction? Ḥasan al-Bannā's Memoirs Revisited'. *Journal of Arabic and Islamic Studies* 15 (2015): 119–226.

The Society of the Muslim Brothers in Egypt. Reading, UK: Ithaca Press, 1998.

Little, Douglas. 'A Puppet in Search of a Puppeteer? The United States, King Hussein, and Jordan, 1953–1970'. *The International History Review* 17, no. 3 (1995): 512–44.

Lucas, Russel E. 'Deliberalization in Jordan'. *Journal of Democracy* 14, no. 1 (2003): 137–44.

Lund, Aron. *Struggling to Adapt: The Muslim Brotherhood in a New Syria*. Washington, DC: Carnegie Endowment for International Peace, 2013.

Lust, Ellen and Sami Hourani. 'Jordan Votes: Election or Selection?' *Journal of Democracy* 22, no. 2 (2011): 119–29.

Lust-Okar, Ellen M. 'The Decline of Jordanian Political Parties: Myth or Reality?' *International Journal of Middle East Studies* 33 (2001): 545–69.

Lybarger, Loren D. *Identity & Religion in Palestine: The Struggle between Islamism & Secularism in the Occupied Territories*. Princeton, NJ, and Oxford: Princeton University Press, 2007.

Lynch, Marc. *The Brotherhood's Dilemma*. Waltham, MA: Crown Center for Middle East Studies at Brandeis University, 2008.

State Interests and Public Spheres: The International Politics of Jordan's Identity. New York: Columbia University Press, 1999.

'Young Brothers in Cyberspace'. *Middle East Report* 245 (2007): 26–33.

Mahmoud, Muhammad. 'Women and Islamism: The Case of Rashid al-Ghannushi of Tunisia'. In *Islamic Fundamentalism*, edited by Abdel Salam Sidahmed and Anoushiravan Ehteshami, 249–65. Boulder, CO: Westview Press, 1996.

March, Andrew F. 'Genealogies of Sovereignty in Islamic Political Theology'. *Social Research* 80, no. 1 (2013): 293–320.

Islam and Liberal Citizenship: The Search for an Overlapping Consensus. Oxford: Oxford University Press, 2009.

Maréchal, Brigitte. 'The European Muslim Brothers' Quest to Become a Social (Cultural) Movement'. In *The Muslim Brotherhood in Europe*, edited by Roel Meijer and Edwin Bakker, 89–110. London: Hurst & Co., 2012.

Markaz Ḥimāyat wa-Ḥurriyyat al-Ṣaḥafiyyīn. *Qamʿ bi-Quwwat al-Qānūn: Ḥālat al-Ḥurriyyāt al-Iʿlāmiyya fī l-Urdunn 2012*. Amman: Markaz Ḥimāyat wa-Ḥurriyyat al-Ṣaḥafiyyīn, n.d.

Marks, Monica. 'Tunisia's Islamists and the "Turkish Model"'. *Journal of Democracy* 28, no. 1 (2017): 102–15.

Massad, Joseph A. *Colonial Effects: The Making of National Identity in Jordan*. New York: Columbia University Press, 2001.

McAdam, Doug. *Political Process and the Development of Black Insurgency, 1930–1970*. Chicago, IL, and London: University of Chicago Press, 1999 [1982].

McCarthy, John D. and Mayer N. Zald. 'Resource Mobilization and Social Movements: A Partial Theory'. *American Journal of Sociology* 82, no. 6 (1977): 1212–41.

McCarthy, Rory. 'Protecting the Sacred: Tunisia's Islamist Movement Ennahda and the Challenge of Free Speech'. *British Journal of Middle Eastern Studies* 42, no. 4 (2015): 447–64.

Meijer, Roel. 'Commanding Right and Forbidding Wrong as a Principle of Social Action: The Case of the Egyptian al-Jamaʿa al-Islamiyya'. In *Global Salafism: Islam's New Religious Movement*, edited by Roel Meijer, 189–220. London: Hurst & Co., 2009.

'The Majority Strategy of the Muslim Brotherhood'. *Orient*, no. 1 (2013): 22–30.

'Moslim Broederschap maakt zich op voor de democratie van morgen'. *ZemZem* 1, no. 2 (2005): 53–61.

'The Muslim Brotherhood and the Political: An Exercise in Ambiguity'. In *The Muslim Brotherhood in Europe*, edited by Roel Meijer and Edwin Bakker, 295–320. London: Hurst & Co., 2012.

'The Political, Politics, and Political Citizenship in Modern Islam'. In *The Middle East in Transition: The Centrality of Citizenship*, edited by Nils A. Butenschon and Roel Meijer, 179–202. Cheltenham: Edward Elgar Publishing, 2018.

Meijer, Roel and Edwin Bakker. 'Introduction'. In *The Muslim Brotherhood in Europe*, edited by Roel Meijer and Edwin Bakker, 1–23. London: Hurst & Co., 2012.

Meijer, Roel and Nils Butenschon, eds. *The Crisis of Citizenship in the Arab World*. Leiden: Brill, 2017.

Meining, Stefan. 'The Islamic Community in Germany: An Organisation under Observation'. In *The Muslim Brotherhood in Europe*, edited by Roel Meijer and Edwin Bakker, 209–33. London: Hurst & Co., 2012.

Milton-Edwards, Beverley. 'Climate of Change in Jordan's Islamist Movement'. In *Islamic Fundamentalism*, edited by Abdel Salam Sidahmed and Anoushiravan Ehteshami, 123–42. Boulder, CO: Westview Press, 1996.

'Façade Democracy in Jordan'. *British Journal of Middle Eastern Studies* 20, no. 2 (1993): 191–203.

Islamic Politics in Palestine. London and New York: I.B. Tauris, 1996.

The Muslim Brotherhood: The Arab Spring and Its Future Face. London and New York: Routledge, 2016.

'A Temporary Alliance with the Crown: The Islamic Response in Jordan'. In *Islamic Fundamentalisms and the Gulf Crisis*, edited by James Piscatori, 88–108. Chicago, IL: American Academy of Arts and Sciences, 1991.

Milton-Edwards, Beverley and Peter Hinchcliffe. *Jordan: A Hashemite Legacy*. London and New York: Routledge, 2001.

Milton-Edwards, Beverley and Stephen Farrell. *Hamas*. Cambridge and Malden, MA: Polity Press, 2010.

Mishal, Shaul. 'The Pragmatic Dimension of the Palestinian Hamas: A Network Perspective'. *Armed Forces and Society* 29, no. 4 (2003): 569–89.

West Bank/East Bank: The Palestinians in Jordan, 1949–1967. New Haven, CT, and London: Yale University Press, 1978.

Mishal, Shaul and Avraham Sela. *The Palestinian Hamas: Vision, Violence, and Coexistence*. New York: Columbia University Press, 2000.

'Participation without Presence: Hamas, the Palestinian Authority and the Politics of Negotiated Coexistence'. *Middle Eastern Studies* 38, no. 3 (2002): 1–26.

Mitchell, Richard P. *The Society of the Muslim Brothers*. Oxford: Oxford University Press, 1969.

Moaddel, Mansoor. *Jordanian Exceptionalism: A Comparative Analysis of State–Religion Relations in Egypt, Iran, Jordan, and Syria*. New York: Palgrave, 2002.

Morris, Aldon D. and Carol McClurg Mueller, eds. *Frontiers in Social Movement Theory*. New Haven, CT, and London: Yale University Press, 1992.

Mottahedeh, Roy P. *Loyalty and Leadership in an Early Islamic Society*. Princeton, NJ: Princeton University Press, 1980.

Motzki, Harald. 'Das Kopftuch – ein Symbol wofür?' *Religion, Staat, Gesellschaft: Zeitschrift für Glaubensformen und Weltanschauungen* 5, no. 2 (2004): 175–201.

Mouline, Nabil. *Les clercs de l'islam: Autorité religieuse et pouvoir politique en Arabie Saoudite, XVIIIe-XXIe siècle*. Paris: Presses Universitaires de France, 2011.

Moussalli, Ahmad S. 'Ḥasan al-Bannā's Islamist Discourse on Constitutional Rule and Islamic State'. *Journal of Islamic Studies* 4, no. 2 (1993): 161–74.

Radical Islamic Fundamentalism: The Ideological and Political Discourse of Sayyid Quṭb. Beirut: American University of Beirut, 1992.

Muir, William. *The Caliphate: Its Rise, Decline and Fall*. Edited by T. H. Weir. Edinburgh: J. Grant, 1915 [1891].

Musallam, Adnan A. *From Secularism to Jihad: Sayyid Qutb and the Foundation of Radical Islamism*. Westport, CT: Praeger Publishers, 2005.

Muslih, Muhammad. 'Hamas: Strategy and Tactics'. In *Ethnic Conflict and International Politics in the Middle East*, edited by Leonard Binder, 307–31. Gainesville, FL: University of Florida Press, 1999.

Nasr, Seyyed Vali Reza. 'Mawdudi and the Jamaʿat-i Islami: The Origins, Theory and Practice of Islamic Revivalism'. In *Pioneers of Islamic Revival*, edited by Ali Rahnema, 98–124. London and New York: Zed Books, 2005.

Mawdudi & the Making of Islamic Revivalism. Oxford: Oxford University Press, 1996.

Nüsse, Andrea. *Muslim Palestine: The Ideology of Hamas*. Abingdon, UK: RoutledgeCurzon, 1998.

Oliver, Pamela E. and Hank Johnston. 'What a Good Idea! Ideologies and Frames in Social Movement Research'. In *Frames of Protest: Social Movements and the Framing Perspectives*, edited by Hank Johnston and John A. Noakes, 185–203. Lanham, MD: Rowman & Littlefield Publishers, 2005.

Opwis, Felicitas. 'New Trends in Islamic Legal Theory: *Maqāṣid al-Sharīʿa* as a New Source of Law?' *Die Welt des Islams* 57 (2017): 7–32.

Pargeter, Alison. *The Muslim Brotherhood: From Opposition to Power*. London: Saqi Books, 2010.

The Muslim Brotherhood: The Burden of Tradition. London: Saqi Books, 2010.

Peter, Anne Mariel and Pete W. Moore. 'Beyond Boom and Bust: External Rents, Durable Authoritarianism, and Institutional Adaptation in the Hashemite Kingdom of Jordan'. *Studies in Comparative International Developments* 44 (2009): 256–85.

Peter, Frank. 'Muslim "Double Talk" and the Ways of the Shariʿa in France'. In *The Muslim Brotherhood in Europe*, edited by Roel Meijer and Edwin Bakker, 127–48. London: Hurst & Co., 2012.

Peters, Rudolph and Gert J. J. de Vries. 'Apostasy in Islam'. *Die Welt des Islams* 17 (1977): 1–25.

Pew Research Center. *The World's Muslims: Religion, Politics and Society*. www.pewforum.org/2013/04/30/the-worlds-muslims-religion-politics-society-overview/ (accessed 24 June 2019), 30 April 2013.

Phelps Harris, Christina. *Nationalism and Revolution in Egypt: The Role of the Muslim Brotherhood.* Stanford, CA: The Hoover Institution on War, Revolution, and Peace, 1964.

Pipes, Daniel. 'Islamism's Unity in Tunisia'. www.danielpipes.org/12103/islamism-unity (accessed 6 September 2018), 30 October 2012.

Podeh, Elie. 'The *Bay'a*: Modern Political Uses of Islamic Ritual in the Arab World'. *Die Welt des Islams* 50, no. 1 (2010): 117–52.

Policy Analysis Unit ACRPS. *Political Reforms and Parliamentary Elections in Jordan: The Trials and Tribulations of Forming a New Government.* Arab Center for Research and Policy Studies: http://english.dohainstitute.org/release/d1297561-3df6-479a-a078-7f59d1b4688a# (accessed 20 March 2013), 6 March 2013.

Rabb, Intisar A. 'Negotiating Speech in Islamic Law and Politics: Flipped Traditions of Expression'. In *Islamic Law and International Human Rights Law: Searching for Common Ground?*, edited by Anver M. Emon, Mark S. Ellis and Benjamin Glahn, 144–67. Oxford: Oxford University Press, 2012.

Rabil, Robert G. 'The Syrian Muslim Brotherhood'. In *The Muslim Brotherhood: The Organization and Policies of a Global Islamist Movement*, edited by Barry Rubin, 73–88. New York: Palgrave Macmillan, 2010.

Rath, Kathrine. 'The Process of Democratization in Jordan'. *Middle Eastern Studies* 30, no. 3 (1994): 530–57.

Reissner, Johannes. *Ideologie und Politik der Muslimbrüder Syriens: Von den Wahlen 1947 bis zum Verbot unter Adīb aš-Šīšaklī 1952.* Freiburg: Klaus Schwarz Verlag, 1980.

Rich, David. 'The Very Model of a British Muslim Brotherhood'. In *The Muslim Brotherhood: The Organization and Policies of a Global Islamist Movement*, edited by Barry Rubin, 117–36. New York: Palgrave Macmillan, 2010.

Roald, Anne Sofie. 'From Theocracy to Democracy? Towards Secularisation and Individualisation in the Policy of the Muslim Brotherhood in Jordan'. *Journal of Arabic and Islamic Studies* 8, no. 7 (2008): 84–107.

Robins, Philip. *A History of Jordan.* Cambridge: Cambridge University Press, 2004.

Robinson, Glenn E. 'Can Islamists be Democrats? The Case of Jordan'. *Middle East Journal* 51, no. 3 (1997): 373–87.

'Defensive Democratization in Jordan'. *International Journal of Middle East Studies* 30, no. 3 (1998): 387–410.

'Hamas as Social Movement'. In *Islamic Activism: A Social Movement Theory Approach*, edited by Quintan Wiktorowicz, 112–39. Bloomington and Indianapolis, IN: Indiana University Press, 2004.

Rock-Singer, Aaron. 'Scholarly Authority and Lay Mobilization: Yusuf al-Qaradawi's Vision of Da'wa, 1976–1984'. *The Muslim World* 106, no. 3 (2016): 588–604.

Rogan, Eugene L. 'Bringing the State Back: The Limits to Ottoman Rule in Jordan, 1840–1910'. In *Village, Steppe and State: The Social Origins of Modern Jordan*, edited by Eugene L. Rogan and Tariq Tell, 32–57. London and New York: British Academic Press, 1994.

Frontiers of the State in the Late Ottoman Empire. Cambridge: Cambridge University Press, 1999.

Rosefsky Wickham, Carrie. *Mobilizing Islam: Religion, Activism, and Political Change in Egypt*. New York: Columbia University Press, 2002.

The Muslim Brotherhood: Evolution of an Islamist Movement. Princeton, NJ, and Oxford: Princeton University Press, 2013.

'The Path to Moderation: Strategy and Learning in the Formation of Egypt's *Wasat* Party'. *Comparative Politics* 36, no. 2 (2004): 205–28.

Rosenthal, E. I. J. *Political Thought in Medieval Islam: An Introductory Outline*. Cambridge: Cambridge University Press, 2009 [1958].

Rotter, Gernot. *Die Umayyaden und der zweite Bürgerkrieg (680–692)*. Wiesbaden: Deutsche Morgenländische Gesellschaft, 1982.

Roy, Sara. *Hamas and Civil Society in Gaza: Engaging in the Islamist Social Sector*. Princeton, NJ, and Oxford: Princeton University Press, 2011.

Rubin, Barry. 'Comparing Three Muslim Brotherhoods'. In *The Muslim Brotherhood: The Organization and Policies of a Global Islamist Movement*, edited by Barry Rubin, 7–18. New York: Palgrave Macmillan, 2010.

Rubin, Uri. 'The "Constitution of Medina": Some Notes'. *Studia Islamica* 62 (1985): 5–23.

Rutherford, Bruce K. *Egypt after Mubarak: Liberalism, Islam, and Democracy in the Arab World*. Princeton, NJ, and Oxford: Princeton University Press, 2008.

'What Do Egypt's Islamists Want? Moderate Islam and the Rise of Islamic Constitutionalism'. *Middle East Journal* 60, no. 4 (2006): 707–31.

Ryad, Umar. *Islamic Reformism and Christianity: A Critical Reading of the Works of Muḥammad Rashīd Riḍā and His Associates (1898–1935)*. Leiden: Brill, 2009.

Ryan, Curtis R. 'Elections and Parliamentary Democratization in Jordan'. *Democratization* 5, no. 4 (1998): 176–96.

'Peace, Bread and Riots: Jordan and the International Monetary Fund'. *Middle East Policy* 6, no. 2 (1998): 54–66.

Jordan and the Arab Uprisings: Regime Survival and Politics Beyond the State. New York: Columbia University Press, 2018.

'Jordan and the Rise and Fall of the Arab Cooperation Council'. *Middle East Journal* 52, no. 3 (1998): 386–401.

Jordan in Transition: From Hussein to Abdullah. Boulder, CO: Lynne Rienner, 2002.

'One Society of Muslim Brothers in Jordan or Two?' *Middle East Report Online*, http://merip.org/one-society-muslim-brothers-jordan-or-two (accessed 2 September 2015), 5 March 2015.

'"We Are All Jordan" ... But Who Is We?' *Middle East Report Online*, www.merip.org/mero/mero071310 (accessed 2 November 2018), 13 July 2010.

Ryan, Curtis R. and Jillian Schwedler. 'Return to Democratization or New Hybrid Regime? The 2003 Elections in Jordan'. *Middle East Report* 11, no. 2 (2004): 138–51.

Sahliyeh, Emile. 'The West Bank and Gaza Strip'. In *The Politics of Islamic Revivalism: Diversity and Unity*, edited by Shireen Hunter, 88–100. Bloomington and Indianapolis, IN: Indiana University Press, 1988.

El-Said, Hamed and James E. Rauch. 'Education, Political Participation, and Islamist Parties: The Case of Jordan's Islamic Action Front'. *Middle East Journal* 69, no. 1 (2015): 51–73.

El-Said, Hamed and Jane Harrigan. 'Economic Reform, Social Welfare, and Instability: Jordan, Egypt, Morocco, and Tunisia, 1983–2004'. *Middle East Journal* 68, no. 1 (2014): 99–121.

El-Said, Sabah. *Between Pragmatism and Ideology: The Muslim Brotherhood in Jordan, 1989–1994*. Washington, DC: Washington Institute for Near East Policy (WINEP), 1995.

Sajid, Mehdi. 'A Reappraisal of the Role of Muḥibb al-Dīn al-Khaṭīb and the YMMA in the Rise of the Muslim Brotherhood'. *Islam and Christian–Muslim Relations* 29, no. 2 (2018): 193–213.

Sakthivel, Vish. *Al-Adl wal-Ihsan: Inside Morocco's Islamist Challenge*. Washington, DC: Washington Institute for Near East Policy, 2015.

Salibi, Kamal. *The Modern History of Jordan*. London and New York: I.B. Tauris, 2006 [1993].

Salvatore, Armando. 'Qaradawi's *Maslaha*: Frome Ideologue of the Islamic Awakening to Sponsor of Transnational Islam'. In *Global Mufti: The Phenomenon of Yusuf al-Qaradawi*, edited by Bettina Gräf and Jakob Skovgaard-Petersen, 239–50. New York: Columbia University Press, 2009.

Satloff, Robert B. *Troubles on the East Bank: Challenges to the Domestic Stability of Jordan*. New York, Westport, CT, and London: Praeger/Washington, DC: The Center for Strategic and International Studies at Georgetown University, 1986.

Schanzer, Jonathan. *Hamas vs. Fatah: The Struggle for Palestine*. New York: Palgrave Macmillan, 2008.

Schwedler, Jillian. 'Can Islamists Be Moderates? Rethinking the Inclusion-Moderation Hypothesis'. *World Politics* 63, no. 2 (2011): 347–76.

'Don't Blink: Jordan's Democratic Opening and Closing'. *Middle East Report Online*, www.merip.org/mero/mero070302 (accessed 12 January 2017), 3 July 2002.

Faith in Moderation: Islamist Parties in Jordan and Yemen. Cambridge: Cambridge University Press, 2006.

'Jordan's Islamists Lose Faith in Moderation'. *Foreign Policy*, https://foreignpolicy.com/2010/06/30/jordans-islamists-lose-faith-in-moderation/# (accessed 3 December 2019), 30 June 2010.

'A Paradox of Democracy? Islamist Participation in Elections'. *Middle East Report*, no. 209 (1998): 25–9, 41.

'Why Exclusion and Repression of Moderate Islamists Will Be Counterproductive'. In *Adaptation Strategies of Islamist Movements*. POMEPS Studies 26, 8–11. Washington, DC: Project on Middle East Political Science (POMEPS), 2017.

Scott, Rachel M. *The Challenge of Political Islam: Non-Muslims and the Egyptian State*. Stanford, CA: Stanford University Press, 2010.

Seeley, Nicholas. 'The Jordanian State Buys Itself Time'. *Middle East Report Online*, www.merip.org/mero/mero021213 (accessed 12 February 2013), 12 February 2013.

Shadid, Mohammed K. 'The Muslim Brotherhood Movement in the West Bank and Gaza'. *Third World Quarterly* 10, no. 2 (1988): 658–82.

Shahin, Emad Eldin. *Political Ascent: Contemporary Islamic Movements in North Africa*. Boulder, CO: Westview Press, 1998.

Shavit, Uriya. 'Islamotopia: The Muslim Brotherhood's Idea of Democracy'. *Azure*, no. 46 (2011): 35–62.

'Is *Shura* a Muslim Form of Democracy? Roots and Systemization of a Polemic'. *Middle Eastern Studies* 46, no. 3 (2010): 349–74.

'The Muslim Brothers' Conception of Armed Insurrection against an Unjust Regime'. *Middle Eastern Studies* 51, no. 4 (2015): 600–17.

Shehata, Samer S. 'Political *Da'wa*: Understanding the Muslim Brotherhood's Participation in Semi-authoritarian Elections'. In *Islamist Politics in the Middle East: Movements and Change*, edited by Samer S. Shehata, 120–45. London and New York: Routledge, 2012.

Shepard, William E. 'Islam and Ideology: Towards a Typology'. *International Journal of Middle East Studies* 19 (1987): 307–36.

Shlaim, Avi. *Lion of Jordan: The Life of King Hussein in War and Peace*. New York: Alfred A. Knopf, 2008.

The Politics of Partition: King Abdullah, the Zionists, and Palestine, 1921–1951. Oxford: Oxford University Press, 1998 [1988].

Shryock, Andrew. *Nationalism and the Genealogical Imagination: Oral History and Textual Authority in Tribal Jordan*. Berkeley, CA, Los Angeles and London: University of California Press, 1997.

Singh, Ranjit. 'Liberalisation or Democratisation? The Limits of Political Reform and Civil Society in Jordan'. In *Jordan in Transition: 1990–2000*, edited by George Joffé, 66–90. London: Hurst & Co., 2002.

Sivan, Emmanuel. *Radical Islam: Medieval Theology and Modern Politics*. New Haven, CT, and London: Yale University Press, 1985.

Skovgaard-Petersen, Jakob. 'Brothers and Citizens: The Second Wave of Islamic Institutional Thinking and the Concept of Citizenship'. In *The Crisis of Citizenship in the Arab World*, edited by Roel Meijer and Nils Butenschon, 320–37. Leiden: Brill, 2017.

Snow, David A., E. Burke Rochford, Jr., Steven K. Worden and Robert D. Benford. 'Frame Alignment Processes, Micromobilization, and Movement Participation'. *American Sociological Review* 51 (1986): 464–81.

Snow, David A. and Robert D. Benford. 'Ideology, Frame Resonance, and Participant Mobilization'. In *International Social Movement Research, Vol. 1 – From Structure to Action: Comparing Social Movement Research Across Cultures*, edited by Bert Klandermans, Hanspeter Kriesi and Sidney Tarrow, 197–217. Greenwich, CT, and London: JAI Press, 1988.

El-Solh, Raghid. 'Islamist Attitudes towards Democracy: A Review of the Ideas of al-Ghazālī, al-Turābī and ʿAmāra'. *British Journal of Middle Eastern Studies* 20, no. 1 (1993): 57–63.

Stacher, Joshua. 'Post-Islamist Rumblings in Egypt: The Emergence of the Wasat Party'. *Middle East Journal* 56, no. 3 (2002): 415–32.

Steinberg, Guido. 'The Muslim Brotherhood in Germany'. In *The Muslim Brotherhood: The Organization and Policies of a Global Islamist Movement*, edited by Barry Rubin, 149–60. New York: Palgrave Macmillan, 2010.

Stillman, Norman A. *The Jews of Arab Lands: A History and Source Book*. Philadelphia, PA, and New York: Jewish Publication Society of America, 1979.

Stowasser, Barbara Freyer. 'Yūsuf al-Qaraḍāwī on Women'. *Global Mufti: The Phenomenon of Yusuf al-Qaradawi*, edited by Bettina Gräf and Jakob Skovgaard-Petersen, 181–211. New York: Columbia University Press, 2009.

Sullivan, Denis J. and Sana Abed-Kotob. *Islam in Contemporary Egypt: Civil Society vs. the State*. Boulder, CO: Lynne Rienner Publishers, 1999.

Tadros, Mariz. *The Muslim Brotherhood in Contemporary Egypt: Democracy Redefined or Confined?* London and New York: Routledge, 2012.

Tadros, Samuel. 'Egypt's Muslim Brotherhood after the Revolution'. In *Current Trends in Islamist Ideology, Vol. 12*, edited by Hillel Fradkin, Husain Haqqani, Eric Brown and Hassan Mneimeh, 5–20. Washington, DC: Hudson Institute, 2011.

'Islamist Responses to the "End of Islamism"'. In *Current Trends in Islamist Ideology, Vol. 16*, edited by Hillel Fradkin, Husain Haqqani, Eric Brown and Hassan Mneimeh, 33–64. Washington, DC: Hudson Institute, 2014.

Tal, Lawrence. 'Dealing with Radical Islam: The Case of Jordan'. *Survival* 37, no. 3 (1995): 139–56.

Tal, Nachman. *Radical Islam in Egypt and Jordan*. Brighton, UK, and Portland, OR: Sussex Academic Press, 2005.

Talhamy, Yvette. 'The Syrian Muslim Brothers and the Syrian–Iranian Relationship'. *Middle East Journal* 63, no. 4 (2009): 561–80.

Tamimi, Azzam S. *Hamas: A History from Within*. Northampton, MA: Olive Branch Press, 2007.

Rachid Ghannouchi: A Democrat within Islamism. Oxford: Oxford University Press, 2001.

Tammam, Husam. 'Yusuf al-Qaradawi and the Muslim Brothers: The Nature of a Special Relationship'. In *Global Mufti: The Phenomenon of Yusuf al-Qaradawi*, edited by Bettina Gräf and Jakob Skovgaard-Petersen, 55–83. New York: Columbia University Press, 2009.

Taraki, Lisa. 'Islam Is the Solution: Jordanian Islamists and the Dilemma of the "Modern Woman"'. *British Journal of Sociology* 46, no. 4 (1995): 643–61.

'Jordanian Islamists and the Agenda for Women: Between Discourse and Practice'. *Middle Eastern Studies* 32, no. 1 (1996): 140–58.

Tarrow, Sidney. *The New Transnational Activism*. Cambridge: Cambridge University Press, 2005.

Teitelbaum, Joshua. 'The Muslim Brotherhood and the "Struggle for Syria", 1947–1958: Between Accommodation and Ideology'. *Middle Eastern Studies* 40, no. 3 (2004): 134–58.

'The Muslim Brotherhood in Syria, 1945–1958: Founding, Social Origins, Ideology'. *Middle East Journal* 65, no. 2 (2011): 213–33.

Toth, James. *Sayyid Qutb: The Life and Legacy of a Radical Islamic Intellectual*. Oxford: Oxford University Press, 2013.

Trager, Eric. 'Egypt's Looming Competitive Theocracy'. In *Current Trends in Islamist Ideology, Vol. 14*, edited by Hillel Fradkin, Husain Haqqani, Eric Brown and Hassan Mneimeh, 27–37. Washington, DC: Hudson Institute, 2014.

Tucker, Judith E. *Women, Family, and Gender in Islamic Law*. Cambridge: Cambridge University Press, 2008.

Tyan, E. 'Bayʿa'. In *Encyclopaedia of Islam: New Edition*, vol. 1, edited by H. A. R. Gibb, J. H. Kramers, E. Lévi-Provençal, J. Schacht, B. Lewis and Ch. Pellat, 1113–14. Leiden: E.J. Brill, 1986 [1960].

Valbjørn, Morten. 'The 2013 Parliamentary Elections in Jordan: Three Stories and Some General Lessons'. *Mediterranean Politics* 18, no. 2 (2013): 311–17.

'Post-democratization Lessons from the Jordanian "Success Story"'. *Foreign Policy*, https://foreignpolicy.com/2010/06/16/post-democratization-lessons-from-the-jordanian-success-story/# (accessed 12 December 2019), 16 June 2010.

Vatikiotis, P. J. *Politics and the Military in Jordan: A Study of the Arab Legion, 1921–1957*. London: Frank Cass, 1967.

Vidino, Lorenzo. 'The European Organization of the Muslim Brotherhood: Myth or Reality?' In *The Muslim Brotherhood in Europe*, edited by Roel Meijer and Edwin Bakker, 51–69. London: Hurst & Co., 2012.

'The Muslim Brotherhood in Europe'. In *The Muslim Brotherhood: The Organization and Policies of a Global Islamist Movement*, edited by Barry Rubin, 105–16. New York: Palgrave Macmillan, 2010.

Wagemakers, Joas. 'Ashqar, ʿUmar Sulaymān'. In *Encyclopaedia of Islam Three*, edited by Kate Fleet, Gudrun Krämer, Denis Matringe, John Nawas and Everett Rowson, 2020-IV, 1–3. Leiden: Brill, 2020.

'Between Exclusivism and Inclusivism: The Jordanian Muslim Brotherhood's Divided Responses to the "Arab Spring"'. *Middle East Law and Governance* 12, no. 1 (2020): 35–60.

'An Inquiry into Ignorance: A Jihādī-Salafī Debate on *Jahl* as an Obstacle to *Takfīr*'. In *The Transmission and Dynamics of the Textual Sources of Islam: Essays in Honour of Harald Motzki*, edited by Nicolet Boekhoff-van der Voort, Kees Versteegh and Joas Wagemakers, 301–27. Leiden: Brill, 2011.

'"The *Kāfir* Religion of the West": *Takfīr* of Democracy and Democrats by Radical Islamists'. In *Accusations of Unbelief in Islam: A Diachronic Perspective on* Takfīr, edited by Camilla Adang, Hassan Ansari, Maribel Fierro and Sabine Schmidtke, 327–53. Leiden: Brill, 2016.

'Foreign Policy as Protection: The Jordanian Muslim Brotherhood as a Political Minority during the Cold War'. In *Muted Minorities: Ethnic, Religious and Political Groups in (Trans)Jordan, 1921–2016*, edited by Idir Ouahes and Paolo Maggiolini. London: Palgrave, forthcoming.

'Legitimizing Pragmatism: Hamas' Framing Efforts from Militancy to Moderation and Back?' *Terrorism and Political Violence* 22 (2010): 357–77.

A Quietist Jihadi: The Ideology and Influence of Abu Muhammad al-Maqdisi. Cambridge: Cambridge University Press, 2012.

'Salafi Scholarly Views on Gender-Mixing (*Ikhtilāṭ*) in Saudi Arabia'. *Orient* 57, no. 2 (2016): 40–51.

Wagner, Mark S. '*Ḥukm bi-mā anzala'llāh*: The Forgotten Prehistory of an Islamist Slogan'. *Journal of Qur'anic Studies* 18, no. 1 (2016): 117–43.

al-Wāʿī, Tawfīq Yūsuf. *Al-Fikr al-Siyāsī al-Muʿāṣir li-Tawajjuhāt al-Ikhwān al-Muslimīn*. Kuwait: Maktabat Ibn Kathīr, 2011.

Waltz, Susan. 'Islamist Appeal in Tunisia'. *Middle East Journal* 40, no. 4 (1986): 651–70.

Warren, David H. 'The ʿUlamāʾ and the Arab Uprisings 2011–12: Considering Yusuf al-Qaradawi, the "Global Mufti," Between the Muslim Brotherhood, the Islamic Legal Tradition, and Qatari Foreign Policy'. *New Middle Eastern Studies* 4 (2014): 2–32.

Warren, David H. and Christine Gilmore. 'One Nation under God? Yusuf al-Qaradawi's Changing Fiqh of Citizenship in the Light of the Islamic Legal Tradition'. *Contemporary Islam* 8 (2014): 217–37.

'Rethinking Neo-Salafism through an Emerging Fiqh of Citizenship: The Changing Status of Minorities in the Discourse of Yusuf al-Qaradawi and the "School of the Middle Way"'. *New Middle Eastern Studies* 2 (2012): 1–7.

Watt, W. Montgomery. *Islamic Political Thought*. Edinburgh: Edinburgh University Press, 2007 [1968].

Muhammad: Prophet and Statesman. Oxford: Oxford University Press, 1961.

Wegner, Eva. *Islamist Opposition in Authoritarian Regimes: The Party of Justice and Development in Morocco*. Syracuse, NY: Syracuse University Press, 2011.

Weismann, Itzchak. 'Democratic Fundamentalism? The Practice and Discourse of the Muslim Brothers Movement in Syria'. *The Muslim World* 100 (2010): 1–16.

'Framing a Modern Umma: The Muslim Brothers' Evolving Project of *Daʿwa*'. *Sociology of Islam* 3 (2015): 146–69.

El-Wereny, Mahmud. 'Reichweite und Instrumente islamrechtlicher Normenfindung in der Moderne: Yūsuf al-Qaraḍāwīs *iǧtihād*-Konzept'. *Die Welt des Islams* 58 (2018): 65–100.

Wiktorowicz, Quintan. 'Islamists, the State and Cooperation in Jordan'. *Third World Quarterly* 21, no. 4 (1999): 1–16.

The Management of Islamic Activism: Salafis, the Muslim Brotherhood, and State Power in Jordan. New York: State University of New York Press, 2001.

Wilson, Mary C. *King Abdullah, Britain and the Making of Jordan*. Cambridge: Cambridge University Press, 1987.

Wood, Simon A. *Christian Criticisms, Islamic Proofs: Rashīd Riḍā's Modernist Defense of Islam*. Oxford: Oneworld, 2008.

Yazbeck Haddad, Yvonne. 'The Qurʾanic Justification for an Islamic Revolution: The View of Sayyid Quṭb'. *Middle East Journal* 37, no. 1 (1983): 14–29.

Zahid, Mohammed. *The Muslim Brotherhood and Egypt's Succession Crisis: The Politics of Liberalisation and Reform in the Middle East*. London and New York: I.B. Tauris, 2010.

Zollner, Barbara H. E. *The Muslim Brotherhood: Hasan al-Hudaybi and Ideology*. London and New York: Routledge, 2009.

'Opening to Reform: Hasan al-Hudaybi's Legacy'. In *The Muslim Brotherhood in Europe*, edited by Roel Meijer and Edwin Bakker, 273–93. London: Hurst & Co., 2012.

'Prison Talk: The Muslim Brotherhood's Internal Struggle during Gamal Abdel Nasser's Persecution, 1954 to 1971'. *International Journal of Middle East Studies* 39, no. 3 (2007): 411–33.

Index

Books in the Series

1 Parvin Paidar, *Women and the Political Process in Twentieth-Century Iran*
2 Israel Gershoni and James Jankowski, *Redefining the Egyptian Nation, 1930–1945*
3 Annelies Moors, *Women, Property and Islam: Palestinian Experiences, 1920–1945*
4 Paul Kingston, *Britain and the Politics of Modernization in the Middle East, 1945–1958*
5 Daniel Brown, *Rethinking Tradition in Modern Islamic Thought*
6 Nathan J. Brown, *The Rule of Law in the Arab World: Courts in Egypt and the Gulf*
7 Richard Tapper, *Frontier Nomads of Iran: The Political and Social History of the Shahsevan*
8 Khaled Fahmy, *All the Pasha's Men: Mehmed Ali, His Army and the Making of Modern Egypt*
9 Sheila Carapico, *Civil Society in Yemen: The Political Economy of Activism in Arabia*
10 Meir Litvak, *Shi'i Scholars of Nineteenth-Century Iraq: The Ulama of Najaf and Karbala*
11 Jacob Metzer, *The Divided Economy of Mandatory Palestine*
12 Eugene L. Rogan, *Frontiers of the State in the Late Ottoman Empire: Transjordan, 1850–1921*
13 Eliz Sanasarian, *Religious Minorities in Iran*
14 Nadje Al-Ali, *Secularism, Gender and the State in the Middle East: The Egyptian Women's Movement*
15 Eugene L. Rogan and Avi Shlaim, eds., *The War for Palestine: Rewriting the History of 1948*
16 Gershon Shafir and Yoar Peled, *Being Israeli: The Dynamics of Multiple Citizenship*
17 A. J. Racy, *Making Music in the Arab World: The Culture and Artistry of Tarab*
18 Benny Morris, *The Birth of the Palestinian Refugee Crisis Revisited*
19 Yasir Suleiman, *A War of Words: Language and Conflict in the Middle East*
20 Peter Moore, *Doing Business in the Middle East: Politics and Economic Crisis in Jordan and Kuwait*
21 Idith Zertal, *Israel's Holocaust and the Politics of Nationhood*
22 David Romano, *The Kurdish Nationalist Movement: Opportunity, Mobilization and Identity*

23 Laurie A. Brand, *Citizens Abroad: Emigration and the State in the Middle East and North Africa*
24 James McDougall, *History and the Culture of Nationalism in Algeria*
25 Madawi al-Rasheed, *Contesting the Saudi State: Islamic Voices from a New Generation*
26 Arang Keshavarzian, *Bazaar and State in Iran: The Politics of the Tehran Marketplace*
27 Laleh Khalili, *Heroes and Martyrs of Palestine: The Politics of National Commemoration*
28 M. Hakan Yavuz, *Secularism and Muslim Democracy in Turkey*
29 Mehran Kamrava, *Iran's Intellectual Revolution*
30 Nelida Fuccaro, *Histories of City and State in the Persian Gulf: Manama since 1800*
31 Michaelle L. Browers, *Political Ideology in the Arab World: Accommodation and Transformation*
32 Miriam R. Lowi, *Oil Wealth and the Poverty of Politics: Algeria Compared*
33 Thomas Hegghammer, *Jihad in Saudi Arabia: Violence and Pan-Islamism since 1979*
34 Sune Haugbolle, *War and Memory in Lebanon*
35 Ali Rahnema, *Superstition as Ideology in Iranian Politics: From Majlesi to Ahmadinejad*
36 Wm. Roger Louis and Avi Shlaim, eds., *The 1967 Arab–Israeli War: Origins and Consequences*
37 Stephen W. Day, *Regionalism and Rebellion in Yemen: A Troubled National Union*
38 Daniel Neep, *Occupying Syria under the French Mandate: Insurgency, Space and State Formation*
39 Iren Ozgur, *Islamic Schools in Modern Turkey: Faith, Politics, and Education*
40 Ali M. Ansari, *The Politics of Nationalism in Modern Iran*
41 Thomas Pierret, *Religion and State in Syria: The Sunni Ulama from Coup to Revolution*
42 Guy Ben-Porat, *Between State and Synagogue: The Secularization of Contemporary Israel*
43 Madawi Al-Rasheed, *A Most Masculine State: Gender, Politics and Religion in Saudi Arabia*
44 Sheila Carapico, *Political Aid and Arab Activism: Democracy Promotion, Justice, and Representation*
45 Pascal Menoret, *Joyriding in Riyadh: Oil, Urbanism, and Road Revolt*
46 Toby Matthiesen, *The Other Saudis: Shiism, Dissent and Sectarianism*
47 Bashir Saade, *Hizbullah and the Politics of Remembrance: Writing the Lebanese Nation*
48 Noam Leshem, *Life after Ruin: The Struggles over Israel's Depopulated Arab Spaces*
49 Zoltan Pall, *Salafism in Lebanon: Local and Transnational Movements*
50 Salwa Ismail, *The Rule of Violence: Subjectivity, Memory and Government in Syria*

51 Zahra Ali, *Women and Gender in Iraq: Between Nation-Building and Fragmentation*
52 Dina Bishara, *Contesting Authoritarianism: Labour Challenges to the State in Egypt*
53 Rory McCarthy, *Inside Tunisia's al-Nahda: Between Politics and Preaching*
54 Ceren Lord, *Religious Politics in Turkey: From the Birth of the Republic to the AKP*
55 Dörthe Engelcke, *Reforming Family Law: Social and Political Change in Jordan and Morocco*
56 Dana Conduit, *The Muslim Brotherhood in Syria*
57 Benjamin Schuetze, *Promoting Democracy, Reinforcing Authoritarianism: US and European Policy in Jordan*
58 Marc Owen Jones, *Political Repression in Bahrain*
59 Dylan Baun, *Winning Lebanon: Youth Politics, Populism, and the Production of Sectarian Violence, 1920–1958*
60 Joas Wagemakers, *The Muslim Brotherhood in Jordan*

CPSIA information can be obtained
at www.ICGtesting.com
Printed in the USA
LVHW081751200920
666588LV00004B/35